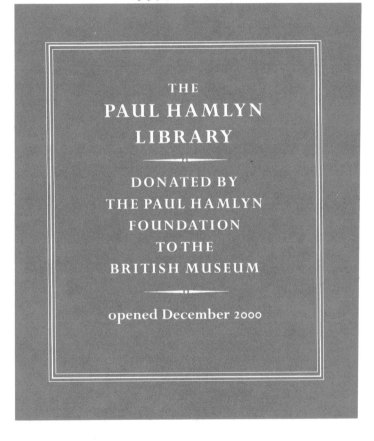

Work in Towns 850–1850

John Sell Cotman's water-colour of *Norwich Market Place* (*c.* 1806) is published by courtesy of the Tate Gallery, London.

WORK IN TOWNS 850–1850

EDITED BY PENELOPE J. CORFIELD
AND DEREK KEENE

Leicester University Press
(a division of Pinter Publishers Ltd)
Leicester, London, New York

First published in Great Britain in 1990 by Leicester University Press
(a division of Pinter Publishers Ltd)

Editorial offices
Fielding Johnson Building, University of Leicester,
University Road, Leicester, LE1 7RH and P.O. Box 197, Irvington, New York

Trade and other enquiries
25 Floral Street, London, WC2E 9DS

British Library Cataloguing in Publication Data
A CIP cataloguing record for this book is available
from the British Library

ISBN 0-7185-1313-4

Library of Congress Cataloging-in-Publication Data
Work in towns, 850–1850/edited by Penelope J. Corfield and Derek Keene.
    p. cm.
Includes bibliographical references.
ISBN 0-7185-1313-4
1. Working class—History—Congresses.   2. Cities and towns-
History-Congresses.   3. Urban economics—History—Congresses.
I. Corfield, P. J. II. Keene, Derek.
HD4841.W67   1990
305.5′62′091732—dc20
                                                        90-33776
                                                           CIP

Typeset by DP Photosetting, Aylesbury, Bucks
Printed and bound in Great Britain by Biddles Ltd.

Contents

Preface

Work is a big subject with extensive ramifications. As a result, its history has often been subsumed into wider social and economic studies. But it deserves attention in its own right. The essays in this volume began as papers at a special conference, held in London in July 1987, on the theme of *Work in Towns*. The agenda was designed to bring together recent research into urban economic life, looking in particular at: the archaeological evidence and other new sources; the impact of trade; the relationship of town and countryside; the range and nature of town work; the role of women; urban and suburban growth; and the meaning of urban occupations. Above all, by covering a very long time-span, the discussions confronted important questions about the extent of change and continuities in urban work throughout many centuries.

The editors wish to extend their warmest thanks to all participants at the conference (listed, x–xi) for three days of intensive and enjoyable debate, which continued long into the evenings. Particular thanks go to the hard-working contributors of papers; and to those colleagues who chaired the individual sessions. In addition, it is a pleasure to acknowledge financial sponsorship for the conference from the Economic and Social Research Council, as well as from Leicester University Press, the History Department of Royal Holloway and Bedford New College, and the University of California, Riverside. The British Museum also gave welcome hospitality, and London University's Institute of Historical Research provided admirable conference facilities.

A study of work need not claim to be effortless. Many expert hands have helped to lighten the labours of producing this volume. The skilled support from Alice Prochaska at the Institute and the organizational flair of Martha Carlin and Olwen Myhill deserve special tribute. Above all, Peter Boulton, the former Secretary to Leicester University Press, played a key role both in fostering the enterprise and providing expert advice throughout.

P.J.C. and D.K.

Contributors

Jan M. Baart is City Archaeologist for the City of Amsterdam and heads the Archaeological Research Division of the Amsterdam Department of Public Works; he is co-author of *Opgravingen in Amsterdam* (Amsterdam, 1977) and other publications in urban archaeology and history.

Penelope J. Corfield teaches history at Royal Holloway and Bedford New College, University of London, and is author of *The Impact of English Towns 1700–1800* (Oxford, 1982) and essays on urban, social, linguistic, and economic history.

Chris Evans is Sir James Knott Research Fellow at the University of Newcastle upon Tyne; he writes on industry, work and radicalism in South Wales, and his study of early industrial Merthyr Tydfil is to be published by the University of Wales Press.

Edmund M. Green is a postgraduate student in the History Department at Royal Holloway and Bedford New College, University of London, researching for a PhD thesis on the political and economic history of eighteenth-century Westminster.

Göran Hoppe is Reader in the University of Stockholm's Department of Human Geography and is co-author (with S. Fogelvik and T. Gerger) of *Man, Landscape and Society: An Information System* (Stockholm, 1981) and studies in education and social mobility, and agrarian change in nineteenth-century Sweden.

Derek Keene is Director of the University of London's Centre for Metropolitan History and author of *Survey of Medieval Winchester* (1985) and *Cheapside before the Great Fire* (1985) and other writings in urban history and archaeology.

Maryanne Kowaleski teaches at Fordham University, New York, and is author of *Local Markets and Regional Trade in Late Medieval Exeter* (forthcoming from Cambridge University Press) as well as articles on urban oligarchies, women, and families in medieval England.

John Langton is Fellow and Tutor at St John's College, Oxford, and University lecturer in Geography; he is author (with Göran Hoppe) of *Town and Country in the Development of Early Modern Western Europe* (Hist. Geog. Research Studies *11*, 1983) and studies in English mining history and historical geography.

John A. Phillips is Associate Professor of History at the University of California, Riverside, and is author of *Electoral Behaviour in Unreformed England* (Princeton, 1982) as well as essays on Georgian and Victorian politics and historical computing.

Michael J. Power is a lecturer in history at the University of Liverpool and has written many essays on Tudor and Stuart London, including a contribution to A.L. Beier and R. Finlay (eds), *London 1500-1700: The Making of the Metropolis* (1986).

Michael Roberts is a lecturer in history at the University College of Wales, Aberystwyth, and writes on the history of work, including an essay in L. Charles and L. Duffin (eds), *Women and Work in Pre-Industrial England* (1985).

Heather Swanson is a Fellow of the Institute for Advanced Research in the Humanities at the University of Birmingham; she is author of *Medieval Artisans: An Urban Class in Late Medieval England* (1989) and articles on medieval urban and social history.

Dominic Tweddle works for the York Archaeological Trust and has published papers on early medieval metalwork as well as editing a forthcoming study of the archaeological evidence for craft production in Viking York.

Conference participants:
Work in Towns Conference, London, 9–11 July 1987

Peter Addyman	York Archaeological Trust
James Alexander	London School of Economics
John Allan	Royal Albert Memorial Museum, Exeter
Jan Baart	City of Amsterdam Department of Public Works
Elizabeth Baigent	St Hugh's College, Oxford
Caroline Barron	Royal Holloway and Bedford New College, London
Maxine Berg	University of Warwick
Jeremy Boulton	Cambridge Group for the Study of Population and Social Structure
Peter Boulton	Leicester University Press
Richard Britnell	University of Durham
Martha Carlin	Rutgers University, New Jersey
John Cherry	British Museum
Penelope Corfield	Royal Holloway and Bedford New College, London
Peter Earle	London School of Economics
Geoffrey Egan	Museum of London
Chris Evans	University of Newcastle upon Tyne
Edmund Green	Royal Holloway and Bedford New College, London
Vanessa Harding	Birkbeck College, London
Edward Higgs	Public Record Office
Rodney Hilton	University of Birmingham
Göran Hoppe	University of Stockholm
Mary Hulton	University of Warwick
Derek Keene	Centre for Metropolitan History, University of London
Maryanne Kowaleski	Fordham University, New York
John Langton	St John's College, Oxford
Paul Laxton	University of Liverpool
John Money	University of Victoria, British Columbia
Robert Morris	University of Edinburgh
David Palliser	University of Hull
John Phillips	University of California, Riverside
Michael Power	University of Liverpool
Stephen Rappaport	New York University
Sarah Rees-Jones	University of York

Michael Roberts	University College of Wales, Aberystwyth
Lyndal Roper	Royal Holloway and Bedford New College, London
Leonard Schwarz	University of Birmingham
Heather Swanson	University of Birmingham
Dominic Tweddle	York Archaeological Trust
Lorna Weatherill	University of St Andrews
Susan Wright	University of Leicester
Tony Wrigley	All Souls College, Oxford.

List of figures

List of tables

Abbreviations

ASA   Association of Social Anthropologists
BL   British Library
n.s.   new series
OED   *Oxford English Dictionary*
PCC   Prerogative Court of Canterbury
           [Some wills are cited according to the traditional names of the PCC volumes in which they were registered; the volumes are now in the PROB 11 class at the PRO, where there is a concordance listing their present numbers]
PRO   Public Record Office
RO   Record Office, as in the form Hants RO
Rot. Parl. *Rotuli Parliamentorum: The Rolls of Parliament* (7 vols, 1793; plus Index, 1832)
SSRC   Social Science Research Council, later renamed as the Economic and Social Research Council (ESRC)
STC   A.W. Pollard and G.R. Redgrave, *A Short-Title Catalogue of Books Printed in England, Scotland, & Ireland, and of English Books Printed Abroad 1475-1640*, second edition revised and enlarged by W.A. Jackson, F.S. Ferguson and K.A. Pantzer (1986)
VCH   *Victoria History of the Counties of England* ('Victoria County History')

Note: In citations that follow, place of publication is within Great Britain, unless otherwise specified.

1 Continuity and development in urban trades: problems of concepts and the evidence

Derek Keene[1]

nullus christianus debet esse mercator[2]

Augustine's precept expresses an attitude prevalent among the early church fathers towards the work which is the subject of this book. It may also reflect a socially dominant attitude within the wider context of the ancient economy.[3] During medieval and later times, by contrast, the work of the merchant, the artisan, and the hired worker, though placed on level inferior to that of men who fought and men who prayed, was acknowledged as lying within the bounds of Christian society. Indeed, by the thirteenth century, the notion of a market in labour, as in any other commodity for sale or for hire, was a well-established one.[4] The Christian, moreover, had a special duty promptly to pay the workers and servants whose labour he had hired, since, as Aquinas said, they were poor and had no other resource.[5]

The wage-labour force with, as we shall see, other attendant features to which some theories attribute a crucial role in the development of the 'modern' or 'capitalist' economy, was thus in being.[6] It was undoubtedly more visible in towns than elsewhere, although in England, as in much of Europe, town-dwellers as yet represented only a small proportion of the whole population. This focuses attention on one of the crucial questions which lie behind the essays in this volume. Over the period of a thousand years which they cover, is it possible convincingly to identify basic structural changes in the organization of work which led, perhaps ineluctably, from 'feudal', 'medieval' or 'small-craft' systems of production, *via* 'mercantile capitalism' and 'proto-industrialization' to the 'modern' system?[7] Or is the period characterized rather by a fundamental continuity in the repertoire of modes of production? If this were so, the changes which certainly did take place should be seen not as denoting stages in the irreversible trajectory of social development, but rather as expressing choice of the appropriate mode according to the situation at the time.[8] Such choices would be made as responses to shifts in the scale of the resource base and of demand for goods (both of which were determined in different ways by levels of population), in the distribution of spending power between social groups, and in the spatial concentration and the regional or international pattern of these forces. Some current thinking suggests that this cycle of responses, containing 'regressive' as well as 'progressive' phases, perhaps only came to be broken in the latter part of our period, towards 1700, with unprecedented advances in agricultural productivity and, in Britain, with the widespread use of mineral fuel for power and heating.[9]

Several obstacles hinder progress towards securing dispassionate answers to these questions. One is the historian's tendency to devote attention to relatively short periods, causing at times the identification as innovations of practices which in fact had continued from previous periods, or which were revivals of earlier, discontinued procedures. This is an understandable, if not excusable, practice. Sometimes it involves unconscious assumptions. Thus in his valuable and characteristically robust account of mid-fifteenth-century Gloucester, Langton, by his use of the word 'already' in a final paragraph, implies that the city was in a precocious state of development.[10] In fact, the evidence he had cited concerning land values and social topography revealed features which had characterized many English towns for several centuries previously, and which in some cases were at a more 'advanced' stage of 'development' at an earlier date.[11]

Another obstacle is the vague and indiscriminate use of a vocabulary derived from theoretical writing on social development. Often enough the theory itself has little relation to demonstrable features of the real world in the past,[12] but even when it may profitably be appropriated by historians to inform their interpretative processes, the terminology is frequently used loosely, as if it were a substitute for rather than an aid to thought. The term 'capitalism' itself has in historians' usage acquired a wide variety of meanings denoting distinctive types of work relationships in towns, yet it is also used both to identify a single major social change which is supposed to have taken place within the long span of the medieval and early modern periods, and, sometimes in virtually the same context, as no more than a chronological indicator.[13]

A third, and the most serious, obstacle is the variation in both the quantity and the quality of the evidence for urban work and working practices. Documentary evidence from before AD 1300 is sparse, but there is an increasing body of evidence in the form of material remains, which can extend our knowledge in the early period and add new dimensions to the existing picture of later ones. Even so, we need constantly to be aware of those aspects of the past which are not recorded in surviving evidence of any type but which nevertheless may have played a key role in historical development. But even when the written records are abundant, their coverage and the meanings of their vocabulary vary over time and from place to place. In the past, historians have not always shown the necessary sensitivity on these matters, and this has compounded the difficulties which arise from assumptions concerning levels of economic or social development. There is an urgent need to develop both powers of basic observation (sometimes, but wrongly, dismissed as 'mindless antiquarianism') and the ability to deploy theoretical concepts in conjunction with them, but in a distanced manner so that each procedure can properly inform the other.

The title, 'Work in Towns', assumes the central role of towns in economic life. For England, and for the period in question, there is little need to justify this assumption, even though the proportion of town-dwellers, and presumably also of those who visited towns, was low at first and increased enormously as time went on.[14] While the focus is on towns, however, there is no intention to divorce them from the setting of which they formed part. Whether we see towns as places where men and women exchanged goods and services, and indulged their propensity to barter, or as places where they congregated for defensive, social, and religious reasons, they could only exist as part of wider communities and landscapes. This book is primarily concerned with towns as places where material goods were exchanged or produced. We should remember, however, that even at the beginning of our period, when defences, crafts, mints, tolls, and borough laws dominate our picture, towns were at least as important as sites for the interchange of information and ideas and the provision of non-material services. Tenth-century Cambridge, Norwich, Ipswich and Thetford, for example, are known to have contributed to the life of their region as places where agreements were given special power to endure.[15] For the medieval period generally, the spiritual services which towns provided for their regions must be counted as a large part of their work. At Winchester about 1400, a cathedral city containing three Benedictine houses, four friaries, and many parish churches, the clerical population, both secular and religious, accounted for four per cent of the inhabitants. If we count each monk, nun, friar or priest as equivalent to the head of a lay household, they probably represented the largest single specialized productive group, greater even than that occupied in the clothing industry.[16]

In the world of material production, towns had a key role as centres for marketing, distribution, and the organization of productive systems, even when manufacturing activities were located in the countryside. During medieval and later periods the activities of many merchants, artisans, and labourers were characterized by a high degree of diversity in the commodities they traded and in the services they provided, and the interests of individuals might shift quite sharply during their careers, according to their personal circumstances or to wider economic trends.[17] In such conditions, towns would have a special importance as places where new opportunities were to be identified, even if those openings might lead to trading relations or to craft activity outside the urban setting.[18] Towns moulded the world beyond their limits in other ways, notably by their requirements for food and the raw materials for manufactures and building. In this way they promoted specialization and commercialization within their regions.[19] Conversely, changes in the agricultural base, a shift in the balance between cereal growing and pastoralism for example, could have a marked influence on the pattern of activities in towns.[20] In their material remains and in the written records of the activities of their inhabitants, towns thus encapsulate an important body of evidence for understanding the agriculture, forestry, mineral workings, and craft production of their regions.[21]

Mobility and the circulation of people, ideas, and goods are essential to the existence and prosperity of towns. The significance of migration to towns, of movement out again, and of visits to market on a daily basis have long been appreciated. More recently, the frequency and patterns of short-distance movement within towns, and their relationship to career cycles and to notions of community and neighbourhood have been elucidated.[22] In this volume a remarkably high degree of mobility is revealed, between farms, hamlets, villages and small towns in southern Sweden.[23] Individual participants in these cyclical patterns of movement would have spent much of their working lives outside the urban setting. The town, however, served as a theatre where they played a distinctive working role. The distinctiveness lay less in the perduring urban lifestyle of individual workers than in the nexus of different activities within the town to which they contributed. Experiences of urban life and of rural life were thus common to many individuals who could practise their skills or provide their labour in either setting. Yet this does not erode the distinction between the two environments, which provided contrasting physical and behavioural sets within which work took place. This particular study provides a rare insight into a style of life which almost certainly was widespread throughout our period.

In considering the development of work in towns, one of the most useful organizing concepts, and one based on straightforward, commonsense observation, is that of the division of labour. For Xenophon, the subdivision of manufacturing into specialized tasks was the means of improving the quality of the product.[24] For Adam Smith, it arose progressively from the expansion of the market. Both writers, in fact, saw it as a response to demand, in each case of a different type, but only Smith was concerned to incorporate the notion into a theory of economic development. Smith also identified an effective administration of justice and public order as one of the circumstances which favoured the growth of the market and hence the division of labour.[25] The importance of this observation requires no emphasis for students of the Middle Ages familiar with the ways in which systems imposed by external authority, as well as the more informal, communally-generated ones, were used to regulate and to promote economic activity in towns. There were mechanisms for validating contracts, and for arbitrating in cases of dispute; lordship played a vital role in providing the circumstances in which markets and fairs could prosper;[26] and late-medieval town courts provided a forum through which regional credit networks were rendered effective.[27] The relationship between such systems on the one hand, and economic activity on the other, was presumably interactive rather than straightforwardly causal. Nevertheless, we need to take them into account, for their possible effect on the size of the market, and on the degree to which productive tasks were subdivided.

Durkheim's view of the division of labour emphasized its roots in social rather than in economic relations.[28] Some aspects of this, notably systems of division by age or gender, he did not develop very far. For our present purposes, however, there is special value in his concern with the link between the level of specialization on the one hand and the scale and concentration of populations on the other, and with the quality of the relations between individual members of those populations. This is a state for which he devised the useful term 'moral density', and which a recent sensitive writer on government has characterized as a 'state of community'.[29] In essence, it is the degree to which individuals living and working within large groups and performing specialized functions can depend upon or predict the actions of their fellows with other specialisms. Without a degree of moral density specialization would be impossible. It was clearly central to the organization of ironworking at Merthyr in the late eighteenth century, in a context which otherwise was remarkable for the savagery and disorder which often characterize episodes of rapid urbanization.[30]

For an earlier period, it is appropriate to use the notion of 'moral density' in conjunction with that of legal change to explore developments which may have come about during the fourteenth and fifteenth centuries. Up to 1300, despite the accumulation of some very large fortunes by a relatively small number of individuals, the production and distribution of goods in towns was characterized by subdivision into minute independent trading units, just as land, buildings, and other interests in real property were divided into small parcels. Later the pattern was reversed. In property holding this can be attributed to depopulation and to the redistribution of resources which accompanied an overall rise in the standard of living. But when population rose again, the former degree of subdivision did not re-emerge. In urban landholding this was due partly to earlier statutory changes but also to the widespread use of systems of management, such as the repairing lease, which were more securely founded in contractual obligation than previous systems.[31] Tenurial relationships, between 'merchant' landlords and 'craftsmen' or 'shopkeeper' tenants for example, may often have mirrored relationships in the manufacture or distribution of goods, as they seem to have done in fourteenth-century Winchester.[32] Changes in landholding may thus stand proxy for similar, though less visible (or less investigated), ones in the patterns of urban work. The shops and warehouses of sixteenth-century London, for example, were, on the whole, larger than their thirteenth-century predecessors and formed part of larger and less tenurially differentiated blocks of land and buildings. The workforces occupying them may likewise have formed productive units which were more tightly organized than the more widespread networks of independent stallholders in earlier times.[33]

Two features which are sometimes identified as characteristic of towns and work during the late medieval and early modern period are a tendency towards a concentration in the control of productive work, and a related enlargement of the wage-labour sector. Occasionally such developments are placed within a context of emerging 'capitalism'. On examination of the evidence, however, it is not at all clear that this is a helpful approach. Even when, as in fifteenth-century Colchester, control of the production of cloth, as indicated by the pattern of sales, was being concentrated in fewer hands, we should not assume that a more productive, efficient, or radically new system was in the course of emerging. It may be more useful to view changes in the terms of a balance of economic advantage between the makers and finishers of cloth on the one hand, and the distributors of the final product on the other.[34] Likewise, the clothiers' wills of the 1520s, which record legacies to their spinners, weavers, fullers, and shearmen, should probably be interpreted not as evidence for the emergence of a new type of labour force employed under the putting-out system, but more an indication of Christian charitable concern, in line with Aquinas's precept and perhaps reflecting a current sense of unease, among those in powerful circles, for a group of workers who were undergoing particular difficulties at that time.[35] Certainly, the numbers of employees or outworkers were very small, and clothiers evidently found it difficult to retain the services of workers in some preparatory crafts for extended periods.[36] A century and more previously similar networks of production were common among workers in the cloth trade in English towns. They involved a score or more workers operating sometimes in close proximity, sometimes in scattered work-shops, sometimes as tenants of clothiers, and sometimes as their employees in the modern sense;[37] we may suppose that independent craftsmen gave more or less of their time to the demands of individual entrepreneurs or to developing their own networks of production and distribution as circumstances dictated.[38]

It is misleading to characterize urban production in this period as dominated by craftsmen who provided their own capital and were constrained by the 'guild system'.[39] Undoubtedly such men were important, and the small-scale, household-based workshop served as the most common working environment, but even in such a modest city as late fourteenth-century Winchester units of production ranged from those which seem to have focused on a single artisan household, to complex entrepreneurial networks like that associated with the leading merchant Mark le Fayre. There was, presumably, a full range of variants between. Le Fayre was active over a period of about fifty years and invested substantially in both distribution and production. He imported wine and exported cloth. In Winchester he owned a tavern and shops, and built a substantial inn. He also organized cloth production both within and outside the city: he put out cloth to be woven, sold cloths, and dealt in dyestuffs. As well as his portfolio of residential property in Winchester (which towards the end of his life had a capital value of about £260), a house in Southampton, and a country estate, he owned a dyehouse in Winchester which he managed directly, paying an annual wage of £1.6s.8d. to the dyer who operated it.[40] Directly or indirectly, he controlled employment in several key areas of the city's economy. For the twelfth and thirteenth centuries it is virtually impossible to reconstruct the pattern of urban work in this way, but the broad similarities in social and economic structure between towns then and in the fourteenth century suggest that enterprises like Mark le Fayre's may have been just as typical of the earlier period. In London at least, it is clear that a developed putting-out system existed both in the clothing industry and in retail trading by the beginning of the thirteenth century, as revealed by the rules governing distress for arrears of rent.[41] This was a time when craftsmen in the city appear to have been losing status in relation to merchants and entrepreneurs,[42] and may, as again in the late fifteenth century, have been forced for the time being into a more dependent economic relationship with them.

Another feature of later medieval urban production sometimes identified as 'progressive' was the combination of several processes within a single workshop.[43] This may often have come about as practitioners of a particular craft made the most of opportunities for diversification and entrepreneurial activities.[44] Even so, the scale of working units was small, and it was presumably equally possible for craftsmen to be forced into diversification by contracting markets and by a fall in the demand for specialized skills.[45] We should remember, too, that we know very little about such aspects of work in English towns before the fourteenth century. A recent archaeological discovery in London, for example, demonstrated the unexpectedly substantial scale of a workshop or group of workshops in use during the late twelfth and early thirteenth centuries. Here, on a site near the waterfront, was a concentration of furnaces almost certainly used in connection with dyeing cloth. They represented a major investment in industrial plant, sustained through several stages of renewal, but how that investment was mobilized and how work on the site was organized remains unknown.[46]

Despite many changes in the size and character of the market over the period covered by this volume, the overwhelming impression is that patterns of urban work, at least up to the eighteenth century, were determined by differing combinations of modes of production used at the same time, rather than by a sequential development from one mode to another. Scale of demand and the shifting pattern of regional and international specialism were the principal factors which determined the combination in use at a particular place and time. In the eighteenth century there may have been signs of radically new developments, but even these were imperfectly developed, far from widespread, and coexisted with older systems.[47]

For most of our period there is no reliable way of establishing absolute measures of the scale of the market served by English towns. On the other hand, estimates of the size of the towns themselves can provide a rough indication. In considering the complexity and the degree of specialization of urban work as well as the overall commercialization of the English medieval urban economy, particularly before 1350, too little weight has been given to these estimates,[48] which in any case are currently subject to revision upwards. Many, if not all of the larger towns, including London, had populations which were greater in 1300 than in 1400 and in the first half of the sixteenth century.[49] English towns were notably wealthy in the eleventh and twelfth centuries.[50] About 1100 the country probably contained a good stock of towns where there is likely to have been a high degree of craft and commercial specialization. London perhaps had at least 20,000 inhabitants and there were four other cities whose populations are likely to have exceeded 5,000.[51] Information on the range of activities practised in this period is hard to come by, but the bynames of Winchester citizens listed in a survey of 1148 incorporate 48 separate occupational terms, and a further 14 occupations are recorded in earlier surveys.[52] Numbers of medieval urban occupations seem broadly to reflect population and commercial development,[53] despite the problems associated with changing patterns of nomenclature. For Winchester about 1300, when the population probably exceeded 10,000 persons, about 70 occupations are recorded. In Norwich, a larger city, 68 trades have been found. Around 1400, when Winchester had about 7,500 inhabitants, the number of recorded occupations was 57. By 1500 it had dropped to 52, but this fall did not equal that in the population.[54] A survey of Gloucester in 1455, when it was roughly comparable to Winchester in size, lists 54 occupations.[55] Tax rolls for London around 1300, when its population may have been more than 80,000, record 175 occupational labels,[56] while similar records for Paris, which was at least twice the size of London, list over 300 occupations.[57] A listing of 1422, when London's population was significantly smaller than in 1300, describes only 111 crafts.[58] At the end of the seventeenth century, when London's population approached half a million, 721 different occupational labels were recorded for taxpayers in the City alone.[59] What is remarkable about these figures, despite all the problems with the sources from which they are derived, is the broad correspondence between population size and specialization. This suggests the value of more systematic exercises, taking factors other than population size into account, and of extending the comparison into the eighteenth and nineteenth centuries, when substantial towns and the specialized occupations within them proliferated to a far greater degree.[60]

Most of these occupations, and the process of their subdivision, were probably generated in response to the internal demands of the towns themselves. But specialist manufactures, meeting a localized demand or finding a niche within the national or international trading network, could produce a particularly high degree of division of labour. The textile industries of the Flemish and Italian towns, for example, contained larger numbers of identified specialist trades than their English counterparts. By the early seventeenth century large numbers of specialized trades were to be found in London's suburbs, where there was a considerable concentration of manufactures.[61] In the eastern parish of St Botolph outside Aldgate, some 280 separate occupations can be identified in about 1600, when the population of the parish was approaching 10,000 persons. Two of the largest manufacturing sectors, each with eleven per cent of the classifiable workforce, were concerned with textiles and metalworking, with 18 and 30 separate trades, respectively. There was a notable armaments industry, stimulated by localized royal demand and comprising six per cent of the classifiable workforce. This contained fourteen separate crafts: not only gunmakers, for example, but also firelockmakers, snaphancemakers, and gunstock-makers. So far as it is possible to tell, these crafts were practised in workshops and working units on a scale no greater than that which could have been found in the medieval city.[62]

Throughout the period up to the later eighteenth century, the household-based workshop was the commonest unit of production. Sometimes, perhaps particularly in metal-working trades, such a workshop might contain about twenty persons.[63] More often, the larger workforces were brought together by an entrepreneur who coordinated the efforts of several workshops. In such cases, the scale and concentration of demand were important in determining patterns of work. The Crown provided the most concentrated demand of all. In 1408–9, for example, the king's embroiderer, while working on a royal contract, employed as many as 85 people at a time, paying them on a daily basis, just as building-workers were paid.[64] It is most unlikely that these people were assembled in a single workplace: they were probably distributed in many domestic workshops where, even during 1408–9, they would also have carried out work for other clients. The largest workforces assembled on single sites in towns were concerned with building.[65] Royal projects were among the largest, and testify to the existence of a substantial pool of labour.[66] Cathedral-building generated a similar demand. In the countryside, mining created a comparable work environment, with gangs of labourers working in close proximity, not unlike conditions in eighteenth-century Merthyr.[67] In towns there was a steady supply of building work and its practitioners moved from site to site participating in teams of varying sizes according to circumstances. The circulation of labour in response to employment opportunities was a distinctive feature of town life, and recognized hiring places for particular types of worker played an important part in the market. With workshop-based production the goods circulated rather than the people, but even there skilled labour circulated in response to demand. The journeyman weavers of fifteenth-century London, for example, had an established place in one of the city's conventual churches where they waited for hire each morning.[68]

The likely size of the pool of labour, as well as the degree of specialization in many medieval towns, has probably been underestimated. This is in part because the work of a large proportion of town-dwellers remains invisible to the historian on account of their poverty or their lack of specialization.[69] Almost equally invisible were those whose work was essential for maintaining the productive and distributive processes, but who received no cash remuneration, or who were accorded only a limited role in the social and administrative structures which generated most of the written records to have come down to us. Married women were by far the largest of these groups, contributing work which sustained households and wider communities, and at the same time participating directly in manufacturing and retailing activity.[70]

The size of urban populations and the degree of urbanization may have been the main determinant of patterns of work in towns, but overall levels of disposable income, and regional shifts in production were also important factors. The rise of the English urban clothing industry during the later fourteenth and the early fifteenth centuries, altering the balance of occupations within towns, promoting new levels of specialization, and perhaps creating new opportunities for independent activity among women, was a response to international changes in the costs of textile production. It took place within the context of an overall fall in population levels, which probably affected even the most prosperous towns, and an overall rise in standards of living for wage earners and craftsmen generally. The latter is likely to have increased demand per head of the population for manufactured items and consumables of all types, promoting a relative increase in specialization and exchange. Not all aspects of this process are thoroughly worked out or understood in terms of the documentary record. Certainly the material remains in English towns and elsewhere seem to support this picture.[71]

Developments such as these are sometimes set in a context of increasing commercialization during the later Middle Ages, a prelude, perhaps an essential prelude, to the 'modernization' which was to follow. It may be more helpful to characterize them as an aspect of the restrictions of the market, in response to the scale and distribution of basic resources, rather than to any fundamental change in systems of production. During the medieval and early modern period technological innovation, relatively slow and small-scale, seems to have responded in a similar fashion. There was a notable exception, however, in the case of the brewing industry. In many English towns during the fifteenth century brewing came to be concentrated in fewer, larger units of production, as beer brewing was introduced. In London, the emergence of the new product, capable of being stored, transported and marketed on a much larger scale than ale, caused some very large enterprises to be established, and the industry was relocated within the city away from the main concentrations of population and business to new sites on the river frontage.[72] This was perhaps the most dramatic change in the pattern and organization of work to have occurred in English towns during medieval and early modern times, yet it seems to have been prompted by a simple technical innovation rather than by any fundamental change in the scale of demand, in the availability of capital, or in the social relations of production.

Assessment of general trends or theoretical possibilities is essential if we are to develop our understanding of work in medieval and early modern towns, especially if we are to see beyond the narrow compartments into which such studies tend to fall. All too often, however, the available evidence is too sparse to bear a conclusive interpretation, or our reading of it is insufficiently informed. Written sources, for example, may give us the names of crafts practised by many individuals in towns, but we remain ignorant of the real character of the day-to-day activities which lay behind the designations. For medieval towns, unlike eighteenth-century Westminster,[73] we do not even know that the occupational designations incorporated in bynames or surnames, or occurring as affixes to them, were those which the practitioners themselves used to describe their daily business. It is necessary to establish with care the context in which the terms were used. Without a knowledge of this context, it is easy to misread the evidence, and to draw inappropriate contrasts and comparisons between different places and different periods.

From the late thirteenth century onwards, occupational labels were employed as a component part of the indicator of the status of many individuals whose names were entered in legal and administrative records. This information is widely used in studies of the urban economy, but often it is a more direct record of social organization than of manufacturing or commercial activity.[74] Before craft guilds achieved an established position in urban constitutions, such occupational labels were more rarely used. For this earlier period a good deal of information on patterns of work can be gleaned from occupational bynames or nicknames, but even then contemporary perceptions of status may skew our picture of urban occupations. The many priests and clerks recorded in twelfth-century Winchester, for example, reflect partly the large numbers of churches and altars in the city, but also the crucial role which clerical status had in notions of social order. At this time a rich variety of terms was used to denote the occupations of townsmen, but since those terms had few, if any, precise connotations of status, we find that many laymen were named or described without reference to their work.[75] Moreover, the meanings of words denoting occupations, in terms of the status or the actual practice of the trade, could change significantly over time; and even a single term in use at one place and at one time could denote several totally different types of activity.[76]

To identify and reconstruct the activities which lay behind even the purely descriptive occupational terms often requires a great deal of labour, investigating cases of debt and broken contract or inventories of stock in trade. More indirectly, patterns of residence and property holding, relations between landlords and tenants, and the proximity of different trades to one another can suggest the existence of particular systems of manufacture or distribution. Such exercises often reveal the variety of occupations which individuals pursued at any one time, or the changes in both residence and trade which could take place at different stages of their careers.[77] Some of these features were as characteristic of eighteenth-century Westminster and of provincial towns in the early nineteenth century as of medieval cities.[78] The more systematic records which survive for these later communities make their study relevant for our understanding of earlier societies too.

Such inquiries demand further examination of the extensive and still underexplored archives of English towns, but in addition another type of evidence, the material remains, is coming to hand in increasing quantities. This has its own problems of interpretation, but offers the possibility of extending our knowledge of towns and of the systems of which they formed part in several otherwise impossible directions. Most obvious is the contribution it can make to knowledge of that substantial period of urban history before c. 1100 when written records begin to give us a detailed picture of working practices. It can do this by establishing the scale and extent of individual urban settlements or by revealing long-distance contacts and local patterns of consumption.[79] Sometimes, as the York evidence makes clear,[80] it can reveal the existence and location of specialized crafts within a town, and the exploitation of the natural resources of the region necessary to supply the raw materials for them. Furthermore, it can provide indications of the ways in which manufacturing processes may have been organized at workshop level. Even for relatively well-documented periods, the material remains can provide evidence for the practice of crafts which made little impression on the written record. A notable example concerns the widespread manufacture of household and personal items out of animal bone, abundantly attested by the survival both of the items themselves and of the waste produced in making them, but hardly at all in documentary sources. In combination with written or place-name evidence, the material remains can be a powerful tool for reconstructing the pattern of work in towns, and its evolution over time.[81]

The Coppergate site in York is of special value for the quantity of its artefacts and for the way in which they could be attributed to structural, chronological and even social contexts.[82] Other, similar sites have provided crucial evidence for urban economic activities and lifestyles.[83] At Winchester there is a fortunate combination of archaeological deposits and written records. All too often, however, the material remains constitute a fragmentary and disturbed body of evidence which occurs in statistically insignificant groups. Even when the material is undisturbed, the very mobility and heterogeneity of the activities which led to its deposition may mean that we should not expect it to reveal the types of topographical distinction which were visible to contemporaries or which can be reconstructed by users of written records. These fundamental characteristics of urban life have caused to founder at least one brave attempt to explore the social and occupational topography of a town through material remains.[84]

There are, however, two rays of hope. One is that opportunities for excavation continually present themselves, so that if they are taken within an appropriate research framework it should be possible to extend the archaeological coverage and make it more representative of the particular features of a town. Secondly, by simply enlarging the quantity of artefactual evidence from contexts which can be dated but which, since they take the form of general rubbish dumps or similar deposits, do not represent any definable social or economic context, we can add substantially to our knowledge of urban activities. With sufficient quantities of such material, as the study of Amsterdam shows, it is possible to trace over several centuries changes in the material equipment of everyday life, in the quality and degree of standardization of the goods, in their origin, and even in the methods of production, as with the involvement of women and children in making them. From this, using the evidence from a single town, it is possible to explore international systems of manufacture and distribution, and the shifts within them which reflected levels of demand, fashion, and transaction costs.[85]

With the different categories of both archaeological and documentary evidence, it is necessary to devise a form of generalization appropriate to each category before proceeding to erect hypotheses which depend upon evidence from several groups of sources. The essays which follow show some of the ways in which these generalizations can be made. In reconstructing past systems from the disparate evidence available, the 'ideal types' and 'modes of production' offered by some branches of social theory can be of great value in organizing preliminary hypotheses, but the tendency to assume that one type necessarily arose from another, in a chronological sequence, has often caused interpretations to be forced into straight-jackets. This has been particularly unfortunate with regard to earlier periods, where the relative absence of evidence has sometimes led to the assumption that their activities were at a correspondingly 'primitive' stage. The growing body of evidence for the extent and complexity of urban life in Britain at an early date, however, should redress this stage of affairs. Nor is it any longer appropriate to view towns as islands of 'advancement' within a more 'backward' rural setting. They performed specialized services, but many of these were in relation to a wide hinterland, and they were often undertaken by individuals whose period of residence within the town was only a part of their career cycle. Now that new types of evidence are coming to hand, and well-known but under-investigated documentary sources are being made to yield new insights, it is time to break free of some traditional constraints concerning social relations and periodization. It is the purpose of this book to assist this process by increasing the 'moral density' among specialists in different disciplines and different historical periods, and so to promote a new understanding of continuity and change in the work of town-dwellers, a crucial facet of economic and social life generally, over a period of nearly one thousand years.

Notes

1. I am grateful to my co-editor for advice, criticism, and above all encouragement, throughout this project.
2. Cited in E. Roll, *A History of Economic Thought* (4th edn., 1973), 45.
3. M.I. Finley, *The Ancient Economy* (2nd edn., 1985), esp. 17–34 and 177–83.
4. For a good summary, which nevertheless in its conclusion tends to play down the significance of the labour market in the medieval urban economy, see B. Geremek, *Le salariat dans l'artisanat parisien aux XIIIe-XV e siècles* (Paris, 1968), esp. 136, 144–7. See also: J. le Goff, 'Le vocabulaire des categories sociales . . .' in *Ordres et Classes. Colloque d'histoire sociale de St. Cloud*, 24–5 May 1967 (Paris, 1973), 73–123; *idem*, 'A note on tripartite society, monarchical ideology and economic renewal in ninth- to twelfth-century Christendom' and 'Licit and illicit trades in the medieval west' in *idem*, *Time, Work, and Culture in the Middle Ages* (Chicago and London, 1980), 53–7, 58–70.
5. Sancti Thomae de Aquino, *Summa Theologiae* (Rome, 1962), 1028, 1031; Aquinas was commenting on Leviticus 19.13 (in the Authorized Version).
6. For the reservoir of wage labour, see the fundamental discussion in M. Postan, *The famulus: The Estate Labourer in the Twelfth and Thirteenth Centuries* (Economic History Review Supplement no. 2, 1954); also J.L. Bolton, *The Medieval English Economy 1150-1500* (reprint, 1985), 111–12; and R.H. Hilton, 'Some social and economic evidence in late medieval English tax returns' in his *Class Conflict and the Crisis of Feudalism* (1985), 253–67.
7. For introductions to these notions and to the debate surrounding them, revealing, perhaps above all, the confusion which sometimes arises from the attempt to impose abstractions on a weak evidential base, see G. Lefebvre et al., *The Transition from Feudalism to Capitalism* with an 'Introduction' by R. Hilton (1978); D.C. Coleman, 'Proto-industrialization: a concept too many', *Economic History Review*, 2nd ser. 36 (1983); L. Clarkson, *Proto-industrialization: The First Phase of Industrialization?* (1985). A valuable case-study, criticizing both Marxist and non-Marxist assumptions concerning 'progress' to industrial capitalism is J. Edwards, '"Development" and "Underdevelopment" in the Western Mediterranean: the case of Cordoba and its region in the late fifteenth and early sixteenth centuries', *Mediterranean Historical Review*, 2 (1987), 3–45.
8. B. Hindess and P.Q. Hirst, *Pre-Capitalist Modes of Production* (1975), seems to move towards this conclusion.
9. E.A. Wrigley, 'Urban growth, and agricultural change, England and the Continent in the early modern period', *Journal of Interdisciplinary History*, 15 (1985), 683–728; R.C. Allen, *The Growth of Productivity in Early Modern English Agriculture* (Dept. of Economics, University of British Columbia, Discussion Paper 86-40, 1986); E.A. Wrigley, *Continuity, Chance and Change: The Character of the Industrial Revolution*

in England (1988). P. Glennie, 'Continuity and change in Hertfordshire Agriculture, 1550–1700: I – Patterns of agricultural production' and 'II – trends in crop yields and their determinants', *The Agricultural History Review*, 36 (1988), 55–76 and 145–61, contains an important survey of the agrarian issues, with bibliographical references to key works.

10. J. Langton, 'Late medieval Gloucester: some data from a rental of 1455', *Transactions of the Institute of British Geographers*, n.s. 2 (1977), 259–77, esp. 275.

11. Compare, for example, the Gloucester data with that for earlier periods in D. Keene, *Survey of Medieval Winchester* (1985) or M. Biddle (ed.), *Winchester in the Early Middle Ages: An Edition and Discussion of the Winton Domesday* (1976).

12. A notable example, still often cited, being G. Sjoberg, *The Preindustrial City, Past and Present* (New York, 1960).

13. A recent case, where a sound empirical study is vitiated in this way, is M.C. Howell, *Women, Production, and Patriarchy in Late Medieval Cities* (Chicago, 1986).

14. Given the current revision of estimates of the size of towns, and of populations generally, before 1500, there is little point in giving figures. For earlier views, based on what are probably underestimates of urban populations, see Hilton, *Class Conflict*, 195; and P.M. Hohenberg and L.H. Lees, *The Making of Urban Europe 1000–1950* (1985), 51–5.

15. E.O. Blake (ed.), *Liber Eliensis* (Camden 3rd series 92, 1962), 100 (no. 26).

16. Keene, *Medieval Winchester*, 252–3, 367.

17. Ibid., 281, 326–7; H. Swanson, *Medieval Artisans: An Urban Class in Late Medieval England* (1989); Swanson, 'Artisans', below, Ch. 3; B. Geremek, *The Margins of Society in Late Medieval Paris*, trans. J. Birrell (1987), 243–69.

18. Kowaleski, 'Town and Country', below, Ch. 4.

19. F.J. Fisher, 'The development of the London food market, 1540–1640', *Economic History Review*, 5 (1935); M. Chisholm, *Rural Settlement and Land Use: An Essay in Location* (1962), esp. 20–32; for a review of current research developments, see B.M.S. Campbell, 'Towards an agricultural geography of medieval England', *The Agricultural History Review*, 36 (1988), 87–98.

20. Kowaleski, 'Town and Country', below, Ch. 4.

21. Tweddle, 'Craft and industry', below, Ch. 2. For timber, see O. Rackham, W.J. Blair, and J.T. Munby, 'The thirteenth-century roofs and floor of the Blackfriars priory at Gloucester', *Medieval Archaeology*, 22 (1978), 105–22. A valuable early study is E.M. Jope, 'Saxon Oxford and its region', in *Dark-Age Britain: Studies presented to E.T. Leeds*, ed. D.B. Harden (1956), 234–58.

22. J. Boulton, 'Residential mobility in seventeenth-century Southwark', *Urban History Yearbook 1986*; *idem*, *Neighbourhood and Society: A London Suburb in the Seventeenth Century* (1987); Phillips, 'Working and Moving', below, Ch. 11.

23. Langton and Hoppe, 'Urbanization', below, Ch. 9.

24. M.I. Finley, 'Aristotle and economic analysis', *Past and Present*, 47 (May 1970), 3–25, places Xenophon's remarks firmly in the category of observation rather than analysis.

25. Adam Smith, *The Wealth of Nations* (Penguin Classics edition, Harmondsworth, 1986), Book 1, chapters I–III (pp. 109–21), IX (esp. p. 198), and X (esp. p. 213).

26. R.H. Bautier, 'Les Foires de Champagne. Recherches sur une évolution historique', *Recueils de la Société Jean Bodin*, 5, *La Foire* (Brussels, 1953), 97–147; R.H. Britnell, 'The proliferation of markets in England, 1200–1349', *Economic History Review*, 2nd ser. 34 (1981), 209–21; *idem*, 'English markets and royal administration before 1200', *Economic History Review*, 2nd ser. 31 (1978), 183–96.

27. Kowaleski, 'Town and country', below, Ch. 4; Keene, *Medieval Winchester*, 20–1, 251–78, 287–9.

28. E. Durkheim, *The Division of Labour in Society*, trans. W.D. Halls (1984), esp. 68–225.

29. M. Taylor, *Community, Anarchy, and Liberty* (1982), esp. 25–33.

30. Evans, 'Work, violence and community', below, Ch. 8. For the notion of 'savage urbanization' applied to medieval towns, see B. Chevalier, *Les bonnes villes de France du XIVᵉ au XVIᵉ siècle* (Paris, 1982), 38, and cf. ibid., 14–17.

31. D. Keene, 'The property market in English towns, A.D. 1100–1600' in *Aux origines de la ville moderne*, ed. J.-C. Maire Vigneur (École Française de Rome, forthcoming).

32. Keene, *Medieval Winchester*, 248–365.

33. The evidence for this change is presented in D. Keene and V. Harding, *Historical Gazetteer of London before the Great Fire, Part 1, Cheapside* (1987). For earlier networks, cf. D. Keene, 'Shops and shopping in medieval London' in *Medieval Art and Architecture in London*, ed. L.M. Grant (British Archaeological Association Conference Transactions, *10*, 1990).

34. Cogently argued in R.H. Britnell, *Growth and Decline in Colchester 1300–1525* (1986), 183–6. In other industries in the same period production increased while the size of the units of production fell: Bolton, *Medieval Economy*, 277–8. The debate is paralleled in current discussions of agrarian productivity between 1300 and 1700, where a strong cases is put that the size of the unit of production (which changed markedly over this period) was less relevant to levels of productivity than the scale and geographical concentration of demand and the availability of labour: see above, n. 9, also, B.M.S. Campbell, 'Agricultural progress in medieval England: some evidence from eastern Norfolk', *Economic History Review*, 2nd ser. 36 (1983), 26–46, esp. 44.

35. Britnell, *Colchester*, 184–5; Keene, *Winchester*, 300, 302.

36. Keene, *Winchester*, 300. Phrases such as 'my weavers and spinners' do not necessarily demonstrate the existence of groups of wage-earners under a single employer (cf. Britnell, *Colchester*, 185), but may rather express the sort of customary, informal relationship between independent, though socially unequal, parties that existed between Samuel Pepys and the tradesmen (or their wives) whom he patronized, and which still exists today in similar contexts. For a fifteenth-century example of the relationship, see N. Davis (ed.) *Paston Letters and Papers of the Fifteenth Century*, I (1971), no. 287; and for a more equal one in the same period, see M.K. Dale, 'Women in the textile industries and trade of fifteenth-century England' (MA thesis, University of London, 1928), 93.

37. Keene, *Winchester*, 399; E.M. Veale, 'Craftsmen and the economy of London in the fourteenth century', in *Studies in London History presented to Philip Edmund Jones*, ed. A.E.J. Hollaender and W. Kellaway (1969), 135–51, esp. 149, 151; cf. Geremek, *Salariat*, 121.

38. Well covered in Geremek, *Salariat, passim*.

39. As, for example, in A.L. Beier, 'Engine of manufacture; the trades of London', in *London 1500–1700: The Making of the Metropolis*, ed. A.L. Beier and R. Finlay (1986), 141–67, esp. 161.

40. Keene, *Winchester*, 514, 1228.

41. M. Bateson, 'A London municipal collection of the reign of John', pt. 1, *English Historical Review*, 17 (1902), 494.

42. C. Brooke and G. Keir, *London 800–1216: The Shaping of a City* (1975), 284–5.

43. See, for example, Bolton, *Medieval Economy*, 265–6.

44. Compare the Winchester fullers in the fourteenth century: Keene, *Winchester*, 305–6.

45. Compare Geremek, *Salariat*, 19–20.

46. *Medieval Archaeology*, 26 (1982), 193 and Plate VII; *Medieval Archaeology*, 27 (1983), 195.

47. N.R. Crafts, *British Economic Growth during the Industrial Revolution* (1984); C. Lee, *The British Economy since 1700: A Macroeconomic Perspective* (1985).

48. The work of Rodney Hilton on small towns has begun to remedy this state of affairs: see above n. 14.

49. For London, see D. Keene, 'A new study of London before the Great Fire', *Urban*

History Yearbook 1984, 11–21. Colchester may have been an exception: Britnell, *Colchester*, 86–98.

50. P.H. Sawyer, 'The wealth of England in the eleventh century', *Trans. Royal Historical Society*, 5th ser. *15* (1965), 145–64; J. Campbell, 'Observations on English government from the tenth to the twelfth century', *Trans. Royal Historical Society*, 5th ser. *25* (1975), 39–54; J.R. Maddicott, 'Trade, industry and the wealth of Alfred', *Past and Present, 123* (May 1989), 3–51.

51. D. Keene, 'Medieval London and its region', *London Journal, 14* (1989), 99–111, esp. 107; Biddle (ed.) *Winchester*, 440, 500–501; Keene, *Winchester*, 366–8.

52. Biddle (ed.), *Winchester*, 428–32.

53. For a recent general survey, see H. Samsonowicz, 'Les villes d'Europe centrale à la fin du Moyen Age', *Annales, 43* (1988), 173–84.

54. Keene, *Winchester*, 250–1 and Table 26 (pp. 352–65); S. Kelly, E. Rutledge and M. Tillyard, *Men of Property: An Analysis of the Norwich Enrolled Deeds 1285–1311*, ed. U. Priestley (1983), 16.

55. Langton, 'Gloucester', Table V (p. 273); for the size of Gloucester, cf. Keene, *Winchester*, 92.

56. Listed in the indexes to E. Ekwall (ed.), *Two Early London Subsidy Rolls* (Lund, 1951); for the size of London see Keene, 'A new study of London'.

57. Geremek, *Salariat*, 15; R. Cazelles, *Paris de la fin du règne de Philippe Auguste à la mort de Charles V 1223–1380* (Paris, 1972), 136.

58. Veale, 'Craftsmen', 139–40.

59. J.M.B. Alexander, 'The economic and social structure of the City of London, *c.* 1700' (PhD thesis, University of London, 1989), 77–9.

60. See Corfield, 'Defining urban work', below, Ch. 12.

61. See Power, 'East London', below, Ch. 7; Beier, 'Engine of Manufacture', 147.

62. Figures based on an analysis of a sample of the St Botolph's parish clerks' memoranda books, 1583–1624. (London, Guildhall Library, MSS 9234/1–8), undertaken in the context of a wider study of the development of the parish: D. Keene, 'The Aldgate Project' (typescript in Institute of Historical Research: 'end of award' report on ESRC-funded project D0023 2027; 1986). cf. below, p. 169.

63. Veale, 'Craftsmen', 149; cf. Keene, *Winchester*, 383, 399.

64. Dale, 'Women', 110–13.

65. Geremek, *Salariat*, 21; L.F. Salzman, *Building in England down to 1540* (reprinted, 1968); Biddle (ed.), *Winchester*, 433–4, 459; Keene, *Winchester*, 283–4; Swanson, *Medieval Artisans*, 82–97.

66. Particularly evident in H.M. Colvin (ed.), *Building Accounts of King Henry III* (1971).

67. Bolton, *Medieval Economy*, 277–8; Evans, 'Work, violence and community', below, Ch. 8.

68. Geremek, *Salariat*, 126–31; F. Consitt, *The London Weavers' Company* (1933), 216.

69. Only about a third of those listed in the tax rolls of late thirteenth-century Paris are identifiable as artisans, and the tax-payers themselves probably represent less than 10 per cent of the population: Geremek, *Salariat*, 13; Cazelles, *Paris*, 136. The proportion covered by the London tax rolls is likely to have been smaller. The size of the pool of labour is indicated by the large numbers of 'poor' (perhaps in the sense in which Aquinas used the term, see above n. 5) who would assemble to receive alms: Veale, 'Craftsmen', 136; J.H. Harvey, 'Richard II and York' in *The Reign of Richard II: Essays in Honour of May McKisack*, ed. F.R.H. Du Boulay and C.M. Barron (1971), 202–17; G. Rosser, *Medieval Westminster 1200–1540* (1989), 295–8.

70. See Roberts, 'Women and work', below, Ch. 6; for a recent study, see D. Frappier-Bigras, 'La famille dans l'artisanat parisien du XIIIe siècle', *Le Moyen Âge, 95* (1989), 47–74. For definitions of work, see Corfield, below, 220–1.

71. Bolton, *Medieval Economy*, 207–319; P. Chorley, 'English cloth exports during the

thirteenth and early fourteenth centuries: the Continental evidence', *Historical Research*, 61 (1988), 1–10; C. Dyer, *Standards of Living in the later Middle Ages* (1989), esp. 188–233; G. Astill, 'Economic change in later medieval England: an archaeological review' in *Social Relations and Ideas*, ed. T.H. Aston *et al.* (1983); Keene, *Winchester*, 219–318; P.J.P. Goldberg, 'Female labour, service and marriage in the late medieval urban north', *Northern History*, 22 (1986), 18–38; *idem* 'Mortality and economic change in the diocese of York, 1390–1514', *Northern History*, 24 (1988), 38–55; Swanson, 'Artisans', below, Ch. 3; J. Allan, *Medieval and Post-Medieval Finds from Exeter 1971–80* (Exeter Archaeological Reports 3, 1984).

72. Power, 'East London', below, Ch. 7; Keene, *Winchester*, 265–9; *idem*, 'Aldgate'; for fifteenth-century riverside beer-breweries in London, see PRO, SC2/191/55–8.

73. Green 'Taxonomy', below, Ch. 10.

74. Swanson, 'Artisans', below, Ch. 3.

75. Biddle (ed.), *Winchester*, 27–8, 193–221, 392–6; A. Rumble, 'The personal name material' in Keene, *Winchester*, 1405–11, esp. 1409.

76. Keene, *Winchester*, 250–336, esp. 289, 304–6.

77. Ibid; Kowaleski 'Town and Country', below, Ch. 4; Swanson 'Artisans' below, Ch. 3; M.J. Bennett, *Community, Class and Careerism: Cheshire and Lancashire Society in the Age of Sir Gawain and the Green Knight* (1983), 114–121.

78. Green, 'Taxonomy', below, Ch. 10; Phillips, 'Working and moving' below, Ch. 11.

79. For two recent studies, see A. Vince 'The economic basis of Anglo-Saxon London', and M. Brisbane, 'Hamwic (Saxon Southampton): an 8th-century port and production centre', both in *The Rebirth of Towns in the West AD 700–1050*, ed. R. Hodges and B. Hobley (Council for British Archaeology Research Report 68, 1988).

80. Tweddle, 'Craft and industry', below, Ch. 2.

81. Keene, *Winchester*, 282, 287–8, 298–300.

82. Tweddle, 'Craft and industry', below, Ch. 2.

83. Brisbane, 'Hamwic'; R.M. Spearman, 'Workshops, materials, and debris – evidence of early industries', in *The Scottish Medieval Town*, ed. M. Lynch, M. Spearman, and G. Stell (1988), 134–47; Allan, *Finds from Exeter*; C. Platt and R. Coleman-Smith, *Excavations in medieval Southampton 1953–69* (1975); M.O.H. Carver, 'Three Saxo-Norman tenements in Durham City', *Medieval Archaeology*, 23 (1979), 1–80.

84. A. Falk and R. Hammel, *Archäologishe und Schriftliche Quellen zur spätmittelalterlich-neuzeitlichen Geschichte der Hansestadt Lübeck: Materialen und Methoden einer archäologish-historischen Auswertung* (Lübecker Schriften zur Archäologie und Kulturgeschichte 10, Bonn, 1987).

85. See Baart, 'Ceramic consumption', below, Ch. 5.

2 Craft and industry in Anglo-Scandinavian York[1]

Dominic Tweddle

For the Early Medieval period the study of the origins, growth and development of towns is as much the province of the archaeologist as that of the documentary historian, and this is more so when dealing with the evidence for work in towns. For most towns the evidence for crafts, industry and trade before the Norman Conquest is exclusively archaeological. The preoccupation of archaeologists in the 1970s and early 1980s with the excavation of urban sites has meant an immense addition to the available corpus of data.[2] Some of the material is as yet unstudied; much is still unpublished, and certainly no general interpretative synthesis has yet emerged. This essay, therefore, concentrates on a single town – York – and within that town principally on a single site, 16–22 Coppergate. Arguably this is the single most important urban excavation on deposits of the pre-Conquest period conducted in this country to date, and one which is especially rich in the evidence for urban crafts. It equally exemplifies some of the difficulties in handling the evidence and its limitations.[3]

York was founded by the Romans about AD 71 as a base for the ninth legion *Hispana*, replaced after AD 122 by the sixth legion *Victrix*. The Romans chose a site on the ridge above the confluence of the rivers Foss and Ouse for their fortress; part of its wall line is incorporated into the medieval walls of the city. Around the fortress to the south-west and south-east developed the *canabae*, a civilian settlement under military control with shops, markets, temples, taverns and workshops providing services to the legion. Across the Ouse to the south-west lay the *colonia*, a self-governing municipality. Fortress and *colonia* were linked by a bridge between the present Lendal and Ouse bridges. The *colonia* was the capital of the province of *Britannia Inferior* and probably possessed both a governor's palace and an imperial palace. Two emperors, Septimius Severus and Constantius I, made York a base for campaigns in the north, and both died there. In AD 306 Constantine the Great was proclaimed emperor in York.[4]

With the break-down of the Roman system of government, York vanishes from the written record only to emerge again in the seventh century; archaeological evidence for this period is equally sparse, consisting only of a handful of pagan Anglo-Saxon objects from the area of the Roman city. In the suburbs and immediate hinterland are a number of cemeteries of this period, on The Mount, at Heworth, and at Castle Yard. Those on The Mount and at Castle Yard are on the site of Roman cemeteries.[5] By the seventh century York appears to have been a centre for the Northumbrian kings – for it was here that St Paulinus baptized King Edwin.

The focus of royal and ecclesiastical activity appears to have been in the old Roman fortress whose defences and *principia* (headquarters building) were still standing and probably in use.[6] Certainly the later Minster occupied the site of the *principia*. Recent excavation suggests that this royal and ecclesiastical centre was complemented by what appears to have been a trading settlement at the confluence of the rivers Foss and Ouse, on the east bank of the Ouse, and outside the area of the medieval walled city.[7]

The coin series in this trading settlement stops about AD 860, the date of the Viking capture of York. The new rulers seem to have reorganized the city radically. Not only was the Anglo-Saxon trading settlement abandoned, but the bridge across the Ouse seems to have been relocated on the site of the present Ouse bridge. A new network of streets was developed leading down to it, particularly on the north-east bank of the Ouse in the area of the *canabae* outside the old Roman fortress wall. As the tenth century progressed, much of the wall on the south-east and the south-west sides of the fortress was demolished, allowing better communication between this new commercial town and the ecclesiastical centre near the site of the Roman *principia*. Many of the streets in this central area of York still bear Anglo-Scandinavian names, identified by the suffix '-gate' (Old Norse *gata*, 'street'). The first elements of some street-names may derive from personal names, such as Goodramgate, from the Old Norse personal name *Guthrun*.[8] Others apparently denote the craft practised there. The first part of the name Coppergate probably derives from the Old Scandinavian *koppari*, a worker in wood who perhaps made turned items, including cups.[9]

The use of street-names derived from Old Norse seems to suggest a considerable Scandinavian influence in York, and this is underlined by a study of the moneyers' names on York coins. For the period of direct Scandinavian rule, AD 866–954 (with short breaks), these are overwhelmingly Scandinavian, with the English element growing after the reform of the coinage in AD 973, at a time when York was ruled by the kings of Wessex.[10] The material culture and art, however, are less distinctively Scandinavian. This is exemplified by the stone sculpture. Both the use of stone as a material and the overall form of the monuments are of Anglo-Saxon inspiration. The iconographic programmes may derive from either culture, from Christian sources or from Scandinavian myth and legend, especially the Sigurd saga; both are found on sculptures from the tenth or eleventh-century graveyard excavated below York Minster. The style of the purely decorative animal ornament draws both on Scandinavian styles, especially the Jellinge style, combined with pre-existing Anglo-Saxon beast chains.[11] The sculpture, like the other material culture of York might, therefore, best be characterized as Anglo-Scandinavian.

The Coppergate site, excavated between 1976 and 1981, lay at the heart of this Anglo-Scandinavian town, on the south side of the street, where the land sloped down towards the River Foss (Figs. 2.1, 2.2). It covered some 1,000 square metres and the archaeological deposits varied from three metres deep at the street front to nearly ten metres on the side closest to the River Foss. Even this large excavation covered only a small sample of the city, representing less than half a per cent of the total area within the medieval walls and, with four house plots, perhaps two per cent of the properties recorded in Domesday Book.[12] Nevertheless, this was a densely-settled area close to the principal economic focus of a city which in 1086 probably had over 10,000 inhabitants.[13]

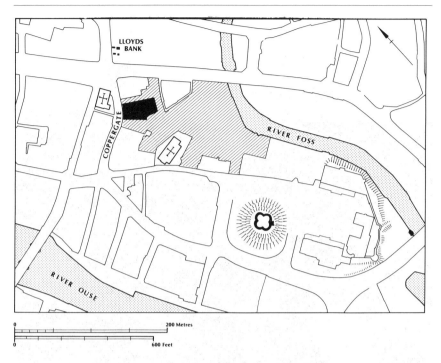

Figure 2.1. Location of the excavation at 16–22 Coppergate, York.

Excavation has revealed a long and complicated sequence of development from the Roman period to *c.* AD 1100; as yet the later medieval and post-medieval sequence has not been fully worked out.[14] Settlement began about AD 100, when the area formed part of the *canabae*; the closest known Roman street lies 100 metres to the south-west, at right angles to Coppergate and approximately on the line of the modern Coney Street and Castlegate. The first buildings were of timber and were located both near the modern street frontage and at the rear of the site. Later, the buildings towards the back of the site were replaced in stone, and at the front of the site there was a mixed inhumation and cremation cemetery (Fig. 2.3).[15] Covering the latest Roman remains was a layer of sterile grey soil, an accumulation of natural deposits transported by wind and water without human interference, representing the period from the end of the Roman city in the early fifth century to the beginning of the Anglo-Scandinavian settlement in the late ninth century. However, the discovery of a scatter of Anglo-Saxon (pre-Viking) objects in later layers,[16] and, of the eighth-century Coppergate helmet (found outside the area of excavation during later building works: Fig. 2.4),[17] demonstrates that there must have been some activity in this area during the intervening period. This was apparently concentrated in the late eighth and in the ninth century. The site contained no evidence for activity between the fifth and the seventh centuries.

Major activity began again on the site in the late ninth century, with the digging of pits and the construction of fences, all still aligned with the Roman layout. A

Figure 2.2. General view of the excavation at 16–22 Coppergate, looking towards the church of All Saints, Pavement.

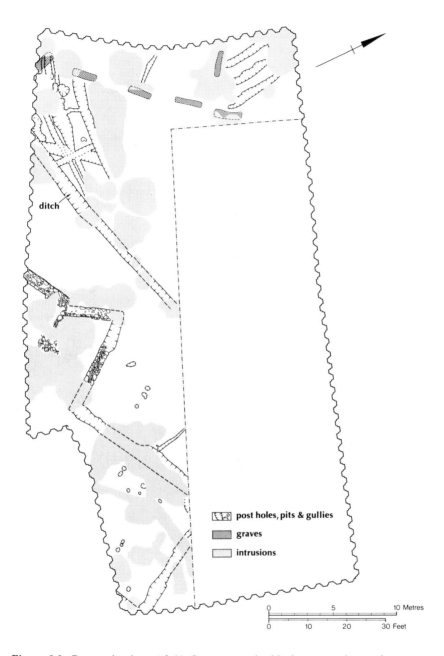

ditch

post holes, pits & gullies

graves

intrusions

0   5   10 Metres

0   10   20   30 Feet

Figure 2.3. Roman levels at 16–22 Coppergate; the blank area to the north was not excavated to this depth.

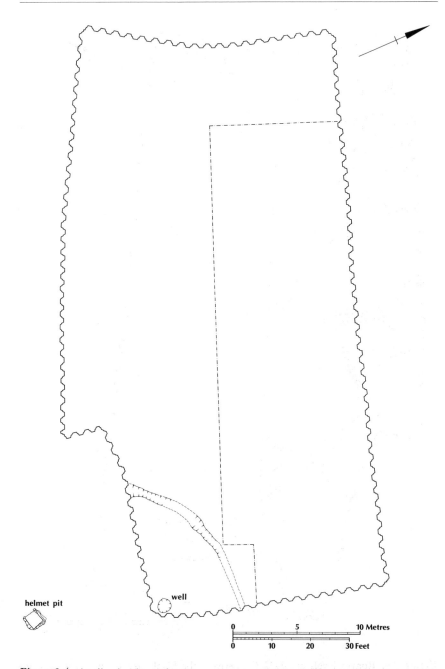

Figure 2.4. Anglian levels at 16–22 Coppergate, and their relationship to the pit in which the Coppergate helmet was discovered.

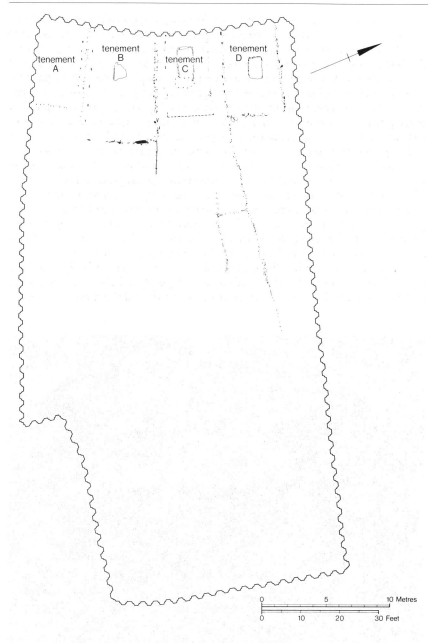

Figure 2.5. Plots laid out at 16–22 Coppergate *c.* 930–5.

small glass-working furnace used to remelt Roman glass, probably for beadmaking, was also constructed, and is the first evidence for early-medieval craft activity on the site. All these features were situated towards the modern street frontage.[18] About AD 900 a comprehensive redevelopment was undertaken. Only slight remains of wattle walls or fences survived from this period, but they were on a new alignment running at right angles to the street frontage of Coppergate. The street itself may have come into existence at this time. It was certainly present by the next phase of development. This took place about 930–5, when house plots about seven metres wide were laid out running back from Coppergate, towards the River Foss (Figs. 2.5 and 2.6). Four plots lay partly or wholly within the area of excavation. They were separated by wattle fences, and each contained a rectangular building of post and wattle construction, situated close to the street frontage and gable end on to it. Each of these houses had a central, rectangular clay hearth edged with wood, stone, or re-used Roman tile.[19] They were rebuilt and modified down to *c*. AD 975, when they were replaced by more substantial structures built of timber uprights with horizontal planking, and partially sunk into the ground (Figs. 2.7 and 2.8).[20] These buildings were also rectangular and placed with gable ends to the street. Each plot now contained a pair of buildings, one on the street frontage, probably a dwelling house, with a workshop behind. Although frequently rebuilt, these structures survived into the eleventh century. In both the wattle and the timber phases the

Fig. 2.6. General view of the wattle-built structures of *c*. 930–5 at 16–22 Coppergate, looking north.

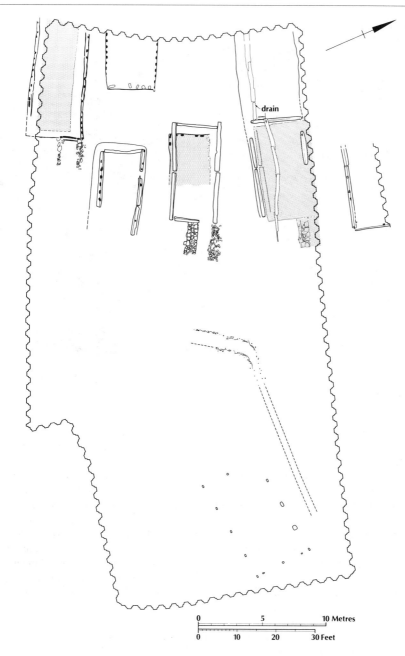

drain

0   5   10 Metres

0   10   20   30 Feet

Figure 2.7. Timber structures of *c.* 975 at 16–22 Coppergate.

Figure 2.8. The north wall of one of the sunken-featured buildings of *c.* 975 at 16–22 Coppergate. The scale measures 1 metre.

yards behind the houses were filled with pits, some of them very large and wattle-lined. Scientific examination of their contents suggests that many of them were cess pits.

Of the 17,000 artefacts recovered from the excavation as a whole, the overwhelming majority are of Anglo-Scandinavian date, and these represent a tremendous diversity of crafts. Iron and non-ferrous metalworking, antler and bone working, amber and jet working, glassworking, woodworking, leather-working, coin minting, and the making of textiles are all represented. Moreover, the waterlogging of the Anglo-Scandinavian deposits means that not only did organic materials, such as wood and leather, survive (which they do not on most other sites), but that other materials, especially the metals, were exceptionally well preserved. The quantity and quality of information which can be obtained from the artefacts is consequently of a different order from that obtained from the equivalent objects on non-waterlogged sites.

Within this great mass of finds, evidence for most of the stages of making a wide range of both everyday and more specialized objects is to be found. In non-ferrous metalworking, for example, there are pieces of the ore galena (lead sulphide usually found mixed with silver sulphide), from which lead and silver were smelted, and ingot moulds made both of stone and of reused Roman tile in which the smelted metal was cast. There are both metal ingots and the fired-clay crucibles in which

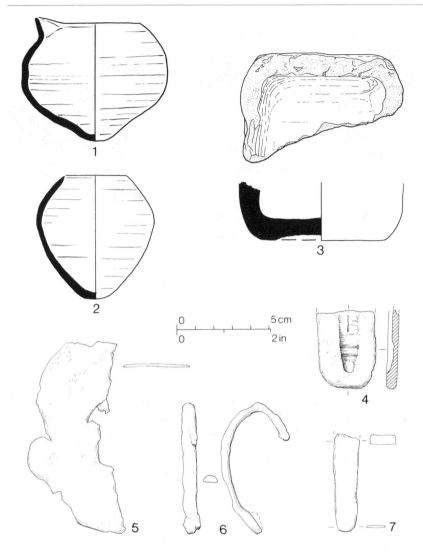

Figure 2.9. Non-ferrous metalworking debris from 16–22 Coppergate, including crucibles (1–3), an iron mould (4), a metal flow (5), and ingots (6–7).

pieces cut from the ingots were remelted to form alloys. There are waste metal flows, fragments of fired clay moulds in which objects were cast, at least one iron mould for the same purpose, and failed castings where the metal did not completely fill the mould, as well as the finished items (Fig. 2.9). That at least some objects were made on the site is suggested by the discovery of groups of finished items which very closely resemble each other. This is the case, for example, with a pair of open-work badges decorated in a version of the Scandinavian Borre style.[21] In addition, there

Figure 2.10. Coins and coin-minting debris from 16–22 Coppergate, including 2 coin dies, and lead trial pieces.

are tools which may have been used for metalworking. These range from small hammers and punches to very specialized tools such as the two dies used for striking coins (Fig. 2.10).[22] The presence of moneyers in Coppergate, which these dies indicate, is a fact of great significance, since at Winchester the moneyers were clearly the most important of the occupational groups among the citizens, with an economic status comparable to that of royal officials. At Winchester, as apparently at York, moneyers were concentrated in the commercial heart of the city.[23]

Evidence for the other crafts is equally abundant, not least with woodworking, the craft after which Coppergate was named. The woodworking tools include axes, shaves and drill bits (Fig. 2.11). The axes could have been used for a wide range of tasks, from felling trees to trimming timbers for building, but the other tools are more specialized. The drill bits come in several sizes, from the small and delicate which could have been used for the making of furniture or in fine carving, to those large enough for use in such heavy carpentry as house- or ship-building. Of the shaves, some are for trimming and shaping wood, like a modern chisel, while others are for shaping staves or planing wood. There are also a tool rest from a pole lathe (the specialized tool of the wood-turner), partly-finished turned vessels, and turning waste (especially the cores of cups and bowls), as well as the finished objects (Fig. 2.12). All this evidence has allowed the process of lathe-turning wooden bowls to be studied in some detail, and a pole lathe of the type used in Anglo-Scandinavian York has been reconstructed and used.[24]

It is salutary to reflect that on sites which are not waterlogged – and this in practice means most archaeological sites – the majority of the evidence for woodworking recovered from the Coppergate site would not have survived. Only the iron tools would have been recovered, but in a badly corroded and even unrecognizable state. At Coppergate the iron tools probably constitute no more than one or two per cent of the objects representing the craft which were originally

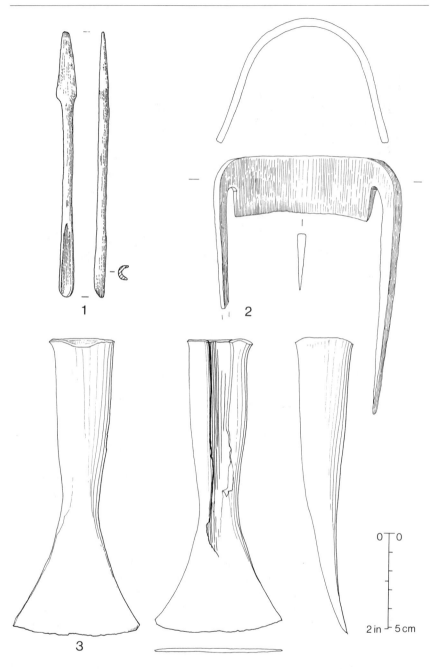

Figure 2.11. Wood-working tools from 16–22 Coppergate, including a spoon bit (1) and two shaves (2, 3), one of which resembles a chisel.

Fig. 2.12. Wood-turning cores, bowls and turned wooden cups from 16–22 Coppergate

buried in the ground. Equally, the Coppergate finds include products of the woodworker which would not normally survive on other sites. These range from the buildings themselves to portable items such as stave-built barrels, buckets and vessels, turned wooden bowls and cups, and shaped objects such as spades, shovels, spoons and implement handles. But even in the excellent preservative conditions of the Coppergate site, some organic materials hardly survived at all, notably horn, and bast fibres such as flax.

Some classes of craft evidence do not appear in the archaeological record because they were never, or only rarely, deposited. This can be documented at Coppergate in the case of the non-ferrous metalworking debris. A superficial examination of this material would suggest that the metals being worked were principally lead and copper alloys. There are only a handful of silver objects, one silver ingot, and a few fragments of silver ore to suggest the working of silver on the site. Only three tiny gold objects were found, and there was no evidence of goldworking visible to the naked eye. Yet, microscopic examination and X-ray fluorescence analysis of the tiny droplets of metal adhering to the insides of the crucibles has shown that most of them were used for melting silver, and that a small but significant number had been used for melting gold. The absence of gold objects can probably be explained by the fact that they were so valuable that if they were lost extraordinary efforts were made to find them again, and by the likelihood that the inhabitants of Coppergate who made objects of gold were not themselves rich enough to own them. The absence of silver objects could be explained in a similar fashion, although it is perhaps more likely that the silver-working debris was associated with the minting of coins rather than with the making of jewellery or other items of personal adornment.

Scientific examination of the objects not only has revealed new information about the types of craft practised on the site, but is also crucial in elucidating the detailed processes involved in manufacture. Such work demonstrates that Anglo-Scandinavian craftsmen, as might be expected, made clear and rational choices about the materials used for particular objects, or parts of composite objects. 'Bone' combs, for example, are usually not made of bone at all, but of antler, usually from red deer. The craftsman fully appreciated that bone is rather brittle and liable to snap when used in thin pieces under intense strain, as in comb teeth. Antler, however, is much more flexible and can absorb much greater strains without breaking.[25] Similarly, in the making of shoes there was a careful selection of the leathers employed. Cattle hide was used for the soles where thickness and hence strength and durability were important; calfskin, sheepskin, or more rarely goatskin, were used for the uppers where greater suppleness was required.

Different materials were also combined in much more subtle ways to achieve a desired effect. Detailed examination of the iron tools from Coppergate, involving the cutting and microscopic examination of etched sections, shows that smiths made their tools of differing qualities of iron. The use of wrought iron for the body of the tool gave it flexibility, while a steel strip, forge-welded on, formed the cutting edge. As steel could only be made in small quantities, this method was economical with a scarce material. Steel is also brittle, so even had it been widely available, tools made completely of steel would have been impractical. Occasionally, even more elaborate effects were achieved, as when numerous strips of iron with differing carbon content and, therefore, differing flexibility and hardness, were forged together to make a tool having just the right combination of these qualities. A steel cutting edge was then added by forge-welding. Qualities which today would be achieved by making an alloy were attained by the Anglo-Scandinavian smith, but by a much more circuitous and laborious method than used today.

While a close examination of objects from the site has allowed the processes involved in numerous crafts to be reconstructed in great detail, the material raises a number of more general questions, although it is not necessarily capable of answering all of them.

One of the most pressing problems for the archaeologist is to define the precise nature of the craft activity on a site. The observation that particular craft processes in particular materials were performed is a simple, and in the end, fairly uninformative one. More importantly, do the objects represent a single event or one-off activity? Or do they represent activity continuing over a long period? Were people producing the objects for their own use? Or were the remains left by specialist craftsmen who made the greater part of their living this way? If this was the case, what was the degree of their specialism? If the craftsmen were specialists, were they active on the site permanently or only seasonally? These questions are crucial for an understanding of how early medieval towns originated, evolved, and functioned. If answers to some of these questions can be squeezed from the relatively well-preserved archaeology of York, then they may help in interpreting the less abundant archaeological record in other towns.

From an examination of both the finished objects and the craft evidence for manufacturing processes from the Coppergate site it appears that there were two levels of craft activity. The first was the making of simple objects for everyday use, which in some materials may have been undertaken in every household. Bone points, scoops, needles and spindle whorls, for example, are ubiquitous and required only the simplest tools and little expertise to make; the raw materials were readily available from food bones. Similarly, evidence for textile making is so widespread, and many of the tools so simple that it seems likely that in nearly every household textiles were made for the everyday use of its members, perhaps leaving specialist weavers to concentrate on the finer, high-value products. The textile implements most commonly found include wool-comb teeth for the combing of the wool to align the fibres, spindles and spindle whorls for spinning the yarn, loom weights and parts of the vertical looms on which the textiles were woven, pin beaters for adjusting the yarn, and lucets for making edge braids. There are also fragments of the dye plants used to colour the yarn or cloth: woad, madder, dyer's greenweed and clubmoss were all present in most of the deposits.[26]

In contrast, some crafts seem to have been the monopoly of specialist craftsmen, a hypothesis which can be advanced on several grounds. For some crafts the raw materials must have been difficult and costly to acquire. The ore galena was brought at least 30–40 kilometres from the Pennines, the nearest source to York. Jet was presumably brought a similar distance from Whitby or the North York Moors: its only other source in Western Europe is in Spain. Antler was collected seasonally in May when it was shed naturally, since little of the antler found in York came from dead animals. All this implies the construction and maintenance of systems to mine or to collect the raw materials and to transport them to the point of use. That in turn implies the investment of time and resources in proportion to the value of the raw material, and probably the establishment of trading networks. Some of the raw materials may have been transported overland, but most will have been moved by water along the Ouse and its tributaries: the Ouse was navigable as far as Boroughbridge, 26 kilometres north-west of York, at this period. Coastal shipping may have been used to transport some raw materials, and some, such as walrus ivory or amber, may have been brought to the city by ocean-going ships.[27]

In addition, some crafts demanded greater complexity than others in the tools or facilities required. The making of furnaces for metalworking, pole lathes for wood turning, and specialist iron tools for most crafts (such as the rasps and small saws needed for antler working) were all in themselves complex tasks. The ceramic crucibles which were brought to York from Stamford, some 160 kilometres away, for the melting of metals again imply the use of capital and exchange systems to acquire resources.[28] Equally, time had to be invested in learning the craft. Many crafts required particular, complex skills which must have taken some years to perfect, as with iron smithing or non-ferrous metalworking.

For these reasons it is probable that most of the craft evidence from the Coppergate site relates to specialist craftsmen. But what was the extent of the specialization? Did individual craftsmen deal with one particular material? With more than one? Or with many? One way to tackle this problem archaeologically is to examine the relationship over time between the house plots on the site, which presumably correspond to units of household workshop activity, and the debris representing each craft. This technique is of particular value on the Coppergate site, where each phase of activity can be narrowed to three or four decades, allowing changes to be traced over relatively short periods of time. This is a laborious exercise which involves the accurate plotting on the appropriate phase plan of every one of the objects from the site, and is not yet complete. There are already, however, clear concentrations of particular categories of craft evidence on particular plots, implying that they were occupied by recognizable craft specialists. For example, in period 4B (from 930–5 to c. 975) there is a concentration of non-ferrous metalworking (represented by crucibles used for melting silver) on properties C and D, especially on property D (Fig. 2.13). Iron-working debris from this period shows a similar distribution, within the sites of the four houses, with a particular clustering on property C (Fig. 2.14). This might suggest that the metalworking crafts, both ferrous and non-ferrous, were practised by the same craftsmen, or by associated craftsmen on the same or adjoining sites. Alternatively, the evidence may reflect the activities of a group of craftsmen, even of a single business, which over a period of about forty years switched from making one type of product to another. That the former is the more likely interpretation is suggested by the distribution of the coin minting evidence (Fig. 2.15). This is present on properties C and D in periods 4A (from c. 900 to 930–5) and 4B (from 930–5 to c. 975), indicating that the craft was long-lived, a fact confirmed by the latest piece of numismatica, a trial piece of King Eadwig dating to 955–9, very close to the end of period 4B.[29] This is virtually conclusive evidence that both coin minting and other forms of metalworking were practised here simultaneously. Indeed, at Winchester and elsewhere at later periods close links are apparent between goldsmiths and the production of coin.[30]

There seems to be good evidence from Coppergate and other early medieval sites for a level of craft specialization. But to what degree was this activity permanently settled on the site? Some archaeologists have been disturbed by the relatively small absolute quantity of craft evidence usually recovered, even where all stages in the manufacturing process are represented. This has led Ulbricht in her study of the Viking-Age antler-working debris from Haithabu (Schleswig-Holstein) to deny that there could be full-time specialist craftsmen at all.[31] Ambrosiani has interpreted the similar and broadly contemporary material from Birka (Sweden) and Ribe (Denmark) differently, suggesting that it was produced not by settled, part-time craftsmen, but rather by full-time craftsmen moving seasonally from town to town.[32]

These interpretations both assume that the quantity of material recovered in excavation forms a relatively large percentage of that originally deposited. In fact this may not be the case. For example, with non-ferrous metalworking (Fig. 2.16), some of the materials, notably gold and silver, were so precious that no waste could be afforded. For the stages where there was bulky waste generated, as with the slag from smelting, it need not have been disposed of on the site where it was generated. Recent excavations behind the Coppergate site, in Piccadilly, on the edge of the river Foss, have shown that in the twelfth century metalworking waste was removed from the Coppergate site and dumped at the edge of the river. Other stages in the manufacturing process produced much less waste. At a time when raw materials were difficult to obtain, manufacturing techniques were very economical, and wastes such as metal spillages and failed castings were generally recycled. But even of that material which was originally deposited on the site, not all will have survived, the survival rate varying according to the type of material and the soil conditions. Certainly, not all the material which survived will have been recovered. With material picked out by the excavators as they trowel, there is a bias towards the recovery of the larger finds. This problem can only be overcome by sieving all the spoil from an excavation, or at least a representative sample of it, an approach

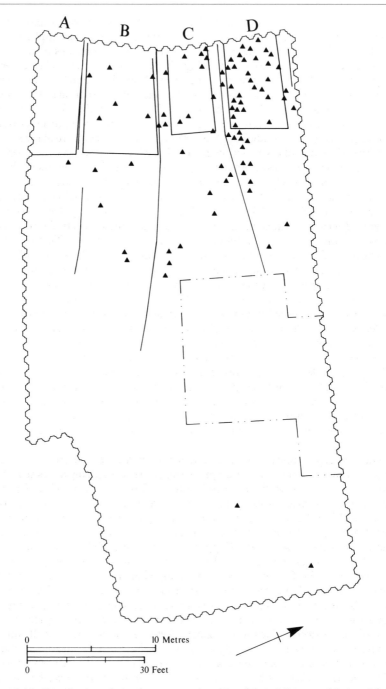

Figure 2.13. Distribution of non-ferrous metalworking debris (silver crucibles) at 16–22 Coppergate. Period 4B.

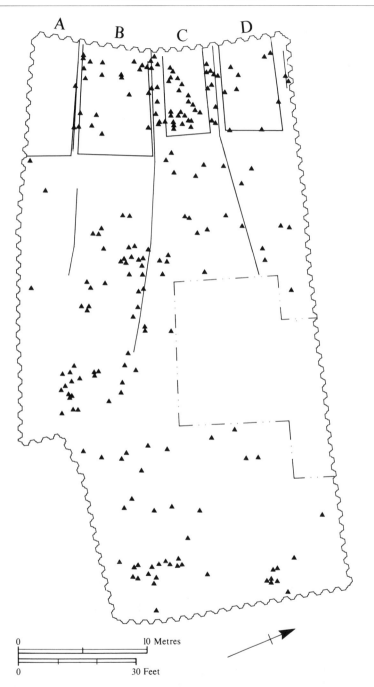

Figure. 2.14. Distribution or iron-working debris (iron strips and plates) at 16–22 Coppergate. Period 4B. The blank area was not excavated to these levels.

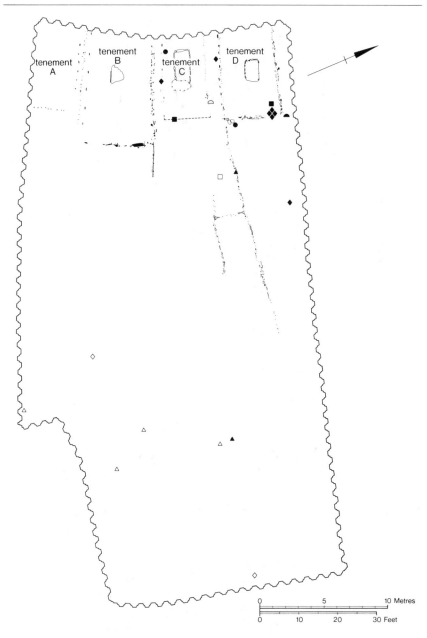

Figure 2.15. Distribution of coin-minting debris at 16–22 Coppergate. Periods 4A and 4B. The debris comprised trial pieces (shown as squares), dies (circles), pennies (lozenges), stycas (triangles), and a foreign coin (half circle); open symbols indicate that the precise find spot is uncertain.

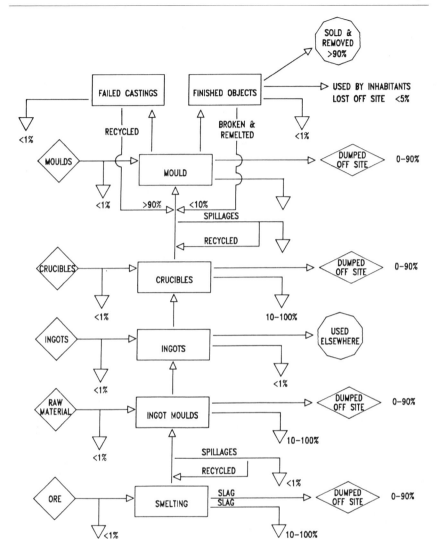

Figure 2.16. Non-ferrous metalworking. Diagrammatic representation of the processes and the types and levels of waste produced.

which is both expensive and laborious. Yet on the Coppergate site, it was only by sieving that it was possible to recover the yellow mineral orpiment (Arsenic trisulphide), used as a colour and inlay on jet, and many of the small offcuts of amber.

These factors suggest that the craft material recovered from most sites represents only a small fraction of that originally produced. The small absolute quantities need not, therefore, be explained away by denying the existence of full-time specialist craftsmen or by suggesting seasonal production. When most stages in the manufacturing process are represented in the material evidence, then the permanent occupation of the site by specialist craftsmen is a plausible, although not the only possible interpretation. It is made even more likely where there are several related crafts represented on the same site since, as seems to be the case at Coppergate, the same craftsmen may have been undertaking them. Almost certainly craft specialization had not yet proceeded to the point where there was necessarily a specialist in a single material, much less in a single type of object or small group of related objects, as there was in the later Middle Ages.

Nor does it appear that there was yet any exclusive zoning of crafts within the Anglo-Scandinavian city. The Coppergate site, despite the street-name, contains evidence for a dozen or so crafts being practised side by side. Distribution plots of the waste from different crafts on a city-wide basis tentatively support this conclusion. For example, antler-working debris is found on virtually every site where Anglo-Scandinavian levels have been excavated in the centre of the modern city (Fig. 2.17). There are two caveats here, however. The evidence for wood-working, at least, does appear to be confined to the Coppergate area. This may be mere chance, or a reflection of the differing degrees of preservation which prevailed

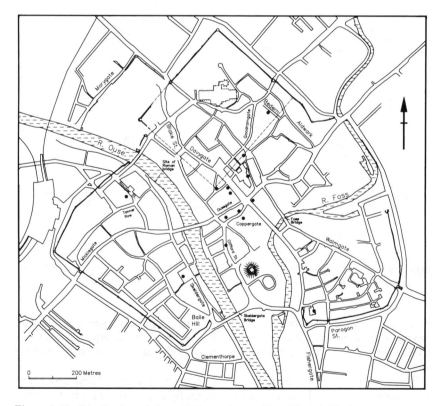

Figure 2.17. Distribution of sites yielding antler-working debris in York.

in different parts of the city, but it may be a genuine pattern. If so, it was presumably the more-or-less unique occurrence of woodworking craftsmen in this district, rather than their numerical predominance over other trades, which gave Coppergate its name. Secondly, there appears to be a concentration in the city centre of crafts which might be classed as socially acceptable, those which neither produced noxious smells and unpleasant fumes, nor required large open spaces. No evidence for pottery manufacture has been encountered in excavations in the heart of the Anglo-Scandinavian city, presumably because this was an essentially rural or suburban craft, and little for the tanning of leather, probably for the same reason. Both Coppergate itself and, close by, the Lloyd's Bank site at 6–8 Pavement have produced evidence of leatherworking. At 6–8 Pavement a leatherworker's workshop was found, but evidence for tanning on both these sites is minimal.[33] It may well be that the Coppergate/High Ousegate/Pavement area was itself distinctive in York as an area where manufacturing crafts of several different types were concentrated. Thus, excavation of Anglo-Scandinavian levels south-west of the River Ouse and in Walmgate has not produced anything approaching the range of craft evidence seen at 16–22 Coppergate and 6–8 Pavement.

Excavations at 16–22 Coppergate and other sites in York have produced clear evidence for the range of crafts practised in the city in the tenth and eleventh centuries and have elucidated the techniques and technologies used to create objects in the period. The careful recording and detailed analysis of the data from 16–22 Coppergate has allowed a number of tantalizing questions about the organization of the crafts and industries of the city to be addressed. Even if the answers are not yet conclusive, the difficulties in arriving at them can be mapped out. What can be said is that there is clear evidence for the existence of complex economic systems to obtain and to transport the raw materials, and presumably to distribute the finished goods. Within the city there were craft specialists, probably permanent residents, who manufactured a wide range of utilitarian and decorative objects, although these specialists were working in a range of allied materials, not, so far as can be seen, just in one. These conclusions, based on York's outstandingly rich archaeology, are probably applicable, at least in England, to other early medieval towns where the archaeology is less well preserved. The analysis of the vast body of data recovered from excavations may be slow, laborious and expensive, but it is virtually the only source of evidence for patterns of work in towns during the early medieval period.

Notes

1. I am grateful to my colleagues and co-workers at the Coppergate project for freely discussing their more detailed research with me, particularly Patrick Ottaway, Penelope Walton, Ailsa Mainman, Arthur MacGregor, Sonia O'Connor, Justine Bayley and Carole Morris. R.A. Hall, the site director, has as ever been ready with help and information. The text has been typed by Karen Smith, the figures were prepared by the York Archaeological Trust Drawing Office, and M.S. Duffy took the photographs. I am indebted to the York Archaeological Trust for permission to publish in advance of the final publication of the Coppergate excavation.

2. For recent overviews, see: C. Dyer, 'Recent developments in early medieval urban history and archaeological research in England'; H. Stephen, 'Urban archaeological research in Germany: a regional view of medieval topographic development'; and H.

Steuer, 'Urban archaeology in Germany and the study of topographic, functional and social structures', all in *Urban Historical Geography: recent progress in Britain and Germany*, ed. D. Denecke and G. Shaw (1988). J. Schofield and R. Leech (ed.), *Urban Archaeology in Britain* (Council for British Archaeology Research Report 61, 1987), and J. Schofield and D. Palliser (ed.), *Recent Archaeological Research in English Towns* (1981), contain useful listings. H. Clarke, *The Archaeology of Medieval England* (1984), esp. 166–94, and M. Biddle, 'Towns' in *The Archaeology of Anglo-Saxon England*, ed. D.M. Wilson (1976), 99–150, are still valuable.

3. Excavations in York are published in the series The Archaeology of York edited by P.V. Addyman (1976 onwards). Recent research is encapsulated in the Ordnance Survey Maps, *Roman and Anglian York* and *Viking and Medieval York*, both published in 1988.

4. Royal Commission on Historical Monuments, England, *An Inventory of the Historical Monuments in the City of York*, I, *Eburacum: Roman York* (1962), xix–xxxix. For more recent reviews, see D.A. Brinklow, 'Roman settlement around the legionary fortress at York' and P. Ottaway, '*Colonia Eburacensis*: a review of recent work', both in *Archaeological Papers from York presented to M.W. Barley*, ed. P.V. Addyman and V.E. Black (1984), 22–7 and 28–33.

5. Some of the material for York's pagan Anglo-Saxon cemeteries is published in B. Eagles, *Anglo-Saxon Humberside* (British Archaeological Reports, British Series 68, 1979).

6. I am grateful to Mr D. Phillips, formerly Director of the York Minster Excavation Unit, for this information.

7. R. Kemp, 'Anglian York – The Missing Link', *Current Archaeology*, 104 (1987), 259–63.

8. D.M. Palliser, 'The medieval street names of York', *York Historian*, 2 (1978), 10.

9. Ibid., 8; A.H. Smith, *The Place-Names of the East Riding of Yorkshire and York* (English Place-Name Society 14, 1937), 285.

10. E.J.E. Pirie, *Sylloge of Coins of the British Isles, 21, Coins in Yorkshire Collections* (1975), 1–1ii.

11. J.T. Lang, 'Anglo-Scandinavian sculpture in Yorkshire', in *Viking Age York and the North* (Council for British Archaeology Research Report, 27), ed. R.A. Hall (1978), 11–20. J. Lang, 'Continuity and innovation in Anglo-Scandinavian sculpture', in *Anglo-Saxon and Viking Age Sculpture and its Context*, ed. J. Lang (British Archaeological Reports, British Series 49, 1978), 145–55.

12. P.M. Tillott (ed.), *A History of Yorkshire: The City of York* (VCH Yorkshire, 1962), 19.

13. For this estimate, cf. F. Barlow, M. Biddle, O. von Feilitzen, and D. Keene, *Winchester in the Early Middle Ages: An Edition and Discussion of the Winton Domesday*, ed. M. Biddle (1976), 440, 468. Winchester probably had a population of at least 8,000 in the early twelfth century, occupying 1,130 properties; York was a larger city, with possibly as many as 13,000 inhabitants occupying its 1,890 properties. See also D. Keene, 'The property market in English towns, A.D. 1100–1600' in *Aux origines de la ville moderne,* ed. J-C Maire Vigueur (École Française de Rome, forthcoming).

14. R.A. Hall, *The Viking Dig* (1984) contains a preliminary general account of the Coppergate excavation. Final publication will be in The Archaeology of York.

15. Hall, op. cit., 15–28, Fig. 8.

16. Ibid, 27–42.

17. D. Tweddle, *The Coppergate Helmet* (1984).

18. Hall, op. cit., 43–5, Fig. 41.

19. Ibid., 49–66, Fig. 50. As a result of recent work this interpretation varies slightly from the published account in the final detail of the phasing and dating.

20. Ibid., 67–80, Fig. 72.

21. A general account of the development of this style in England is provided by D.M. Wilson, 'The Borre style in the British Isles' in *Minjar og menntir*, ed. K. Eldjárn (Reykjavik, 1976), 502–9.

22. E.J.E. Pirie, *Post-Roman Coins from York Excavations* (The Archaeology of York, *18/1*, 1976), 396–422.

23. F. Barlow *et al.*, op. cit., 400–22.

24. For an account of the wood-turning debris from 16–22 Coppergate, see C. Morris, 'Aspects of Anglo Saxon and Anglo-Scandinavian lathe-turning' in *Woodworking Techniques before AD 1500*, ed. S. MacGrail (National Maritime Museum, Greenwich Archaeological Series, 7; British Archaeological Reports International Series, *129*: 1982), 245–61.

25. A. MacGregor, *Bone, Antler, Ivory and Horn* (1985), 25–9.

26. P. Walton, *Anglian and Anglo-Scandinavian Textiles from 16–22 Coppergate* (The Archaeology of York, *17/6*, forthcoming).

27. See D.M. Palliser, *Tudor York* (1979), 186–9; *VCH York*, 472–5.

28. A. Mainman, *Anglian and Anglo-Scandinavian Pottery from 16–22 Coppergate* (The Archaeology of York, *16/5*, forthcoming).

29. Pirie, *Post-Roman Coins*, 39–40, Fig. 7, Pls vii, ix.

30. Barlow *et. al.*, op. cit., 421–2; P. Nightingale, 'Some London moneyers and reflections on the organization of English mints in the eleventh and twelfth centuries'. *Numismatic Chronicle, 142* (1982), 34–50.

31. I. Ulbricht, *Die Geweihverarbeitung in Haithabu* (Die Ausgrabungen in Haithabu, 7, Neumünster, 1978).

32. K. Ambrosiani, *Viking Age Combs, Comb Making and Comb Makers in the Light of New Finds from Birka and Ribe* (Stockholm, 1981), 40–54, 157–8.

33. A.R. Hall *et al.*, *Environmental and Living Conditions at Two Anglo-Scandinavian Sites* (The Archaeology of York, *14/4*, forthcoming) and P.V. Addyman, *Excavations at 6–8 Pavement* (The Archaeology of York, *8/4*, forthcoming). The so-called tanning pits recorded by Benson in his 1903 excavations at High Ousegate (G. Benson, 'Notes on excavations at 25, 26 and 27 High Ousegate, York', *Yorkshire Philosophical Society Annual Report for 1902* (1903), 64–7) have been reinterpreted by R.A. Hall as sunken-featured buildings of the tenth century, similar to those from 16–22 Coppergate.

3 Artisans in the urban economy: the documentary evidence from York

Heather Swanson

The image of the medieval master craftsman, in command of his own workshop, making shoes or horseshoes, purses or pots, for retail sale in his shop, is something of a commonplace. Many different manufacturing specialities can be isolated and listed to illustrate the diversity of urban enterprise. Such a picture leaves a great many assumptions unchallenged; it is the purpose of this essay to make a closer examination of some of those assumptions which relate to craft ascriptions, and to question their reliability as a guide to the industrial structure of the medieval town.[1] Obviously, the appearance and disappearance of individual crafts in urban records were related to changes in the economy. But alterations in the meanings of craft ascriptions, and in the status of specific crafts, were not always determined by economic change; they might equally well be the result of political or social change. The first part of this essay analyses some of the craft ascriptions so readily attached to the men, and sometimes to the women, of later medieval York, in order to see how far their meanings changed in changing circumstances. Throughout, the word 'artisan' has been used to describe these people, rather than the more familiar term craftsman, because the first, and most consistent misapprehension most likely to arise from medieval craft ascriptions is that men and women generally did different kinds of work. The second part goes on to challenge the assumption that a profile of the urban economy based on these craft ascriptions offers an adequate approach to the understanding of the industrial function of the town.

I

Population statistics for late medieval towns have to be largely guesswork, but as a rough guide York had a population of about 13,000 in the late fourteenth century, somewhat larger than Bristol, Coventry and Norwich, which had populations of over 8,000. Some forty English towns at this time had populations of over 2,000, although there was a continuum down to small market towns, definitely urban in character, with no more than 1,000 inhabitants.[2] A combination of factors brought about the decline in the size and prosperity of some towns, among them York, in the later fifteenth century, so that by the early sixteenth century its population was around 8,000, placing the city well down on a listing of towns ranked either by size or by wealth. York, nevertheless, still predominated in the north.[3] Most of the discussion in this essay applies to towns with about 2,000 to 15,000 inhabitants. In considering urban artisans, it should be emphasized that there was a qualitative difference between London and the large provincial towns of late medieval England, stemming from the great size and status of the capital. The scale of economic activity found in London was inevitably reflected in the relationships between artisans and merchants.[4] In contrast York, although the first city of the north, had much in common with places like Coventry and Bristol. A detailed study of artisans in York can therefore fairly confidently be said to reflect the experience of artisans in other provincial towns. Comparisons with London have to be made more cautiously.

Evidence for urban manufacturing has in the past been taken from what might generally be called 'public' records, primarily records of administration. These include composite volumes such as the York Memorandum Book, Coventry Leet Book, and the Little and Great Red Books of Bristol that preserve the major administrative decisions of corporate bodies.[5] Where registers of freemen have survived, historians have used them to draw up league tables of crafts.[6] The main problem with these documents is precisely that they were administrative. Although their subject-matter is often the urban workforce, they were drawn up in terms of political and social preoccupations. Essentially, they record how the ruling class of the town sought to govern the community. Such documents can provide evidence of occupational structure, but only obliquely, and such evidence cannot be taken at face value. It follows that what appear to be changes in the economy between the early fourteenth and early sixteenth centuries may in fact be no more than changes in administrative or social concerns. To a large extent court records can flesh out this rather limited view and such records, along with those of property holding, have been used to analyse the occupational structures of Winchester and Colchester, for example.[7] The problem for many large towns is that judicial records do not survive, whereas small market towns, subject to local lords, often do have detailed and revealing court rolls.[8] York is one of those towns where court records are missing. In this case the wills and inventories of artisans have been used to lend perspective to the official records. Some 1,100 wills survive, mostly those of men, dating from between 1320 and 1534. In contrast, there is only a handful of inventories, twenty-four in all, but the range of dates and occupations that they cover is sufficiently wide to provide a useful basis for comparison. There are a great many limitations to using wills, but handled with caution they can provide some valuable insights into the lifestyle of artisans.[9]

The range of specialized industries in the larger provincial towns was very wide, exemplifying the characterization of the town as a place with a diversity of occupational structure. The York Register of Freemen produces the names of such engaging trades as *mynstrall and brewer*, or specialists such as *sheregrynder* and *colourmaker*.[10] This variety is, unfortunately, very easily lost sight of in attempts to impose a structure on medieval industry, for example by tabulating evidence of occupation into sectors such as 'textiles', 'clothing', 'leather', 'services' and the like. It can be argued that the historian is no more than following the example of the medieval record makers, who were anxious to corral as many male artisans as possible into identifiable groups for their better regulation.[11] But by doing so an over-rigid framework is imposed on the process of urban manufacture, thereby obscuring some of its essential features – the flexibility of employment, the constantly fluctuating boundaries between crafts, and the multi-occupational household.

Evidence for the industrial structure of York has tended to place a great deal of emphasis on statistics drawn from the Register of Freemen, because during the course of the later Middle Ages an increasing proportion of those who took out the freedom had a craft ascription assigned to them. But a town's register of freemen was not primarily an economic document; it can be better characterized as a register of those who had rights, but more importantly obligations, as members of the urban community. The precise meaning of this freedom will be discussed later; the point to be made here is that although an increasing number of freemen had a craft ascribed to them, the choice of this ascription may have been dictated by social or political considerations. In addition, the meaning of these ascriptions changed over time and from place to place. The status and content of each occupation have to be seen in the context of the specific local society in which it was pursued. Furthermore, it has to be recognized that differences in terminology in the records may amount to no more than the idiosyncracies of the enrolling clerk, particularly in a service industry such as medicine. In York only six treaclers, makers of herbal medicine, appear in the Register of Freemen, all of them between 1411 and 1430. The ambiguity of medical terminology is evident in the history of Nicholas Wodhill, made free in York in 1435, when he was described as *medicus*. In 1440 he received a royal pardon for various offences in which he was described as 'alias Nicholas Leche, late of London, alias late of York, leche, alias of York, surgeon'.[12]

Table 3.1 Proportion of York freemen with no trade ascription

	Total free	Those with no craft ascription	Percentage
1273–1300	541	207	38
1301–1350	2,756	694	25.2
1351–1400	4,811	398	8.3
1401–1450	4,978	445	4.5
1451–1500	3,534	69	2.0
1501–1534	1,810	25	1.4

Where apparently identical crafts have different trade ascriptions it cannot always be assumed that these were synonymous. Although shoemakers and cobblers, described variously as *cordwaner, allutarius, cobler*, seem to be undifferentiated in York, the same cannot be said of marshals and smiths. The marshals and smiths resolutely attempted to keep two separate crafts despite the virtually identical nature of their work, until forced into an unhappy union by the city council in the mid-fifteenth century.[13] The potters and founders, who both cast bronze vessels, likewise maintained a distinction throughout the later Middle Ages which seems to have rested more upon social and geographical than upon industrial grounds. Other terms used for casters of bronze were brazier and bell-founder, and it was usual in provincial towns for one guild to embrace the handful of men who practised these crafts. In Coventry, pewterers and braziers were united in the fifteenth century.[14] Despite the difference in techniques involved, one man might undertake the manufacture of pewter and bronze vessels, as did Nicholas Green, a leading citizen of sixteenth-century Worcester.[15] In York there were crafts of pewterers, potters, and founders. Of the latter two, potters appear first; in the early fourteenth century they boasted such eminent practitioners as Richard Tunnock, mayor and donor of the celebrated bell-founders' window in the Minster. Such evidence as there is suggests that other potters in the first half of the fourteenth century were of similar status to Tunnock. The potters of the late fourteenth and fifteenth centuries do not seem to have been so prominent, although some amongst them still had respectable livelihoods. They undoubtedly lost out to some extent to the founders, parvenus of the late fourteenth century. The difference in work between the two crafts is hard to discern, although surviving founders' inventories from the early sixteenth century suggest that they concentrated on small domestic utensils. The only appreciable distinction between them is that potters lived on one side of the river Ouse and founders on the other.[16]

The proliferation, or conversely the disappearance, of crafts is obviously related to some extent to the state of the economy. This was the background to the expansion of manufacturing by workers in non-ferrous metals: the reduction in population brought about by the Black Death and succeeding plagues resulted in a considerable improvement in living standards in later generations and increased demand for consumer durables.[17] But social considerations were equally significant in determining the form of organization among potters and founders. Likewise alterations in the status of the craft and the meaning of craft ascriptions might be accomplished by political change. One such change was in the nature of the franchise of the city, for in the late thirteenth and early fourteenth centuries the freedom of York carried different implications from that of the later Middle Ages. Professor Dobson has demonstrated the way in which the expansion of the freedom in the years after the Black Death was one aspect of the 'fiscal tyranny' of the late medieval civic authorities.[18] Purchase of the freedom was extended, in theory, to become an obligation on all artisans setting up in business in the city, although, unlike London, the franchise was not tied to membership of a specific craft.[19] In practice, there were a great many groups who did not have to take out the freedom: those who worked in the liberties outside the city's jurisdiction, as well as piece workers, and most obviously women. Those artisans who were free benefited not only from the right to buy and sell retail, but equally importantly from the right to trade free of toll. These benefits were matched by obligations to contribute to the city's finances and for many artisans the 'privilege' of freedom must have been a dubious one.

The freedom of the early fourteenth century, being more restricted, was a more genuine privilege. Entries in the Register of Freemen before 1350 contain a high proportion of victuallers and leather workers, compared to a noticeable absence of builders and textile workers. It is no accident that the two best-represented groups were those who bought their materials locally and benefited by freedom from tolls. The point has previously been made, but needs re-emphasizing, that power and profit in medieval towns came not from manufacture but from trade, and this applies as much to local as to long-distance markets.[20] In this context the artisans who bought the freedom in the early fourteenth century can be seen as those who were most likely to be engaged in trade.

Certain occupations, such as the cutlers and the girdlers seem to have had a genuinely mercantile dimension at this time. Cutlers, for example, took out the freedom in great numbers in early fourteenth-century York, accounting for some 25 per cent of all metalworkers made free. They included men such as Adam del Ireland, free as a *cotoler vel haberdasscher*.[21] Cutlers supervised the assembly of knives whose component parts might also be made by other artisans, such as bladesmiths and sheathers. They were accustomed also to sell imported knives and daggers, and serious competition in this quarter came from merchants in the fifteenth century. Ordinances of 1445 required that all sellers of knives and sheaths in York, except, significantly, the members of the mercers' guild, were to contribute to the cost of the cutlers' Corpus Christi pageant.[22] Other competition came from bladesmiths, who by the end of the fifteenth century had effectively distinguished themselves from cutlers. The net result was that whereas 62 cutlers took out the freedom in the years between 1301 and 1350, in the period 1451–1500 the number was 15, a mere 4.5 per cent of all metalworkers. The figure does not, of course, say anything about the amount of knife-making and -selling in the city, but it speaks volumes about the status of the cutlers. The history of the girdlers' craft follows much the same pattern. The failure of both the cutlers and the girdlers illustrates the very change in urban society which brought about the extension of the franchise, and which can be characterized as the growing polarization of merchants and artisans. In York this was bound up with the extraordinary growth in the operations of denizen (i.e. non-alien) merchants, a growth that has been amply demonstrated, but as yet only in part explained.[23] Economic power brought political power as the merchants evolved a classic oligarchic system of government in York, as in so many other towns.[24] It seems reasonable to assume that these merchants would not have extended the franchise if such a change represented a commercial threat.

The change in the meaning of the freedom is paralleled by that undergone by the craft guilds in the later Middle Ages. Some crafts had a long history of association, not just the textile guilds made famous by Carus-Wilson, but leather workers and some victuallers as well.[25] The organizations of the textile workers, originally intended as a protective measure, arguably came to be used as a vehicle for taxation and exploitation. Organizations among other crafts were by no means ubiquitous, but were found among the most prosperous and numerous groups of artisans in early medieval towns. In York there was a guild of leather workers by 1181 and a butchers' fraternity in the late thirteenth century. The earliest recorded craft ordinances were those of the girdlers in 1307.[26]

Such self-regulating groups had enormous potential as part of the administrative system of the city, and it is inconceivable that a powerful oligarchic council could have ignored this potential. The craft regulations recorded in York, and indeed in town after town in the late fourteenth and fifteenth centuries, make it clear that they were enrolled at the mayor's pleasure and that he could 'amende, correcte and refourme it and every parcell thereof at his pleiser'.[27] As I have argued elsewhere, whatever the origins of the guild and the fraternal feeling harboured between brothers, there is strong evidence to suggest that the extension and organization of the guild system were undertaken by city councils in the later Middle Ages as a method of policing industry.[28] Certainly, the proliferation of craft guilds in one town as opposed to another may say more about the organization of the administration than about the economy. In Norwich, each small craft was to be associated with a larger 'mystery' for better organization.[29] By contrast, in York the council allowed the proliferation of guilds, registering ordinances for small and barely viable crafts, such as the saucemakers and the bowstring-makers.[30]

Changes in the power structure, and increasing regulation, led to changes in the status of artisans; the decline in importance of the girdlers and cutlers has already been described. Similarly, the status of many victuallers altered during the later Middle Ages. Victualling was just one part of the commercial operations undertaken by the civic élite in the early fourteenth century. A notorious York guild, dissolved in 1306 because of the way it had abused and manipulated power, had included among its members at least two bakers, four fishmongers, a cook, four taverners and six brewers.[31] Victuallers in York in the later Middle Ages did not have this kind of standing. Merchants might undertake brewing or act as taverners as a sideline, but butchers, bakers, fishmongers and cooks were corralled into craft organizations and isolated from the élite; the butchers in particular faced discrimination.[32] The use of the term 'fishmonger' illustrates the ambiguity of craft nomenclature very well. By the fifteenth century in York, it no longer described wholesale dealers in fish. Those fishmongers who left wills were, with one exception, only moderately well off. Their craft regulations deliberately excluded them from travelling to the coast to buy fish and they were essentially retailers in the city.[33] Moreover, all kinds of artisans dealt in fish, and strenuous efforts were made to get these dealers under control as well. The result was that, at a time when the population of the city was falling, the number of fishmongers taking out the freedom rose dramatically from 60 between 1351 and 1400 to 108 between 1451 and 1500.

The case of the fishmongers demonstrates a further point about the craft guilds. Whatever view is taken of their origin and function, without question guilds imposed an artificial framework on manufacturing artisans. The boundaries between crafts could not be sustained. Cooks sold fish, butchers sold fish, indeed almost anyone sold fish.[34] In other industries, interests constantly overlapped. Fullers sheared cloth; woollen weavers made linen cloth; the dyeing of cloth and wool was not the monopoly of the dyers. There were crafts of pinners, cardmakers and wiredrawers, but wiredrawers made both pins and cards.[35] A girdler's stock in 1439 contained latten and iron wire, daggers and knives, while the girdlers' ordinances of 1475 refer to a variety of goods such as *daggar chapes, purse knoppes, bulyons, book claspes, dawkes, dog colers, girdilles* and *other maner gere or harnesse of laton, stele or yren.*[36] By the late fifteenth century the combination of occupations was to some extent becoming evident in the Register of Freemen. Entries appear such as *barber and waxchandler, chapman and inholder, textwriter and book binder, blaksmith, loksmith and lorimer*; and in 1499 Robert Daglase became free as *bower, patoner, boteller and boggemaker.*[37] Detailed examination of the histories of these occupations has shown that the only novelty about such combinations was that they were now being declared.

So far the emphasis has been on the artisans of York. The meaning of craft terms could also vary considerably from place to place as the status of artisans depended on the function of the town. The social and political factors which came into play in one town might not be relevant in another. If, for example, the local market was more important than long-distance trade, then those artisans who obtained their supplies locally would be in a relatively strong position. The status of tanners and butchers in a market town such as Romford was much higher than that of their counterparts in York; indeed it is doubtful if the butcher/graziers of small towns can be called artisans at all.[38]

Differences in status are best observed in the leather trades. Cow and ox hides were supposed to be tanned only by tanners, then passed to curriers to be rendered supple. Tanned leather was then made up into shoes by cordwainers. Alternatively it was made into bottles, bags and trunks. According to the ordinances of the York bottlemakers, this might be done *within the houses or chambres of [any] tanner, shomaker, glover, whitetewer, couurour or girdiller* in the city.[39] At a national level, constant efforts were made to keep tanners, curriers and cordwainers to their crafts. In practice, curriers seem to have worked mainly for cordwainers, the most important consideration being that their work was distinguished from that of the tanners.[40] The curriers were usually the losers. In York they were poor, working on piece rates defined in very great detail. Many were women.[41] Curriers make little impact on the records in most late medieval towns, the exception being Winchester. There, surprisingly, curriers appear as significant property-holders at a time when the holdings of tanners were declining; somehow they had acquired a slice of the profits to be made in leather.[42]

Cordwainers, being banned from tanning leather, sought in many towns to exercise some control over tanners by claiming the right to search, that is examine the standard of, tanned leather.[43] Any expectations they may have had of profiting from these rights, were generally disappointed. Comparison of the status of cordwainers in various towns in the early sixteenth century shows that in Norwich, Shrewsbury and Worcester they were poor, while the tanners were rich.[44] However, the York cordwainers were surprisingly successful and included a number of very substantial men. In the 1524 subsidy returns for York, cordwainers make a strong showing, with six being assessed on over £10 worth of goods as compared to five tanners.[45] The fifteenth century in York had been punctuated by spectacular conflicts between the tanners and the cordwainers, the cordwainers being at one point excluded from the freedom of the city *en masse*.[46] It seems that the council ultimately must have favoured the cordwainers, and it is suggested that this line was taken deliberately to neutralize the tanners.

II

A bald craft ascription rarely gives an adequate impression of the status or activity of the artisan to whom it was applied. It hides the great gulf that could lie between two artisans who apparently practised the same craft or, conversely, the similarities between two who claimed completely different occupations. A list of the leading crafts of a town, based on enumeration of specific crafts, is inevitably somewhat misleading in this respect. It is more profoundly misleading in another way. Because some sort of statistics are available for manufacturing artisans, the temptation is to refine these statistics and to improve definitions in order to get a better social and economic profile of the town. A rather more profitable exercise is to see the manufactures of a town in a wider context. It is a truism to say that industry and trade are two sides of the same coin, and that the manufacturing function of the town was dependent on its role as a market on a local, regional and international level. Unfortunately, this truism is all too often ignored in analysing urban industry. There are few records of regional trade where there are abundant records of craft guilds, and placing too much emphasis on this latter group of records gives a very lop-sided view of the economy. Great sections of urban enterprise thus come to be underestimated. This applies not only to the supply of materials and the marketing of produce, but also to the multitude of service industries, which grew up to satisfy the needs of the constant stream of visitors to the medieval town as well as the requirements of the local inhabitants.

The greatest profit did not come from manufacture, but from trade. Some artisans, those who sold into what might be called the 'bespoke' market, provide something of an exception to this rule. The early fourteenth-century York bellfounders and armourers, or the goldsmiths, could sometimes build up a profitable network of regional contacts. Most artisans were not in such a fortunate position; they remained subordinate to the merchants who controlled the marketing network. One of the best ways for an artisan to get a foothold in the distributive trades was by trading in victuals.

The inventory of a York mason, Hugh Grantham, demonstrates very clearly how, by diversifying into victualling, an artisan could build up a respectable fortunate.[47] Grantham, who died in 1410, had built up a sufficiently good reputation as a mason to do work on contract rather than for a wage. At the time of his death he was putting in a window at the church of All Saints North Street, employing three servants to assist him, and in addition paying casual labour to carry stone. Both the stone and the lead for the window he had bought himself, though he had not yet paid for them when he died. He also had agricultural interests. He owned cattle and sheep and had extensive dealings in grain. At the time of his death he had just negotiated the carriage of six cartloads of grain from the nearby village of Pocklington, where he rented a grain store. Most of the grain he handled was barley, and this he sold to a variety of people, including York bakers and presumably brewers: for example Agnes, wife of the cutler John Waghen, owed him 20s. for barley; John Welburn, baker, owed him £9, presumably for grain; another £3 was owed by 'diverse' debtors, also for grain. In all, his debtors owed him £85 17s.10d., mostly for grain, although £9 12s. 4d. was outstanding for the sale of cloth. Grantham dealt extensively on credit and was a source of loans. He had advanced £16 on an unspecified obligation to William Robynson of Kirkby Hall. He himself borrowed money; John Kendale, one of the Vicars Choral of the Minster, lent him £20, and he owed smaller sums to two other masons.

To call Hugh Grantham a mason does not do credit to his multifarious activities; only the chance survival of his inventory does that. What makes Grantham unusual is the scale of his operations. The resources of most artisans could not stretch to wholesaling; their wealth was to be reckoned mainly in household goods and the contents of their workshops. For such people extensive credit was unlikely to be forthcoming. But it seems reasonable to suggest that for nearly every artisan, selling food or services, even on a very small scale, offered a practicable means of supplementing income. Indeed the extensive and significant role of women as small-scale hucksters and traders in medieval towns has long been recognized.[48] Yet women make very little impact on the administrative records surviving from York, because they had no political status, nor were they obliged to be free of the city in order to work.[49] They were members of craft fraternities but had no formal role in the mystery, the regulatory side of the craft organization. Yet women shared the running of the family business, the domestic industrial unit, on which urban industry was based. They worked on equal terms with men, not always as servants, but often heading their own enterprises.

These enterprises could be quite separate from the occupation of the head of the household and are perhaps most frequently to be found in the victualling and service industries. The most obvious example is in the provision of lodgings and the running of inns. Innkeeping simply does not appear as a significant occupation in the York Register of Freemen.

Table 3.2 Hostellers and innkeepers made free in York between 1301 and 1534

1301–50	1351–1400	1401–1450	1451–1500	1501–34
–	2	7	17	24

Quite obviously these figures do not reveal the whole truth about innkeeping in medieval York. Winchester deeds and court records show how numerous inns were at this time, but for York no figures are available until the mid-sixteenth century.[50] By then there were beds for over 1300 visitors: this at a time when the population was possibly only half of what it had been in the late fourteenth century.[51] To some extent, the absence of innholders from the Register reflects contemporary prejudice; it does not seem to have been an occupation held in very high regard in the early sixteenth century, when John Petty, appointed alderman, was told to 'leve his kepyng of hostery'.[52] However, other ill-favoured occupations make a good showing in the records and the more probable explanation of the absence of innkeepers is that they undertook this occupation in conjunction with another craft, or simply as an extension of the household economy.

This can be demonstrated from the list of hostellers (as innkeepers were known) prosecuted in York in 1301 for alleged malpractice.[53] The presence of the king and court in York at this time must have put pressure on accommodation, giving the hostellers a chance to inflate prices. Of the forty-five hostellers charged, eleven were women, one of whom, Alice Manners, ran a hostel in William Fader's house. There is very little other evidence of innkeeping in York before the late fifteenth century. Thirteen hostellers were listed in the poll tax of 1381.[54] Three of them were described elsewhere as mercers, and it seems very likely that other merchants utilized their large houses for the same purpose. So too did the more prosperous artisans. John Stubbs was described in the Register of Freemen and in his will (made in 1450) simply as a barber. Only the chance survival of his inventory shows that he and his wife ran a thirty-six-bed inn, complete with brewery and grain store. Despite his six bedrooms he was apparently so short of space that he stored a mattress and sixteen pairs of sheets in the bolting house, where flour was sifted.[55] Stubbs was operating on a large scale, but it seems likely that many smaller properties could prove equally elastic in their provision of bed and board. John Grene, a glover (d.1525), had, in addition to his personal chamber, a room specifically designated 'gestes chamber'.[56]

It is only in the sixteenth century, when it became more common for innkeeping to be declared as an occupation, that the true scale of this business in York begins to emerge. John Fernelee became free in 1502 as a 'yoman, inholder and smyth'; two men were made free in 1504 as 'haberdasher and inholder'.[57] In 1526 Agnes Johnson took out the freedom as an innholder, being described in the Register as 'widow of William Briggs, tailor'. Another widow who inherited an inn was Joanna Ellis who in 1510 took over the Three Kings in Micklegate from her husband William.[58]

John Stubbs, as well as running an inn, had a brewery. Brewing, it is well known, was a common secondary occupation in urban households. Work on Norwich, Winchester and York has shown just how wide a variety of artisans from glaziers to fullers brewed beer.[59] However lucrative the occupation may have been, few people in York described themselves as full time brewers, as shown in Table 3.3.

Table 3.3 Entrants to the freedom as brewers in York between 1301 and 1534

1301–50	1351–1400	1401–1450	1451–1500	1501–1534
3	8	32	23	18

By comparison, in 1450–1 221 people were fined in York for breaching the assize of ale.[60] Of these 221, only seven had been made free of the city as brewers. In the circumstances it is not surprising that there was not a craft of brewers in York. The same was the case in many other provincial towns. Nor are leading citizens often described specifically as brewers. One exception was Oxford, a town so dominated by the university in the later Middle Ages that its economy was almost entirely directed to servicing the needs of scholars. These needs manifestly included large quantities of drink, for brewers, vintners and taverners dominated the city government in the fifteenth century.[61]

Despite the absence of full-time brewers from the records of many provincial towns, the scale of brewing could be formidably large, providing an important source of income for women in particular. John Lepyngton was an ironmonger who died in 1332; he left to his daughter Margaret brewing equipment that included a seventy-gallon lead vessel, another of thirty-eight gallons, and a third of thirty gallons.[62] Not surprisingly, Hugh Grantham's brewery had over £9 worth of brewing equipment, which incidentally amounted to more than the total value of the estate of William Coltman, a brewer who died in 1481.[63] Grantham's brewery also included £42 worth of grain. The vessels and utensils in his house, which together with £40 were bequeathed to his wife, ensured her a continued livelihood.[64]

Among the multiplicity of customers in the inns and alehouses of York were many who were brought there on a variety of church business. As well as attracting streams of pilgrims, there were those men and women, willing and unwilling, who came to the church's courts of ecclesiastical and secular jurisdiction. Many came in connection with the economic demands of ecclesiastical institutions large and small, and the church as a major landholder was of course as dependent on the regional marketing network as any lay lord. Obviously such a huge topic as the church's involvement in the urban economy cannot be tackled here, but attention needs to be drawn to the way that ecclesiastical capital could help artisan enterprise.

Professor Dobson has emphasized the 'quite remarkable value' of the incomes of the Minster clergy, which put them on the same footing as the leading lay magnates.[65] These incomes were not always accumulated as dead money, and there is good reason to see the clergy as one of the most important sources of loans for the merchant class. Whereas large-scale credit was primarily extended to merchants, the most successful artisans were also likely to look to the clergy as a source of funds. Hugh Grantham, as has been seen, borrowed from one of the Vicars Choral of the Minster. Another Vicar Choral, Dom. Richard Sutton, was owed £8 by the skinner, Roger Burton, who died in 1428. Thomas Grissop, a chapman (d. 1446), had borrowed £13 from Mag. John Castell, clerk.[66] Masons like Grantham, who frequently worked for ecclesiastical employers, were particularly well-placed to capitalize on their connections for the purpose of trading. The same may well prove to be true of other building workers who were unusually wealthy. Another artisan, William Barton, vestmentmaker of York, seems also to have profited by his contacts with the clergy, for he had acted as receiver to the abbot of St Mary's Cirencester.[67] Possibly the most fruitful opportunities for trading lay in the marketing of tithes on behalf of the rectors of rural parishes. Evidence of such dealings survives from early fourteenth-century York and there is no reason to suppose that they did not persist throughout the later Middle Ages.[68]

As well as selling, the clergy also bought on a huge scale. Many of the religious houses in Yorkshire bought quantities of goods in York: Selby Abbey, for example, purchased footwear, cloth and fish as well as more exotic spices.[69] The demand for more luxury items or specifically ecclesiastical products, such as vestments and church ornaments, often brought purchasers from as far afield as Durham and the North West.[70] It was the continued demand for these items that helped sustain the wide manufacturing base to be found in York, even when the city's international trade was faltering. But the health of the urban economy did not only depend on the large-scale buying and selling of institutions and wealthy individuals. Equally significant, but far harder to document was the trade generated by the demands of ordinary consumers.

It is a point that can be illustrated obliquely from the status and lifestyle of artisans in the late fifteenth century, when, despite difficulties in certain sections of the urban economy, the demand for goods and services remained high. It is now generally accepted that the reduction of the population in the Black Death and succeeding plagues contributed to improving the standard of living of the majority of the survivors, with the most significant proportionate increase in income being among the wage-earners at the bottom of the social hierarchy.[71] As a result the demand for mundane household items such as brass cooking vessels and cheap textiles increased and they became something of a commonplace in inventories of even the poorer peasants. Inventories of artisans of even limited means list impressive amounts of 'consumer durables'. Thomas Cok, a York carpenter who died in 1510, had goods worth 94s. in his small rented house; these included 20s. worth of pewter.[72] The growth of the pewter industry itself is good evidence of improvement in standards of living. Pewter offered an attractive alternative to treen and earthenware, at prices which made it far more accessible than silver. In consequence it was rapidly adopted in houses at every level of society, including those of artisans and wealthy peasants.[73] The first pewterer to take out the freedom in York did so in 1349. The craft grew rapidly after 1400, and in the second half of the fifteenth century, when the number of freemen in most industries was falling, the number of pewterers continued to rise: forty-five took out the freedom between 1451 and 1500, making them at this stage more numerous than goldsmiths.

The changing relations between crafts in the late fifteenth century may often have been connected to the continued high level of local demand in contrast to the failure of the export market. By the end of the fifteenth century, York was a very different place from what it had been a hundred years earlier, one where local and regional demand played a much more significant part in determining individual fortunes. From the 1470s onwards, competition from London merchants and the closing of trading opportunities in the Baltic combined to cut savagely the profits and resources of many York merchants.[74] Both in overall numbers and in the size of their personal fortunes, the York merchants of the late fifteenth century were pale shadows of their counterparts in the late fourteenth century. This in turn brought a revision in the status of artisans. Weavers, who had made broadcloth for export, were in fairly dire straits, but tapiters, who made furnishings and bedhangings, were among the most prosperous of early sixteenth-century artisans. The drapers as a distinct group virtually disappeared from York, absorbed by the tailors who in turn became so affluent that they referred to themselves as merchant tailors.[75] The tailors did not necessarily give employment to manufacturing artisans in the city. John Carter, a York tailor who died in 1485, had a shop full of West Riding and southern cloth.[76] The most noticeable rise in status occurred among the victuallers and in this respect York came to resemble more closely the smaller provincial towns where victuallers had always formed an integral part of the civic élite.

Some, but not all of these changes can be detected in the statistics of men taking out the freedom of the city. Much of this essay has been devoted to criticizing the validity of the Register of Freemen of York, and by implication the registers of other towns, as an accurate indicator of the nature of urban industry or as a reliable guide to the occupations of the urban workforce. Obviously to pursue this line much further would be merely perverse; undeniably the Register of Freemen is a very profitable source of information. But like many other surviving records generated by civic authorities it only tells part of the story. This essay has been concerned to emphasize those things that the administrative records omit, and thereby to give an impression of the vitality, variety and flexibility of employment among urban artisans in the later Middle Ages.

Notes

1. Much of the evidence for the arguments pursued here is elaborated in my *Medieval Artisans: An Urban Class in Late Medieval England* (1989).
2. H.C. Darby (ed.), *A New Historical Geography of England before 1600* (1973), 243; R.H. Hilton, 'Lords, burgesses and hucksters', in his *Class Conflict and the Crisis of Feudalism* (1985), 194–204. See D. Keene, *Survey of Medieval Winchester* (1985), 367–9, for a calculation of Winchester's size which suggests that these figures for other towns may be underestimates; see also above, pp. 7, 18.
3. For York generally, see P.M. Tillott (ed.), *A History of Yorkshire: The City of York* (VCH Yorkshire, 1961); D.M. Palliser, *Tudor York* (1979). For a summary of the arguments concerning the decline of York in the late fifteenth century, see Swanson, *Medieval Artisans*, Ch. 12.

4. For the crafts of London, see E.M. Veale, 'Craftsmen and the economy of London in the fourteenth century', in *Studies in London History*, ed. A.E.J. Hollaender and W. Kellaway (1969), 133–51. For its size, see D. Keene, 'A new study of London before the Great Fire' in *Urban History Yearbook 1984* (1984), 11–21.

5. M. Sellers (ed.), *York Memorandum Book* (2 vols, Surtees Society *120, 125*, 1912, 1915) hereafter *YMB*; A. Raine (ed.), *York Civic Records* (8 vols, Yorkshire Archaeological Society Record Series, *98, 103, 106, 108, 110, 112, 115, 119*, 1938–52); M.D. Harris (ed.), *Coventry Leet Book* (Early English Text Society, *134, 135, 138*, 1907–9); F. Bickley (ed.), *Little Red Book of Bristol* (2 vols, 1900); E.W.W. Veale (ed.), *Great Red Book of Bristol* (3 vols, Bristol Record Society Publications, *2, 4, 8*, 1932–38).

6. F. Collins (ed.), *Register of the Freemen of the City of York* (Surtees Society 96, 1897); for a critical analysis of the value of freemen's registers for this purpose, see R.B. Dobson, 'Admissions to the freedom of the city of York in the later Middle Ages', *Economic History Review*, 2nd. ser. *26* (1973), 1–21.

7. Keene, *Survey of Medieval Winchester*; R.H. Britnell, *Growth and Decline in Colchester 1300–1525* (1986).

8. Hilton, 'Lords, burgesses and hucksters' (see n. 2 above).

9. Borthwick Institute (hereafter BI): Prob. Reg. 1–9; Dean and Chapter Original wills and inventories; York Minster Library, L2/4, L2/5a (hereafter D/C Prob. Reg. 1, 2). The wills used were made by men and women primarily involved in some form of production for the market and exclude those employed wholly in service industries, and all 'professions'. For the incidence of will-making in York and associated problems, see H.C. Swanson, 'Craftsmen and industry in late medieval York' (unpublished D. Phil. thesis, University of York, 1981), 405–14. Will-making was apparently more common in the southern province: R.S. Gottfried, *Epidemic Disease in Fifteenth-Century England* (1978), 22–3.

10. *Register of Freemen*, 218, 162, 89 (1494, 1444, 1391).

11. See below p. 46; see also H.C. Swanson, 'The illusion of economic structure: craft guilds in late medieval English towns', *Past and Present, 121* (1988), 29–48.

12. *Register of Freemen*, 149; *Calendar of Patent Rolls 1436–41*, 483.

13. *YMB*, II, 176–82.

14. *Coventry Leet Book*, 554.

15. He died in 1541: A.D. Dyer, *The City of Worcester in the Sixteenth Century* (1973), 127.

16. For a description of these crafts, see Swanson, *Medieval Artisans*, Ch. 6; for Tunnock see W. Page (ed.), *The Victoria History of the County of York*, II (1912), 449.

17. C. Dyer, *Standards of Living in the Later Middle Ages* (1989), *passim*; see also below page 52.

18. Dobson, 'Admissions to the freedom', (see n. 6 above) 20.

19. For the London franchise, see S. Thrupp, *The Merchant Class of Medieval London* (Ann Arbor, 1948), 3–4.

20. M. Dobb, *Studies in the Development of Capitalism* (1946), 97–103; R.H. Hilton, 'Towns in English feudal society' in his *Class Conflict and the Crisis of Feudalism*, 181–2.

21. *Register of Freemen*, 130.

22. *YMB*, I, 136–7.

23. *VCH, City of York*, 100–5; R.B. Dobson, 'The risings in York, Beverley and Scarborough, 1380–1381', in *The English Rising of 1381*, ed. R.H. Hilton and T.H. Aston (1984), 119–20.

24. For a general survey of late medieval urban government, see S. Reynolds, *An Introduction to the History of English Medieval Towns* (1977), 171–7.

25. For textile workers, see E.M. Carus-Wilson, *Medieval Merchant Venturers* (1954), 223–38; for early leather guilds, see *Pipe Roll 7 Henry II* (Pipe Roll Society, *4*, 1885), 26; *Pipe Roll 27 Henry II*, (Pipe Roll Society, *30*, 1909), 41.

26. *YMB*, I, 180–1.
27. *YMB*, I, 186.
28. Swanson, 'The illusion of economic structure' (see n. 11 above).
29. W. Hudson and J.C. Tingey (ed.), *Records of the City of Norwich* (2 vols, 1906–10), II, 280.
30. *YMB*, I, 155–6, II, 122–3.
31. G.O. Sayles, 'The dissolution of a gild at York', *English Historical Review*, 55 (1940), 83–98; M. Prestwich, *York Civic Ordinances, 1301*, (Borthwick Paper 49, 1976), 22–8.
32. Swanson, *Medieval Artisans*, Ch. 2, 9.
33. No major importer of fish recorded in the Hull customs accounts described himself as a fishmonger. For fishmongers' ordinances, see *YMB*, I, 224. The exception was William Muston: BI, Prob. Reg. 3, fos. 605–606v.; his sales to Selby Abbey are recorded in G.S. Haslop (ed.), 'A Selby kitchener's roll of the early fifteenth century', *Yorkshire Archaeological Journal*, 48 (1976) 124–5.
34. *YMB*, I, 221.
35. *YMB*, II, 297–8; H.R. Schubert, 'The wiredrawers of Bristol 1312–1797', *Iron and Steel Institute Journal*, 159 (1948), 16–22.
36. *YMB*, I, 187; BI, D/C Original wills and inventories.
37. *Register of Freemen*, 218, 219, 226, 223.
38. M.K. MacIntosh, *Autonomy and Community: The Royal Manor of Havering 1200–1500* (1986), 154–5.
39. *YMB*, II, 142.
40. 13 Richard II, st. I c. 12, 4 Henry IV c. 35, 2 Henry VI c. 7: *Statutes of the Realm* (1810–17), II, 65, 142–3, 220. *YMB*, II, 69–70.
41. *YMB*, I, 65.
42. Keene, *Survey of Medieval Winchester*, 288.
43. E.g. Exeter cordwainers: L.T. Smith (ed.), *English Gilds* (Early English Text Society 40, 1870), 332; *YMB*, II, 162–6; *York Civic Records*, II, 56–9, 74; *Coventry Leet Book*, 227.
44. J.F. Pound, 'The social and trade structure of Norwich, 1525–75', *Past and Present*, 34 (1966), 56; W.A. Champion, 'Shrewsbury lay subsidy 1525', *Transactions of the Shropshire Archaeological Society*, 64 (1985), 41; Dyer, *Worcester*, 122.
45. Swanson, *Medieval Artisans*, Ch. 11.
46. *YMB*, II, 162–6; *York Civic Records*, II, 56.
47. BI, D/C Original wills and inventories.
48. R.H. Hilton, 'Women traders in medieval England', in his *Class Conflict and the Crisis of Feudalism*, 205–15.
49. For an excellent account of women's work in the medieval town, see M.C. Howell, *Women, Production and Patriarchy in Late Medieval Cities* (1986). For women in York, see P.J.P. Goldberg, 'Female labour, service and marriage in the late medieval urban north', *Northern History*, 22 (1986), 18–38. See also M. Kowaleski, 'Women's work in a market town; Exeter in the late fourteenth century', in *Women and Work in Pre-Industrial Europe*, ed. B. Hanawalt (1986), 145–64.
50. Keene, *Survey of Medieval Winchester*, 164, 274–5.
51. Palliser, *Tudor York*, 166.
52. *York Civic Records*, III, 10.
53. Prestwich, *York Civic Ordinances*, 28.
54. J.N. Bartlett (ed.), 'Lay poll tax returns for the city of York', *Transactions of the East Riding Antiquarian Society*, 30 (1953).
55. BI, D/C Original wills and inventories.
56. BI, D/C Original wills and inventories.
57. *Register of Freemen*, 226, 228.
58. *Register of Freemen*, 237.
59. BI, Prob. Reg. 8, f. 63; Hilton, 'Women traders', 209.
60. York City Archives, Cc1a(i), fos. 35–7.

61. A. Crossley (ed.), *A History of the County of Oxford* (VCH Oxfordshire), IV, *City of Oxford* (1979), 48.

62. BI, D/C Prob. Reg. 1, f. 11–11v.

63. Coltman's goods were worth £8 1. 2d. in all: BI, D/C Original wills and inventories.

64. BI, D/C Prob. Reg. 1, fo. 154.

65. R.B. Dobson, 'The later middle ages', in *A History of York Minster*, ed. G.E. Aylmer and R. Cant (1977), 61.

66. BI, D/C Original wills and inventories.

67. *Calendar of Patent Rolls 1429-36*, 483.

68. Swanson, *Medieval Artisans*, ch. 10.

69. J.C. Atkinson (ed.), 'Account roll of Selby Abbey, 1397-8', *Yorkshire Archaeological Journal*, *15* (1900), 415.

70. J.T. Fowler (ed.), *Extracts from the Account Rolls of the Abbey of Durham*, II (Surtees Society *100*, 1899), 383, 549, 551; Palliser, *Tudor York*, 185–92.

71. Dyer, *Standards of Living in the Later Middle Ages*, esp. chs. 6, 7, 8.

72. BI, D/C Original wills and inventories.

73. J. Hatcher and T.C. Barker, *History of British Pewter* (1974).

74. J.I. Kermode, 'Merchants, overseas trade and urban decline: York, Beverley and Hull, *c.* 1380–1500', *Northern History*, *23* (1987), 51–73.

75. B. Johnson, *Acts and Ordinances of the Company of Merchant Tailors* (n.d.). William Huby, horner, was described in the will of Robert Rede, girdler (d.1505) as 'horne and tayler merchand': BI, Prob. Reg. 6, f. 200.

76. *Testamenta Eboracensia*, III, ed. J. Raine (Surtees Society *45*, 1865), 301-3.

4 Town and country in late medieval England: the hide and leather trade*

Maryanne Kowaleski

The fundamental importance of commercial and industrial links between the urban and rural sectors of the medieval economy has been acknowledged by many scholars but explored in detail by few. Because of the disparate sources extant for boroughs and manors, we have been inclined to study singly either towns or the countryside. Such an approach, however, tends to conceal the complexities of the medieval economy by neglecting the interaction between these sectors. The study presented here aims to address, in part, this neglect by examining the hide and leather trade in medieval England. By focusing on the marketing of hides and skins we can learn much about the commercial links between agricultural production, urban consumer demand, and urban industry. An analysis of this trade will also show how developments in the countryside could exert a strong influence on urban occupational structures and on work in the urban leather industry in particular. The nature of work in towns – the number, organization, status, and location of specific occupations – could clearly be affected by changes in the rural sector. Finally, this essay also aims to emphasize the importance of the under-studied leather trade and to point to its significance in the medieval economy, particularly in towns.

Leather was an essential and ubiquitous material in the Middle Ages. In an era without plastic and rubber, protective rain- and work-gear was made of leather, as were shoes, gloves, hats, purses, and belts. Other leather articles included bottles, buckets, coffers, saddles, harness, scabbards, helmets, and armour. Blacksmiths used leather bellows, scribes wrote on parchment leaves, books were bound in boards covered with leather, and children played games with leather balls.[1] The leather industry, in fact, ranked second only to the cloth industry in medieval England, and the occupational profile of medieval towns reflected its importance. Craftsmen making or using leather made up the third (and sometimes even the second or first) largest occupational group in most towns, outnumbered only by the victuallers and cloth workers. In late fourteenth-century Exeter, for example, about 15 per cent of householders worked in the leather crafts and in Oxford they comprised 13 per cent of the occupations stated in the 1381 poll tax.[2] Occupational figures derived from studies of freedom registrations or of property-holders, both of which tend to include only the more substantial citizens, also point to the prominence of the leather crafts in medieval towns.[3]

Despite the obvious importance of the leather industry in medieval England, scholars have rarely turned their attention to this trade. We know something about the structure and organization of the leather-working occupations because of their visibility within urban economies. But compared to the scholarly attention paid to workers in the cloth industry, we really know only the bare outlines of the history of these crafts. Even less is understood about the trade in the raw materials (hides, skins, bark) used by leather workers. Yet this trade clearly played a significant part in the marketing of agricultural (especially pastoral) goods, and linked rural production and industry with urban and even international networks of trade. This essay will concentrate on the trade in basic materials, especially hides, because this was the crucial link between rural producers and urban crafts and consumers, and because we know least about this aspect of the industry. Much of the information used arises from a larger study of the market town of Exeter and its region in the late Middle Ages.[4] With a population of about 3,000 in 1377, Exeter ranked only twenty-third in size among English towns; but as the seat of a bishopric, as an administrative centre for the king's itinerant justices, and as a thriving seaport, the city served as the chief market town of the south-western peninsula of England.

The medieval leather industry was generally divided into the heavy and the light trades, depending on whether hides or skins were used.[5] In the heavy leather trade, raw hides from larger animals, mainly cattle, underwent a lengthy tanning process of about a year in which prepared hides passed through a series of tannin solutions (usually made from water and oak bark) in various pits. This produced a strong, durable, and waterproof leather for use by shoemakers and saddlers after it had been curried or dressed. Calf and sheep skins could also be tanned in the Middle Ages. Tanned sheepskins, called 'bazan' or 'bazil', were considered an inferior product, and many towns passed regulations forbidding shoemakers from substituting bazan for higher-quality hide leather when making shoe soles. But the frequent presentments in borough courts concerning shoemakers who used bazan in shoes indicates that the practice continued and may have been typical in the manufacture of cheaper shoes.[6]

It was more common, however, for skins from smaller animals such as sheep, calves, goats, and pigs to undergo a simpler process of preservation typical of the light leather trades. These skins were generally made into leather within a matter of weeks by tawing with alum or with oil. Alum-tawing produced a relatively thin white leather which could be made more water-resistant if dressed with oil. Tawed leather, which could easily be dyed, was commonly used in gloves, most leather garments, pouches, laces, and shoe uppers. Furriers and skinners also employed the services of tawyers to dress their skins. While technically not leather, parchment and vellum were related to the light leather trades since they were made from sheep and calf skins and were subjected to some of the same processes like dehairing and fleshing.

The marketing chain for leather began with the sale of raw hides and skins, the supply of which was largely dependent on the slaughter of animals for meat, since 'dead' hides (from animals which died of natural causes) did not make a satisfactory leather. As a result, the vast majority of hides came onto the market in towns, where the greatest quantity of meat was consumed. Municipal ordinances required butchers, in fact, to bring carcasses into the market along with the hides or skins, or face stiff penalties.[7] Such ordinances aimed both to channel the raw hide and skin trade to towns and to regulate this trade in the urban market-place, making easier the authorities' efforts to collect customs, to ensure quality, and to control prices. These regulations also made butchers the primary sellers of raw hides and skins, thereby adding considerably to their commercial diversification and profits. The butchers' share in this trade is obvious in their regular involvement with tanners, curriers, cordwainers and saddlers among the debt cases enrolled in borough courts.[8]

The central role played by butchers in the marketing chain of hides and skins can be illustrated through an analysis of 577 fines assessed by the Exeter courts between 1370 and 1390 on those who sold raw hides and skins (mainly wool fells) outside the town's appointed market-place.[9] These fines, most of which concerned the trade in raw hides, were basically a type of licensing fee for sales outside the official market-place (in private houses, inns, and in illegal markets near city gates). The court's presentments show that over 95 per cent of the sales of hides and skins by Exeter residents were made by butchers.[10] Sellers who did not reside in Exeter also tended to be butchers; all but one of the 22 identifiable (of a total 49) non-Exeter sellers practised this trade.

More interesting than the preponderance of butchers as sellers of hides and skins is the fact that more than half of the vendors came from outside Exeter (see Fig. 4.1). Most of these non-resident sellers were butchers who came from villages and

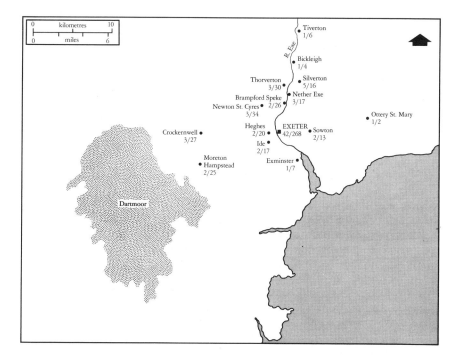

Figure 4.1. Sales of raw hides and skins in Exeter, and the origins of the vendors, 1370–90. In each case the first figure represents the total number of vendors from that place who were fined at the Exeter Mayor's Tourn, and the second figure the total number of sales represented by the fines, in the form vendors/sales.

small towns within a fifteen-mile radius of Exeter, in particular from places in the Exe valley – like Silverton, Thorverton, Nether Exe, Brampford Speke, and Newton St Cyres – where cattle were probably driven for fattening.[11] These butchers were regular traders in Exeter since many of them paid annual rents for stalls in the city's Fleshfold (meat market) and appeared as litigants in Exeter's courts. Matthew Spencer and his son William, for example, were butchers from the small hamlet of Ford (in Newton St Cyres) who sold hides in Exeter from 1372 until at least as late as 1392, when William paid a 5s. rent for a stall in the Fleshfold. William was sued for debt five times in Exeter in 1387–90, often by other butchers, or for animals he purchased, for sums ranging from 6s. to over 38s. The Spencers were presumably prominent members of their own community since Matthew served as a sub-collector for the 1377 poll tax at Ford.[12]

Buyers differed from sellers of hides and skins in several ways. Their identity can be ascertained through a set of 976 presentments in the Exeter courts between 1370 and 1390 concerning persons who purchased hides or skins either outside the official market-place or without being freemen of the city. As a group, buyers were both more numerous and more diversified than sellers, since among them they practised at least twenty-four different occupations.[13] Of those buyers with known occupations, 30 worked in the heavy leather trades, 24 were skinners, 11 laboured in the light leather crafts, 15 were butchers, 9 were innkeepers or taverners, 7 were involved in clothing manufacture, and 9 others pursued miscellaneous occupations like chandler and victualler.[14] The diversity of occupations reflects the large number of urban craftsmen involved in this aspect of the trade; almost 75 per cent of the buyers lived in Exeter.

A substantial portion of the buyers, however, resided outside the city of Exeter (see Fig. 4.2). In contrast to the sellers, they often came from more distant places within a 30-mile radius of the city. The greatest distances were travelled by skinners like John atte Forde, a man of some stature who served as portreeve (the chief administrative officer) for the borough of Tavistock, over 30 miles from Exeter on the other side of Dartmoor. His trading activities in Exeter are reflected in his debts with butchers, tanners, and cordwainers there, as well as his imports of hides through the port of Exeter. The Exeter authorities clearly recognized the status of atte Forde because, while they presented him in court eighteen years in a row for buying hides without being a freeman of the city, they never fined him, preferring instead to forgo the fines, on occasion 'by grace of the mayor'.[15] Skinners like atte Forde were active at the quality end of the leather business; their primary concern was with the fur trade which brought them sizeable profits and allowed them to expand the regional scope of their commercial activities. Many of the eleven buyers from the small town of Tiverton, about thirteen miles north of Exeter, were also skinners who in all likelihood catered to the Earl of Devon's large household there. But even skinners from as far away as London traded in Exeter, and Exeter skinners were active in such distant towns as Wilton and London.[16]

While non-Exeter buyers represented about one-quarter of all customers of hides and skins, the frequency and number of their purchases may have been greater than that of residents since they were responsible for almost 40 per cent of the fines. This regional marketing pattern resulted in part from the substantial presence of tanners amongst the buyers of hides. Indeed, these tanners were more likely to dwell outside Exeter than in the town. Even the tanners resident in Exeter tended

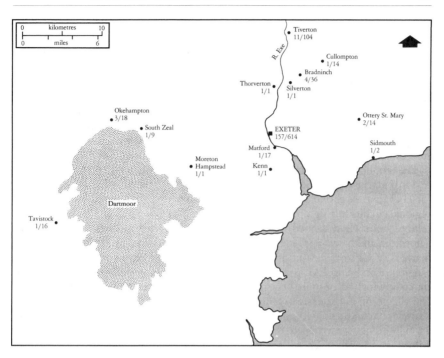

Figure 4.2. Purchases of raw hides and skins in Exeter, and the origins of the buyers, 1370–90. In each case the first figure represents the total number of buyers from that place who were fined at the Exeter Mayor's Tourn, and the second figure the total number of purchases represented by the fines, in the form buyers/purchases.

to live beyond the West Gate by the River Exe, outside the city's jurisdiction. Municipal authorities, in fact, often restricted the industrial activities of tanners to areas on the fringes of the town because of the extremely annoying smells and pollution generated by their work.[17] But tanners may themselves have preferred suburban, or even out-of-town locations for several reasons: access to running water without the interference and complaints of town authorities, avoidance of the increasing efforts of leather-workers to regulate their work, and proximity to sources of bark. Bark was certainly not in short supply in Devon; there was a tanning (bark-grinding) mill at Tavistock as early as 1291 and another one in fourteenth-century Okehampton, a small town on the edge of Dartmoor containing 135 taxpayers in 1377, which sent three purchasers of hides to Exeter during this period.[18] Nor were streams and rivers scarce in Devon. Rural tanneries in Devon, like the one with four pits in fourteenth-century Bradninch, were located close to river banks.[19] John Tannere and Roger Tannere of Bradninch were both regular purchasers of hides in Exeter.[20] Such rural tanneries had a long history in Devon; as early as 1207, the men of Axmouth in east Devon paid 20s. to have tanneries there.[21]

It is striking that tanners from livestock-rich areas like Okehampton and Tiverton had to travel miles to Exeter to acquire hides for their trade. This regional network of contacts, however, clearly illustrates the pull of the urban market-place, as well as the secondary character of the hide trade as a by-product of urban meat consumption. The evidence provided by bones recovered from archaeological excavations in Exeter and other towns shows that slaughtered cattle must have been in good supply; over 70 per cent of the meat consumed (by weight) in late medieval Exeter was from cattle, mainly mature animals.[22] Thus the concentrated supply in towns of the essential raw material of the leather industry – hides and skins – channelled traders in these items, particularly tanners, to the urban market-place and promoted networks of trade which extended out to towns and villages in the surrounding countryside.

The tanners of late fourteenth-century Lincolnshire followed a similar pattern of regional marketing. In the sessions of the peace, accusations levelled against tanners for charging excessive prices on tanned hides show that tanners travelled on regional circuits buying up raw hides in market-places (mostly in towns) and then selling them when tanned in the same markets. Three tanners from Grimsby, Thornton, and Newsham, for example, were accused of buying raw ox-hides in the markets of Caistor, Barton on Humber, Glandford Brigg, and Limber for prices ranging from 8d. to 12d. and then selling them tanned to shoemakers throughout the county for 16d. or more per hide.[23] The marketing circuit formed by these towns and villages in north-eastern Lincolnshire encompassed about 50 miles. There was a similar circuit further south centring on Sleaford, another on Horncastle, and yet another to the east which included Mablethorpe, Greenfield, Markby, Hanby, Alford, and Louth.[24] These itinerant Lincolnshire tanners thus used a variety of market-places not only for the purchase of raw hides, but also for the sale of the finished product to the shoemakers, saddlers, and other craftsmen who used it.

A further insight into the marketing of hides and skins can be gained from an analysis of the Southampton Brokage Books, which recorded a variety of municipal customs on incoming and outgoing merchandise.[25] In three years covered by some of the earliest surviving books (1430–1, 1439–40, and 1443–4), at least 25 different individuals carried 107 loads of 688 hides into Southampton.[26] Tanners from outlying towns and villages like Romsey, Winchester, Salisbury, Swaythling, Wickham, Newbury, and Southwick were responsible for at least three-quarters of this trade in what were clearly tanned hides. Almost all of these tanners travelled to Southampton regularly, occasionally renting a place in the market where they could display their wares. Many others, however, probably had customers already lined up, as was the case at Exeter where at least one leather craftsman sued a supplier of hides and skins for breaking an agreement to provide him with all the supplier's skins.[27] Such prior arrangements must account for the large percentage of trips in which tanners brought only one or two hides into Southampton. Indeed, on only about 10 per cent of the trips were more than ten hides carried in. A fairly typical example were the twelve journeys to Southampton made in 1430–31 by John Noble, a tanner from Romsey, about seven miles away. He brought hides to Southampton on 26 October (with three hides), 12 November (three), 24 November (two), 26 November (two), 28 November (two), 8 January (three), 11 January (two), 14 January (four), 16 July (ten), 30 July (one), 2 September (two), and 14 September (four). Since tanning was a long but not exactly-timed process, and since tanners sold in a variety of markets, the clustering of Noble's visits was probably related to the demands of his clients in Southampton.

Tanners also dominated the out-going trade in hides, but not to the same extent that they commanded the in-coming trade. Hides, probably untanned, were usually carted out of Southampton in large loads of 30 to 100 hides. Skins (mostly lamb and calf) were also carried out from (and into) the town in even larger numbers, by professional carters who worked for local English and Italian merchants, and for glovers from cities like Winchester and London. The Brokage Books, in fact, suggest a rather different marketing pattern for skins than for hides. Apart from the difference in the personnel involved in the trades, the supply of raw skins was also more subject to seasonal variations than the hide trade since lamb and calf skins often came onto the market in the spring; about 85 per cent of the skins brought into Southampton during these three years arrived between April and June.

The involvement of Italian merchants in the Southampton skin trade points to the extension of the marketing system for skins and hides into the network of overseas trade. At times the trade in skins through the port of Southampton was quite impressive. In 1435–36, for example, well over 38,000 skins of sheep, lamb, calf, rabbit, kid, stag, fox, and goat were imported, while over 27,000 skins were exported.[28] Hides were also shipped by sea, although by this date not in such substantial amounts as skins. In 1,435–36, 1,408 hides were imported and 194 exported at Southampton. Many of the imported hides may have originated in Wales or Ireland, both known for their cattle husbandry.[29] But they could equally have come from Cornwall and Devon, each of which had a long tradition of coastal trade with Southampton. Cargoes of hides were regularly shipped out through the south-western ports of Fowey, Plymouth, Dartmouth, and Exeter. In 1350–1, for example, the primarily Cornish ports of the Duchy of Cornwall exported over 3,000 hides.[30]

These shipments of hides and skins show the regional dimension of English coastal trade, as well as the international aspect of the hide and leather trade. Both this evidence and that concerning the local and regional marketing of hides and skins vividly illustrate the crucial role played by urban merchants and the urban market-place in this trade. Indeed, the English import and export trade in hides deserves further study from historians. What little scholarly comment that exists on this trade consists largely of negative comparisons with wool exports. Such comparisons do not do justice to the significance of this trade which ranked for many years as the second most important export effort of medieval England.[31] We also need to keep in mind that the wool fells exported from England were undoubtedly used for their skin as well as for their wool content. Yet historians have, for the most part, considered only the potential wool value of the fells.

Furthermore, we need to examine more closely the fluctuations in hide and skin exports in medieval England, because they appear to be symptomatic of major changes in the domestic leather industry. In the late Middle Ages, for example, hide exports decreased, and numbers were substantially less than the thousands exported annually in the late thirteenth and early fourteenth centuries.[32] This decline in exports, however, did not necessarily signal a decline in the English leather trades. Rather, in a development analogous to that of the cloth industry, it may reflect a relative increase in the manufacture and consumption of leather goods at home. The late-medieval domestic leather industry, unlike that of the pre-plague era, probably absorbed most of the country's surplus hides and skins. During the late Middle Ages, this surplus may actually have grown in relative terms, taking into account the reduction in human population and the expanding pastoral economy of England at this time.[33] These late medieval developments were the basis of the expansion of the domestic leather industry in the early modern period, developments outlined in some detail by L.A. Clarkson.[34] Fundamental to this expansion were agricultural changes which affected the supply of hides and skins and, in turn, the pattern of work in the urban leather trades.

The great drop in population, after the Black Death and other pestilences, reduced demand for cereal crops and at the same time raised the price of labour. Landlords and peasants alike increasingly found it more lucrative to concentrate on pastoral farming rather than the more labour-intensive and less profitable arable production. This trend and its effects, through the increase in wool production, on the rise of the domestic cloth trade have received much detailed scholarly attention. Scholars have also examined the growth of cattle farming in terms of the rise of the butcher or yeoman-grazier and the growing emphasis upon stock raising specifically for the market in meat.[35] Rather less attention, however, has been paid to the effect that the expansion of both cattle and sheep raising had on the leather trades.

These agricultural changes in the overall supply of hides and skins must also be considered in the light of the immediate supply of these raw materials to the leather crafts, which was largely a function of urban meat consumption. At first glance it would seem that the population decline or stagnation of many of England's larger cities in the late Middle Ages reduced demand for meat, and that this in turn would have influenced the supply of available hides and skins. But there is evidence that improved standards of living in the late medieval period led to dietary changes and increased consumption of meat per person.[36] Indeed, archaeological analyses of the bone evidence indicates that late medieval people also showed a preference for greater diversity in kinds of meat (particularly veal which would account for more calf skins), thus making available a wider variety of animal skins.[37] The expansion of dairy farming in the late medieval and Tudor periods might also have added to the supply and assortment of animal skins.

Changes in demand may also have increased the consumption of leather products, although this development is harder to document than changes in supply. We know that wage-rates for agricultural and building work rose substantially in the late Middle Ages while food prices, particularly for cereals, generally fell in the same period.[38] These factors worked together to raise the standard of living for most English people, leaving them with a larger disposable income after meeting basic expenses.[39] Some of this additional income could have been spent on relatively low cost leather goods. In the late fourteenth century, for example, a pair of men's shoes cost about 5d. or 6d. and a pair of stout leather boots ranged from 8½d. to 3s., at a time when even a common labourer on a building site earned between 3d. and 4d. a day. By the mid-fifteenth century, when the common labourer was making over 4d. and the skilled mason over 6½d. per day, the price of shoes and boots remained stable.[40] Gloves in the 1450s cost as little as 2d., or as much as 2s.10d. when made for an important personage such as the bishop of Lincoln. The work gloves worn by many field labourers were priced at under 3d. a pair in 1436. Other leather goods, with the exception of highly decorated items and saddles, also sold for relatively low prices. In the 1440s, four pairs of harness cost 8d., and two horse-collars the same. A leather 'jack' (a large drinking mug or pitcher) sold for 11d., three-gallon leather buckets fetched 1s.6d., and a half-gallon bucket sold for 1s. in the period between 1478 and 1483. The cost of these items was kept low, despite the general rise in wage-rates, because of the relatively low (and perhaps even falling) price of hides and skins, the basic raw materials of the industry.[41]

The rise in living standards was the most important, but probably not the only, reason behind an increased demand for leather products. Certain late-medieval fashion trends probably augmented the demand for leather. These included the popularity of extremely pointed shoes and leather pattens, the growing use of long boots for walking as well as for riding, the prevailing taste for the belted gown with a purse or pouch of leather slung from the belt, the adoption of the short jacket or jerkin, and even the introduction of the cod-piece.[42] Yet more significant may have been the demand for leather goods generated by medieval warfare.[43] Leather was used to cover shields, for the linings of metal helmets and helms, and even for the helmet itself if *cuir bouilli* (an extremely hard leather made by soaking tanned cattle hide in water and then moulding and drying it) was employed. Belts, sheaths, scabbards, gauntlets, harness, saddlery, flasks, many types of body armour, all footwear, and many tents and wagon-covers were constructed of leather. The various pieces of a knight's armour were fastened together by leather laces and points. Most of the infantry, too poor to afford metal armour, made do with leather armour in the form of the cuirass, protective leather leg-guards and hand-guards, and leather helmets. As the role of the infantry increased in late medieval armies, moreover, its demand – from archers, crossbowmen, pikemen, and artillerymen – for leather armour, stout footwear, and other leather goods must have also grown.[44] Certainly, the hostilities of the Hundred Years War and the Wars of the Roses ensured a steady if not rising demand by soldiers and armies for leather goods.

This potentially greater demand for leather goods, coupled with the greater supply and increased variety of hides and skins, encouraged both relative growth and diversification in the late medieval leather trades. Before the late fourteenth century, the leather trades consisted primarily of tanners, shoemakers (cordwainers, cobblers, corvisers, souters), saddlers, glovers, and skinners. From the late fourteenth to the sixteenth century, however, the numbers of people who were recorded as bottlemakers, coffermakers, curriers, girdlers, leathersellers, pointmakers, pouchmakers, and sheath- and scabbard-makers mounted significantly in many towns. Especially noticeable was the proliferation of leather-dressing occupations like curriers and whitetawyers.[45] This diversification in the leather trades was reflected in national and municipal legislation which, for example, required the separation of tanning from leather-working crafts like shoemaking, or forbade cordwainers to curry leather.[46] Craft guilds of leather workers, often reflecting the various divisions of labour involved in the entire leather-manufacturing process, were also established in much greater numbers in the century after the Black Death, although this may reflect social rather than purely economic developments.

To a large extent this diversification, regulation, and organization of the leather trades represent phenomena which also occurred in the textile trades and in other urban industries in the late medieval and early modern period. But we should not assume that the factors which facilitated these developments, or their effects on the pattern of work within the leather trades, were always identical to those discerned for the more-studied textile trades. Both the cloth and leather industries received a boost when the shift to pastoral farming increased the relative supply of their raw materials. But the marketing pattern for hides and skins as a by-product of urban meat consumption differed greatly from the marketing of wool, whose value was also markedly higher than that of hides and skins.[47] The markets for the finished goods of these two industries also diverged; the medieval leather industry never produced goods for the export market on the scale of the cloth industry. Nor were the profits derived from the cloth trade ever matched by the leather trades.

These changes in late medieval and early modern urban industries were also accompanied by developments which altered the work profile of specific occupations within the leather trades. The increased specialization and competition within the leather crafts during this period, for example, had a particular impact on tanners. As the number of trades using the product of the tanner grew in both number and type, they sought to exercise more stringent control over the quality and price of their raw material, and hence, over tanners. In towns like London, York, and Exeter, cordwainers, curriers, saddlers, girdlers, and bottlemakers sought and received the right to search the products of tanners to check for quality.[48] In York, a tanners' seld, to which tanners were required to bring their tanned hides for inspection and sale, appeared in order to make easier the supervision of this craft.[49] Indeed, much of the guild, municipal, and national legislation regarding the leather industry aimed primarily to regulate the tanning trade, thus making tanning subject to more regulation than any of the other leather crafts. These regulations, combined with the greater availability and possibly lower prices of their primary raw material may also have tended to lower the profits of tanners. It may be significant that proceedings under the Statute of Labourers (1351) and at Sessions of the Peace often targeted tanners for charging excessive prices for the cost of their labour.[50] Since tanners represented the crucial link between the raw material and the leather manufacturers, it is possible that their labour costs were more tightly controlled than those charged by other occupations.

Increased urban regulation and the resulting tension between tanners and those trades which purchased their products probably encouraged tanners to move to areas not directly under the control of urban authorities. This regulation, combined with the decline of the earlier export market for hides, also worked to lower the status of urban tanners in the late Middle Ages.[51] There is good evidence, in fact, that tanners became both relatively less numerous and less prominent (in terms of wealth and municipal office) in the larger towns of the late Middle Ages than they had been in such towns before the Plague. The occupational figures based on entries to the York freedom show, for example, that a number of tanners admitted between 1350 and 1500 only doubled while, in sharp contrast, the number of glovers more than quadrupled, the number of skinners tripled, and the number of shoemakers almost tripled as well.[52] Similar hints of a drop in the relative status of urban tanners appear in other towns. There was a marked decline in the number of tanners in late medieval Winchester accompanied by a general decrease in the average number of properties they held.[53] A comparison of occupations mentioned in Coventry deeds shows that tanners appeared only half as often in the deeds of the fourteenth and early fifteenth centuries as they had in the deeds of the twelfth and thirteenth centuries. And in the list of Coventry trades contributing armour in 1450, tanners ranked below nineteen other trades (including five other leather crafts) in the number of members who contributed.[54] The number of tanners allowed to join the élite freedom organization of Exeter also dropped precipitously in the late

Middle Ages: before 1350, sixteen tanners entered the freedom, but between 1350 and 1500, only one entrant gave his occupation as tanner.[55] There was a similarly sharp decline in the number and status of Norwich tanners. In the late thirteenth and early fourteenth centuries, tanners represented the single largest leather-working occupation and many belonged to the city's most prominent and wealthy families. Their numbers had decreased considerably by the late fourteenth century, however, and by the end of the fifteenth century, according to one study, only three tanners can be identified as property-holders in Norwich. No tanners held city office in the fifteenth century and they ranked low in the order of precedence for the procession on Corpus Christi, the most public expression of the relative standing of crafts and other social groups.[56] The lowered status of late medieval tanners may also be reflected in the small number of guilds of tanners which emerged in late medieval towns, by contrast with the proliferation of guilds for leather dressers and the manufacturers of leather goods.

Thus, changing markets, lower profits, a greater availability of hides and skins, and the diversification and growth of leather-using crafts, whose practitioners were intent on regulating the source of their raw material, all worked together to lower the relative status of urban tanners. This increasingly marginalized group may have been prompted to settle in the villages and small towns of late medieval England rather than in the greater centres. Then, too, tanning was an occupation easily practised in the countryside and not uncommonly combined with more purely agricultural work.[57] The relative growth of small towns from the fifteenth century onwards (at least in counties like Devon and Hampshire), combined with the growth in pastoral farming, may have also made available to tanners a regular supply of hides outside the larger urban centres, thus removing one of the forces which drew tanners to settle in such places. Indeed, as the evidence presented from Exeter, Lincolnshire and Southampton illustrates, tanners commonly participated in regional networks of trade, a trend which may have intensified as market networks became more sophisticated in the sixteenth and seventeenth centuries. In the leather trades, as in other sectors of the economy, the character of such networks and the changing specialisms of individual markets within them, emerge as a critical factor in determining the opportunities presented to urban artisans.

We should not conclude, however, that all late medieval and early modern tanners avoided urban locations and never held municipal office or enjoyed great wealth and status. The London suburbs of Bermondsey and Southwark became renowned for their tan-yards, for example, because of the large number of hides and skins which came out of the city's meat markets.[58] Elsewhere, a Leicester tanner actually served as mayor of his city on three occasions in the late sixteenth century, and Chester tanners also enjoyed some prominence within their town in the sixteenth century.[59] But such examples are not common and tend to occur mainly in the sixteenth and seventeenth centuries, when regional specialization and commercial capitalization had become more highly developed than in the late Middle Ages.

The changes affecting tanners were not the only ones to occur within the leather crafts. Certain trades, for example, began to dominate other leather workers and grew wealthier by acting as middlemen and wholesalers of both raw materials and finished products. The glovers and leathersellers of London in particular were well situated to take advantage of a growth in the market for high quality items and the expansion of London's overseas trade.[60] In provincial towns, such as Oxford in the fifteenth century and Chester in the sixteenth, glovers emerged as the wealthiest and most powerful representatives of the leather crafts.[61]

These developments in the medieval leather trades deserve further investigation. Throughout much of the Middle Ages, leather was the basis of England's second largest urban industry and hides were its second most important export. This business played an integral role in the expansion and diversification of work in pre-industrial towns, and in the emergence of individual provincial towns as specialized centres of production and marketing. Analysis of the trade enhances our understanding of crucial links between town and country. We have seen how transformations in late medieval agriculture, such as the shift from arable to pastoral husbandry, affected patterns of work in the urban leather trades. In the other direction, urban demand, particularly for the consumption of meat, channelled hides through the urban market-place while commercial and port facilities linked together local, regional, and international marketing networks for both the raw materials and finished products of the industry. Few trades more clearly illustrate the dynamic interchange between town and country than that in hides and skins.

Notes

*   Research for this article was funded by the National Endowment for the Humanities and by Fordham University, whose support the author gratefully acknowledges.

1. For illustrations of these items and an idea of the range of leather products used for both decorative as well as domestic, everyday purposes, see J.W. Waterer, *Leather in Life, Art and Industry* (1946), 33–53; idem, *Leather and Craftsmanship* (1950), 1–25; idem, *Leather and the Warrior*, ed. Lysbeth Merrifield (1981); London Museum, *Medieval Catalogue* (1954), 185–99; Jane Cowgill, Margrethe de Neergaard and Nick Griffiths, *Knives and Scabbards* (Medieval Small Finds from Excavations in London, 1987); Clare E. Allin, *The Medieval Leather Industry in Leicester* (Leicestershire Museums Archaeological Report, 3, 1981); Janet Russell, 'English medieval leatherwork', *Archaeological Journal*, 96 (1940), 132–41; D.E. Friendship Taylor, 'The leather', in J.P. Allan, *Medieval and Post-Medieval Finds from Exeter, 1971–80* (1984), 323–33; Herbert Norris, *Costume and Fashion*, II, *Senlac to Bosworth 1066-1485*, (2nd ed., 1940), 257–65, 273–4, 420–8, 449–53; C. Willett Cunnington and Phillis Cunnington, *Handbook of English Medieval Costume* (Boston, Mass., 1969), 85–6, 105–11, 136–47, 174–9.

2. Maryanne Kowaleski, *Local Markets and Regional Trade in Late Medieval Exeter* (Cambridge University Press, forthcoming); Janet Cooper and Alan Crossley, 'Medieval Oxford: economic history', in *The Victoria History of the County of Oxford*, IV, *The City of Oxford*, ed. Alan Crossley (1979), 45; I include in this total three hosiers, a bookbinder, and three parchment-makers counted in other categories by Cooper and Crossley.

3. Derek Keene, *Survey of Medieval Winchester* (1985), 285–91, 356–7; Heather Crichton Swanson, 'Craftsmen and industry in late medieval York' (D. Phil. Thesis, University of York, 1980), 23–6; A.F. Butcher, 'Canterbury's earliest rolls of freemen admissions, 1297–1363: a reconsideration', in *A Kentish Miscellany*, ed. F. Hull (Kent Archaeological Society, 1979), 9; Joan C. Lancaster, 'The city of Coventry: crafts and industries', in *The Victoria History of the County of Warwick*, VIII, *The City of Coventry and the Borough of Warwick*, ed. W.B. Stephens (1969), 152–5; Miller

Christy, 'Industries', in *The Victoria History of the County of Essex*, II, ed. William Page and J. Horace Round (1907), 458–9.

4. Kowaleski, *Local Markets and Regional Trade*.

5. The best descriptions of leather manufacture are found in: Roy Thomson, 'Leather manufacture in the post-medieval period with special reference to Northamptonshire', *Post-Medieval Archaeology*, 15 (1981), 161–75; L.A. Clarkson, 'The organization of the English leather industry in the late sixteenth and seventeenth centuries', *Economic History Review*, 2nd ser., 13 (1960–61), 245–53; Waterer, *Leather in Life, Art, and Industry*, 136–53. A good summary of the archaeological evidence may be found in John Cherry, 'The medieval leather industry', in *English Medieval Industries*, ed. John Blair and Nigel Ramsay (Hambledon Press, forthcoming).

6. See, for example, Devon Record Office (DRO) Exeter West Quarter Mayor's Tourn (WQMT), 1374–6, 1385, East Quarter (EQMT) 1389–92; and Waterer, *Leather in Life*, 66, 80. Bazan was also commonly used for shoe linings and shoe uppers.

7. P.E. Jones, *The Butchers of London* (1976), 146; DRO, Exeter South Quarter (SQ) MT, 1391–93. These ordinances also aimed to prevent butchers from plucking and selling separately the valuable wool attached to sheepskins.

8. For example, butchers' debts with leather craftsmen in Exeter appear in: DRO, Exeter Provosts' Court Roll (PCR) 8 Feb. 1379, 24 Mar. 1384 and 8 Jan. 1387 (selling skins), 6 Oct. 1384 (debt with a souter), 4 Oct. 1386; DRO, Exeter Mayor's Court Roll (MCR) 8 Sept. 1385 (with saddlers), 22 Dec. 1382 (with skinners). For similar relationships in Winchester, see Keene, op. cit., 288.

9. DRO MT 1370–90. Almost all butchers paid these fines (ranging from 2d. to 20d. but averaging about 6d.) annually for the length of their working life.

10. Exeter residents accounted for 268 of the fines; 32 butchers were charged with all but 5 per cent of these fines. The remaining 5 per cent of fines or 'sales' by Exeter residents were made by two cordwainers and eight persons whose occupations are unknown; most of these non-butcher sellers were accused of selling bazan for cordwain (i.e., passing off inferior quality tanned sheepskin for higher quality tanned cattle hides).

11. For a more detailed description of the regional network of butchers and traders in hides and skins centred on late fourteenth-century Exeter, see Kowaleski, *Local Markets and Regional Trade*. Keene, op. cit., 256–7 and 289 also notes the regional nature of the butchers' trade in Winchester.

12. DRO, SQMT 1372–93; PCR 18 April 1387; MCR 17 Feb. 1388, 1 Jun. 1388, 29 Aug. 1390; DRO, Book 53A, f. 76; PRO, E179/95/55/2. The hamlet of Ford had a tax-paying population of 34 in the 1377 poll tax.

13. Like the fines assessed on sellers, these annual payments were essentially a licensing fee to pursue supposedly 'illegal' activities. But these fines are less representative of buyers than sellers of hides and skins, since Exeter freemen who never purchased hides in illegal places escaped the notice of the court. This omission, however, merely intensifies the differences noted here between the buyers and sellers since almost all of the freemen were residents of Exeter.

14. Occupations are known for 61 per cent of Exeter residents but only 17 per cent of non-Exeter residents. Note also that certain occupations like butchers and skinners are easier to identify because of more numerous references in the Exeter documents.

15. DRO, SQMT 1370–87; PCR 19 Jan. 1380, 22 Mar. 1386; MCR 21 Oct. 1381; DRO, Exeter Port Customs Accounts (PCA) 1370/71, 1372/73; R.N. Worth (ed.), *Calendar of Tavistock Parish Records* (1887), 70. In late fourteenth-century Exeter, only a small group of Exeter residents enjoyed the freedom of the city: 4 per cent of the total population of the town in 1377, or about 21 per cent of the householders, belonged to this privileged group; Maryanne Kowaleski, 'The commercial dominance of a medieval provincial oligarchy: Exeter in the late fourteenth century', *Mediaeval Studies*, 46 (1984), 355–84.

16. DRO, MCR 15 Nov. 1389; PRO, C131/38/21–22; R.B. Pugh (ed.), *Wiltshire Gaol Delivery and Trailbaston Trials 1275-1306* (Wiltshire Record Society, *33*, 1977), 149, 160. The occupational profile of medieval skinners is discussed at length in Elspeth M. Veale, *The English Fur Trade in the Later Middle Ages* (1966).

17. For the extra-mural location of Exeter tanners, see DRO, ED/M/336, and E. Carus-Wilson, *The Expansion of Exeter at the Close of the Middle Ages* (1963), 22. Winchester tanners also settled near water, downstream and downwind to avoid polluting the city; see Keene, op. cit. 287–8. Canterbury tanners were also situated near the river; see William Urry, *Canterbury under the Angevin Kings* (1957), 122. During the Middle Ages, London tanners frequently located in suburban areas near the Fleet stream and to the north of the city, and later along the south bank of the Thames, in Bermondsey; see Derek Keene and Vanessa Harding, *Historical Gazetteer of London before the Great Fire, Part I, Cheapside* (1987), no. 104/42; and Waterer, *Leather in Life*, 107–8. For a similar situation in Leicester, see Allin, op. cit., 4–5. In Oxford, the authorities even tried to move the parchment-makers outside the city because of the smell: see Keene, op. cit., 287.

18. H.P.R. Finberg, *Tavistock Abbey* (1969), 153–4, 196. The Okehampton mill was noted in PRO, C135/260 (inquisition taken in 1377) and was being leased out in 1424–5 for 2s.8d.; see BL, Add. Charter 64,663. The poll tax is in PRO, E179/95/54/6. The Okehampton buyers were John Breghe, John Sampson, and John Staundon; DRO, SQMT 1370-78. For the influence investment in tanning mills could have on local leather industries, see Eleanor Searle, *Lordship and Community: Battle Abbey and its Banlieu 1066-1538* (Toronto, 1974), 299–303.

19. PRO, SC11/802 m.3. Duchy of Cornwall Record Office (DCO), Duchy Ministers' Accounts 32/22, 32/25.

20. DRO, SQMT 1370–78, 1382–86; PCR 8 May 1378.

21. A. Mary Kirkus (ed.), *The Great Roll of the Pipe for the Ninth Year of the Reign of King John* (Pipe Roll Society, *60*, 1946), 184.

22. Mark Maltby, *Faunal Studies on Urban Sites: The Animal Bones from Exeter 1971-75* (1979), 22, 31–2.

23. Elisabeth G. Kimball (ed.), *Records of Some Sessions of the Peace in Lincolnshire 1381-96*, I, *The Parts of Lindsey* (Lincolnshire Record Society, *56*, 1962), 69. I am grateful to Larry Poos for pointing out these Lincolnshire records to me.

24. R. Sillem (ed.), *Records of Some Sessions of the Peace in Lincolnshire 1360-75* (Lincolnshire Record Society, *30*, 1937), 49–50, 62–3; Kimball (ed.), op. cit., 199–200.

25. The following is based on data drawn from three Brokage Books: Southampton Record Office, SC5.5/1 (1430–31); Barbara D.M. Bunyard (ed.), *The Brokage Book of Southampton from 1439-40*, (Southampton Record Society, *30*, 1941; Olive Coleman (ed.), *The Brokage Book of Southampton 1443-44* (Southampton Records Series, *4* and *6*, 1960–1).

26. These entries underestimate the trade since dues were not collected on goods owned by a person exempt from the local custom who carried his goods on his own horse. Since most of the trade by cart is recorded, however, these figures probably present a fairly accurate view of bulk trade in hides by land. The figures presented here do not include calf skins, which could be tanned or tawed.

27. DRO, MCR 11 July 1390.

28. These and the following figures were compiled from Brian Foster (ed.), *The Local Port Book of Southampton for 1435-36* (Southampton Record Series, *7*, 1963). An exact count of the skins traded is not possible since indeterminate measures like the fardel and sum were often used.

29. Caroline Skeel, 'The cattle trade between Wales and England from the fifteenth to the nineteenth centuries', *Transactions of the Royal Historical Society*, *9*, (1926), 135–58; E.A. Lewis, 'A contribution to the commercial history of medieval Wales', *Y*

Cymmrodor, 24 (1913), 86–188; W.R. Childs and T. O'Neill, 'Ireland's overseas trade in the later Middle Ages', in *A New History of Ireland*, **II**; *Medieval Ireland 1169-1534*, ed. Art Cosgrove (1987), 501-2; Kathleen Ryan, 'Cattle-keeping in ancient and medieval Ireland: the archaeological evidence', (Unpublished paper presented at the 20th International Congress on Medieval Studies, Kalamazoo, Michigan, 1985).

30. PRO, SC6/817/1, m. 14; for other Duchy accounts of hides, see DCO, Duchy Minister's Accounts, under the 'Cokett' entries and the relevant SC6 accounts in the PRO. For other ports in Devon and Cornwall, see the relevant PRO, E122 accounts and the DRO Exeter Port Customs Accounts which commence in 1302. Both tanned and raw hides were shipped although raw hides (probably salted) predominated. Some of these ports also exported finished leather products, such as shoes, but the import trade in such finished leather goods as points, laces, saddles, and armour was more substantial. I intend to examine these aspects of the trade in more detail in future publications.

31. Ports like Newcastle, for example, exported over 15,000 hides a year in the late thirteenth century; see R.A. Pelham, 'Medieval foreign trade: the eastern ports', in *An Historical Geography of England before 1800*, ed. H.C. Darby (1936), 314-16.

32. H.L. Gray, 'English foreign trade from 1446 to 1482', in *Studies in English Trade in the Fifteenth Century*, ed. Eileen Power and M.M. Postan (New York, 1966), 4, 361, n. 6; compare these figures with those of the thirteenth century in note 31, above, and with J. Conway Davies, 'Wool customs accounts for Newcastle upon Tyne for the reign of Edward I', *Archaeologia Aeliana*, 4th series, 32 (1954), 220-97. The Exeter customs accounts show a similar decline; see especially PRO, E122/40/1, 40/1A, 40/3, 40/7, 40/7A-B.

33. Given the difficulties of measuring the absolute production of hides, skins, or finished leather manufactures, it is impossible at this time to say if or when such production in the late Middle Ages may have surpassed that of the thirteenth and early fourteenth centuries. It is very likely, however, that the supply of the raw materials (and probably of leather goods) increased relative to the population in the later period.

34. L.A. Clarkson, 'The leather crafts in Tudor and Stuart England', *Agricultural History Review*, 14 (1966), 25-39; and 'Organization of the English leather industry'. For the strength of the urban leather trades in early modern England, see also D.M. Palliser, *The Age of Elizabeth: England under the Later Tudors 1547-1603* (1983), 242-5; D.M. Woodward, 'The Chester leather industry, 1558-1625', *Transactions of the Historical Society of Lancashire and Cheshire*, 119 (1967), 65-111.

35. B.H. Slicher Van Bath, *An Agrarian History of Western Europe (500-1850)* (1963), 164-6, 170-83; R. Trow-Smith, *A History of British Livestock Husbandry to 1700* (1957), 106-13; Christopher Dyer, *Warwickshire Farming 1349 - c. 1520: Preparations for Agricultural Revolution* (Dugdale Society Occasional Papers, 27, 1981). The expansion of the continental cattle trade during the late Middle Ages and the early modern period was even more dramatic and has received detailed scholarly attention; see, for example, Ian Blanchard, 'The continental European cattle trades, 1400-1600', *Economic History Review*, 2nd ser., 39 (1986), 427-60 and the essays in E. Westermann (ed.), *Internationaler Ochsenhandel 1350-1750* (Stuttgart, 1979). But these and other works on the continental cattle trade make only passing references to the potential effect of this growing trade on the leather industry.

36. Christopher Dyer, 'English diet in the later Middle Ages', in *Social Relations and Ideas: Essays in Honour of R.H. Hilton*, ed. T.H. Aston *et al.* (1983), 191-216, and 'Changes in diet in the late Middle Ages: the case of harvest workers', *Agricultural History Review*, 36 (1988), 21-37.

37. Maltby, op.cit., 83-93.

38. John Hatcher, *Plague, Population and the English Economy 1348-1530* (1977), 48-51; D.L. Farmer, 'Crop yields, prices and wages in medieval England', *Studies in Medieval and Renaissance History*, n.s., 6 (1983), 117-55.

39. A.R. Bridbury, *Economic Growth: England in the Later Middle Ages* (2nd ed., 1975); Hatcher, op.cit., 44–50. Falling rents and the greater availability of property during much of this period also worked to augment living standards for many.

40. For these prices and those noted below, see James E. Thorold Rogers, *History of Agriculture and Prices in England* (7 vols, 1866–1902), II, 615; III, 551–8. Additional information and confirmation of some of these prices have been kindly furnished by Chris Dyer. For wages, see Hatcher, op. cit., 48.

41. Rogers (op.cit., I, 328–9, 451; IV, 326–8, 376–7) notes that prices of ox and cow hides were less in the late fourteenth century than they had been in the early part of the century; thereafter they rose, although not as much as livestock prices. The prices offered by Rogers, however, need to be treated with extreme caution since his figures were frequently derived from manorial accounts which usually sold 'dead' hides from diseased animals rather than hides from animals recently slaughtered for meat. Regional variations could also be quite significant and need to be taken into account. The prices quoted (for 1450–1649) by Peter Bowden, 'Agricultural prices, farm profits, and rents', in *The Agrarian History of England and Wales*, IV *1500–1640*, ed. Joan Thirsk (1967), 602–5, 646–8, and his 'Statistical Appendix' Table V, 838–45, show that hide prices remained low and changed little in comparison with the prices of livestock and other animal products from the 1450s to 1490s. Thereafter hide prices rose although not at the rate of the price of livestock. Clarkson, 'Leather crafts', 26, notes that the prices of hides and skins in the seventeenth century fell so low on occasion (because of the ample supply derived from the growth in meat consumption) that the surplus was buried. The greater availability and lower prices of hides in the late Middle Ages may also have been responsible for the growing use of cattle hides in shoe uppers instead of sheep or goat hides, and for the decline in finds of repaired or reused uppers in archaeological excavations; see Francis Grew and Margrethe de Neergaard, *Shoes and Pattens* (Medieval Finds from Excavations in London, 2, 1988), 44–6. This issue of prices and its effects on consumption requires further study.

42. Cunnington, op.cit., 85–6, 105–11, 136–47; Norris, op.cit., 257–61, 273–4, 423–6, 449–52; Grew and Neergaard, op.cit., 28–46, 101, 112–22.

43. For the following description of leather items used in warfare, see Waterer, *Leather and the Warrior*, 21–76, 83–7; and Claude Blair, *European Armour circa 1066 to circa 1700* (1958).

44. For the rise of the infantry in late medieval armies, see Philippe Contamine, *War in the Middle Ages*, trans. Michael Jones (1984), 132–72.

45. This diversification of the leather trades can be seen in lists of, for example, those joining town freedoms; see Swanson, op.cit., Table 3.3, pp. 119–22; see also above, p. 48. Compare also the eleven leather and allied occupations listed for Norwich residents mentioned in deeds from 1285 to 1311 in Serena Kelly, Elizabeth Rutledge and Margot Tillyard, *Men of Property: An Analysis of the Norwich Enrolled Deeds 1285–1311* (1983), 34–5, with the eighteen noted as entering the Norwich freedom in the sixteenth century, in J.F. Pound, 'The social and trade structure of Norwich, 1525–75', *Past and Present*, 34 (1966), 67–9. There are, of course, problems of interpretation involved in such comparisons of different sources.

46. L.A. Clarkson, 'English economic policy in the sixteenth and seventeenth centuries: the case of the leather industry', *Bulletin of the Institute of Historical Research*, 38 (1965), 149–62; one set of fifteenth-century regulations relating to the leather crafts was repeated in many urban record books of the period; see R.H. Britnell, *Growth and Decline in Colchester 1300–1525* (1986), 240 and Hugh R. Watkin, *Dartmouth* (Parochial Histories of Devonshire, 5, 1935), 251–2.

47. T.H. Lloyd, *The English Wool Trade in the Middle Ages* (1977); Eileen Power, *The Wool Trade in English Medieval History* (1941).

48. Waterer, *Leather in Life, Art, Industry*, 108; L.F. Salzman, *English Industries of the*

Middle Ages (1964), 248-9; for Exeter see DRO, MCR 25 Nov. 1387 for the selection of two cordwainers to supervise souters and tanners; Maud Sellers (ed.), *York Memorandum Book, Part II: 1388-1493* (Surtees Society, *125*, 1915), 162-6. It is significant that earlier ordinances regulating the tanners in York allowed tanners themselves to supervise the craft; see Michael Prestwich, *York Civic Ordinances, 1301* (Borthwick Papers, *49*, 1976), 14.

49. Swanson, op. cit., 97-8.
50. See Kimball (ed.), op. cit.; Sillem (ed.), op. cit.; Bertha Haven Putnam, *The Enforcement of the Statutes of Labourers* (New York, 1908).
51. This earlier export market was probably more lucrative to tanners than the more highly regulated domestic market. The involvement of tanners in this export market, however, needs to be clarified since many if not most of the exported hides were probably untanned. For the profits accrued by urban merchants who exported hides in the late thirteenth and early fourteenth century, see C.M. Fraser, 'The pattern of trade in the north-east of England, 1265-1350', *Northern History*, *4* (1969), 44-66.
52. Swanson, op.cit., Table 3.3, 119-22; but cf. above, p. 48.
53. Keene, op.cit., 285-91, 356-7; Keene, op. cit., 251 and 289, attributes the decline of urban tanners in Winchester to the migration of tanners, pressed by the expansion of the cloth industry, into suburbs outside the city's jurisdiction and therefore outside the view of his sources, as well as to the contraction of the city's cattle trade and a migration of tanning to rural centres.
54. Lancaster, op.cit., 153-5; the Coventry deeds mentioned eighteen tanners in the first period compared to nine in the later period (all of whom lived outside the city gates).
55. Margery M. Rowe and Andrew M. Jackson (ed.), *Exeter Freemen 1266-1967* (Devon and Cornwall Record Society, extra series, *1*, 1973), 1-63. A search of the municipal election returns for Exeter from 1350 to 1405 also shows that no tanners held municipal office during this period.
56. Helen Sutermeister, 'The merchant classes of Norwich and the city government 1350-1500' (Typescript in the Norfolk Record Office, *c.* 1970-79), chapter 5, 1-6. See also Kelly et al., op. cit., 22-3.
57. Clarkson, 'Leather crafts', 30-8; Clarkson, 'Organization of the English leather industry', 248, 252.
58. Montague S. Giuseppi, 'Industries: leather', in *The Victoria History of the County of Surrey* (1905), II, 329-41; Clarkson, 'Leather crafts', 26-7.
59. Clarkson, 'Organization of the English leather industry', 248; Woodward, 65-111.
60. Clarkson, 'Organization of the English leather industry', 251-2; Salzman, op. cit., 252.
61. Woodward, op. cit., 79-84, 100-11; Cooper and Crossley (ed.), op. cit., 47.

5 Ceramic consumption and supply in early modern Amsterdam: local production and long-distance trade*

Jan M. Baart

This study examines two key aspects of the general theme of 'Work in Towns'. In the first place, it looks at one specific kind of data: that is, archaeological data as a source for historical inquiry. Secondly, it considers the general framework within which the development of urban work can be analysed, setting the study of Amsterdam in the period from 1500 to 1800 into the context of long-distance trade.

In recent years, historians have become increasingly interested in archaeological evidence as a source for the study of medieval and early-modern society. The problem is that the value of this source, although widely recognized, has not always been defined clearly; nor has it been widely used by non-archaeologists: hence, this analysis of the possibilities and limitations of the material record. The discussion also draws upon the large number of written sources relating to Amsterdam in this period, in order that both categories of data can be mutually verified and mutually supplemented.

The development of work needs its historical context. In Amsterdam, excavations show that a pre-urban settlement had emerged by the late twelfth century. The first written sources date from 1275 onwards. At that time, the inhabitants of the county of Holland were farmers living on isolated farms, spread out across the boggy terrain behind the Dutch coastal dunes. They grew some grain, and kept some cattle. They made all kinds of household articles themselves. Their farms were more or less self-sufficient units that knew only few commercial transactions, confined chiefly to the exchange of a small range of luxury goods and the payment of rents. To judge from the metal slags or refuse found on many of these sites, even metal work was quite widely carried out on individual farms.

This community had initially colonized the vast bog, as peat-cutters, from about AD 900 onwards.[1] Work was organized according to a sexual division of labour, sustained by custom rather than by any intrinsic requirements of the different tasks. Women did the spinning and weaving, ground the corn, extracted salt, baked bread, made pottery and shoes, brewed ale, grew vegetables, made candles, and attended to medical care and teaching. Meanwhile, men performed manorial duties and military service, built the boats that were vital for farms surrounded on all sides by water, tended and slaughtered their cattle, and worked the fields.

The evolution of the pre-urban agricultural settlement into the town of Amsterdam was a long process, not completed until the fourteenth century. As it grew, the urban centre saw a redistribution of work specialisms. The first changes can be observed during the eleventh and twelfth centuries, when tasks originally performed by women were taken over by men. Early examples were weaving, pottery, and shoe-making. Then followed, in the period from 1200 to 1400, milling, salt-extraction, baking, brewing, teaching, and medical care. At the same time, a monetized economy evolved, in which goods and services were paid for in coin. Women had sold goods produced by men and thereby played an important role in commercial life. That role was curtailed deliberately in the fifteenth and sixteenth centuries by urban guild regulations, which specified that transactions involving money were to be carried out by men.

Initially, the market for specialized products was small. For instance, Amsterdam itself had no more than 1,000 inhabitants in *c*.1300, although a century later their number had risen to about 5,000. Only a few more consumers lived within a radius of five to ten miles from the urban centre. In this period, craft guilds came into existence and, with the authority of the city council, obtained monopolies over production and – to a lesser extent – over retail distribution.[2] At the same time, women's membership of the guilds was restricted; and there was a ban both on the production of competitor goods in the surrounding countryside and upon their sale in the city, except on designated market days. Many tasks previously performed by men as part of a household production system – such as grain-growing, boat-building and metallurgy – were taken over by specialist producers. One consequence of this was that rents came to be paid in coin, rather than in kind.

The tasks that were thus lost to men and women, within the framework of the domestic production system, were taken on not only by male specialists in the city, like the miller, baker, butcher, potter, weaver and ship's carpenter, but also by specialists abroad. That gave an enormous stimulus to long-distance traffic in goods. Apart from luxury items, which included handsome pottery, international commerce now supplied many elementary necessities of life. By the end of the fifteenth century, Amsterdam depended heavily upon imported grain from Germany and Poland,[3] beer from Hamburg, and wool from England. Because such commodities usually had to be traded for other goods, that stimulated in turn new urban work specialisms, especially in the textile industry.

In the light of these changes, there were two further developments in the system of production itself. First, there was a steady growth in the number of specialist workers: chiefly men who ran small workshops in Amsterdam itself. In the second place, the increase in the scale of the market, facilitated by the growth of long-distance trade, led to regional concentrations of specialist craftsmen and also to the emergence of large-scale enterprises, employing relatively large numbers of waged employees. In Hamburg, for instance, some tens of small brewers but also a few larger brewers, employing groups of labourers, supplied Amsterdam with high-quality German beer.[4] The same applied to the textile industry in Amsterdam and other Dutch cities. There were even special locations in the city, where the clothier could recruit labour each morning from the waiting workforce of men and women.[5]

Amsterdam then grew dramatically in the sixteenth and seventeenth centuries. It housed approximately 14,000 citizens by c.1500; 65,000 by 1600; something over 170,000 by 1650; and as many as 200,000 by 1700.[6] Such headlong growth, which drew thousands into town from the surrounding countryside, was accompanied by further changes in patterns of work and trade.

For this period, there is a considerable range of archaeological data;[7] and, selecting from this abundance of material, the detailed discussion will focus upon one product: pottery. Earthenware has long attracted exhaustive survey, while in recent decades other industrial goods, such as those produced by the textile and leather industries, are now getting more specialist research attention.

To start with earthenware: strictly speaking, no more than about one per cent of disposable income was used for this product in the early modern period (as in modern times). Economically, therefore, it did not constitute an extensive sector. On the other hand, there were many ramifications to its production and use. For example, a major function of earthenware was its deployment in the preparation and consumption of food. And food was one of the main items in family disposable income, comprising anything from 70 to 80 per cent in the early modern period.[8]

Archaeologists excavate used products. Investigation starts with the study of the distribution of artefacts in the ground. Then comes consideration of their provenance. A full analysis of Amsterdam's earthenware, therefore, directs attention not only to local production within and around Amsterdam but also – and as significantly – to the many foreign industries that supplied the city.

In order to chart changes in consumption patterns and in competition between the rival production centres, a series of quantitative tests has been undertaken of earthenware from every twenty years throughout the city's history. The various earthenware groups excavated in Amsteredam have been compared typologically and petrographically with pottery wasters found at the different production centres. Indeed, modern earthenware research has developed such technical expertise that virtually all pottery groups can be traced to their place of origin.

The resulting picture shows that between 1200 and 1500 most of the earthenware in use – between 70 and 80 per cent of the total – was locally produced.[9] This pottery was made from local clays; and the resulting products were red or grey, depending on the firing techniques used. Between 15 and 25 per cent of the remaining earthenware was imported from Germany, and another small percentage mainly from Spain. Here the archaeological record notably extends the information available from written sources, although documentary evidence sometimes supplies valuable information on the location and processes of production.

Technological research also proves informative. The involvement of men, women, and children in the production processes can be established by studying the size of fingerprints in the clay. For example, this shows that the ceramics produced in the eleventh and twelfth centuries were made by women, who shaped the pots by hand. The pots were then fired in small quantities in an open fire. Consequently, there have never been any large finds from this period, either in Amsterdam or in other Dutch cities. That is because large quantities of wasters are the results of mistakes in production by specialist potters, who worked with kilns.

By these means, interesting comparisons can also be made with reference to earthenware imported from Germany. From documentary sources, it was already known that Siegburg (near Bonn) had developed its own concentration of specialist potters, whose market in the period between 1200 and 1500 reached as far as England, Scandinavia, and Poland.[10] Children's fingerprints appear very regularly on early thirteenth-century pots from this site, indicating details of the production process: the transport of the freshly-turned pots to the drying areas, making child labour in those specialized production units literally visible.

Similarly, another German earthenware centre, at Langerwehe (near Aachen), supplied more German pots for import to Amsterdam. It is interesting to find that this industry was a completely rural one. Farmers dug claypits in winter to get at the fine clay. Nex, specialized potters processed the clay into pots, and others fired them.[11] Production presumably fluctuated throughout the year, according to the seasonal patterns of the rural economy; but otherwise the product and market were like those of Siegburg. Thus in both small township and countryside, industrial development burgeoned in the context of expanding long-distance trade.

Technical changes also played a role in the growing predominance of men in the processes of industrial production: the rise of the potter's wheel and the kiln, or that of windmills for the grinding of corn, and ovens for the baking of bread. These more complex means of production demanded more advanced knowledge and larger financial investment, and consequently fitted less and less well into the household production system.

Discussion of industrial production must also note the important élite market for manufactured goods. Court and church demanded their own status symbols. For example, Theophilus in *De Diversis Artibus* described one such workshop, which was aimed at the production of luxury goods, and was presumably situated near a great church or court.[12] All kinds of specialists gathered to supply the social and political élites. Not only at Amsterdam but also at Utrecht, the centre of ecclesiastical government, and at Rijnsburg, where the counts of Holland held court, handsome fourteenth-century tiles have been recovered in excavations. It has recently been established, on the basis of excavated production waste, that these tiles were made in Utrecht. Tiles of this provenance have not been found in other Dutch cities. The same holds true for Germany and Belgium, where similar fourteenth-century luxury ceramics have been found near ecclesiastical centres in Hamburg and Ghent respectively. The manufacturing centres for these products were exceptional in north-west Europe for that time, in their use of a tin glaze. This was a specialist technique, that had probably been imported from Italy.[13]

Furthermore, religious communities themselves could serve as production centres. In early fifteenth-century Amsterdam, at least sixteen *Begijnhof* or communities of women were established, purchasing groups of houses in which they could live a self-sufficient existence.[14] Here women from the upper class earned a living by writing, among other activities; while the larger numbers of lower-class women applied themselves to the production of textiles and beer. Between them, these communities housed around 10 per cent of the marriageable women, whereas there were few comparable groups for men. Some of these women also employed their own male workforce, such as weavers with specialist skills, to increase manufacturing output. Indeed, it is interesting to note that not only were these communities important as industrial centres but their buildings, even after the Reformation, often played a significant role as centres for new industrial activities.

A major discontinuity in the development of production and consumption in Amsterdam followed in the course of the sixteenth century, but became even more pronounced in the seventeenth century. In the excavated material, that discontinuity is demonstrated by the much larger variety of products, from a much wider range of countries. Apart from the ceramics that were made locally or which came from other specialized production centres in the Netherlands, there were products from Italy, Spain, Portugal, France, England, Germany, Denmark, China, and Japan. By contrast, during the medieval period, only Germany and Spain, outside the Netherlands, had supplied pottery to Amsterdam. Indeed, it is possible, from the archaeological material, to measure the proportionate significance of the different production centres for ceramic consumption in Amsterdam and to establish how those proportions changed over time – again information that cannot be obtained from written sources.

Layers of wasters and sometimes even kiln constructions have been excavated in the most important places for earthenware production in the countries listed above. Generally, speaking, the state of this research has progressed so far that it is possible to attribute individual finds to a specific production centre. This research has permitted the analysis of distribution and production; it then has to be matched with examination of the organization of production itself. Here the emphasis shifts from the archaeological data to include archival evidence.

During the period from 1300 to 1500, fine tableware – a luxury article – was exported from Spain to Amsterdam and to most north-western European cities. These products were made in Malaga, Manises (near Valencia) and Seville,[15] using a technology originally introduced by Muslim artisans and imitated by the Spaniards in thirteenth- and fourteenth-century Andalucia, where Muslims and Christians worked closely together. The glazed Spanish majolica wares included plates, bowls and pitchers.

From about 1500 onwards, Italian majolica was also imported regularly to Amsterdam from Montelupo, near Florence. The latter centre played a significant role in this trade: merchants from Florence contracted with a group of majolica potters for a certain volume of goods. A system of production was thereby organized so that a concentration of specialists in one place, Montelupo, could produce sufficient goods to supply a market that stretched across a large part of north-western Europe – and ultimately, after 1600, embraced North America as well.[16] The merchants exercised control over the potters by means of disciplinary clauses in the contracts between them.[17] Indeed, modern petrographical research has been able to identify the special care that went into the preparation of the basic raw materials, the high-quality clays from the neighbourhood of Montelupo. Decorations on these products show influences variously from the Italian Renaissance, Persian and Chinese porcelain, and Christian symbolism. Thus by 1500 the inhabitants of Amsterdam were brought into contact with Renaissance motifs and oriental patterns of decoration, before the influence of the Italian Renaissance, in any deeper cultural sense, began to manifest itself in the Netherlands, and well before ships from Amsterdam sailed to China.

By the sixteenth century, if not before, the production of majolica in Spain was organized in a way similar to that in Italy. In addition, it is known that, in Manises, the merchants who ordered the majolica also supplied the basic materials and paints, so that the potters there depended upon the merchants to an even greater extent.

If Montelupo had a European-wide importance by 1500, a more elaborate mode of production, based upon the same markets, developed in the course of the sixteenth century in Liguria: especially in and around Albisola. Here the entire region dedicated itself to the production of faience wares, with many specialist trades involved in the constituent processes: workshops that processed the clay, and mills that took care of the preparation of clay and pigments.[18] This system may be termed one of regional specialization. In Amsterdam, the net effect was a rise in the Italian share of total earthenware sales, from one or two per cent at the start of the sixteenth century to a good five per cent.[19] Indeed, this method of production can be taken as the direct forerunner of the factory, in which all these specialized processes were later brought together under one roof and the control of a single entrepreneur.

Meanwhile, a number of Italian majolica potters migrated to settle in various cities in the Low Countries, including Amsterdam, bringing with them their fund of technological know-how. These potters ran small workshops with sales initially in the city, but they soon began to cater also for markets in neighbouring cities, the countryside, and eventually the export trade. Only a few people worked in the business. Together, they were able to produce for an international market (England, Scandinavia, Germany, Poland), just like the potters of Montelupo. However, there is no surviving documentation of the Dutch contracting system.

France also had a production centre in Saintonge, where several workshops delivered the wares to merchants, just as in Montelupo. As the production of refined tableware demanded a particularly high quality, specialist designers were to be found here. One such was Palissy,[20] who influenced the style of all the potters in Saintonge. Here again, the market embraced the whole of north-western Europe. However, the proportion of consumption in Amsterdam that was accounted for by these French wares was low: never more than about one per cent.

By the end of the sixteenth century, therefore, an Amsterdam consumer could choose his or her tableware from an impressive array of products: from Montelupo, Albisola, and Faenza in Italy; from Valencia, Seville, and Talavera (near Madrid) in Spain; from Saintonge in France; from Amsterdam itself and from other Dutch cities; and from China. In the seventeenth century, porcelain from Japan and faience from Portugal were also available.[21] All these countries had production centres that were especially geared to long-distance trade and the large-scale production attendant upon it.

In the latter half of the seventeenth century, however, the indigenous Dutch industry underwent an important organizational change, with the advent of a more handsome product: faience. That entailed larger manufactories, where some fifty labourers carried out specialized part-processes. The first such establishment came into existence in Haarlem around 1640, and the next in Amsterdam at the end of the century. Moreover, a situation arose in Delft from the 1650s onwards that can be compared with the state of the industry in Albisola in Italy. A great concentration of workshops formed in effect a regional specialization. Some workshops – sometimes with a handful of labourers – were dedicated to one process, such as the preparation or supply of foreign clays, while others undertook the entire production process. This regional specialization in Delft attracted a specialist workforce from other cities and in that way enlarged production on an extraordinary scale. Hence, in the later seventeenth century, that one city accounted for a product which was carried across almost the entire globe, wherever the Dutch traded.[22]

The development of the Dutch faience industry promptly brought an end to imports from Montelupo, Albisola, Saintonge, and Lisbon. It was a clear case of import substitution. Likewise, the earlier success of the Portuguese faience on the international market has to be seen in the context of the glamour of imported Chinese porcelain. Portugal had been the first European country to supply this product in the course of the sixteenth century. Chinese porcelain was expensive and was brought to Europe only in small quantities, even sometimes patterned to order. It was a luxury item, a status symbol on the tables of the European élite. Several potters in Lisbon had therefore taken the initiative to make an imitation Chinese porcelain.[23] In 1619, there were 28 small specialist workshops, concentrated at Lisbon. Plates, bowls and pitchers were produced, with Chinese decorations in faience-techniques: attractive and relatively cheap tableware for the emergent 'middle classes' of Europe and the New World. These Portuguese wares were particularly successful in Amsterdam in the years from 1600 to 1660.[24] Thereafter, Lisbon faience faced competition from the Italian faience from Liguria, and both were in turn replaced on the Amsterdam market by faience from Delft.

Meanwhile, from the beginning of the seventeenth century, Portugal's role as the chief importer of Chinese porcelain began to wane, while Amsterdam merchants began to play an increasing part. Larger quantities were imported than ever before, but the product still remained expensive, and the average consumption per household in Amsterdam remained very restricted.[25] When, however, at the end of the seventeenth century, the drinking of coffee and tea became widespread among all social classes, Chinese porcelain moved into first place in Amsterdam: constituting some 30 to 40 per cent of the total consumption of earthenware and pottery.[26] It had become a mass product.

The organization of the Chinese industry was the most highly developed, in terms of the division of labour, technology, and management. For the first time, it is appropriate to talk of something like modern factories. One merchant/manager stood at the apex of the organization, owning a gigantic kiln complex, and employing in turn labourers to prepare the kaolin (the basic raw material), painters in the workshop, and many other specialists. A similar development also took place in Japan between 1650 and 1680, with, however, a smaller export trade.[27] In that case, the Japanese manufacturers quickly imitated the Chinese porcelain, in order to take advantage of the unstable political situation in mid-seventeenth-century China.

Amidst this proliferation of trade, there were many different markets with differing demands and price-levels. Germany supplied the pitcher for the Amsterdam table or the jar for storage of beer or wine.[28] Siegburg, famous in medieval times but subsequently in decline, by this time supplied only mugs and beer-jugs, albeit still very handsomely modelled. These were made in small and specialized stoneware workshops. As still happens today in the cycle of industrial development, a highly specialized industry survived as the final stage of a formerly all-round manufacturing enterprise. However, this particular production centre finally went out of business in the seventeenth century. Instead, from 1500 onwards, Cologne emerged as a production centre for jars that were exported to international markets. Production was again organized into small workshops, concentrated in a few streets, while Dutch merchants entered into contracts with potters in Cologne, as earlier in Siegburg, in order to ensure supplies. There were also some similar products made in rural Raeren, as well as in urban Cologne, indicating the locational diversity of industrial production in this era. However, by the seventeenth century, these specialist potters began in turn to move away from Cologne, Raeren, and Siegburg, to settle at new centres at Frechen and Westerwald.[29]

Another key product was a plain red earthenware, used for cooking pots. Throughout the sixteenth and seventeenth centuries, this was manufactured in Amsterdam workshops, especially established just outside the city walls, as had been the case in medieval times. Remarkably, however, just as Delft had concentrated national production of faience, so Bergen-op-Zoom managed the same feat by about 1500, with reference to the production of these plain cooking pots.[30] Amsterdam therefore used wares from Bergen alongside its own manufactures. The organization of the Bergen industry, which was concentrated in some ten workshops, was particularly notable in that the potters themselves ensured by means of guild regulations that the volume of trade and distribution were satisfactory. They also made direct arrangements for transport with skippers from Amsterdam. The reason for the emergence of this industry was the presence of the directly-usable good clays around Bergen. Like Delft, it developed a world-wide export trade, England being one of its major markets.

Also on sale in the eighteenth century were cheap products of red or white earthenware. These pots, produced on farms in the neighbourhood of Frankfurt-am-Main, flooded the Amsterdam market. Wages and living-standards were then relatively high in Amsterdam, so that the German wares could be sold below the price of similar goods produced in Amsterdam itself.[31] Red earthenware had comprised about 70 to 80 per cent of the pottery market in medieval times; this percentage remained high in the sixteenth century (at about 80 per cent); but dropped significantly in the seventeenth century to an average of 50 per cent, and even further in the eighteenth century, to no more than 10 to 20 per cent.[32] Until 1700, however, this red earthenware remained a staple article in Amsterdam's export trade.

Another distinctive product was the cheap black cooking-pot from Denmark. These pots were regularly found in Amsterdam, as well as in large areas of north-western Europe, throughout the sixteenth, seventeenth and eighteenth centuries. They did not claim a very large slice of the market (less than one per cent of surviving archaeological material), and the pots were probably bought for very specific cooking purposes. This kind of earthenware was produced mainly in the countryside, and exclusively by women, using old-fashioned techniques and working part-time to gain additional income.[33] That is to say, the pots were shaped by hand, and fired in an open fire. The extreme cheapness of these primitive wares enabled them to keep their niche in the highly-competitive urban markets, which were otherwise dominated by the products of much more complex manufacturing and trading systems.

Technological innovations in early seventeenth-century Amsterdam mainly took place via the recruitment of foreign labour, as in the case of Dutch majolica production. Such a change occurred in yet another specialist ceramic manufacture, with the migration of a number of English pipe makers. Most of these men had been mercenary soldiers in origin, whose wives had taken over production to provide for themselves in wartime. The new industry produced at least one major business. In the case of Edward Bird, an initially small workshop grew into a decentralized manufacturing establishment with a truly international market, reaching as far as the colonies. At Bird's death in 1670, the warehouse behind his house alone contained contained some 500,000 pipes awaiting transport.[34]

The intricate networks that serviced demand for ceramics in Amsterdam have revealed fluidity and competition in both trade and manufactures. Growth and specialization responded to the expanding size of markets; but were not invariably sustained.

Hence, the Dutch ceramics industry began to falter in the later eighteenth century. The reasons behind this decline were political as well as economic. As a world power, the Dutch Republic was fast being eclipsed.[35] Meanwhile, Britain had emerged. One important factor in this change was Britain's access to new markets in overseas colonies. Yet of still greater importance was innovation in the organization of work. The advent of early industrialization was certainly visible in the English pottery areas – in places like Leeds and Liverpool, and, above all, in Staffordshire. Their factories, their many innovations in techniques and fashion, their large-scale labour processes and production runs, their enormous markets and advanced sales techniques, announced a major new development in European manufactures.[36]

From about 1750 onwards, therefore, English wares were found in Amsterdam, where they were sold in special shops. Indeed, these products can now be found at excavations all over the world. English pottery presented very serious competition both to Delft faience and to Chinese porcelain, for the English goods were stylish but relatively inexpensive: about a third the price of Chinese porcelain and almost the same price as Delft faience, which was visibly of poorer quality.

In consequence, the purchase of red earthenware cooking pots ceased in eighteenth-century Amsterdam, and the industry disappeared completely from the city. At the same time, the manufacture of faience tableware also dwindled, as Dutch production became concentrated at Delft. Attempts were made to combat these developments, but industrial success was not easily borrowed. Two new factories, with some fifty labourers, were set up in eighteenth-century Amsterdam. One of these, sponsored by a well-intentioned minister, attempted to revive the production of faience. As the product was old-fashioned, the initiative proved hopeless and led to bankruptcy after a few years.[37] A second factory made hand-painted porcelain but that proved extremely expensive, costing at least fourteen times as much as the English wares. Consequently, it was sold solely to the Amsterdam élite. But such a small (and indeed shrinking) market provided too narrow a basis for success, and this project met the same end as the faience factory.[38] Not until the years after 1840 did Dutch industrialization eventually lead to developments similar to those in England; but then the new industry was not established at Amsterdam but at Maastricht.

In sum, therefore, by collating archaeological and archival sources for Amsterdam ceramics, three key stages can be identified. In the initial period, from 900 to 1200, household production was predominant. It was mainly small-scale, and based upon female labour. Luxury goods, manufactured by specialist potters, were imported from Germany, or came from newly-developing potteries in Dutch cities.

A subsequent period, from 1200 to about 1500, saw the development of much greater specialization: with small domestic workshops, staffed exclusively by men. There were some regional concentrations of potteries, especially in Germany, geared to international export markets – including those of Amsterdam itself, with its fast-growing population of eager consumers. Finally, in the years from 1500 to 1800, these specialist craft production shops in turn went into decline. They now faced competition from a literally world-wide range of increasingly sophisticated industries and eventually from modernized and large-scale factory production. All that occurred within a highly competitive market – not just in Amsterdam but on a truly international scale – as demand for both plain and luxury pottery continued to expand among all social classes.

Archaeologists like to 'look beyond the fragments'. Those from Amsterdam ceramics reveal a long and intricate history of competition and change in patterns of industrial production and of long-distance trade. In those changes, both traditional methods of work and increasing specialization, stimulated by expanding markets, had a part to play in supplying ceramics to consumers in early modern Amsterdam.

Notes

* The text of this essay has been translated from the Dutch by J.J.M. Houtkamp and edited by P.J. Corfield and D. Keene.
1. For further discussion, see J.M. Baart, 'Werkzeug, Gerät und Handwerksarten in der Stadt um 1200', in *Zur Lebenweise in der Stadt um 1200: Ergebnisse der Mittelalter-Archäologie*, ed. H. Steuer (Cologne, 1986), 379–88.
2. N. de Roever, 'De Amsterdamsche gilden van voorheen', in *Uit onze oude Amstelstad, 4* (Amsterdam, 1893), 65–116.
3. Information on trade is available in B. Zientara, 'Die Entwicklung der Städte im Niederoderraum im 13 Jahrhundert im Zusammenhang mit den Anfängen des Kornexports', *Lübecker Schriften zur Archäologie und Kulturgeschichte, 7* (Bonn, 1983), 147–57; and N.W. Posthumus, *De geschiedenis van de Leidsche lakenindustrie* (The Hague, 1908), I, 74.
4. H.J. Smit, *De opkomst van de handel in Amsterdam* (Amsterdam, 1914), 30–133.
5. Posthumus, op.cit. in n. 3 above, I, 37.
6. Figures for Amsterdam's population growth are indicated in J. de Vries, *European Urbanization 1500-1800* (1984), 271.
7. For further information, see J. Baart, W. Krook and A.C. Lagerweij, 'Opgravingen aan de Oostenburgermiddenstraat', in *Van VOC tot Werkspoor*, ed. J.B. Kist (Utrecht, 1986), 83–151.
8. See on this, L. Noordegraaf, *Hollands welvaren? Levensstandaard in Holland 1450-1650* (Bergen-op-Zoom, 1985), 15.
9. J.M. Baart, 'Ceramiche Italiane rinvenute in Olanda e le prime imitazzioni Olandesi', *Centro Ligure per la Storia della Ceramica Albisola, 16* (Albisola, 1985), 161–187, esp. 187.
10. H. Stephan, 'The development and production of medieval stoneware in Germany', in *Ceramics and Trade*, ed. P. Davey and R. Hodges (1983), 99–100.
11. For further information, see J. Schwarz, *Die Langerweher Töpferei im Spiegel der Sprache* (Langerwehe, 1982), 5–11.
12. Text available in numerous editions, as in C.R. Dodwell (ed.), *Theophilus: De Diversis Artibus* (1961).

13. Baart, 'Ceramiche Italiane', 165.
14. These are discussed in I.H. Van Eeghen, *Vrouwenkloosters en Begijnhof in Amsterdam van de 14de eeuw tot het einde der 16de eeuw* (Amsterdam, 1941).
15. See variously: J.G. Hurst, D.S. Neal, and H.J.E. van Beuningen, 'Pottery produced and traded in north-west Europe, 1350–1650', *Rotterdam Papers, 6* (Rotterdam, 1986), 38–88, esp. 38–67; and A. Ray, 'Fifteenth-century Spanish pottery: the blue and purple family', *Burlington Magazine, 5/129* (May 1987), 306–9.
16. For further details, see F. Berti, *The Montelupo Ceramics* (Montelupo, 1986), 27.
17. G. Cora, *Storia della Maiolica di Firenze e del Contado* (2 vols, Florence, 1986), 361–3.
18. See D. Restagno, 'La Ceramica della scavo della cattedrale di Savona sal Priamar', *Atti del V Convegno Internazionale della Ceramica* (Albisola, 1972), 147–72.
19. Baart, 'Ceramiche Italiane', 161–87.
20. Hurst et al., op. cit. in n. 15 above, 83–8.
21. J.M. Baart, 'Dutch material civilisation – daily life between 1650–1776: evidence from archaeology', in *New World Dutch Studies*, ed. R.R. Blackburn and N.A. Kelley (Albany, 1987), 1–13, esp. 1–7.
22. This is given detailed discussion in J.W. van Dam, 'Geleyersgoet en Hollands porceleyn, ontwikkelingen in de Nederlandse aardewerkindustrie, 1560–1660', *Mededelingenblad Nederlandse vereniging van vrienden van de ceramiek, 108/4* (1982), 1–93.
23. See comment in R. dos Santos, *A Faiança Portuguesa Séculos XVI e XVII* (Lisbon, 1960), 33.
24. J.M. Baart, 'Faiança Portuguesa escavada no solo de Amsterdão', in *Faiança Portuguesa 1600–1660*, ed. C. van Lakerveld and T. Oliveira-van Royen (Amsterdam and Lisbon, 1987), 18–27.
25. C.J.A. Jorg, *Porselein als Handelswaar* (Groningen, 1978), 5–32.
26. Baart et al., op. cit., in n. 7 above, 94.
27. A comprehensive account is available in T. Volker, 'Porcelain and the Dutch East India Company, as recorded in the Dagh Registers of Batavia Castle, those of Hirado and Deshima and other contemporary papers, 1602–82', in *Mededelingen van het Rijksmuseum voor Volkenkunde, 11* (Leiden, 1971).
28. Baart, 'Ceramiche Italiane', 187.
29. See variously K. Gobels, *Rheinisches Töpferhandwerk* (Frechen, 1971), 119; and G. Reineking-von Vock, *Steinzeug* (Cologne, 1971), 30–8.
30. L.J. Weijs, 'Techniek en produkten van de Bergen-op-Zoomse potmakers', in *Tussen Hete Vuren*, ed. C.F.J. Slootmans, L.J. Weijs, and C.J.J. van de Watering (2 vols, Tilburg, 1970), I, 13–15.
31. J. de Kleyn, *Volksaardewerk in Nederland 1600–1900* (Zeist, 1965), 39–46.
32. Baart, op.cit., in n. 21 above.
33. For further information, see the account in A. Jensen, *Jydepotten* (Copenhagen, 1924), 1–173.
34. M. de Roever, 'The Fort Orange "EB" pipe bowls: an investigation into the origin of American objects in Dutch seventeenth-century documents', in Blackburn and Kelley (ed.), op. cit. in n. 21 above, 51–61.
35. For discussion of the relative eclipse of the Dutch Republic, see variously J. de Vries, *De economische achteruitgang der Republick in de achttiende eeuw* (Amsterdam, 1958); C.R. Boxer, *The Dutch Seaborne Empire 1600–1800* (1973 edn.), 302–31; A.C. Carter, *Neutrality or Commitment: The Evolution of Dutch Foreign Policy 1667–1795* (1975); A. van der Woude, 'La ville Néerlandaise', in J. Meyer *et al.*, *Études sur les villes en Europe occidentale: milieu du XVIIe siècle à la veille de la Révolution Française* (2 vols, Paris, 1983), II, 323–38; and J. Israel, *Dutch Primacy in World Trade 1585–1740* (1989).
36. See L. Weatherill, *The Pottery Trade and North Staffordshire 1660–1760* (1971); and

also N. McKendrick, 'Josiah Wedgwood and the commercialization of the Potteries', in N. McKendrick, J. Brewer and J.H. Plumb, *The Birth of a Consumer Society: The Commercialization of Eighteenth-Century England* (1982), 100–45.

37. W.F.H. Oldewelt, 'De aardenwerkfabriek Blankenburg', in *Jaarboek Amstelodamum, 27* (1930), 313–17.

38. W.M. Zappey, 'Porceleinwerkers aan de Amstel', in *Mededelingenblad Nederlandse vereniging van vrienden van de ceramiek,* 86/87 (1977), 2–3.

6 Women and work in sixteenth-century English towns[1]

Michael Roberts

In October 1582, a woman named Alice Wynn was expelled from Liverpool by the town's authorities. Welsh Alice, as she was known, had been lodging for some time with a local married woman, amongst whose other guests were noted Manx, Irish and 'northern men', described scathingly by the authorities as 'loiterers and quaines'.[2] The expulsion was a perfectly ordinary occurrence. Liverpool, like many other English towns in the later sixteenth century, pursued a policy of carefully scrutinizing newcomers to assess their potential contribution to the town's economy. Unless they could find someone to vouch for their good character and perhaps to guarantee them work, or to support them in sickness and unemployment, the newcomers would be turned away. It was a difficult policy to enforce, because landlords busily converting barns into cottages and erecting new small dwellings for the poor were not opposed to newcomers. Nor were solitary widows always reluctant to receive and accommodate a stranger for some small help or payment.[3] In Liverpool even a former mayor, Alexander Garnett, had been reported in 1565 for his failure to expel unwelcome immigrants,[4] and Alice Wynn seems to have been scraping a living in the town for at least four years before her expulsion in 1582.

The pressures brought by subsistence migration to many towns in the late sixteenth and early seventeenth centuries impelled their inhabitants towards some difficult decisions about the kinds of social and economic behaviour they wanted to encourage.[5] In confronting them, they articulated a conception of the urban economy in which a woman's work, her sexuality and her marital status were intricately intertwined within the confines of the household. The offences of the Liverpool 'inmates' like Alice Wynn were those of women who did not observe the disciplines of domestic life appropriate to their age: young women who worked as 'char-women' on a daily basis, refusing to enter service: and others, perhaps older, who were variously described as 'light', 'unchaste', or evil-disposed. One, again harboured by another woman, was stigmatized in 1577 as 'a woman [who] maye worke great inconvenience to this towne'. Prominent among such inconveniences was the bearing of illegitimate children, for whom maintenance would have to be found. But women at work on their own terms could untie the bands of domestic discipline in more subtle ways; and that is why the authorities lost patience with

Alice Wynn. For, having failed to break into the victualling trade as an unlicensed brewer and baker, she had turned to a more insidious form of petty trading by 'intysinge mens children, servantes and apprentices to buy thinges unlawfull, as salte etc'. By doing so she not only breached municipal marketing controls, but also undermined the domestic authority of the youngsters' proper households, where the provision of food was the responsibility of the householder's wife, and where money was not supposed to be available for the purchase of sweetmeats by children.[6]

This essay examines more examples of the work undertaken by sixteenth-century urban women, and the framework of assumptions, rules and customs which gave it shape. The contemporary evidence affords an access to the subject which is unprecedented in its richness, though sixteenth-century experiences and attitudes need not be regarded as themselves unprecedented or unique. From this vantage-point we can look out across longer spans of time, and frame questions about the history of women's work on that basis. The particular experiences of Alice Wynn take us straight to some of the crucial issues: how was a townsperson's contribution to the work of the community defined in this period, and what part was played in that definition by a sense of gender? It is worth insisting on the term gender, as a reminder of the cultural, rather than natural, origin of these distinctions. Contemporary dramatists had much to say about different gender roles, but none of the parts they wrote actually played on stage by female actors. In this sense, concepts of gender are quite separable from the 'natural' facts of human biology. As far as 'work' is concerned, there is also a problem of definition, made all the more urgent by the organization of much recent research into the history of women's work around particular themes which take the meaning of *work* itself for granted: the life cycle,[7] or stages in the cycle such as widowhood;[8] or the process of competition for work of 'high status';[9] or stoical improvisation in adversity, managing an 'economy of makeshifts'.[10] We surely need to ask ourselves first of all how the notion of work *in general* was being constructed and transformed in this period, and in exploring this question our guides must include anthropologists as well as economists, historians and social theorists.

The anthropologist's cross-cultural comparisons can alert us to the great variety of ways in which work has been defined in the past, and to the need to understand the processes by which such definitions are maintained, and how they change.[11] When viewed in this light, the men and women of the later sixteenth century may be said to have grounded their approach to work on the twin foundations of material scarcity and religious plenty. The pressures which came from the one direction were interpreted with resources drawn from the other, so that at its most poetic, the combined legacy of humanist thought and Protestant theology offered a unifying characterization of all human activity as a form of blessed labour. To express it in our terms, men and women were seen to be undertaking three kinds of work or labour: the creation of new human beings through reproduction; the production of food, clothing and other goods; and the reproduction of social relations, through their management of household, kin and community interaction.[12] Against the background of contemporary Christian teaching, the process of human reproduction was not of prime importance; for the central miracle was, rather, God's creation of the world and his support for man's place in it with the earth's natural bounty. These gifts were in turn considered, particularly after the

Reformation, to be fructified by the spiritual nourishment of Christ's gospel.[13] Of the three kinds of labour, therefore, the highest status was given to the second, the production of necessary sustenance. That was the activity in which men predominated (in public at least), as against the crucial contribution of women to both biological and social spheres of reproduction.

Alongside these questions of definition, two further general issues should be noted. First, although in studying this period we can now build on the achievements of a generation of urban historians, the length and intensity of any late medieval urban 'crisis' are still in dispute.[14] One conclusion to be drawn from the experience of Alice Wynn and her many sisters may indeed be that our concepts of urban decay or crisis could be enriched by the introduction of an analysis of gender relations, such as has recently been developed for late sixteenth-century rural communities.[15] A second, related, issue is raised by the Cambridge school of historical demographers: how were the social and cultural determinants of household formation linked to changing levels of prosperity in this and other periods?[16] Or, to turn again to Liverpool, how far was the attitude of scepticism towards immigrant women, with their 'light and unchaste conversation', a product of identifiable features of the town's economic development? It is not unlikely that the severity with which courtship, or female behaviour in general, were subjected to control was related in some way to cycles of prosperity and recession. But this has to be demonstrated rather than assumed, and the number of theories seeking to explain the links between economic systems and patterns of gender inequality remind us that both the evidence and the conceptual problems involved in its interpretation are complex.[17]

With these points in mind we can return to the 'shaping' of work in sixteenth-century towns, to ask how far that shaping involved a sense of gender. Until quite recently, it would have seemed that our most obvious starting point was the recorded occupational structure, with its promise of an authentic contemporary classification of work. However, it has become increasingly apparent that the occupational structure visible to us in the public records of towns was a form of political and cultural display, whose relationship to economic activity was not always very close.[18] Yet the public representation of work through the craft guilds, as an array of occupations or mysteries, clearly did have practical consequences, not least for women. When demographic stagnation and competition from rural industry made trading conditions difficult in many towns during the fifteenth century, the implementation of the guild rules which had been evolving over the preceding centuries could be restricting. At the same time, the internal organization of the guilds themselves was becoming more hierarchical, and the rules governing access to urban freedom and trading privileges were also being more clearly defined, if not more harshly applied.[19] One outcome may have been a somewhat firmer sense of the individual occupation.[20] Another was an enhanced identification of the occupational structure with the urban social order in general. As the translator of a work dedicated to Elizabeth I on her accession put it,[21] what body politic could survive:

> whiche is not compacte and measured ... Wherein the Smith leavyng his owne occupation, wil labour to plaie the Tailour, and contrary the Tailour will medle with the forge, the Shomaker will in hand with linne[n] Draperie, the private man entermedle

with the officer, . . . to disturbe & dissolve the worke of God, that is the frame of the common weale.

The identification between political and economic roles required of each household head an occupation; sometimes, as in Beverley, forcing a man to acknowledge the authority of the craft 'he most gets his living by', and in other places maintaining the consistency of the *occupational* requirement by actually recognizing the pursuit of more than one occupation.[22] Men required such an identity as the public face of the household, as those who engaged in our second sort of productive work. Women did not. The proper roles of man and wife, explained Sir Thomas Smith[23] around 1565, were:

Figure 6.1. *Woman Cooking beside an Unmade Bed* (1656) by Esaias Boursse. The exploration of gender roles, which was vividly dramatized on the Elizabethan stage, was also a key theme in the visual art of seventeenth-century Dutch towns. This quietly-brooding domestic interior by the Amsterdam-born genre painter, Esaias Boursse, shows a woman sitting meditatively at the hearth, amidst the tokens of her unfinished chores of cooking, cleaning, and childcare.

Reproduced by permission of the Trustees, The Wallace Collection, London (Wallace Collection, P/166).

the man to get, to trauaile abroad, to defende; the wife, to saue that which is gotten, to tarrie at home to distribute that which commeth of the husbandes labor . . . and to keepe all at home neat and cleane.

But the development of a self-conscious, politically-informed sense of occupational identity also held implications for the practical opportunities available to women, to participate in the work of the crafts whose public image remained resolutely male. The formulation of the guild rules made possible the articulation of assumptions about the sexual division of labour which in the earlier Middle Ages may have admitted of more flexibility. Women were unusual as urban office-holders in the fifteenth and sixteenth centuries, and there were few guilds, or guild-like associations, of women such as were to be found in some European cities.[24] What is more, it is generally argued that women's access to craft work under the auspices of the guilds was diminishing over the course of this period. In York, for example, a high point of independent female economic activity has been identified from franchise, testamentary and employment evidence in the first half of the fifteenth century, and the franchise evidence at least shows a much reduced role for women by the end of the sixteenth century.[25] Two interconnected factors have been adduced to explain such changing patterns of activity: the prosperity of the town concerned, and the comparative availability of labour. Similar patterns have also been tentatively identified for other towns: Abingdon, Coventry, London, Oxford, Salisbury and Warwick.[26] As those familiar with the interpretation of freemen's records will recognize, however, it is difficult to associate admissions to freedom with actual levels of activity and prosperity in any straightforward way. In the case of women, the exercise is rendered even more problematic by the small numbers involved: 44, for example, from a total of 6,231 admissions to freedom in sixteenth-century York.[27]

For reasons of this kind, historians of women's work have increasingly seen the need to probe behind the more formally-documented areas of urban life, to try to establish how often men were actually to be found 'travailing abroad', and their wives 'tarrying at home'. The craft guilds can again provide a starting point, since the exercise of economic, social and spiritual functions across the entire spectrum of medieval guilds had firmly embedded 'work' in a broad family and community context. That went some way towards effacing in practice the separation of male and female roles, which occupational terminology implied. Wives and daughters were thus often exempted from guild restrictions on the employment of female labour.[28] But the craft organizations were in their turn influenced by concepts of gender permeating society as a whole, and which were sustained by the asymmetry of gender roles within the household. The employment of female weavers in Bristol was decried in 1461 for casting into destitution men who might be called upon for military service. In Coventry, female activity at the broad loom was deemed 'a geyn all goode order and honeste' in 1453. Looms were barred to women in Norwich in 1511, since they were thought to lack the strength required to produce decent cloth, as were boys under the age of fourteen.[29] Restrictions of this kind are sometimes viewed as a kind of patriarchal camouflage, behind which men could guarantee for themselves the monopoly of well-paid, high-status work in difficult times. But the interplay between strength, status, gender and remuneration may well have been more subtle, as the exclusion of boys from weaving suggests, and as is indicated in another context by the association of urban privileges for either sex with morally acceptable or 'chaste' behaviour.[30]

If craft rules reflected assumptions about gender current in the wider society, however, the rules also served in their turn to sustain the family as a social institution. Female apprentices were rare in the sixteenth century, but daughters do not seem to have been normally excluded from the informal acquisition of craft skills via instruction by their fathers.[31] The length of male apprenticeships was in any case determined by the need to guarantee the employing craftsman some profit from the labour of his trainee during the later years of his term, as much as by the time required to perfect the learned techniques.[32] Women, who acquired such skills informally, were an undoubted asset to families relying, as many in the towns and suburbs increasingly did, on an improvisational shifting of personnel across a number of activities, both on a seasonal basis, and from one phase of economic activity to another. Widows' rights to engage in trade and production seem similarly to have rested on the assumed priority of family survival, whether this was expressed by protecting a male heir's right ultimately to inherit the family business, or by affording the widow and her children an income from the labour of her husband's apprentices. Where the question of establishing a new productive unit arose, however, either by the entering of fresh apprentices in the widow's name, or by transferring trading privileges to another husband, the rules were tighter.[33]

Against this background of rules and assumptions, then, women's independent participation in the sixteenth-century town's formal economy was greatest in two areas: first, in those spheres where formal regulation was poorly developed or difficult to enforce consistently;[34] and, secondly, in those occupations that specialized in production of the kind undertaken by women for centuries on an informal domestic basis.[35] The question of independence, of holding the initiative and being able to acquire capital, to employ labour and to achieve status, is certainly an important one. This was all the more true after the dissolution of the nunneries closed off one numerically modest, but symbolically important, arena for women's endeavour. Though fewer than 2,000 individual women were directly involved, their reluctance to abandon their houses at the Dissolution, in contrast to the willingness of at least some of their continental sisters, may indicate something of the self-esteem which their communities had continued to sustain.[36] Whether the growth of a capitalist market economy in this period was also tending to limit the opportunities for female initiative has long been subject to dispute.[37] However, an area in which we *can* see the pressures of demography and commerce bearing down heavily on women over the course of the sixteenth century is in the market for servants.

Far more women experienced a period of work in service than could ever aspire to urban freedom. It is tempting to define their work as 'domestic', perhaps even as 'drudgery',[38] but the range of activities undertaken by such women was wide and varied in character, and included participation in industrial production.[39] Some historians have identified a long-term tendency towards the 'feminization' of household service between the fifteenth and eighteenth centuries, suggesting that this was accompanied by a consequent reduction in occupational status for the domestic servant.[40] But within that process there was another tendency, towards the subdivision of functions within the domestic labour force. This might involve the subordination of male apprentices to female servants,[41] and also a developing sense of hierarchy within the female servant group itself, so that in larger households at least maidservants in the seventeenth century characteristically specialized in certain aspects of household work.[42] In smaller households, with perhaps only a single servant, the range of work undertaken by individual women must have been greater. Those who worked for the aged, for instance, might find nursing added to their tasks.[43]

As a characteristic employment of women in the late 'teens and early twenties, service offered the opportunity to experience life in a succession of different domestic environments, as well as time to broaden the pool of suitable marriage partners, and to acquire a stock of clothes or savings with which to embark on adult life. For those who travelled some distance to enter service, there may have been some of that excitement experienced by female migrants to the towns in the developing world.[44] But the shape of service as a form of work was becoming less predictable during the course of the sixteenth century, as the problems of landlessness and rural migration to the towns increased. Municipal authorities had sought since the fourteenth century to regulate the terms of employment for servants, in order to accommodate an effective period of training for the young with shifts in the demand for labour and in urban prosperity.[45] There are signs that it was becoming more difficult to tie both parties down to an annual contract by the later sixteenth century. As farmers shifted their preferences from husbandry servants to the employment of cheaply-available casual labour,[46] so in the towns we hear more about charwomen and 'journeymaids'. These women worked by the day, or for irregular periods of 'service', like that undertaken by the York servant Anne Godfray, who owned only the clothes 'whiche she had apon hir back', and of whom her employer, a tiler's wife, said 'she is but my servant for a whyle, and I cannot tell when she will go away, for she will be here to nyght and away tomorrowe'.[47] The insecurity of this form of employment was all the greater because the influx of indigent girls to the towns proved tempting to would-be employers who could themselves barely scrape a living.[48]

One consequence was an increase in the number of 'quasi-uxorial relationships' between migrant women and single male employers, a phenomenon which spurred on the town authorities to enforce their measures against inmates.[49] The number of such relationships is difficult to measure with any precision, since their well-being partly depended on the ability to avoid official detection and censure. They were certainly not a novel feature of this period,[50] and may have been more common, or at least more visible, in towns whose economies also supported a substantial population of single males. Ports as varied in size as Liverpool (with a population of around 1,000 in 1600) and Southampton (four times as large) took regular steps to discourage liaisons between townsmen, some of whom were certainly mariners, and their washerwomen.[51] But comparison with the experience of certain modern African towns suggests that in the difficult economic circumstances of the late sixteenth and early seventeenth centuries, such relationships may have offered substantial material benefits to those involved, even outside the ports.[52] In early seventeenth-century Salisbury even the overseers of the poor were accused of showing undue sympathy for their charwomen when allocating pensions.[53] But these relationships were also vulnerable to exposure, particularly by an unwanted pregnancy. The pattern of liaisons which can be reconstructed from bastardy cases in seventeenth-century Essex, in which female servants figure prominently among the mothers but poor men are under-represented among the fathers, suggests that for some women at least intimacy with an 'employer' may have represented a high-risk strategy for the acquisition of economic security.[54]

Whether there was also an increase in prostitution in this period is more difficult to establish, partly because of the structure of the authorities' assumptions. These tended to identify the unemployed 'singlewoman' with prostitution, and the employed 'maid' with chastity,[55] and thus effectively to construct an occupational category on moral grounds. With the exception of London, however, it would seem that most extra-marital encounters took place on a casual rather than a regular or professional basis.[56] That we know very little about the possible range of fees involved need not be of great significance, given the importance in the early modern economy of transactions in kind. We do, on the other hand, have the later voice of Ann Morgan of Wells, who refused 1s from a client in 1649 and insisted: 'No, I will have eighteen pence for thou hast torn my coat and has hindered me the knitting of half a hose'. The same woman would have had to spend a day and a half making hay to earn as much as the client had originally offered.[57]

The decreasing security of service in the later sixteenth and early seventeenth centuries coincided with that tendency towards specialization within the household which we have already noticed. One consequence was the disaggregation of household tasks and the growth, or further development, of specialist jobs around the key practices of sick care, washing, cleaning and even the provision of accommodation.[58] Certain roles, like that of the laundress who had serviced the medieval palace or monastery, were of some antiquity. But the growth in the size and complexity of many towns, and particularly of London, in this period brought new opportunities for specialization outside the framework of an annual service contract. Consider, to take one example, the £6 bequeathed in his will by the London merchant William Lambe in 1580 to buy 120 pails for poor women, who might then supplement their incomes by water-carrying.[59] At this social level, at least, necessity stimulated a realistic evaluation of a woman's labour value, as the women in poorer households were equipped with what was, in effect, an occupation from which they could earn a living for themselves and their families.[60] Although the developing concept of an 'occupation' bore a heavily guild-orientated character at the beginning of the sixteenth century, by its end women's work was to a limited extent sharing in that general proliferation of occupational roles with which these later years have been identified.[61]

There was, however, one field of activity in which a more regular female involvement had never been welcome. Sixteenth-century townswomen, like their thirteenth-century predecessors, developed their everyday marketing experience in a number of directions, to obtain an additional income by offering specialized services to a range of targeted customers. They bought up produce in bulk to sell it again in smaller units to purchasers with little to spend, and sometimes offered credit to their customers.[62] In some cases that kind of activity was officially condoned, as in Hull, where the bakers' ordinances of 1598 provided for the marketing of loaves by poor women, who were given thirteen for the price of a dozen. Though the middleman was often the butt of rioters in this period, there was also a contemporary conception of the benign and useful intermediary, able to save the poor time and trouble, and willing to extend their effective purchasing power through credit.[63] But the opportunities for exploitation, and the political sensitivity of the food supply were such that much of this dealing was frowned upon by the authorities. There was indeed much scope for disapproval, from the selling of fruit to apprentices, and the resale of butter having made it 'smaller', to the pawning of goods and the selling of secondhand clothes at more than one penny in the shilling profit.[64]

The prominence of women in this vast, and three-quarters hidden, field of activity earned them a form of muted occupational recognition as herb wives, oyster wives, tripe wives and the like. Many appear to have operated in partnership with their spouse, perhaps shifting capital from one partner's activity to the other's as seasons changed,[65] though since the fourteenth century married women in several towns had been empowered to enter commercial bargains independently of their husbands.[66] In some places there are even suggestions of female control over the market itself, as is the case in many modern African towns.[67] The shrewd and articulate women who operated in the streets and 'women's markets' of the late-sixteenth-century English town must undoubtedly have developed skills of bargaining and negotiation, in the appraisal of market conditions and the avoidance of sudden disaster which resembled those familiar to students of women's work in the modern Third World. But these were activities which, given sixteenth-century assumptions, could not very easily be dignified as 'work'.

The impact of demographic growth and the associated scarcity of resources which bore down on most English towns after around 1570 were extremely unsettling experiences for the generations which lived through them. The symbolic resources to which preachers and town fathers made appeal in the struggle to maintain order in those circumstances unfortunately directed attention precisely to the most vulnerable threads in the social fabric: the cultural assumptions which underpinned the shape of the early modern family. The woman's 'domestic' position in the household had to be emphasized, at just the time that female economic activity of all kinds appeared to be spilling over into the streets and lanes as never before. The generally deteriorating circumstances of the urban poor likewise drew forth an emphasis on the importance of confining procreation within marriage. Yet this was a time when a particularly severe run of bad harvests, by frustrating planned marriages, could push the proportions of illegitimate births and of women never marrying to a new peak.[68] That something like this had occurred before, in the fourteenth century, may have been of comfort to the Elizabethan legislators, who built on fourteenth-century precedents, or to the readers of *The Vision of Pierce Plowman* and its derivatives, had they been aware of it.[69] But the sixteenth-century Piers was rather a reminder of all that stood to be lost in the ungodly present: an image of household government, rooted in God's sustaining earth, which had already been threatened once before in mid-century:[70]

> when I Piers scripture myghte reade, and render and reporte to my wyffe and to my barnes, it semed then a goodly lyffe a houshold then to kepe and feade, both with broth and bacon, and bread of the Byble, to tel forth Christes trade, and trade of oure Christenyng (before were we called Chrysten, and knewe of Christe nothyng), then was I syr, then was I father, then was I shepherd and all.

The poverty and migration of the late sixteenth century called into question such images of the household as had been painfully constructed during the Reformation.

For towns, whose growth and prosperity depended ultimately on the influx of rural strangers to replenish the loss of population through disease, the tensions along the line of gender in this period were especially poignant. In London, whose size and complexity were admittedly unusual, the emergence of the commercial theatre provided one particularly complex, and often disturbing, arena for the dissection and reassembling of woman's proper role.[71] But everywhere there was a struggle to reconcile the ideal of the household with the wayward but necessary improvisations of working women.

In part, as we have seen, this entailed a 'professionalization' of certain long-established domestic female activities. When Elizabeth I visited Norwich in August 1578, a tableau representing good order in the commonwealth was presented by living actors, among whom were girls spinning yarn and making hose.[72] These were industrial skills whose importance for the employment of poorer women grew tremendously in the coming century, as England's first consumer boom took off. Yet in the public image of the household, distribution rather than manufacture continued as the principal female task. The adopted Londoner Peter Erondell put it this way in his characterization of the River Thames in 1605:[73]

O Thames, Thames! Thou art a provident husband, which bringest innumerable riches to thy famous spouse London, . . . who as a true oeconome and huswife doth distribute her goods to th'other partes of the realme, as a naturall mother to her beloved children.

This image would not have pleased the merchants of the outports, nor could its conception of the domestic division of labour have appealed much to the urban poor. For the majority of households, in fact, inflation and violent fluctuations in the price of food meant that it was impossible to confine the distributive role within the home, not least because individual households were interconnected by networks of rent and rate payments, doles, and informal assistance. Household incomes ebbed and flowed across the threshold between cash and kind, and in the management of the associated pawns and credit dealings women were the experts. Their expertise in social organization, however, too easily paralleled their reproductive role, and to accord an occupational dignity to the one threatened to do so to the other, as in Iago's image of Bianca: 'a huswife that by selling her desires/ Buys herself bread and clothes'.[74] So the pressure to find fit work for women which built up powerfully in the towns in the years between 1570 and 1650 pushed women towards occupational experience, without ever fully endowing them with the distinctive independence associated with the male craftsman and householder. For the menfolk in poorer households, of course, that independence may well have grown increasingly illusory over the same period; whilst for the married women from the urban élites alone did actual experience come close to Sir Thomas Smith's ideal of a woman who 'tarries at home'. Both circumstances strengthened the tendency to equate female domesticity with good social order.

As it was experienced and interpreted in contemporary terms, then, what might almost be called the late sixteenth-century urban 'crisis of gender' was a significant challenge. Its ramifications extended far beyond the formal niceties of urban occupational terminology, to embrace the norms of social behaviour in general.[75] Viewed with hindsight, it can be seen to have shared characteristics with other phases of difficult urban change; and the cultural resources through which sense had to be made of the experience included some very ancient components. Continental comparisons show, too, that such experiences were by no means confined to England even in the sixteenth century.[76]

Indeed, because the categories of work and gender are so fundamental to the analysis of any past European society, to study their interrelationship in towns is inevitably to be forced away from a linear, progressive reading of urban history, towards its cyclical rhythms and impermeable structural features. But the significance of gender, as one factor which gave to work its meaning, was always also a new experience. That was especially so in the towns, whose continuing existence so often depended on novelty, from the freshness of the faces on their streets, to the elaborated representations of social life in their theatres. The particular experiences of this period thus gave fresh meaning to the inherited distribution of roles between women and men at a number of levels. Perhaps most enduring was the acknowledgement by the newly-developed system of poor relief of woman's place as a deserving claimant, by virtue of her restricted earning power and occupational opportunities.[77] But almost equally compelling was the rehearsal in contemporary literature and drama of the tensions to which such a situation could give rise. In this sense, the period's most characteristic legacy was its representation of men and women's activities in works such as Thomas Deloney's *Thomas of Reading*, or in Shakespeare's *The Taming of the Shrew*. For it is through evidence of this sort above all that the historian is faced with the full challenge of understanding how notions of 'work', sexuality, and personal identity were constructed in the past.[78]

Notes

1. I am extremely grateful to the editors of this volume, and to those who attended the Conference for which this paper was originally prepared, for their comments on its earlier drafts.
2. J.A. Twemlow (ed.), *Liverpool Town Books*, (2 vols, 1935), II, 308, 397, 423. The woman, described as the wife of George Assheton, may have been the second wife and widow of the shipowner and bailiff George Assheton, who died in 1577. A widow Ashton was fined for flax-drying in her house in 1577, and later for keeping inmates: ibid., II, 264, 538, 597.
3. J.W. Horrocks (ed.), *The Assembly Books of Southampton* (Southampton Rec. Soc., 4 vols, 1925), I-III, *passim*; R.C. Anderson (ed.), *The Book of Examinations and Depositions 1622-44* (Southampton Rec. Soc., 1931), II, 15; M. Bateson (ed.), *Records of the Borough of Leicester*, III, *1509-1603* (1905), 102, 201; W.H. Stevenson *et al.* (ed.), *Records of the Borough of Nottingham* (6 vols, 1889), IV, 112, 260, 305-6, 311-15 et seq.; E.I. Fripp (ed.), *Minutes and Accounts of the Corporation of Stratford-upon-Avon* (Dugdale Society, 4 vols, 1921-9), I, 70; R.S. Ferguson (ed.), *A Boke off Recorde of Kirkbie Kendall* (Cumb. and Westm. Ant. and Arch. Soc., e.s. VII, 1892), 136; R.S. Ferguson and W. Nanson (ed.), *Some Municipal Records of the City of Carlisle* (Cumb. and Westm. Ant. and Arch. Soc., e.s. IV, 1887), 70, 272, 274; N. Goose, 'Household size and structure in early Stuart Cambridge', *Social History*, 5 (1980), 356-7: citing cases from London, Worcester, York, Sandwich, Winchester, Chester and Oxford as well as Cambridge; I. Roy and S. Porter, 'The social and economic structure of an early modern suburb: the Tything at Worcester', *Bull. Inst. Hist. Research*, 53 (1980), 210; P. and J. Clark, 'The social economy of the Canterbury suburbs: the evidence

of the census of 1563', in *Studies in Modern Kentish History*, ed. A. Detsicas and N. Yates (1983), 74; J. Boulton, *Neighbourhood and Society: A London Suburb in the Seventeenth Century* (1987), 36, 129, 132, 272–3; P. Slack, *Poverty and Policy in Tudor and Stuart England* (1988), 68.

4. *Liverpool Town Books*, I, 265.

5. For the concept of subsistence migration, and the decline in its incidence after the mid-seventeenth century, see Peter Clark, 'The migrant in Kentish towns, 1580–1640', in *Crisis and Order in English Towns 1500–1700*, ed. P. Clark and P. Slack (1972); and P. Clark, 'Migration in England during the late seventeenth and early eighteenth centuries', *Past and Present, 83* (1979).

6. *Liverpool Town Books*, II, 264, 397. Salt was a proverbial symbol of hospitality on the one hand, and of childish futility on the other: *O.E.D.* s.v. Salt, 2; cf. Elizabeth and Paul Rozin, 'Some surprisingly unique characteristics of human food preferences', in *Food in Perspective*, ed. Alexander Fenton and Trefor M. Owen (1981), for the taste for chilli among Mexican children.

7. Natalie Zemon Davis, 'Women in the crafts in sixteenth-century Lyon', in *Women and Work in Preindustrial Europe*, ed. B. Hanawalt (Bloomington, Indiana, 1986); Sue Wright, '"Churmaids, Huswyfes and Hucksters": the employment of women in Tudor and Stuart Salisbury', in *Women and Work in Pre-Industrial England*, ed. L. Charles and L. Duffin (1985).

8. Barbara J. Todd, 'The remarrying widow: a stereotype reconsidered', in *Women in English Society 1500-1800*, ed. Mary Prior (1985); Vivian Brodsky, 'Widows in late Elizabethan London: remarriage, economic opportunity and family orientations', in *The World We Have Gained*, ed. Lloyd Bonfield, R.M. Smith and K. Wrightson (1986).

9. Martha C. Howell, 'Women, the family economy, and the structure of market production in the cities of northern Europe during the late Middle Ages', in Hanawalt (ed.), *Women*; and her *Women, Production and Patriarchy in Late Medieval Cities* (Chicago, 1986); M.E. Wiesner, *Working Women in Renaissance Germany* (Brunswick, N.J., 1986); her 'Women's work in the changing city economy', in *Connecting Spheres*, ed. Marilyn J. Boxer and Jean H. Quataert (1987); and her 'Spinsters and seamstresses: women in cloth and clothing production', in *Rewriting the Renaissance: The Discourses of Sexual Difference in Early Modern Europe*, ed. Margaret W. Ferguson *et al.* (Chicago, 1986); and Judith C. Brown, 'A woman's place was in the home: women's work in Renaissance Tuscany', in ibid.

10. Merry Wiesner Wood, 'Paltry peddlers or essential merchants? Women in the distributive trades in early modern Nuremberg', *Sixteenth-Century Jnl., 12* (1981). For the view that multiple occupations reflected not so much women's ingenuity as their inability to obtain one decent income, see Maryanne Kowaleski, 'Women's work in a market town: Exeter in the late fourteenth century', in *Women*, ed. Hanawalt, 158; cf. Mary Prior, 'Women and the urban economy: Oxford, 1500–1800', in Prior (ed.), *Women*, 95.

11. Michael Roberts, '"Words they are women, and deeds they are men": images of work and gender in early modern England', in *Women*, ed. Charles and Duffin, 154–5. Cf. Patrick Joyce (ed.), *The Historical Meanings of Work* (1987), 2–10. For attempts to wrestle free of a strictly 'economic' perspective, see Howell op.cit., and Brown op. cit., both in n. 9 above.

12. For a justification of such a broad definition, see the contributions to Sandra Wallman (ed.), *Social Anthropology of Work* (A.S.A. Monograph *19*, 1979); cf. Robert Dingwall, '"In the beginning was the work ...": reflections on the genesis of occupations', *Sociological Rev., 31* (1983), 622, n. 6.

13. See for example the writings of Clement Armstrong during the 1530s, in R. Pauli, 'Drei volkswirthschaftliche Denkschriften aus der Zeit Heinrichs VIII. von England', *Abhandlungen der königlichen Gesellschaft der Wissenschaften zu Göttingen* (Göttin-

gen, 1878), 22 et seq.; or those of Edward VI in the 1550s: W.K. Jordan (ed.) *The Chronicle and Political Papers of King Edward VI* (1966), 159–67. For the impact of humanist thought on Protestant attitudes towards work, see M. Todd, *Christian Humanism and the Puritan Social Order* (1988), Ch. 5.

14. For those unfamiliar with this debate, D.M. Palliser, *The Age of Elizabeth* (1983), Ch. 7 provides a summary. See also Heather Swanson's essay in this volume. For reasons of space, the related question of how far gender helped *define* sixteenth-century towns *as* urban communities can only be hinted at below.

15. David Underdown, *Revel, Riot and Rebellion* (1985), 36–9; his 'The taming of the scold: the enforcement of patriarchal authority in early modern England', in *Order and Disorder in Early Modern England*, ed. A.J. Fletcher and D. Stevenson (1985); S.D. Amussen, 'Gender, family and the social order, 1560–1725', in the same volume; S.D. Amussen, *An Ordered Society: Gender and Class in Early Modern England* (1988). The urban 'crisis' of the 1590s has hitherto been interpreted without reference to questions of gender: Peter Clark, 'A crisis contained? The condition of English towns in the 1590s', in *The European Crisis of the 1590s,* ed. Peter Clark (1985); M.J. Power, 'London and the control of the "crisis" of the 1590s', *History*, 70 (1985), 230.

16. See David Weir, 'Rather never than late: celibacy and age at marriage in English cohort fertility, 1541–1871', *Jnl. Family Hist.*, 9 (1984); Roger Schofield, 'English marriage patterns revisited', *Jnl. Family Hist.*, 10 (1985); and J.A. Goldstone, 'The demographic revolution in England: a re-examination', *Population Studies*, 49 (1986).

17. For a recent summary, see Sylvia Walby, *Patriarchy at Work* (1986), ch. 2.

18. John Patten, 'Urban occupations in pre-industrial England', *Trans. Inst. British Geographers*, n.s., 2 (1977); and Heather Swanson, 'The illusion of economic structure: craft guilds in late medieval English towns', *Past and Present, 121* (1988). See also above, Ch. 3.

19. Susan Reynolds, *An Introduction to the History of English Medieval Towns* (1977), 165–7.

20. Although this idea already had a long pedigree, the specifically occupational emphasis seems greater in sixteenth-century cases than it had been two centuries earlier, when the concept of occupation or calling was even more intermingled with those of estate or degree. The 1363 instruction to craftsmen to 'hold them every one to one Mystery' needs perhaps to be read as more of an *ad hoc* exception rather than the general rule. Cf. R.H. Tawney (ed.), *Studies in Economic History: The Collected Papers of George Unwin* (2nd edn. 1958), 124–5, and Statute 37 Edward III, c. 6; *Rot. Parl.*, II, 278, 286; Statute 38 Edward III, c. 2. The 'fine social distinctions' of the fourteenth-century sumptuary laws dealt with broad occupational groups such as farm-workers and artificers, not with individual occupations: R.H. Hilton, *The English Peasantry in the Later Middle Ages* (1975), 25; but cf. his *Class Conflict and the Crisis of Feudalism* (1985), 222, 251. I am grateful to Professor Hilton for making me think more carefully about this question, though I am not sure he would share my conclusions.

21. *A Woorke of Ioannes Ferrarius Montanus, Touchynge the Good Orderynge of a Common Weale*, translated by William Bavande (1559 = *STC*, no. 10831), f.17. Ferrarius died in 1558. A copy of the original 1556 Latin edition of his work was owned by Thomas Egerton, Elizabeth's future Lord Keeper, some time after his entry into Lincoln's Inn in 1559: *The National Union Catalog Pre-1956 Imprints*, vol. 170 (1971), no. 0100901.

22. Margaret Pelling, 'Occupational diversity: barber-surgeons and the trades of Norwich, 1550–1640', *Bull. Hist. Medicine*, 56 (1982), 503.

23. Sir Thomas Smith, *De Republica Anglorum* (1583), 12.

24. There were none in sixteenth-century York: D.M. Palliser, *Tudor York* (1979), 78; but women had access to the role of bailiff in Grimsby: E. Gillett, *A History of Grimsby* (1970), 57. For the inheritance of office, see *Liverpool Town Books*, I, 352. As for

women's guilds, see Alice Clark, *Working Life of Women in the Seventeenth Century* (1919; 2nd. ed. 1982), 138 (silkwomen in London), 195-6 (wool packers in Southampton). For women's guilds in medieval Paris, see: E. Dixon, 'Craftswomen in the *Livre des métiers*', *Econ. Jnl.* 5 (1895); and in Cologne: M. Wensky, 'Women's guilds in Cologne in the later Middle Ages', *Jnl. Eur. Econ. Hist.*, 11 (1982).

25. P.J.P. Goldberg, 'Female labour, service and marriage in the late medieval urban north', *Northern Hist.*, 22 (1986), 35; Prior, 'Women and the urban economy', 110; and cf. Diane Willen, 'Guildswomen in the City of York, 1560-1600', *The Historian*, 46 (1984).

26. Todd, 'The remarrying widow', 77-8; C. Phythian-Adams, *Desolation of a City* (1979), 271 et seq.; Kay E. Lacey, 'Women and work in fourteenth and fifteenth-century London', in *Women*, ed. Charles and Duffin, 25; Wright, '"Churmaids"', ibid., 116.

27. Palliser, *Tudor York*, 150.

28. For medieval cases, see Howell in *Women*, ed. Hanawalt, 164, n. 59. For the sixteenth century: W. Hudson and J.C. Tingey (ed.), *Records of the City of Norwich* (2 vols, 1910), II, 308-9, for daughters; Phythian-Adams, *Desolation*, 87, for wives.

29. Clark, *Working Life*, 103; Phythian-Adams, *Desolation*, 87-8, suggesting problems with skirts; *Records of Norwich*, II, 376, 378.

30. *Liverpool Town Books*, I, 325, for 'a woman of an unchaste conversacion, and not worthie to have the fredome of this towne'. Male privileges were also vulnerable to a tarnished reputation, of course; for the loss of office, see *Records of Leicester*, III, 318; *Boke off Recorde of Kirkbie Kendall*, 119-20, 132-3, and cf. 146, for male vulnerability to gossip.

31. Brodsky, 'Widows', 141; Phythian-Adams, *Desolation*, 87, 272-3; *Records of Norwich*, II, 308-9.

32. See the papers on apprenticeship in PRO, SP 12/93/26, 33 and in R.H. Tawney and E. Power (ed.), *Tudor Economic Documents* (3 vols, 1924), I, 355-6 (item 9).

33. Prior, 'Women and the urban economy', 107-8; Goldberg, 'Female labour', 34; Palliser, *Tudor York*, 150; Brodsky, 'Widows', 141-2.

34. For examples in the ale trade, or in teaching, see: Peter Clark, *The English Alehouse: A Social History 1200-1830* (1983), 82; and his *English Provincial Society from the Reformation to the Revolution: Religion, Politics and Society in Kent 1500-1640* (1977), 192.

35. Compare the situation in Cologne: Howell, in Hanawalt (ed.), *Women*, 213-14.

36. David Knowles, *The Religious Orders in England* (3 vols, 1948-59), II, 260-1, III, 311; G.W.O. Woodward, *The Dissolution of the Monasteries* (1966), 2, 73-4, 141-3.

37. For a summary see Joan Thirsk, 'Foreword' to Prior (ed.), *Women*.

38. Goose, 'Cambridge', 374; Clark and Clark, 'Canterbury suburbs', 73.

39. Marjorie K. McIntosh, 'Servants and the household unit in an Elizabethan English community', *Jnl. Family Hist.*, 9 (1984), 12, for Romford in Essex.

40. Dorothy Marshall, *The English Domestic Servant in History* (1949), 6-7; Ralph A. Houlbrooke, *The English Family 1450-1700* (1984), 172; Goldberg, 'Female labour', 35. A similar tendency has been noticed in eighteenth-century France: Sarah C. Maza, *Servants and Masters in Eighteenth-Century France* (Princeton, N.J., 1983), 277-8. Such a tendency was by no means inevitable; for the reverse in late fifteenth-century Florence, see Christiane Klapisch-Zuber, *Women, Family and Ritual in Renaissance Italy* (Chicago, 1985), 176-7.

41. Sir William Davenant, 'The Long Vacation in London', in *The Penguin Book of Everyday Verse*, ed. D. Wright (1976), 253, for apprentices 'who seven long years did never scorn/ To fetch up coales for maids to use, Wipe mistress's and children's shoes.' See also S.R. Smith, 'London apprentices as seventeenth-century adolescents', *Past and Present*, 61 (1973).

42. For a well-known case, see R. Latham and W. Matthews (ed.), *The Diary of Samuel Pepys* (11 vols), x (1983), 195-6.

43. For the reverse, with widows in effect fostering servants, see Brodsky, 'Widows', 152.

44. Kenneth Little, *African Women in Towns* (1973), 23–4; W. Watson, *Tribal Cohesion in a Money Economy* (1958), 45; Ximena Bunster and Elsa M. Chaney, *Sellers and Servants* (New York, 1985), for a less sanguine view of Lima, Peru.

45. For an excellent example of the municipal registration of servants over a long period, see South Humberside Area R.O., Great Grimsby Court Books, for the sixteenth and seventeenth centuries.

46. A. Kussmaul, *Servants in Husbandry in Early Modern England* (1981), 100. In conditions of labour scarcity, however, such as prevailed in the century or so after the Black Death, the impetus for shorter contracts may have come more from the employees' side. See for example Marjorie McIntosh, *Autonomy and Community: The Royal Manor of Havering 1200–1500* (1986), 161.

47. Alan D. Dyer, *The City of Worcester in the Sixteenth Century* (1973), 154–5; *Assembly Books of Southampton*, II, 53; Palliser, *Tudor York*, 132.

48. J.M. Guilding (ed.), *Reading Records* (4 vols, 1892–6), II, 146, for the itinerary of Agnes Gregory of Ripon; and 170, for the employment without pay of Mary Cooke. See also J.F. Pound (ed.), *The Norwich Census of the Poor, 1570* (Norfolk Rec. Soc., 40, 1971), 28, for the maid of unemployed H. White.

49. Little, *African Women*, 86, for the term; *Liverpool Town Books*, II, 212–13, 717, and *passim* for examples.

50. Cf. the suggestive examples of late thirteenth- and early fourteenth-century female behaviour, in R.H. Hilton, 'Small town society in England before the Black Death', *Past and Present*, 105 (1984), 65–8.

51. *Liverpool Town Books*, I, 243, for a woman of unchaste conversation 'maynteyned and kepte at the charges of a Spaniarde called John de Careno'; and G.H. Hamilton (ed.), *The Southampton Books of Examinations* (Southampton Rec. Soc., 1914), I, 62, for the relationship between a mariner on the ship 'Demon' and his washerwoman. Cf. the value placed on female companionship in the African 'Men's towns': Little, *African Women*, 80, n.5.

52. Ibid., 86, for the exchange of meals for firewood between African women and their regular male visitors. Some English towns sought to provide stocks of wood and coal for the poor on a regular basis: Clark, 'A crisis contained?', 60. The importance of payments in food, to those who found work as servants during the difficult 1590s, is noted by R.B. Outhwaite, 'Dearth, the English crown and the "crisis of the 1590s"', in Clark (ed.), *European Crisis*, 38.

53. Slack, *Poverty and Policy*, 190.

54. J. Sharpe, *Crime in Seventeenth-Century England* (1983), 59–60, although this is not the explanation advanced there by Dr Sharpe. For the use of such a strategy by eighteenth-century French servants, see Maza, *Servants and Masters*, 68–72.

55. Compare the earlier treatment of single women in Coventry: Phythian-Adams, *Desolation*, 87, with the strikingly similar attitudes in parts of Africa: Little, *African Women*, 82.

56. Goldberg, 'Female labour', 36; McIntosh, 'Servants', 21; Clark, *Alehouse*, 84, 148–9, 236; Sharpe, *Crime*, 58; G.R. Quaife, *Wanton Wenches and Wayward Wives* (1979), 247, suggests a rather more professional approach in the Somerset towns.

57. Little, *African Women*, 84–6; Quaife, *Wanton Wenches*, 150. For local wage levels, see Somerset R.O., Q/SM 1645–55, Easter 1648 Session.

58. For the importance of washing as a female occupation, for example, see Margaret Pelling, 'Appearance and reality: barber-surgeons, the body and disease', in *London 1500–1700: The Making of the Metropolis*, ed. A.L. Beier and Roger Finlay (1986), 93; for Southwark women 'which live by washing', Boulton, *Neighbourhood*, 82.

59. W.K. Jordan, *The Charities of London 1480–1660* (1960), 99.

60. Thus Mary Harrison was ordered by the Reading authorities in 1626 'to be taught to

spin and earne her living', *Reading Records*, II, 294; cf. Wiesner, 'Women's work', 67 for the reluctance to concede such occupational entitlements to any women but the authorized poor.

61. Jack A. Goldstone, 'Urbanisation and inflation: lessons from the English price revolution of the sixteenth and seventeenth centuries', *American Jnl. Sociology*, 89 (1984), 1148–51.

62. For women dealing in small lots in fourteenth-century Colchester, see R.H. Britnell, *Growth and Decline in Colchester 1300-1525* (1986), 40–1. For the reduction in size of the standard loaf by some 60 per cent when food was scarce in London during the 1590s, see Power, 'The "Crisis" of the 1590s', 374–5.

63. J. Malet Lambert, *Two Thousand Years of Gild Life* (1891), 307; J. Walter and K. Wrightson, 'Dearth and the social order in early modern England', *Past and Present*, 71 (1976), 30–1; Ray Bromley and Chris Gerry (ed.), *Casual Work and Poverty in Third World Cities* (1979), 56.

64. *Records of Nottingham*, IV, 112, 153–4; *Records of Leicester*, III, 147. The Liverpool market seems to have been regularly supplied by traders, who 'forestalled' the arrival of produce 'at the townes end crosse' or on the heath outside, and 'which use to bring butter to theire oulde customers'. Of the 125 individuals who were fined for this 'offence' between 1583 and 1602, 110 were women (including 48 stated to be wives, 13 widows, 9 daughters and 7 servants): calculated from *Liverpool Town Books*, II.

65. Sidney W. Mintz, 'Men, women and trade', *Comp. Studies in Soc. and Hist., 13* (1971), 257, for Third World parallels.

66. Kay E. Lacey, 'Women and work in fourteenth- and fifteenth-century London', in *Women*, ed. Charles and Duffin, 42–5.

67. For widows in control of market rents, see *Reading Records*, II, 258; *Records of Leicester*, III, 426. For the housewives' or women's market, see also *Records of Leicester*, II, 240, 242–3, 268.

68. Keith Wrightson, *English Society 1580-1680* (1982), 145–6; E.A. Wrigley and R.S. Schofield, *The Population History of England 1541-1871* (1981), 257–69.

69. *The Statutes or Ordinaunces Concernynge Artyficers* (1550 and 1562); *The Vision of Pierce Plowman* (1550); *Piers Plowmans Exhortation* (?1550); *A Godly Dyaloge and Dysputacyon betwene Pyers Plowman, and a Popysh Preest* (c.1550).

70. *I playne Piers which can not Flatter* (?1550), Sig. Avi; cf. *A Glasse for Housholders* (1542), Sig. Eiiii, for the neglect of breast-feeding, a maternal work whose labour should ultimately be repaid by the sustaining work of children in the parents' old age.

71. Juliet Dusinberre, *Shakespeare and the Nature of Women* (1975); Simon Shepherd, *Amazons and Warrior Women: Varieties of Feminism in Seventeenth-Century Drama* (1981); Leonard Tennenhouse, *Power on Display: The Politics of Shakespeare's Genres* (1986), 160 *et seq.* For the uniquely charged symbolic role of the theatre in this period, see Jean-Christophe Agnew, *Worlds Apart: The Market and the Theatre in Anglo-American Thought 1550-1750* (1986).

72. D.M. Bergeron, *English Civic Pageantry 1558-1642* (1971), 39.

73. Palliser, *Age of Elizabeth*, 234.

74. W. Shakespeare, *Othello*, IV, i 94–5.

75. This is indicated by Underdown and Amussen in the works cited in n. 15 above, although their emphasis is on 'a period of strained gender relations' at the heart of a more general 'crisis of order'. The theme was first explored, in the case of early modern France, by Natalie Zemon Davis: 'Women on top', in her *Society and Culture in Early Modern France* (1975).

76. For late thirteenth- and early fourteenth-century English parallels, see Hilton, 'Small town society'; and *idem, The English Peasantry*, Chs. 5 and 6; *Class Conflict*, Chs. 13, 15 and 16. Cf. W. Thwaites, 'Women in the market place: Oxfordshire, c. 1690–1800', *Midland History*, 9 (1984). There are many suggestions of a similarly highly-charged

interrelationship between female migration, work and sexuality in the literature on Europe, though often as a long-standing feature rather than a component of 'crisis'. Much still needs to be done before we fully understand the meaning of these experiences for the women concerned. For sixteenth-century France, see Natalie Zemon Davis, *Society and Culture in Early Modern France* (1975), Ch. 5 and pp. 50, 69, 291 n. 15; Leah L. Otis, *Prostitution in Medieval Society* (Chicago, 1985), 63–5. Cf. Ruth Pike, *Aristocrats and Traders: Sevillian Society in the Sixteenth Century* (Ithaca, N.Y., 1972), 207; cf. also Olwen Hufton, *The Poor of Eighteenth-Century France* (1974), 97–103; Eugen Weber, *Peasants into Frenchmen* (1977), 283.

77. Slack, *Poverty and Policy*, 180.

78. See Underdown, 'Taming of the scold', 117–18; Roberts, '"Words"', 122–6; *idem*, 'Work, the body and feelings in early modern England: the case of *Thomas of Reading*' (forthcoming); and, more generally, the contributions to Ferguson *et al.* (ed.) *Rewriting the Renaissance*. Consider, too, the positioning of the figures and domestic accoutrements in the painting by Boursse (Fig. 6.1, above).

7 The East London working community in the seventeenth century

Michael J. Power

London was a phenomenon in early-modern Europe. In a period of great urban change it outgrew rivals by a spectacular margin. Twelfth in size among European cities in 1500 it climbed to third by 1600, and first by 1700, outdistancing previous giants such as Paris and Naples. Its growth in the sixteenth century was part of a European-wide demographic and economic expansion, but its continued growth in the seventeenth century marked it out as one of the few capital and trading cities which ran counter to the trend of stagnation and decline.[1] In number, Londoners increased from *c.*200,000 in 1600 to *c.*500,000 in 1700.[2] In comparison with other cities in England, London stands as even more of a Goliath: about seventeen times the size of the next towns, Norwich and York, in 1600, and by 1700 greater in population than all the major provincial towns put together.

The nature of the economy of such a unique city is clearly of great significance. De Vries suggests that the few large seventeenth-century cities which continued to grow in Europe enjoyed the stimuli of centralizing governments or a burgeoning Atlantic trade.[3] Both factors operated strongly in London, and it has been argued recently that a third, its development as an 'engine of manufacture', was equally important.[4] These three dynamos of work, government, trade and manufacture, suffused the metropolis, but tended to be brightest in particular areas: government held sway in Westminster; trade was organized by merchants in the central City, though commodities were carried by men from the eastern suburbs and Southwark; manufactures were well distributed, large numbers of craftsmen inhabiting the City and the northern and eastern suburbs and Southwark. What is notable about this geographical pattern of work is the significance of the suburbs to London. In 1600, the central City still housed the major part of the London population, *c.*100,000 people compared to *c.*85,000 in the suburbs. But, by the 1630s, the situation was reversed and by the late seventeenth century the 105,000 City centre residents were quite outnumbered by the 330,000 in the suburbs.[5]

It is on one part of this fast-growing suburban area that this essay concentrates: the East End, comprising the parishes of Stepney and Whitechapel. These had already experienced rapid urban development in the sixteenth century, by 1600 containing 20,000 people. During the continued urbanization of the seventeenth century this population grew to about 90,000 and created a dynamic suburb of a

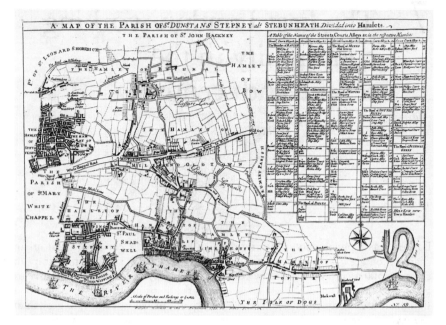

Figure 7.1. Stepney in the early eighteenth century. From *Survey of the Cities of London and Westminster . . . by John Stow . . .*, corrected and enlarged by John Strype (6th edition, 2 vols, 1754–5), vol. 2, Book IV, at p. 47 (1755). The map was first printed for the original edition of Strype's version of Stow's *Survey*, vol. 2 (1720), Book IV, at p. 47, and is a reduced and simplified version of Gascoyne's map of 1703, for which see W. Ravenhill, 'Joel Gascoyne's Stepney: his last years in pastures old and new', *Guildhall Studies in London History* 2.4 (1977), 200–12.

The map shows three distinct areas of settlement: the eastern part of the extra-mural sprawl which extended along Whitechapel Road from Aldgate (Mile End New Town); the semi-rural hamlets to the north of the ancient parish church (Mile End Old Town and Bethnal Green); and the riverside zone of industrial activity, extending yet further east along Poplar High Street to the East India Company's yard at Blackwall. Areas not within the parish of St Dunstan, Stepney, in 1703 are shown as blank on this map.

Reproduced with the permission of the Greater London Record Office.

remarkable city.[6] A study of the work done by East Londoners forms an important component of an understanding of the developing economy of the capital, for they carried the greater part of London's overseas trade, as well as developing an 'engine of manufactures'. This essay approaches this subject by investigating the occupation structure of the largest parish in East London, Stepney, by analysing its parish registers between 1610 and 1690. It then discusses the location of workers, to discover the extent to which the common pre-industrial pattern of domestic work was giving way to work outside the home. Finally, it attempts to assess the wealth and status of different groups of workers. In many ways, the structure of the East London working community emerges as highly specialized, and the organization of its work more complex than in the central City.

I

For the years 1610–90, the burial registers of Stepney parish note the occupation of almost three-quarters of the deceased or the deceased's head of family.[7] These are Anglican burial records, of course, but they probably included the vast majority of Stepney people who died in the seventeenth century.[8] Such data are not ideal for

Table 7.1 Occupational groups in seventeenth-century London (percentages)

	Stepney[1] 1610–90	Cripplegate[2] 1654–93	London[3] Extra-mural 1601–1700	London[3] Intra-mural 1601–1700
Commerce/Professional:				
Dealers	2	3	2	20
Victuallers	7	9	15	10
Professions	3	8	2	11
Total	12	20	19	41
Crafts:				
Shipbuilding	6	0	0	0
Wood	3	5	3	4
Metal	3	6	9	9
Textiles	17	17	24	21
Leather	3	9	10	7
Miscellaneous	1	2	4	1
Total	33	38	50	42
Building	5	6	7	6
Agricultural	2	2	0	0
Carriers:				
Marine	35	1	0	0
Land	1	7	11	5
Total	36	8	11	5
Miscellaneous	12	26	13	6
Total	100	100	100	100
	(n 3087)	(n 12004)	(n 13660)	(n 2219)

Sources: 1 Stepney burial registers. A sample of entries from January to June every tenth year was analysed. Greater London Record Office (GLRO), P93/DUN.

2 T.R. Forbes, 'Weaver and cordwainer: occupations in the parish of St Giles without Cripplegate, London, in 1654–93 and 1729–43', *Guildhall Studies in London History*, 4 (1980), 120–7.

3 A.L. Beier, 'Engine of manufacture: the trades of London', in A.L. Beier and R. Finlay (ed.), *London 1500–1700: The Making of the Metropolis* (1986), 148. London Extramural includes the Stepney sample.

reconstructing the occupation structure of a community. They are biased towards the adult males who were heads of households and only rarely give the occupations of women and younger workers such as apprentices. But, in the absence of census data or any other detailed listings, they are the best guide we have.[9] One bonus of using the Stepney burial data is that they can be compared with the similar data for Cripplegate, assembled by Forbes, and with a sample of City and suburban parishes, analysed by Beier. The results, shown in Table 7.1, show clearly the distinctive characteristics of the Stepney working community.[10]

The categorization of occupations is invariably difficult. The first group, Commerce/Professional, is intended to capture the urban élite and includes traders, who sometimes commanded considerable capital resources, and professional people, lawyers, clergy and the like. Hiding in this group, too, are gentlemen, though there were no aristocrats. Whether there was any real homogeneity in the group (the gentlemen prevent a description of it as a middle class) is doubtful. But most of its members would have been distinguished from the rest of the community in wealth, educational background or status. The second category, crafts, seems at first less problematical, containing a range of artisans who made up a humbler 'blue-collar' stratum. Though this was true of some, particularly in the leather and textile crafts, it was not true of others, especially in shipbuilding which was carried on by substantial businessmen. The imprecise nomenclature of occupations in a parish register makes it often impossible to distinguish the entrepreneur-manufacturer from the jobbing artisan. 'Shipwright', for example, is a term applied to major ship contractors and small boat repairers alike. Unless we have additional information about such men's work it is difficult to use the work label for anything other than the most general analysis. The other categories are, perhaps, less problematical, the work of builders and carriers being more defined, and agriculturalists too small in number to be significant in a town.[11]

Bearing these problems in mind, the figures in Table 7.1 allow a crude comparison of the dominant occupations in Stepney and elsewhere in London. What first strikes the eye is how deficient Stepney appears to be in the Commerce/ Professional group. With only 12 per cent of its working population designated as such it lags behind the other suburbs (about 20 per cent), and far behind the heavy representation of the group in the central City (41 per cent). Commercial and professional weight was clearly concentrated there. When we turn to crafts Stepney is more in line with other suburbs and the City (33 per cent compared with 38–50 per cent) but even here there are significant differences. Shipbuilding and its associated crafts (6 per cent) are prominent in Stepney as might be expected in a parish largely composed of riverside hamlets, Wapping, Shadwell, Ratcliff, Limehouse and Poplar. A large textile sector is common to Stepney and everywhere else. But metal and leather crafts are far less represented in Stepney than elsewhere. The craft structure is thus skewed towards marine-oriented manufacture. And it is the demand for men to man ships that is the most powerful influence on Stepney's workforce and makes its occupation structure unique. Mariners, who dominate the Carriers group, make up over one third of the work-force. In this respect Stepney demonstrates a specialization characteristic of port towns, such as Plymouth and Portsmouth.[12]

The extent to which specialization intensified during a century which witnessed a large increase in both military and commercial seagoing can be tested by analysing

Table 7.2 Occupational groups in Stepney, every tenth year, 1610–90 (percentages)

	1610	'20	'30	'40	'50	'60	'71*	'80	'90
Commerce/Professional:									
Dealers	2	1	1	2	1	1	5	2	1
Victuallers	5	6	6	7	7	9	8	8	5
Professions	4	4	4	2	1	5	3	3	4
Total	11	11	11	11	9	15	16	13	10
Crafts:									
Shipbuilding	4	12	8	9	7	8	6	5	3
Wood	3	1	4	2	4	2	2	5	2
Metal	5	4	4	4	2	3	3	4	2
Textiles	7	13	10	10	10	7	15	21	33
Leather	2	3	3	4	2	3	2	2	2
Miscellaneous	1	1	1	1	2	0	1	0	2
Total	22	34	30	30	27	23	29	37	44
Building	1	2	3	4	4	2	9	7	4
Agricultural	3	4	5	3	1	2	0	1	1
Carriers:									
Marine	20	33	35	38	50	49	37	32	32
Land	1	0	0	1	1	0	1	1	2
Total	21	33	35	39	51	49	38	33	34
Miscellaneous	42	16	16	13	8	9	8	9	7
Total	100	100	100	100	100	100	100	100	100
	(n 100	175	315	398	209	442	487	567	584)

Source: Stepney burial registers, GLRO P93/DUN. The register is defective in 1670 and 1671 was substituted (*). Figures are adjusted after 1660 when Shadwell became a separate parish from Stepney by the proportions of each group accounted for by the hamlet in 1660.

the occupational structure every decade (see Table 7.2). The demands of the sea did not, in fact, lead to any linear trend towards increased specialization in Stepney. Shipbuilding crafts peaked in 1620 and thereafter remained high until towards the end of the century. Down-river competition at Deptford and Chatham, as well as in other shipbuilding towns, clearly had an effect. The mariners increased their dominance from about a third of the workforce to about half in mid-century, but then slipped back to their former position. Other equally interesting developments occurred. The Commerce/Professional group increased its importance towards the end of the century, largely because of the increase in the number of victuallers. More obviously, the craft groups increased in significance towards the end of the century. The major component of this increase was in textile manufacture, as the Spitalfields silk-weaving industry grew with Huguenot immigration.[13] Its proliferation from

1671 was the most obvious example of growing occupational specialization in Stepney, more than compensating for the relative decline in shipbuilding and metalworking. A classic sign of rapid urbanization, the growth of building workers at the expense of agricultural workers, was also evident, particularly in the second half of the century.

There were, therefore, some signs of increasing specialization: mariners from 1640 to 1660, builders from 1660 to 1680, and weavers from 1671 to 1690. But Stepney's economy remained throughout dominated by carrying and craft occupations which ebbed and flowed in response to demand at different times. If there was one overall trend it was perhaps in the reduction of the Miscellaneous group, principally made up of labourers and servants. Could it be that the suburban workforce was becoming more skilled as the century wore on, with an ever greater proportion of workers being engaged in identifiable occupations and fewer employed in menial roles? Or, was it simply that parish clerks switched to identifying labourers and servants by more specific occupational labels?

II

The analysis of the occupational structure of Stepney suggests that the East London working community was unusually dominated by fairly humble manual workers. What can be learned of the nature and conditions of their work? A useful way into this will be to tackle the question of where it was done. It is a commonplace that work in pre-industrial towns was predominantly domestic. Unwin distinguished three stages in the evolution of manufacture: a handicraft phase in which goods were made by a family in the home for local consumption; a domestic phase in which manufacture was still in the home, but organized on a large scale with journeymen and apprentices to supply a dealer who would sell the goods to a wider market; and a factory phase when the process would take place away from the home in large premises, and would involve a more complex capital, management and sales structure. These three stages were not mutually exclusive and could coexist.[14] In seventeenth-century East London, this seems to have been the case. Most work was done at home, falling into either the handicraft or domestic phase, but much more employment was undertaken away from the home – voyaging or in specialist industrial premises – than was common in most seventeenth-century English provincial towns.

Most obviously was this true of mariners, who were peculiar in working far away from home for long periods either in commercial ships or in the Royal or Commonwealth Navy. Some commanded East India Company ships; others were Royal Navy captains.[15] A few held shares in their own ships, often privateering vessels, and ran them independently.[16] There was clearly a substantial number of this officer class living in East London. During the Civil War the constable of Ratcliff submitted to parliament a list of 21 captains in the parish who were fit for a command.[17] And in the late 1660s the corporation of Trinity House, the chartered body that controlled English navigation, issued 61 certificates of competence to Stepney mariners qualified to serve as masters.[18]

Such master mariners were heavily outnumbered by the large mass of ordinary seamen who lived in the area. The national government counted on being able to press men into service whenever necessary, and as early as the year of the Armada exempted the riverside hamlets of Stepney from conventional naval or military musters because of their service in providing men for ships in wartime.[19] At such times a proclamation was read along the streets of East London from East Smithfield to Blackwall, masters were ordered to make lists of their seamen, and constables collected the names of all mariners lodging in the area to be sent to Trinity House.[20] The fact that a plentiful supply of sailors was assumed to be always available suggests that at any time there were Stepney seamen on leave or unemployed, reinforced no doubt by mariners from elsewhere, resting between voyages. How willing they were to be impressed was another matter. In 1667 Lieutenant Boulter and six seamen of the ship *Henrietta* were attacked by 40 to 50 mariners whom they were trying to press in Wapping, and in the ensuing fracas Boulter was killed.[21] And in April 1673, when constables in East London were again ordered to search for seamen and watermen, including those skulking in disguise, musketeers were posted by the government at strategic points to prevent trouble.[22]

How many East Londoners were away at sea at any one time can only be established occasionally. A muster of seamen taken on 12 February 1628 suggests that 1,423 out of 2,268 East London mariners (some 63 per cent) were away at sea. And some idea of what impact this might have made on the total working community is given by the Protestation Return of 1641, a list of signatories pledging loyalty to the reformed Church, which notes that 483 of the 1,859 working men of Ratcliff and Limehouse hamlets were away at sea, over a quarter of the adult male workforce.[23] If this was typical such absence must have created a quiet atmosphere in the riverside hamlets of East London in sharp contrast to the volatile events during impressment or demobilization.

Prolonged absence posed problems for wives and families left at home. Elizabeth Chambers of Shadwell enjoyed married life for only four days before her husband, William, left for a spell of duty lasting almost three years. Accused of adultery by neighbours, she was thrown out by her husband on his return in 1639.[24] Worse still, seamen did not always return. John Dodson of Ratcliff was captured by the Turks in 1624 with a ransom of £160 on his head; William Brousey of Wapping was imprisoned by the Dutch and his wife tried to arrange an exchange with a Dutch prisoner.[25] Others could be maimed or killed in service, leaving widows with children to petition the government for relief. There is no evidence, unfortunately, of whether such widows were able to support themselves by working. But that many were not is suggested by a proposal of Secretary Jenkins in August 1682 for setting up a hospital for housing such families.[26]

The dominant occupational group in East London was, therefore, peculiar in its pattern of work. Mariners worked far away from home for extended periods and were at risk of captivity, injury and death. Their families faced economic and social risk. Even when ashore mariners faced problems of unemployment and the temptations of disposing of their pay too quickly among the riverside alehouses. The size and characteristics of the group must have created some instability within the East London community.

Of more significance for the economic development of the eastern suburbs was the substantial number of men who worked on shore but outside their homes. Though the age of large-scale factory employment was yet to come, some industrial and commercial enterprises in East London gathered men together in purpose-built or adapted workplaces. Shipyards are the most obvious examples. The largest was the yard built by the East India Company at Blackwall in 1614. It covered ten acres and comprised a wet and dry dock and storehouses, and within four years was enclosed by a wall. As early as 1618 there was a labour force of 232 men. They were provided with a taphouse, meals and a barber-surgeon, and some were accommodated in lodgings in the yard to save them the journey home each evening.[27] The storehouses were used for shipbuilding materials, food and gunpowder, and theft from them became a major problem necessitating the appointment of a watch.[28]

This formidable plant was leased and then sold to Henry Johnson in the years 1652 to 1656.[29] When Johnson took Francis Barham as a partner in 1658 it comprised, in addition to the docks, launching places, two cranes, workshops for plumbers, ironworkers, blockmakers, sailmakers and carvers, a rigging house and a taphouse.[30] A new dock was built in 1660, described as the largest in England.[31] Such details, the size of the plant, the number of men, the taphouse, the pilfering of stores, all suggest a quasi-factory concern. Under Johnson's direction Blackwall Yard functioned as a complete shipbuilding enterprise, producing some 31 ships in 42 years, most of them for the Royal Navy, some for merchants and companies.[32] The journey to work must have become a feature of many men's lives after 1614.

How capital was amassed to run such large concerns is a difficult question to answer. Many shipyards were built up by family dynasties over time. Blackwall Yard itself was passed on by Henry Johnson to his son in 1683.[33] A more dramatic example of a shipbuilding dynasty was the Pett family. Peter Pett (d. 1589), the son of a sixteenth-century Harwich shipbuilder, established a yard in Limehouse. Two of his sons, William (d. 1587) and Joseph (d. 1605), continued to work at Limehouse; a third, Peter (d. 1631), set up a yard in Wapping. In turn his son, also named Peter (d. 1652), set up as a master shipwright in Ratcliff and he passed on the yard to his nephew Phineas (d. 1678).[34] Altogether four generations of Petts built ships in East London, as well as elsewhere, notably at Deptford, Woolwich and Chatham, and the passing on of expertise, contacts and capital must have been the basis of their continued success. A third notable shipbuilding family was the Graves. Thomas Graves of Limehouse, shipwright, died in 1603 and his brother John continued shipbuilding there. On his death, in 1637, John left two docks in Limehouse to his three sons, William, Abraham and Nathaniel, and William at least was producing ships into the 1650s.[35]

Such large-scale family businesses grew up in response to the growth in trade which was so notable a feature of the late-seventeenth-century English economy. The building of great ships which necessitated large yards also influenced the various supply crafts. Ropemakers, mastmakers and sailmakers needed space to make or store their merchandise. Most remarkable were the timber importers, entrepreneurial giants of their time. Sir William Warren of Wapping imported timber from Germany, Sweden and New England in the 1660s and 1670s.[36] William Wood of Wapping also imported masts from the New World and operated from a deal yard and mast yard in Wapping, and a yard and jetty in Rotherhithe across the river.[37] Both men were main suppliers to the Navy Commissioners and they dealt in business worth thousands of pounds. By the nature and scale of their trade their organization must have been more than domestic, involving extensive yards and many workmen, though no detailed evidence of these has come to light. It is more difficult to establish the scale of business which the multitude of humbler shipwrights and suppliers operated, often from their homes or backyards along the riverside. The will of Edward Arlibeare of Wapping, for example, gives some idea of the number of smaller ship-related enterprises in Wapping in 1667. A mastmaker, Arlibeare left a mastyard fronting the Thames, containing tenements and sheds. Nearby he owned another yard and wharf, rented to Guildford Elvey, a shipwright, which abutted to the east on the house of John Moore, another shipwright, and to the west on a mastyard occupied by Edward Grey. Arlibeare bequeathed a third piece of land nearby occupied by John Wright, a shipwright, on which stood two tenements and a mastyard.[38] These craftsmen were living side by side in the congested alleyways of riverside Wapping. They were humbler men than the Johnsons or the Petts, often living in a house adjoining their yards, but it is as difficult to classify them as domestic craftsmen, because of the size and scale of their materials, as it is to describe them simply as business entrepreneurs.

Shipbuilding may have been the most dramatic large-scale industry but it was not the only one. Brewing was a craft which could either be carried out at home on a modest scale for local consumption, or in large brewhouses for a wider market.[39] The area east of the Tower, St Katharine's and East Smithfield, had a cluster of them: the Red Lion,[40] the Hart's Horn, and the Three Kings all produced beer and ale on Thames-side sites used for large-scale brewing since the mid-fifteenth century.[41] Further north, in Spitalfields, Joseph Truman established a brewing business in Brick Lane before 1683 and began the business of building up the Black Eagle Brewery, one of the great eighteenth-century breweries.[42] There are two pointers to the scale of these concerns. One is the extent of the property they covered. The Red Lion in St Katharine's contained a vinegar yard, stables, a stillhouse, a brewhouse and some 60 messuages in 1661.[43] The other is the market they served. In the late sixteenth century, the Hart's Horn brewery was exporting beer to Northern Europe.[44] Such slim details do not tell us much about the organization or workforce of these breweries, but are enough to differentiate them from the plethora of domestic brewhouses along the riverside which catered only for the local alehouse trade.

A third industry, which may have broken out of the domestic framework, was founding. A bellfounding business established by Robert Doddes in Whitechapel in Elizabeth I's reign continued to operate throughout the seventeenth century, and indeed into the twentieth. Some 80 bells surviving to the twentieth century were cast there by Robert Mot (d. 1605), Doddes's successor; 13 more were cast by William Carter (to 1616); Thomas Bartlett produced 30 (to 1632); and 127 were made by John Clifton (to 1647), Anthony Bartlett (to 1676) and his son, James (to 1700).[45] It is possible, of course, that these were cast in domestic premises, and our lack of information about the scale of the plant and size of the workforce prevents our being sure what kind of manufactory this was.

A similar difficulty arises with the gunfounders attached to the Ordnance Office on Tower Hill and the Minories, the main supplier of guns to the Royal Navy. Situated in an area where gunfounding skills were traditional, and close to the government market it supplied, the office owned various houses which it reserved for gunmakers and other artificers. Henry Pitt, gunfounder to His Majesty (d. 1612) was just one of the craftsmen engaged there. But we do not know whether the Ordnance Office under the Master of the Ordnance employed such craftsmen in some organized manufacturing process, or simply provided houses and premises for independent workmen, who contracted to make guns and other items to order.[46] If that was the case the gunfounders of the Ordnance Office would have worked in domestic premises that were, however, owned by a larger organization: a half-way house between domestic and factory organization.

No such ambiguity arises over the alum works established by William Turner, George Low and Thomas Jones in Wapping in 1626. They built a large timber house equipped with three furnaces for boiling urine. The messy process undertaken in this purpose-built industrial plant aroused protest among some thousands of neighbouring inhabitants in 1627, who complained about air and river pollution; and an investigation by the College of Physicians led to the Privy Council ordering its closure. Though this order was issued in July 1627, the plant seems to have been still operating two years later, a comment on early-Stuart government ineffectiveness in enforcing its will.[47]

Various other premises were built or adapted in East London during the late-sixteenth and seventeenth centuries, with names which imply manufactories rather than domestic crafts. There were glass houses in Ratcliff, one established in a gunpowder mill,[48] sugar houses established by aliens in Ratcliff and St Katharine's,[49] and starch houses in East Smithfield, St Katharine's, Whitechapel and Poplar.[50] Flemish dyeworks and copperas works were set up in Poplar by the River Lea.[51] Limeburning kilns were established in Bethnal Green and Mile End, and brickmaking developed near Brick Lane.[52] Though we know little of the size and organization of most of these, often gleaning clues to their existence only from their appearance on maps, most seem, by the nature of the process, to have involved the use of furnaces in special premises. The number of such quasi-factory industries established in seventeenth-century East London suggests that the area was particularly suitable for a variety of large-scale enterprises.

To concentrate on these manufactories is perhaps to misrepresent the typical environment of the suburban worker. Altogether they probably employed less than 1,000 men out of a working population of perhaps 10,000 in mid-seventeenth-century East London.[53] And, as we have seen, some apparent manufactories might have been situated in domestic premises, uncomfortable and dirty though this must have made them. The majority of craftsmen would still have carried on their work in their homes. Weavers are an obvious example. Many Spitalfields silkweavers used the garrets of their houses for their looms. Tailors, shoemakers and smiths plied their crafts at home. Most provisioners, bakers, victuallers, vintners and the like, did the same. Brewers did not all work in large breweries. Some were like William Sommer in Shadwell who ran his business in a small brewhouse, stable and hayloft behind his house.[54] Soapmakers and tanners frequently carried on their messy crafts in back sheds in riverside hamlets such as East Smithfield and Shadwell.[55] More unwisely, so did gunpowder-makers and sellers in Whitechapel, Wapping and Ratcliff, with occasional disastrous results. One explosion in Wapping caused damage of over £9,000 to 846 neighbouring houses in 1657.[56]

The tendency for men and women to work at home is confirmed by a parliamentary survey of properties in the riverside hamlet of Shadwell in 1650. Among the 703 dwellings there were 55 shops and 44 alehouses or taverns in which, by definition, the house-holder worked at home. Of the 112 residents whose occupations were identified in other sources, the majority of the 48 per cent who were not mariners seem to have worked at home. Even where the survey described distinct manufacturing or commercial premises, such as roperies, tan yards, brewhouses and timber yards, these usually adjoined the house of the worker involved. It was such small craftsmen who, in a petition for a Stepney market in 1665, called attention to the '12,000 seamen, rope-makers or others using poor manufactures, as ribbonmakers, silkweavers, knitters and the like, whose whole livelihood depends on the management of a very small stock by their own hands'.[57] This was certainly the only context in which casual labour could flourish. We know very little about the numbers of servants, lodging-house keepers, and victualling-house workers, many of whom would have been women. The scope for casual work, feeding, accommodating and entertaining a large seafaring population must have been not inconsiderable. Such occasional opportunities, largely hidden from the historian's eye, must have propped up many a household economy. The norm seems still to have been domestic employment.

Enough has been said, however, to suggest that the working population of East London did not all conform to the characteristic domestic pattern of employment of the pre-industrial city. The largest single occupational group, mariners, are a case apart in working quite outside the home. And a significant minority of craftsmen, because of the scale of their product, or the plant required, or the heat and dirt associated with the process, worked in yards or manufactories. The suburban scene anticipated, to some extent, the industrial characteristics of the nineteenth-century pattern of work, with men journeying to work in purpose-built or adapted manufacturing buildings. A description of this particular London suburb as pre-industrial would therefore be only partly true.[58]

III

Very little direct evidence survives of the wealth and style of life of East Londoners at this period, certainly not enough to rank different occupation groups in a pecking order. Surviving wills are disappointingly few and all too often too unspecific in their bequests to be of much use in such an investigation. But some general points can be made.

It is, first, difficult to generalize about the wealth and status of the dominant group because the term 'mariner' was applied to a wide range of people, from admirals and masters of Trinity House to humble deckhands. While captains and shipowners could be well off, they too could face destitution when sickness, accident or unemployment struck, or when they suffered losses at sea. Captain Thomas Marryott, for example, spent much of the year 1657 trying to get his pay from the Admiralty Commissioners for his service in the *Dunbar*, during which time his family were 'in dire straits'.[59] The humble mariner no doubt oscillated from brief periods of affluence, when coming ashore (sailors' wages were reasonable by the standards of seventeenth-century workers),[60] and poverty while waiting for pay, or being unemployed. Unfortunately we have little idea of how common or long-lasting unemployment could be. It is difficult to be at all precise, therefore, about the economic gain or loss to East London of having so large a marine workforce.

The second point to be made is the existence of a definite industrial élite in East London, the owners of the 'factory' enterprises that have been noted. Henry

Johnson, the shipwright, paid £4,350 to buy Blackwall Yard in 1656, and his son could endow his daughter with a £60,000 portion on her marriage to the Earl of Strafford in the late seventeenth century.[61] John Graves, shipwright, left in his will his Limehouse yard, £526 in cash, shares in several ships, and perhaps 20 properties in East London, the City and Kent in 1637. Fortified with this wealth, his son William was able to buy one of the family's leased yards in Limehouse from the Earl of Cleveland, lord of the manor of Stepney, for £800.[62] Pepys's scoffing comment, 'what shipwrights, new or old, have ever raised estates by this trade', clearly did not apply to all.[63] Associated trades, such as mastmaking and timber importing, involved transactions of many thousands of pounds and control of considerable property. Edward Arlibeare, the mastmaker of Wapping, left £1,000 and much property (as already noted) on his death in 1667.[64] William Wood of Wapping, the timber importer, left yards at Wapping, Poplar and Rotherhithe, tenements in Wapping, and a sum of £800 to his family.[65] Brewing, too, could be an avenue to wealth and recognition. Sir John Parsons, owner of the Red Lion brewery in St Katharine's, became Lord Mayor of London in 1703.[66] But such wealth and recognition were unusual. Few East Londoners were knighted or aspired to become aldermen of the City as a result of their successful entrepreneurship. And social contact between the East-End élite and the gentry, government servants and lawyers of the West End seems not to have been common.

Nevertheless, such men stand out as moguls amongst the generality of East London workers. The third point to be made about the domestic and small-scale craftsmen is their modest means. Textile workers are the most obvious example. John Strype in 1720 described the immigrant silkweavers who settled in Spitalfields in the late-seventeenth century as 'patterns of thrift, honesty, industry and sobriety'.[67] It seems to have done them little material good. Weavers' inventories rarely list more than half a dozen looms in a house,[68] and the poorly-built houses rapidly thrown up in Spitalfields and Mile End New Town to be rented to weavers suggest a working population with limited resources.[69] More striking is the evidence of hardship and discontent among weavers at the time. The introduction of the Dutch or Swivel Engine loom in the 1670s provoked fierce resistance from weavers who saw the increased production of the machine (estimated to produce twenty times the output of a handloom weaver) as a threat to their employment. On 9 August 1675, William Piercey and 40 others broke into the house of John Hascar and set fire to an engine loom, and, the riot growing, a mob of 100 went to John King's house to destroy five more. A day later, Digby Miller and 200 rioters broke into Robert Bowes's house and destroyed ten engine looms and silk worth £120.[70] Bowes was clearly a man of substance operating on a larger scale than most textile workers in the area. These days in August were dangerous ones and it took the mobilization of the trained bands, a military reserve often used to restore order, to subdue the handloom weavers' unrest.[71]

More trouble, of a different kind, occurred in 1683 when, again in August, one Cantrell, a glover of Spitalfields, threatened to lead a rabble against French weavers who, it was complained, failed to employ English workers. Once again military intervention was needed, and a troop of horse was quartered around Mile End and Hackney on 9 August.[72] The early years of the 1680s were stressful, with a succession of cold winters and high prices. Poverty did not, however, always show itself in riot and some textile workers fell on hard times quietly. The lustring weavers of Spitalfields were one such group. Sir William Trumble wrote to the Lord Mayor of London in November 1696 drawing his attention to their necessitous condition and ordered a collection for their relief.[73] Such evidence suggests that poverty, or at least unequal prosperity, was common among the Spitalfields textile workers of the late seventeenth century. It was perhaps the large number of weavers which led to fierce competition for available work, while the 'Luddite' riots suggest great uncertainty of employment.

Analysis of selected groups such as mariners, entrepreneurs and weavers does not give a satisfactory overall view of wealth and status in the community. But this can be approached by the indirect means of examining which occupational groups achieved local office on Stepney vestry.[74] It is, at best, an imperfect way into the

Table 7.3 The representation of occupational groups on Stepney Vestry (percentages)

	Stepney vestry[1] 1600–1662	Stepney as a whole[2] 1610–90
Commerce/Professional:		
Dealers	10	2
Victuallers	8	7
Professions	17	3
Total	35	12
Crafts:		
Shipbuilding	14	6
Wood	1	3
Metal	3	3
Textiles	2	17
Leather	0	3
Miscellaneous	1	1
Total	21	33
Building	1	5
Agricultural	5	2
Carriers:		
Marine	38	35
Land	0	1
Total	38	36
Miscellaneous	0	12
Total	100	100
	(n 200)	(n 3087)

Sources: 1 Stepney vestry minutes and footnote identification by G.W. Hill and W.H. Frere, *Memorials of Stepney Parish: The Vestry Minutes from 1579 to 1662* (1890–1).
2 Stepney burial registers, GLRO, P93/DUN.

problem, for appointment to a vestry reflected the social respect afforded to men, their literary skills and longevity and stability within the community, as well as wealth. The representatives of the community chosen to sit on the vestry, some forty in Stepney from 1599, carried out a responsible local duty. They appointed vestry officers such as churchwardens, sidemen, parish clerks and sextons, and superintended the work they carried out, the upkeep of the church and church services, the collection of local taxes and disbursements to the poor. Table 7.3 shows the percentage of each occupational group represented on the vestry, alongside the percentage of the same group in the population at large.

Even making allowances for the crude data, the comparison of vestrymen and their occupations with occupations in the population as a whole produces very clear indicators of a pecking order. As we might expect the Commerce/Professional group is heavily over-represented on the vestry – wealth and professional skills clearly weighed when vestrymen were chosen – and so too are shipwrights and associated workers, ropemakers, pulleymakers, and the like. Their economic importance in the parish was clearly matched by a local political role. In contrast, textile and leather workers are almost completely absent from the vestry (remarkable in the case of textile workers who made up so large a percentage of the workforce), and their status and influence are apparently negligible. Finally, the representation of mariners on the vestry roughly equals their proportion of the workforce, though significantly three-quarters of the vestry mariners were captains. Authority on deck was matched by influence in the parish community. In short, men who employed or commanded others in their work tended to fill a similar role in governing the local community.

This essay has revealed the unusual occupational structure and patterns of work in the East End of London in the seventeenth century. The area was peculiar in being dominated by marine occupations, and by having a high proportion of men working outside the home, at sea, or in industrial premises. The variegated pattern of work – marine, domestic, and quasi-factory – made the East London economy quite different from that in the central City and added another dimension to the capital.[75]

It is perhaps in the nature of suburbs to develop particular specializations. The concentration of a few dominant occupations in East London, a large area comprising many hamlets, is brought home when the workforce of still smaller areas is examined. Shipbuilding, for example, was concentrated in Poplar and Limehouse, 15 per cent of the workers there being engaged in the craft. Mariners clustered in four contiguous riverside hamlets, Wapping, Shadwell, Ratcliff and Limehouse, making up between 46 and 61 per cent of their workforce. Spitalfields was dominated by weavers who made up 59 per cent of its working population.[76] Other examples, numerically not so striking, founders in East Smithfield and Whitechapel, brewers in St Katharine's and East Smithfield, for example, can be invoked to add to the impression of local suburban communities in which particular types of work were dominant.

Why specialization was so marked is a complex question. The Thames and easy access to it clearly attracted mariners and marine craftsmen who could not employ riverside plots in the City, already densely quayed and built on, nor in the West End where great houses and institutions fronted the river. Riverside industry, whether shipbuilding or brewing, could only develop in East London or on the Southwark bank. Equally important in encouraging large-scale enterprise, was space to build premises, yards and slipways, and cheap houses for a fast-growing labour force. Land was not only plentiful but also cheap, in sharp contrast to the central City. The area was ideal for experiments in establishing plants for producing new or noisome products which would not have been tolerated in the more densely built-up City, with its closer guild and municipal control. The East End was physically and institutionally open to development. It was also strategically located. The raw materials of its industry could be brought in on the flow tide, the products despatched on the ebb. Yet it lay adjacent to the City and within easy reach by river of the centre of government in Westminster.

For such reasons, East London, like some other suburbs, developed working patterns which were quite different, more variegated, and faster growing, than in the City. A study of work in such peripheral areas is therefore of particular importance in an attempt to analyse seventeenth-century urban development.[77] East London is only one example of a suburb which, in developing, added a dynamic element to the economy of a great metropolis.

Notes

1. J. de Vries, *European Urbanization 1500-1800* (1984), 255–8, appendix 1.
2. R. Finlay and B. Shearer, 'Population growth and suburban expansion', in *London 1500-1700: The Making of the Metropolis* (1986), ed. A.L. Beier and R. Finlay, 39.
3. J. de Vries, op. cit., 257.
4. A.L. Beier, 'Engine of manufacture: the trades of London', in Beier and Finlay (ed.), op. cit., 142.
5. The City's jurisdiction extended over 113 parishes inside and just outside the walls; further suburbs stretched along the Thames, east and west of the City, and across the river in Southwark: Finlay and Shearer, op. cit., 45.
6. M.J. Power, 'The urban development of East London, 1550–1700' (PhD thesis, University of London, 1971), 39.
7. Greater London Record Office (GLRO), P93/DUN.
8. E.A. Wrigley and R.S. Schofield regard the problem of non-Anglican burials as insignificant before the 1690s: *The Population History of England 1541-1871: A Reconstruction* (1981), 92. Dissenters did increase in Stepney in the reign of Charles II, but few other than Jews and Quakers would have escaped Anglican burial: Power, op. cit., 267–72.
9. An analysis of occupations in the baptism register, 1606–10, was attempted but was thought to be representative of a more limited sample of the population, those who were young, married and child-bearing, and, moreover, might fail to capture many in-migrants: East London History Group, 'The population of Stepney in the early-seventeenth century', *East London Papers*, 2 (1968), 82–3.
10. T.R. Forbes, 'Weaver and cordwainer: occupations in the parish of St Giles without Cripplegate, London, in 1654–93 and 1729–43', *Guildhall Studies in London History*, 4 (1980), 120–7; A.L. Beier, 'Engine of manufacture', 148. It was necessary to make some adjustments to the categories used by Forbes and Beier to make comparison possible. The adjustment to Forbes was complex but consisted mainly of categorizing his Clothing and Headwear as Textiles; Beverages and Food as Victuallers; Church, Law, Health, Writing, Gentlemen as Professions; Footwear as Leather; Furniture as Wood; Tools, Weapons as Metal; Domestic Accessories as Miscellaneous Crafts; Soldiers,

Labourers, Pensioners as Miscellaneous. Beier's categories were more comparable, with his Clothing categorized as my Textiles; Decorating/Furnishing as Wood; Labouring, Miscellaneous Services as Miscellaneous; Miscellaneous Production as Miscellaneous Crafts; and Officials as Professions.

11. My categories are drawn mainly from J. Langton, 'Residential patterns in pre-industrial cities', *Transactions of the Institute of British Geographers*, 65 (1975), which attempts to distinguish selling groups from making groups. The same attempt is made for London by Beier, op. cit., 150. But the neat-sounding division between selling and making is misleading. For a discussion of the problems involved see J. Patten, 'Urban occupations in pre-industrial England', *Trans. Inst. Brit. Geog.* n.s. 2 (1977).

12. P.J. Corfield, *The Impact of English Towns 1700-1800* (1982), 44-6.

13. R.D. Gwynn, *Huguenot Heritage: The History and Contribution of the Huguenots in Britain* (1985), 75-6, 67-8, 102.

14. G. Unwin, *Industrial Organization in the Sixteenth and Seventeenth Centuries* (1904), 1-8.

15. William Swanley of Ratcliff, David Carpenter, John Gosnoll and William Curtis of Poplar, were all East India Company captains; Sir Henry Palmer, Anthony Tutchin and Robert Dennis served in the Royal or Commonwealth Navy: G.W. Hill and W.H. Frere, *Memorials of Stepney Parish: The Vestry Minutes from 1579 to 1662* (1890-1), 120, 31, 245, 6, 22, 105, 190.

16. William Wildey of Stepney and William Lewes of Ratcliff left wills referring to shares in ships: PRO, PCC 61 Newell; PCC 83 Irby. Privateers included Captain Thomas Davis of Ratcliff, Captain William Mainard of Ratcliff and Captain Edward Johnson of Limehouse: Hill and Frere, op. cit., 169, 178.

17. N.G. Brett-James, *The Growth of Stuart London* (1935), 210.

18. *Calendar of State Papers Domestic (CSPD) 1660-85, Additional*, 418-20; *CSPD 1663-4*, 78, 96; *CSPD 1664-5*, 61, 279; *CSPD 1665-6*, 136, 315, 371; *CSPD 1667-8*, 401; *CSPD 1668-9*, 211, 299; *CSPD 1660-70, Additional*, 103; *CSPD 1660-85, Additional*, 110.

19. *Acts of the Privy Council 1588*, 40-1.

20. *CSPD 1633-4*, 541.

21. *CSPD 1666-7*, 509.

22. *CSPD 1673*, 191-2.

23. PRO, SP 16/135. I am grateful to Dr J. Boulton of the Cambridge Group for the Study of Population and Social Structure for this reference. House of Lords Record Office: Papers 1641-2, Protestations Middlesex; fos. 208-19; 249-60.

24. *CSPD 1639-40*, 208.

25. *Historical Manuscripts Commission: Eighth Report*, 24lb; *CSPD 1658-9*, 453.

26. *CSPD 1682*, 352-3.

27. W. Foster, *John Company* (1926), 138-44.

28. E.B. Sainsbury (ed.), *A Calendar of the Court Minutes of the East India Company 1635-39* (1907), 280, 295, 340; J.C. Jeaffreson (ed.), *Middlesex County Records* (1887-92), II, 126; III, 8-9, 10, 103-4.

29. Foster, op. cit., 148-9.

30. British Library, Additional Charter 13685.

31. Ibid., 13686, 13687, 13688; and H. Green and R. Wigram (ed.), *Chronicles of Blackwall Yard* (1881), 11, 16.

32. Power, op. cit., 212.

33. Green and Wigram, op. cit., 20.

34. W.G. Perrin (ed.), *The Autobiography of Phineas Pett*, (Navy Records Society, no. 51, 1918), 149, 1, 1i.

35. Guildhall Library, Commissary Court of London, MS 9171/19, f. 348; PRO, PCC 163 Goare; *CSPD 1654*, 501.

36. R. Davis, *The Rise of the English Shipping Industry in the Seventeenth and Eighteenth Centuries* (1962), 96; *CSPD 1667-8*, 185; *CSPD 1668-9*, 345; *CSPD 1660-70, Additional*, 456, 471, 551; *CSPD 1672-3*, 102-3, 560; *CSPD 1673*, 21-2.

37. PRO, PCC 135 Reeve; *CSPD 1655-6*, 423; *CSPD 1666-7*, 572-3; *CSPD 1672*, 283; *CSPD 1672-3*, 252; *CSPD 1665-6*, 516.

38. PRO, PCC 60 Hene, 1.

39. For the shift from domestic brewing-retailing to large-scale breweries, see P. Mathias, *The Brewing Industry in England 1700-1830* (1959), xii–xiii, 4–6, and P. Clark, *The English Alehouse: A Social History 1200-1830* (1983), 99–101.

40. H. Llewellyn-Smith, *The History of East London* (1929), 217.

41. *Calendar of Patent Rolls, Elizabeth*, II, 127; PRO, PCC 25 Watson.

42. Llewellyn-Smith, op. cit., 217; F.H.W. Sheppard (ed.), *Survey of London*, XXVII: *Spitalfields and Mile End New Town* (1957), 116–19.

43. Historical Manuscripts Commission, National Register of Archives, file no. 4624.

44. *Calendar of Patent Rolls: Elizabeth*, II, 127; and J.L. Archer, 'The Industrial history of London, 1603-40, with special reference to the suburbs' (MA thesis, University of London, 1934), 28.

45. A.D. Tyssen, 'The history of the Whitechapel bell foundry', *Transactions of the London and Middlesex Archaeological Society*, n.s. 5 (1929), 197–200; Anthony Bartlett's will, Guildhall Library, MS 9177/35, f. 493.

46. Llewellyn-Smith, op.cit., 214; *Calendar of Patent Rolls, Elizabeth*, IV, no. 810; *CSPD 1601-03*, 172; *Acts of the Privy Council 1619-21*, 237-8; Pitt's will, PRO, PCC 24 Rudd; Power, op. cit., 228.

47. J. Stow, *Survey of London*, ed. J. Strype (1720), II, iv, 39–43; *Acts of the Privy Council 1627*, 433-5; ibid., *1627-8*, 169–70; ibid. *1629-30*, no. 248.

48. Ibid., *1580-1*, 351; Archer, op. cit., 20–1; J. Gascoyne, *Map of Stepney*, 1703 (see Fig. 7.1, above).

49. *CSPD 1595-7*, 97; J. Gascoyne, *Map of Stepney*, 1703; *Acts of the Privy Council 1621-3*, 253.

50. Archer, op.cit., 19, 68; Jeaffreson, op. cit., I, 261.

51. S. Smiles, *The Huguenots: Their Settlements, Churches and Industries in England and Ireland* (1870), 88; J. Gascoyne, *Map of Stepney*, 1703; J. Stow, *Survey of London*, ed. J. Strype (1720), II, Perambulation, ii, 102.

52. J. Gascoyne, *Map of Stepney*, 1703; GLRO, M93/158, f. 13.

53. These are estimates based on a total population of about 50,000 in the mid-seventeenth century, and the assumption that one person in five was in full-time work. There were 47 'factory' enterprises traced of which we have a figure of the workforce of only one, Blackwall Yard, with 232 men. Assuming that the six other shipyards employed 30 men each adds 180. Assuming that all other enterprises employed 10 men (18 ancillary ship enterprises, 4 foundries, 4 breweries, 3 alum or dye works, 9 glass, starch and sugar houses, 2 lime or brick works) adds 400. This all adds up to a total of 812 in such industries.

54. Deed of sale of Shadwell, 22 November 1650, consulted in St Paul's Cathedral Library, press E, drawer 5, f. 7. The St Paul's manuscripts are now in the Guildhall Library.

55. Ibid. An abbreviated transcript of this document is contained in Power, op. cit., 311–46.

56. *CSPD 1639*, 86-7; *CSPD 1656-7*, 168; *CSPD 1657-8*, 350, 497.

57. M.J. Power, 'Shadwell: the development of a London suburban community in the seventeenth century', *The London Journal*, 4 (1978), 36–40; PRO, SP 29/94/53.

58. East London was not unique in this respect. Port towns such as Chatham, Plymouth and Portsmouth, as well as fast-growing industrial towns like Halifax shared the specialization, the larger units of production and the rapid housing development experienced in East London: see P. Clark and P. Slack, *English Towns in Transition 1500-1700* (1976), 41-2; and Corfield, op.cit., 44-6.

59. *CSPD 1656-7*, 488, 542, 548, 560; *CSPD 1657-8*, 405.
60. C. Lloyd, *The British Seaman 1200-1860* (1968), 48-9.
61. Foster, op. cit., 146-51.
62. PRO, PCC 163 Goare; *Calendar of the Committee for Compounding 1643-60*, 2160.
63. Davis, op. cit., 56.
64. See above, p. 111, and n. 38.
65. PRO, PCC 135 Reeve.
66. See above, n. 43.
67. Stow, op.cit., II, iv, 48.
68. See, for example, the inventories of Richard Alchurch and Robert Bell, in Guildhall Library: MS 9174/1; and of Henry Wheele, John Wolfinden, — Gaspard, in Guildhall Library: MS 9177/9.
69. See, for example, the building on the Wheler estate in Spitalfields in the 1650s and 1660s: Sheppard, op. cit., 97-9.
70. Jeaffreson, op.cit., IV, 61-3.
71. *CSPD 1675-6*, 257; see A. Plummer, *The London Weavers' Company 1600-1970* (1972), 162-6, for the context of these riots. See, also, T. Harris, *London Crowds in the Reign of Charles II* (1987), 191-6.
72. *CSPD July-Sept 1683*, 267, 330, 422, 433.
73. *CSPD 1696*, 438; Harris, op. cit., 205-07.
74. Hill and Frere, op. cit.
75. See the analysis of the occupational structure of 20 City parishes in 1666 in M.J. Power, 'The social topography of Restoration London', in Beier and Finlay (ed.), op. cit., 212-15.
76. Percentages derived from Power, PhD, thesis, 179-80.
77. See the model study recently published on Southwark: J. Boulton, *Neighbourhood and Society: A London Suburb in the Seventeenth Century* (1987).

8 Work, violence and community in early industrial Merthyr Tydfil[1]

Chris Evans

> At a time when the ravages of war are desolating many other countries, it is not an unpleasing contrast to see in our own, trade flourishing, and towns, in consequence, springing up in places where before there existed only a few scattered houses.

So wrote a correspondent to the *Monthly Magazine* in 1799.[2] His reflection had been prompted by a visit to a new and rapidly-growing town in the 'midland parts of Wales, which twenty years ago deserved scarcely the name of a village'. Two years later the first census confirmed Merthyr's sudden acquisition of urban status when the parish was found to harbour nearly 8,000 inhabitants.

The emergence of Merthyr as a thriving industrial town was abrupt and unexpected. It was, as one commentator justly observed, 'the triumph of fact over probability',[3] for the area was bereft of urban antecedents. The old village was positioned at the northern end of a huge, elongated upland parish – divided into five hamlets – which stretched down the valley of the Taff. It was situated in the 'Hills', as the contemporary English rendering had it, a region which encompassed both the 'Valleys' of modern South Wales and the massif of the Brecon Beacons. Accordingly, its own agriculture was meagre and its hinterland threadbare. It had only the most limited significance as a centre for distribution, still less for consumption. Nor had Merthyr ever been the seat of any judicial or administrative function.

Work, the working of iron, was its sole justification as a town. At Merthyr urban accomplishment waited, always belatedly, on industrial prowess. In its early nineteenth-century heyday the town's retail and professional sectors remained, on a generous estimate, rudimentary.[4] Civic improvements which Swansea, Cardiff and even the minuscule Glamorgan borough of Llantrissent were making in the 1760s and 1770s – street-lighting and paving, new town halls and the like – were not to feature in Merthyr until the second half of the nineteenth century when its industrial decline had set in.[5] So deficient was Merthyr in the varied and sophisticated facilities that were increasingly evident in urban society elsewhere in Britain that some visitors doubted its entitlement to urban credentials. 'Notwithstanding its magnitude and commercial consequence', wrote one, 'Merthyr Tydfil is but a village, although by courtesy it enjoys the title of town.'[6] Indeed, so exclusive was the settlement's dependence on the iron industry that when the last furnaces were damped down in the 1930s it was seriously mooted that the town should simply be wiped off the map and its population removed *en bloc* to a new coastal site.[7]

In the last years of the eighteenth century, however, the erection of furnace batteries around the village propelled Merthyr from obscurity to a world centre of iron production. These were years of unparalleled prosperity for the British iron industry as a whole, but no region could match the explosive growth of South Wales. In 1788, a mere 12,500 tons of pig iron was cast there, only half the output of Shropshire, the then premier iron district. By 1796, production had topped 34,000 tons to overtake Shropshire, and by 1806 exceeded 78,000 tons.[8] The breakthrough of South Wales to the head of the national iron industry was itself spearheaded by the four major ironworks which encircled Merthyr village: Cyfarthfa, Plymouth, Penydarren and Dowlais.[9] Between 1785 and 1811 the number of blast furnaces in the parish increased from three to seventeen, while individual furnace capacity probably doubled in the course of the French wars. Such evidence as there is suggests that the Merthyr works contributed at least one third of the regional 'make' of pig iron in these years. In the refining of cast to wrought iron Merthyr's dominance was still more pronounced, accounting for approximately 70 per cent of the wrought iron rolled in South Wales in 1812.[10]

Merthyr was the beneficiary of the key technological changes which transformed the eighteenth-century iron industry, those centred on the supersession of charcoal by mineral fuel. After 1750 coke ousted charcoal as the principal fuel of blast furnaces. Then, in the 1780s, Henry Cort perfected the process of 'puddling', the long sought-after technique of converting cast to wrought iron that was both coal-fired and reliable. These developments opened the way for large, integrated ironworks where furnaces, forges and rolling mills, hitherto dispersed, could be closely combined, adjacent to coal reserves.[11] At Merthyr the contiguity of coal, ironstone and limestone deposits provided the ideal locale for ironworks of the new configuration.

The ironmasters exercised to the full what Trotsky, in a parallel context, once termed the 'privilege of historic backwardness'.[12] They adopted the new techniques and standards with an unmatched thoroughness, and vaulted over their better-established English rivals. They did not have to switch from smaller, disparate charcoal-fuelled plant. Their furnaces were coke-fired from their inception and built to the latest design. From the outset the Merthyr works displayed what amounted to industrial gigantism by the standards of the day. By 1794, '400 men and boys . . . exclusive of familys' were employed at Dowlais.[13] The larger Penydarren works gave employment, on one sober estimate, to over 900 men, women and children ('reckoning in the miners') by 1802.[14] Richard Crawshay's Cyfarthfa works was bigger still, reputedly being the largest single ironworks in the world by 1800.[15]

Work at Merthyr had a palpable, not to say overwhelming presence. The ironworks comprised vast structures, where a single furnace dwarfed any building to be found in the place. Work and town were indissociable. Whether through the smoke which shrouded the place by day, the furnace flare that illuminated it by night, or the beat of the forge hammers that thundered ceaselessly, industry made itself inescapably manifest. The performance of labour was rarely a hidden, private affair. In contravention of Defoe's famous suggestion, made after observing the

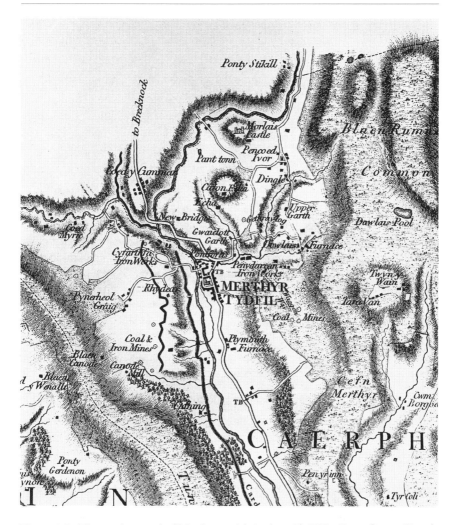

Figure 8.1. The northern end of Merthyr parish in the mid-1790s. From George Yates's map of Glamorgan, 1799. The village lies on the east bank of the Taff, with the Glamorgan Canal running parallel to the river on the west. The four ironworks are clearly marked: Cyfarthfa at the head of the canal; Plymouth to the south, alongside the Cardiff turnpike; Penydarren and Dowlais on rising ground to the east of the village.
Copyright: Glamorgan Archive Service.

textile manufactures of the West Riding, that industrial activity depopulated the landscape, immuring workers within cottages and workshops, production at Merthyr was almost always open to view. Much of what was misleadingly termed 'mining' was performed in the open air, with the result that the hillsides behind the different works teemed with labourers. Ironstone (or 'mine') was commonly obtained by forms of surface excavation such as 'scouring' or 'patching' – so much

Figure 8.2. The Cyfarthfa ironworks *c.* 1825, painted by Penry Williams (1798–1885), from the east bank of the Taff. A forge and mill occupy the right foreground, their roofs studded with the chimneys of balling furnaces. The main body of the works comprises a battery of blast furnaces, each fronted by a casthouse, with engine-houses and smiths' shops to the left, and an additional forge or mill extending away to the right.
Copyright: Cyfarthfa Castle Museum, Merthyr Tydfil.

so that the superintendent of miners at Cyfarthfa in the 1780s was equipped with a telescope as an aid to supervision.[16] Coal also outcropped across the district, and where extensive underground workings were necessary they were entered by levels driven horizontally into the mountain rather than pits.

The hub of iron production itself, the furnace-forge complex, although encased in an imposing masonry shell, was by no means enclosed. The difficulties of ventilating a choking area of work ensured that forge and mill buildings were tall, open-sided structures into which 'strangers' might peer or wander at will. Moreover, the convulsive spurt of expansion in the last years of the eighteenth century produced an industrial environment of extreme disorder. 'Modern' industry brought no segregation of work and leisure. Rather, sites of work and areas of residence and recreation were promiscuously intermixed and continually encroached on one another. Squatter cottages were put up on mine patches, built from the rubble that was strewn across those shattered landscapes; dwellings were squeezed between calcining kilns and coking ovens; even the crevices between the blast furnaces were colonized.

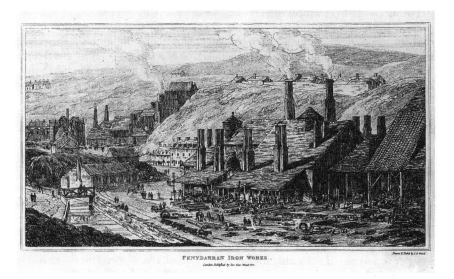

Figure 8.3. Penydarren ironworks: the Penydarren forge as sketched by John George Wood in or shortly before 1811. In the foreground, the Morlais brook flows down towards its confluence with the Taff. The blast furnace complex is further up the valley, half-obscured by a spur of high ground.

I

Work in Merthyr was performed at the behest of four immense and cohesive blocs of capital. Yet the direction of work was not subject to a searching, centralized control. Instead, the productive process was enveloped in a web of subcontracting agreements, or similar *ad hoc* arrangements. As is well recognized, subcontracting was a very widespread form of work organization in eighteenth-century industry, and at Merthyr it was pervasive.[17] Richard Crawshay found it impossible to give an estimate of the numbers he employed 'as he had captains under him, who had each agreed to furnish him with a certain number'.[18]

Crawshay's admission points to one of the foremost advantages of subcontracting for the ironmaster: he was at a stroke released from the responsibility of recruiting and supervising labour. At the same time, a degree of certainty was introduced into his cost calculations: he was able to fix in advance a whole range of outlays as the 'bargains' were negotiated. The ironmasters were also granted flexibility: highly specific bargains, such as for the supply of sand to the casthouse of a blast furnace for the duration of a single 'campaign', facilitated the attraction or repulsion of labour according to the peculiar seasonal rhythms of ironmaking. Above all, the system carried within it a guarantee that the contracting master would attain at least a rudimentary level of productivity. Inhabiting as he did a precarious and ambiguous territory between capital and wage labour, the subcontractor had the keenest interest in keeping his labourers to their tasks.[19]

Forms of indirect employment flourished, especially in the extraction and preparation of raw materials. Naturally, there was considerable variation in the concrete detail of bargains. They were the outcome of complex negotiations in which the monetary rate for the job was only one of a series of contingent factors. Thus, in the 1760s three colliers contracted to take on a coal working for Cyfarthfa, being 'well Skilled in Works of that nature'. They agreed to get the raw coal and deliver it – ready coked – to the furnace bank 'for the Consideration of four shillings per Dozen'. They were to be supplied with 'all the nesissary Tools that is Mandrelles Picaxes Weges & Hamers', and were to be awarded some allowance for opening up the workings. Thereafter the four shilling rate was to cover the getting and processing of the coal, while extra expenses incurred in sustaining the fabric of the colliery were to be reviewed and haggled over at the end of each month.[20]

The prosperity of a master collier or miner depended on just such a specific distribution of responsibilities: on the size of the cash advance given for opening up a 'patch', on the distance rubbish had to be wheeled, on shifting the onus of supplying pit timber or candles onto the ironmaster. A miner who engaged to raise a thousand tons of mine for Dowlais in 1814 settled on a rate of '7/9 per Ton, vizt., 7/6 per ton to be paid Monthly for the Mine Raised, and 3$^{d.}$ per Ton to remain in the Dowlais Iron Company's hands until the said 1000 tons be raised'. The man was to find his own tools for the labourers he took on, but the Company was to bear the costs of fetching the mine from the workings and dressing it for the furnace. A final clause stipulated that the company's hauliers were to remove the mine to the furnace bank within two months of its being dug and stacked; if they failed to do so the miner was still to be paid the full tonnage regardless of any deterioration which the raw mine had suffered when exposed to the elements.[21]

These bargains, most of which were never committed to paper, were endlessly diverse. There were numerous hybrid forms. Master puddlers or rollers, the pivotal figures in the organization of work in the forge, were the directors of the labour process, but not always its paymasters. Forgemen and rollers were often paid directly by the iron company according to a multiplicity of piece rates. However, the procedures of payment often parodied the subcontract form, emphasizing the leadership of the master workman, not the ironmaster. At Dowlais in 1804 William Corns and 'his men' – a team of sixteen ball-furnacemen – were all paid by the Company on an agreed rate for every ton of iron they processed. Yet Corns also received his 'profit' from each man, a farthing per ton which each of them offered up as a tribute to his authority as a master ironworker.[22] Such authority was not derived from his being a petty capitalist, nor from the completion of any formal qualification. Formal apprenticeship was almost unknown, presumably because for centuries previously the mysteries of ironmaking had characteristically been practised in scattered, forest locations, beyond the purview of town-based regulatory bodies.

Instead, the jurisdiction of a man like William Corns was grounded in the common, unspoken recognition of his status as a master, a standing rooted in technical virtuosity and versatility. A master puddler was marked out not just by his expertise at working a puddling furnace, but by a capacity to build, repair or adapt that furnace. He was the real guarantor of successful production, deploying an experience that had often been gained in the English iron districts along the arc of the Severn, in Shropshire and south Staffordshire. The ironmaster ceded to him the hiring of labour in the confidence that the master workman could command the fealty of a gang of 'hands' gathered about him. This was customarily the case, for the ordinary hand gained a vicarious recognition as a reliable and worthy workman by his attachment to a master, as well as some fixity of comradeship and solidarity.

It is not difficult to detect a strong communal ethos among those who had been 'bred up' (to use that very apposite eighteenth-century notion) to one of the iron crafts. Such was its strength, that the ironmasters could not arbitrarily infringe upon the prerogatives of the cadre of skilled ironworkers who *de facto* ordered the working environment. 'I cannot help thinking', William Taitt, the most astringent of the Dowlais partners, told his manager, 'that you may compel the Rollers to put on another set of hands (2 extra each turn) . . . unless we do so we shall never be able to get on, we are not to sacrifice our own interest to their profit only.'[23] Taitt used the language of compulsion, but in less exasperated moments he recognized that the labour process could not be shaped by dictation. It had to be meticulously constructed with blandishments, cajolings and threats; the ironmaster could not take hasty sanctions against men of scarce and valued talents. Rather than assert their domination, the ironmasters had, more often than not, to proclaim their own participation in the knowledge which their workmen put into practice, affirming that they too had been inculcated into the mysteries of the iron crafts, and so had earned inclusion in the community of the trade.

The signal feature of work relations at Merthyr was then the diffusion of authority through a varied body of intermediaries, each of whom asserted at autonomy of sorts. This loose and shifting structure of employment imposed bounds on the power of the ironmasters: their ability to enforce the pace and form of work was compromised. Now, this in itself was unexceptional. Indeed, it has been suggested that the 'persistent tendency of the British working class to erect informal structures at the workplace that resist and impede capitalist domination of the labour process might be seen as a distinctive national peculiarity.'[24] Even so the shortfall of control which the Merthyr ironmasters experienced was marked. They were effectively excluded from the self-sufficient workplace culture of the furnace-yard and the forge, and in the field of mineral excavation their purchase on the working environment, comprising dozens of small and scattered workings, was always uncertain.

Disruption in the getting of raw materials could certainly acquire significant scale. When Richard Hill, the Plymouth ironmaster, contracted with one William Thomas Griffiths to take on a mine working in March 1790 he advanced the miner five guineas. Having pocketed the advance however, Griffiths did nothing for three months, while Hill was 'in the utmost distress for mine' and forced to cut his make of iron by a fifth.[25] This episode not only indicates the size of the losses that might be sustained through the caprice of a contractor, but it reveals as well the limited efficacy of the means of redress available to the ironmaster.

Hill commenced a suit for the recovery of damages from Griffiths. That was the standard procedure for regulating a contractual agreement between two ostensibly equal parties: the ironmaster and the contracting miner. However, civil proceedings, which might be drawn-out and costly, could not offer a simple and immediate instrument of discipline and retribution. More seriously, a suit might founder on the lack of correspondence between the individualist idiom in which contractual agreements were framed, and the collectivism of the work gang which cloaked the perpetration of fraud and sharp practice in the workplace. This was impressed upon one of the Dowlais partners who wished to punish three miners, a father and his two sons, who had committed one of the most commonplace mining dodges. They had been 'overpaid on the Mine Castings by their putting Stones, & Earth, in the middle of the Heaps in order for it to be paid for as ironstone'.[26] A suit against the father would obtain recompense, but allow his sons – judged to be his hired workmen – to evade punishment, although their complicity in this most time-honoured of frauds was evident.

The command of the ironmaster was, then, thought to be especially precarious in the coal and mine workings. The accessibility of the latter left them exposed to depredation, while the expansion unleashed by coke technology at Merthyr, where furnaces of unprecedentedly high capacity were now concentrated, stimulated their multiplication on the slopes about the town. In these circumstances, so flimsy was the force of authority perceived to be that the ironmasters contemplated a legislative solution to their disciplinary conundrum. 'I believe twill be necessary to have a Law in the Iron trade', Crawshay announced in 1797.[27] And indeed, in 1800 the Merthyr ironmasters were among the sponsors of the 'Act for the Security of Collieries and Mines and the Better Regulation of Colliers and Miners'.[28] They had hoped to redefine the appropriation of coal from levels as a felony, and although they were thwarted in this, their Act – the first in English law to deal exclusively with matters of discipline in collieries – did succeed in subjecting a range of workplace disobediences to summary justice.

II

The sketch of work relations in the iron industry presented here has emphasized amorphousness as the chief characteristic: organization was fluid and lines of authority were tenuous. Yet this impression jars against that feature of early industrial Merthyr which historians and contemporary observers alike have insisted on – the solidity of allegiances to particular ironworks. Gwyn A. Williams, the outstanding historian of the town and its politics in the early nineteenth century, has commented on the 'tribal' quality of 'a commitment to "Dowlais" or "Cyfarthfa"'.[29] As early as 1803 William Taitt took such loyalties to be axiomatic: 'a few of ours, Penydarran & Cyfarthfa men will never meet together without some Jealousies.'[30] Indeed, the animosities developed a proverbial ferocity, and were to become, as more settled communities congealed around each works, entrenched local traditions. But whatever momentum the traditions of interworks rivalry later acquired, the conditions of their formation remain to be explored.

In a sense, the antipathies that fractured urban society at Merthyr can be attributed to those elements of 'paternalism' which informed work relations – the articulation of loyalties centred on the figure of the ironmaster, and buttressed by a panoply of extra-economic practices and provisions. Certainly, men like Crawshay or Samuel Homfray were commanding individuals who sedulously cultivated personae in which the requisite qualities of potency and solicitude were blended. Yet the Merthyr ironmasters were probably no more demanding of loyalty from their workforces than were other industrialists of the time.

The ironmasters did, it is true, assume considerable prominence in local affairs.

They were compelled by the very absence of an urban infrastructure at Merthyr to intervene extensively in the lives of their workers. For one thing, the influx of men and women rapidly outstripped the capacity of the existing apparatus of supply to import the necessaries of life. The availability of work at Merthyr sucked in labour from adjacent parishes, and, via the ancient drovers' tracks which passed across the country to the north of the town, men and women who had tramped from the overburdened counties of west Wales. To these were added the recruits from the industrial districts of western Britain: the leaven of English ironworkers from Shropshire or the forges of the Stour valley, and the Cornish engineers who crossed the Bristol Channel with the cargoes of copper ore for the smelters of South Wales. In the face of this immigration the ironmasters were, from the early 1790s, obliged to underwrite the subsistence of their workforces, organizing enormous shipments of foodstuffs. By the winter of 1792–3, Crawshay was importing whole cargoes of American flour direct to Cyfarthfa. The Dowlais Company began to bring in provisions on an extended scale at the same time, and a works shop was opened at Penydarren in the course of the following winter.[31] The ironmasters also provided housing for their more prized workers. A squad of English forgemen, brought to Penydarren in the 1780s, was accommodated in 'Row y Saeson' (Saxon Row), while dwellings were being built at the cost of thirty guineas per unit at both Dowlais and Cyfarthfa in the mid-1790s.[32]

All of this would seem to emphasize the active role of the ironmasters in nurturing a community about their works. On the other hand, it is clear that the efforts to keep Merthyr provisioned were undertaken without enthusiasm. There were even those who, conscious of the strong corporate identity of the iron trade, felt that by dealing in groceries they were 'degrading ourselves, as ironmasters'.[33] Nor is there any reason to view their arrangements as conflict-free. When rioting swept Merthyr during the dearth of 1800, one of the first acts of the crowd was the razing of the Penydarren shop. In the aftermath of the disturbances, it was agreed that payment in copper tokens and credit notes issued by the ironmasters, and hence the constraints these placed on consumer choice, had been high among the rioters' grievances.[34] Again, the matter of company housing is less clear-cut than at first it seems. Shelter was provided only for a small minority. In the late 1790s, when perhaps a thousand people were employed at Cyfarthfa, Crawshay could dispose of fewer than sixty dwellings.[35] Above all, the turnover of labour, now impossible to quantify, but which all the impressionistic evidence suggests was vast, would seem to have militated against the easy growth of community at any one works.

III

If neither provisioning nor housing, the putative material mainstays of 'paternalism', were of decisive importance in cementing loyalties, a cogent guide to the divisions of Merthyr can be located in the fraught and violent atmosphere which characterized the performance of work. Indeed, a close examination of work practices reveals the profound and very direct influence they exerted on social relations.

In part, the very primitivism of extractive techniques was responsible for the air of acrimony. Scouring, the favoured method of working accessible beds of mine, was of particular significance here. It involved no more than putting up makeshift dams across the hillsides to create artificial ponds. Once a sufficient volume of water had collected, the dam could be breached and the torrent would rip away the topsoil and dislodge mine from the lower slopes. Scouring was an effective technique, but it was also immensely destructive, churning up common grazing and ravaging fields. The resentment it incurred among the freeholders and small farmers of the parish can be readily imagined.[36] And the acrimony which it generated in the district was reflected in a rich crop of writs and threats. So bitterly was it resented that, when Richard Crawshay was interviewed before a committee of the Board of Trade in 1786, he could think of no assistance which the iron trade required of government, other than 'a Stop by Act of Parliament to litigious Suits, created by very small individuals in the Hill Counties of Wales . . . for obtaining the mine by scowering away the Earth from it'.[37]

One of these suits, in 1782, reveals the impact that such disputes could have on social relations. In July that year writs were served on John Guest of Dowlais and two of his master miners by Rowland Williams of Gwernllwyn Uchaf, a neighbouring farmer who charged them with knowingly damaging certain of his meadows. Guest's response was to despatch the two miners to the distant anonymity of Bristol, where they were to be supported at the Company's expense until the crisis had passed. It was an astute move. While Rowland Williams's suit languished for want of the two most material witnesses, Guest took steps to secure the allegiance of the remaining miners. They were stiffened against intimidation with free liquor and indemnified against any future legal action, since Williams had threatened:[38]

> . . . to send them to Jail & otherwise punish them if they shou'd dare to Scour from the Mountains, which threats have so much intimidated them that the greater number have left me . . . I was in danger of losing the remaining Workmen – they all refusing to Work had I not call'd them together & given them a good treat – likewise I was Compelled to give them a written indemnity . . . otherwise I must soon have stood still.

These circumstances are instructive. They indicate that antagonism was engrained in the very mode of working in the Merthyr district from an early date. Exposure to legal harassment, if not bodily violence, became a routine accompaniment to the conduct of work. In consequence, the ironmasters were obliged to augment the cash nexus with physical sanctuary and legal succour if they were to attract and retain labour.

Tensions in the district, with all the reciprocities between ironmaster and workman which they implied, took on a qualitatively new aspect from the mid-1780s. Hitherto the adversaries of the ironmasters had been those 'very small individuals', the freeholders and tenants who held the ninety-three farms in Merthyr parish. Then, in 1785, the Penydarren works went into blast for the first time. And in 1786 Plymouth and Cyfarthfa, which had formed a single combine, were relaunched as separate concerns. Henceforth, the important contests were to be between the four great ironworks themselves. As the upward trajectory of local iron production steepened in the late 1780s, the ironmasters were pitched into conflict. With the extension of the ironworks, the existing patchwork of leases was strained and tightened, and an already complex division of property was further obscured beneath a thickening matrix of roads, tramways, watercourses, and cinder tips. Amid so claustrophobic a concentration of industry, contentions became inevitable as the mounting demands for coal, mine and motive power drove up the incidence of trespass, lease infringements and damage to property.

The prudent ironmaster extended his aid and protection to the gangs of workmen who supplied him with raw materials; he also held them ready as a means of harassing his neighbours should the need arise. An incident in 1806 illustrates the mechanisms at play. Samuel Homfray of Penydarren engaged a miner to 'get a certain quantity of mine at 6/- per ton' from disputed ground adjacent to the Dowlais works. Although the Dowlais Company had laid a railroad over the land, connecting its furnaces and collieries with a newly-built forge, the Penydarren Company held 'an unquestionable Title' to the mine beneath the surface. Accordingly, Homfray let it be known that, if the railroad was not dismantled, he would give his miner 'full liberty to stop it up by throughing rubbish upon it, provided it is in doing his duty according to his agreement ... if the Dowlais company think themselves injured and resent it, he will support the man thro' the action'.[39]

In summary, the struggle for local advantage found expression in the contentious behaviour of the rival workforces. Obstructive activity was furthered and endorsed by the ironmasters. The effect was to enforce a closer identification between the plethora of work gangs and the ironmaster who employed them at one remove. It established a structure of tension and antagonism into which the workman or woman entered as an unavoidable corollary of their employment. In this view the paradox of early industrial Merthyr, its combination of rigid alignments with great labour mobility, can be resolved.

By the early 1790s two persistent points of conflict can be identified. The emergence of the first, between Cyfarthfa and Plymouth, was precipitated in 1790 by the commencement of the Glamorgan Canal linking Merthyr with Cardiff. The rival ironworks were sited on opposite banks of the Taff, and both drew heavily on its water for power. However, the diversion of water to the canal threatened to deprive the Plymouth works, downstream on the river, of power. Although the Plymouth furnace was guaranteed an adequate water supply by the authorizing canal Act (30 Geo.III c.82), Richard Hill was soon at loggerheads with Richard Crawshay, who held a controlling interest in the canal company and which he ran as an adjunct to his Cyfarthfa works. Hence ensued the legal contest which reached the Court of Chancery in 1794. But Hill soon despaired of legal remedies, remarking[40] to his attorney that his opponents 'keep such a pack of *Affidavit men* that was I under the necessity to blow out they would Swear I had water enough tho' not a Drop scarce coming to me – this has been nearly the Case Since Saturday last'. Besides, any judgment or arbitration award woud be rendered obsolete by the expansion of furnace capacity at Plymouth and the growing demands on power which this entailed. Since the law could not keep pace with the changing situation on the ground in Merthyr, access to the waters of the Taff was disputed to the accompaniment of smashed locks and stopped-up sluices, the whole performance being punctuated with scuffles and fracas. In these the Plymouth ironmaster played a leading role, lending heart to those of his men who quailed at the might of Crawshay. On a night in June 1794, Hill broke open the No. 3 lock on the canal in person, and, in the wake of another confrontation at No. 3, it was his eldest son,

Richard Hill junior, who was arraigned for assaulting the lock-keeper. The keeper was, in the judgment of Hill senior, 'a worthless Dog: perhaps there does not exist a worse character in the principality'. Yet as he recognized, 'the Canal Co. undertake it for him, and prosecute it to give protection to their Serv.$^{ts.}$'[41] That, precisely, was the effect of the struggle for resources at Merthyr: each of the ironmasters had his powers of leadership, patronage and protection tested in such a way as to bind together the men and women who laboured on his behalf.

The other zone of friction separated Dowlais and Penydarren. As can be seen from George Yates's map of Glamorgan, prepared in the mid-1790s, the two works were built in close proximity, their tenancies sitting cheek-by-jowl along the Morlais and Dowlais brooks. The streams served as receptacles for the waste of both works and so their courses were constantly shifting. Since the stream beds delineated boundaries between the mineral holdings of the two ironworks, they sparked a series of aggressive exchanges. Moreover, Dowlais and Penydarren were ensnared in a tangle of ambiguous leases, most spectacularly at Pwllywheaid farm where the former held the rights to dig coal and the latter the title to the mine deposits. As the unwilling partners in an interlocking embrace the rival works were quickly drawn into a bitter and recurrent feud.

As early as February 1786 William Taitt found cause for complaint to Samuel Homfray, the Penydarren ironmaster:[42]

> ... your miners Viz Lewis Griffiths and his men go upon the mountain & turn the water towards their workes by which they not only invade our property, but have damaged the road so much by scouring down one of the bridges that it is render'd impassable ... be Assur'd that the next Complaint I receive against any of them for the like offence shall instantly be follow'd by an Action against them.

By 1791 Samuel Homfray was making a public avowal 'that he will try whatever *he* can do towards taking down the Dowlais Furnaces'. The Cardiff diarist who recorded this declaration found it inexplicable, for the ground being contested by Homfray and Dowlais 'was not worth 6^d to any person but themselves'. It could be, he thought, 'no more than the effect of a gust of passion'.[43] Yet in the fraught atmosphere of Merthyr, Homfray's pugnacity was readily comprehensible. Although Homfray was a notoriously irascible personality, the Dowlais partners were equally prepared to countenance extreme measures. Their works manager was to suggest a striking expedient to pressurize Homfray into relinquishing the disputed spot. Since the ground in question was defined by the course of the Morlais brook, long choked and contorted by debris, he recommended an attempt to turn the stream towards its original channel:

> ... we may make weares to turn it towards the old course, and it is then their business to protect themselves; I can make a Wear in three or four days in a place that is directly on our premises, that will find its own way to the Level they have drove before the Workmens Houses, fill that and all the Houses in a few hours and go into the Lower Forges if not upper ones and the Furn[ace]s.

He concluded triumphantly: 'in short a were would stop all their works'.[44] This was no idle threat. The proposal to wreck one of the greatest ironworks in the kingdom was canvassed quite ingenuously among the Dowlais partnership, and work on a weir was finally begun in August 1794. And to effect; Homfray was forced to capitulate.[45]

Hostilities between the two works, and their workforces, continued for over two decades. They reached a climax in 1809 when the Dowlais Company attempted to stop Penydarren miners from dumping rubbish in the brook opposite the Dowlais forge, a practice which this time threatened the Dowlais works with inundation. Josiah Guest countered the danger by throwing a brick arch over the brook to prevent the dumping, and having a culvert dug to speed the stream past the works. At Penydarren his actions were seen as an intolerable curb on a longstanding custom, and the culvert as a trespass on Homfray's mine patches. As a result, David Foulkes, an under-manager at Penydarren, led a troop of workmen to demolish the culvert. He was opposed, on the night of 15–16 November 1809, by Guest, who marshalled a smaller number of his own men to repel the attack.

Since a number of the participants in the ensuing disturbances, including Josiah Guest, were later indicted for riotous assembly and assault, this incident is unique in that the testimony of several plebeian combatants was recorded.

Thomas John Harry, a senior Dowlais miner, watched Foulkes arrive with an estimated 150 men:

> ... all Penydarren Workmen among whom were Sawyers, Miners, Colliers & Labourers ... Some of them had Mandrelles others Picaxes & Smiths Sledges.

Evan Davies, a miner who was digging in the culvert, was first alerted by the resounding cheer of the Penydarren men as they rushed to smash down the planking:

> Immediately after they began Foulkes & his men huzza'd – & they huzza'd after they had pull'd down the fence ... The Dowlais Workmen were all at that time working in the Culvert & they were forc'd to go away or they wo'd have been killd & many of them left their Cloaths in the Culvert which was cover'd by the Earth.

Jane Griffiths was also working in the culvert. According to her deposition:

> A great many Penydarren people came there & frightened her very much – they pull'd down the Culvert – the Witness reced a Blow fm some of the Penydarren men on her Head & was kick'd on her Leg – they used very bad Language to the Witness.

Margaret Lewis, another miner, watched the melee from a nearby patch. The commotion drove her from her work in terror:[46]

> She ran away & fell down – She did not faint – She was frightened & everyone ought to be so – She was afraid of her Husband's fighting She tho.t it wo'd be a Rebel – There was no Riot on the Dowlais side ... She heard the Noise, the Women tho.t Mr. Guest would be kill'd.

Margaret Lewis added that she had never seen the Penydarren men 'come up in so large a Body & at such a time of night before'. Nor was she to witness such a sight again, for the pattern of inter-works aggression sponsored by the ironmasters dissolved quite suddenly afterwards. Although Dowlais and Penydarren were embroiled in yet another dispute within the year Homfray was now unusually pacific, urging recourse to a legal settlement:[47]

> 'I think this will be more becoming than what you are now pursuing, by subjecting poor ignorant workmen to danger in consequence of their opposed to each another'.

A year later, the two companies appointed teams of mineral agents, surveyors and attorneys, to settle all their outstanding differences.

IV

Clearly, there was, about 1810, a sea change which swept away the viability of the systematic disturbances that had afflicted the town and its environs for the previous quarter century. The transmutation was simultaneously urban and industrial in character. To deal with the urban aspects first: the fundamental fact of Merthyr as an urban community in the early 1800s was the massive and unrelenting inflow of migrants. The population of the parish increased by 44 per cent between 1801 and 1811. At the third census in 1821 the number of inhabitants had passed 17,000 after a decennial increase of 56 per cent.

The point at which the strains engendered by this prodigious immigration were sensed to be insupportable was signalled by a concatenation of initiatives at the end of the first decade of the nineteenth century. The town's minute and hitherto inconspicuous middle class, huddled in the parish vestry, began to seek the means to penalize proletarian lawlessness. In 1808 the vestry voted funds for building a 'place of confinement for disorderly people'.[48] In 1809, a Court of Requests was established to ease the recovery of small debts.[49] It was complemented within weeks by a 'Society for the Protection of Property in Merthyr Tydfil' to speed the prosecution of felons.[50] The vestrymen were also exercised by the need to shore up the tottering apparatus of parochial administration. During 1811 and 1812, strenuous efforts were made to bolster the beleaguered constabulary, while the revamping of the system of poor relief was proclaimed with the appointment of a salaried general overseer to supervise the overseers of each hamlet.[51]

This burst of parochial activism signalled that it was now inadmissible for the ironmasters to wink at – still less foment – repeated breaches of public order. And, given the increasing tautness of work relations within the giant ironworks, it was doubtful whether they were still in a position to mobilize their workmen as foot soldiers in Merthyr's border wars. By the second decade of the nineteenth century, the earlier buoyancy of the iron industry was faltering as the national economy staggered under the successive impacts of the blockades and counter-blockades that now attended the war against Napoleon, the embargoes which sealed the United States, and the collapse of the South American market in 1810. At the Merthyr works, retrenchment now became the urgent priority: 'the days of pride and profusion are over', it was said at Cyfarthfa, '& a tenacious look out on the contrary tack must take place'.[52]

The drive to economize, whether through direct cuts in piece rates or through the forced redistribution of responsibilities within the workplace, inevitably provoked discord. At Dowlais, the ball-furnacemen went on strike in April 1810 rather than pay their juvenile assistants out of their own pockets, as the Company now insisted.[53] Of course, strikes were no novelty at Merthyr, but from 1810 disputes became sustained and recurrent. Significantly, the stoppage of April 1810 came to be remembered as the 'first' strike. Stoppages by forgemen took on the character of calendar events. By 1813, all the Merthyr works were involved in a strike – or rather, a concerted lock-out – of their puddlers. The response was concerted also. The puddlers, apparently of all the works, bound themselves by what William Crawshay termed a 'Luddite Oath', and sent communiqués into Staffordshire to pre-empt the recruitment of blacklegs.[54]

That conflict was symptomatic of the altered social relations which emerged in Merthyr after 1810. The iron industry continued to enjoy spectacular periods of growth, but these were now interspersed with convulsive downturns. There was no return to the sustained expansion of Merthyr's formative years, when the first fruits of coal technology had coincided with the limitless demands of a war economy. It was during these years of breakneck expansion that the distinctive urban identity of Merthyr Tydfil had evolved, an identity which endured into the mid-Victorian era.[55] It combined a strong sense of 'belonging' to a distinct works-community (nourished by a generation or more of intra-urban conflict) with an equally strong sense of separation from the ironmasters (deriving its strength from the craft protocols of the iron trades).

In explaining this, the categories of 'work' and 'town' are of considerable value. As has been seen, the forms of working that were prevalent in the district were of great moment in the formation of social relations. But it was the *urban* concentration of industry that gave special weight to certain working practices. It is by reference to this urban 'whole' that the peculiarity of the parts is to be best understood. It is not enough to exhume the internal regimes of the different ironworks; their violent interaction must be grasped. For, when a new phase in Merthyr's development opened in the 1810s, modes of working had not been transformed, but they were now practised within changed economic and urban parameters.

Notes

1. This paper is based on research funded by the Economic and Social Research Council between 1984 and 1987, the results of which I have presented more fully in 'Work and authority in an iron town: Merthyr Tydfil, 1760–c.1815' (unpublished PhD thesis, University of London, 1988). I am greatly indebted to the editors of this volume and other participants at the 'Work in Towns' conference for their many helpful comments. Penelope Corfield, in her supervisory capacity, merits special thanks.
2. 'Account of Myrther-tedvel', *Monthly Magazine*, 7 (1799), 356.
3. B.H. Malkin, *The Scenery, Antiquities and Biography of South Wales* (1804), 170.
4. H. Carter and S. Wheatley, *Merthyr Tydfil in 1851: A Study of the Spatial Structure of a Welsh Industrial Town* (University of Wales/Board of Celtic Studies, social science monograph no. 7, 1982), 18.
5. See P. Jenkins, *The Making of a Ruling Class: The Glamorgan Gentry 1640-1790* (1983), 247. And for wider comparison, P.J. Corfield, *The Impact of English Towns 1700-1800* (1982), 168-9.
6. J.G. Wood, *The Principal Rivers of Wales Illustrated* (2 vols, 1813), I, 57.

7. This astounding proposal is recorded in K.O. Morgan, *Rebirth of a Nation: Wales 1880-1980* (1982), 219.

8. M. Atkinson and C. Baber, *The Growth and Decline of the South Wales Iron Industry 1760-1880: An Industrial History* (University of Wales/Board of Celtic Studies, social science monograph no. 9, 1987), 5; and B. Trinder, *The Industrial Revolution in Shropshire* (2nd edn., 1981), 34.

9. J. Lloyd, *The Early History of the Old South Wales Iron Industry 1760-1840* (1906) remains useful: esp. 20–91 for details of the four Merthyr works.

10. Glamorgan RO, D/D G (Dowlais MSS) 1817 (3) G, fo.366, G. Gilpin to W. Wood, 23 September 1817.

11. The standard accounts are T.S. Ashton, *Iron and Steel in the Industrial Revolution* (1924), and A. Birch, *The Economic History of the British Iron and Steel Industry 1784-1879* (1967).

12. L.D. Trotsky, *The History of the Russian Revolution* (1965), 26.

13. National Library of Wales (NLW) Maybery 1904, quoted in H. Jones, *Accounting, Costing and Cost Estimation: Welsh Industry 1700-1830* (1985), 113, n. 46.

14. E.T. Svedenstierna, *Svedenstierna's Tour of Great Britain 1802-3: The Travel Diary of an Industrial Spy* (1973), 55.

15. Statistics collected within the iron trade in 1796 ranked Cyfarthfa as the largest ironworks in the United Kingdom. Its make of 7,204 tons exceeded that of its nearest rival (the Old Park works in Shropshire with an output of 5,952 tons) by a considerable margin. According to the same source, the average yearly make at a British ironworks was 1,562 tons: see Science Museum Library, Weale MSS, 'Account of Furnaces . . . in the year 1796'.

16. Gwent RO, D2.162 (Richard Crawshay's letterbook 1788-97), fo. 35, R. Crawshay to J. Cockshutt, 24 December 1788.

17. For general surveys, see S. Pollard, *The Genesis of Modern Management: A Study of the Industrial Revolution in Great Britain* (1965), and J. Rule, *The Experience of Labour in Eighteenth-Century Industry* (1981).

18. J.H. Manners, *Journal of a Tour through North and South Wales* (1805), 66.

19. See the discussion in S. Pollard, *Genesis*, 38–48.

20. PRO, E112/2094/75.

21. Glamorgan RO, D/D G 1814 A–P, fo. 57, R. Francis to J. J. Guest, 28 February 1814.

22. Glamorgan RO, D/D G 1804 A–W, fos. 181 and 183, W. Taitt to T. Guest, 24 and 26 June 1804.

23. Glamorgan RO, D/D G 1803 R–W, fo. 637, W. Taitt to T. Guest, 16 January 1803.

24. R. Price, 'Structures of subordination in nineteenth-century British industry', in *The Power of the Past: Essays for Eric Hobsbawm*, ed. P. Thane, G. Crossick and R. Floud (1984), 119.

25. NLW, Maybery 2448, R. Hill to W. and J. Powell, n.d.

26. Gloucestershire RO, Hale MSS D1086/F116, W. Lewis to J. Blagden Hale, 12 March 1785.

27. Gwent RO, D2.162, fo. 215, R. Crawshay to J. Wilkinson, 15 February 1797.

28. Statute 39 & 40 Geo.III c. 77. The draft bill was approved at a meeting of ironmasters and coal-owners at the Star Inn, Merthyr in April 1800. Glamorgan RO, D/D G 1800 A–T, fo. 69, printed circular dated 3 March 1800.

29. G.A. Williams, *The Merthyr Rising* (1978), 52. This book is a summation of Professor Williams's extensive researches and writings in his native town, writings which have inspired and influenced me far more than a single footnote can suggest.

30. Glamorgan RO, D/D G 1803 R–W, fo. 713, W. Taitt to T. Guest, 1 September 1803.

31. Gwent RO, D2.162, fo. 136, R. Crawshay to Lord Hawkesbury, 6 May 1793; BL, Add. MS 38,229, fo. 36, R. Thompson to R. Crawshay, 13 May 1793; and Glamorgan RO, D/D G 1793 P–W, fo. 525, W. Taitt to R. Thompson, 2 November 1793.

32. C. Wilkins, *The History of Merthyr Tydfil* (2nd ed., 1908), 245; Glamorgan RO, D/D G copy letters 1782–94, fo. 518, R. Thompson to W. Taitt, 8 March 1793; and J.H. Manners, *Journal*, 66.

33. Glamorgan RO, D/D G 1801 B–T, fo. 405, W. Lewis to T. Guest, 29 May 1801.

34. D.J.V. Jones, 'The Merthyr riots of 1800: a study in attitudes', *Bulletin of the Board of Celtic Studies*, 23 (1969), 166–79.

35. Glamorgan RO, Q/SR 1797 C, fo. 49, appeal against the poor rate for Gellideg hamlet, dated 1 July 1797.

36. B.S. Osborne, 'Patching, scouring and commoners: the development of an early industrial landscape', *Industrial Archaeology Review*, 1 (1976), 37–42, is, to my knowledge, unique in giving a proper recognition to the importance of these extractive techniques.

37. BL, Add. MS 38,347, fo. 9, 'Examination of Mr. Richard Crawshay and Mr. Joseph Stanley 11th August 1782'.

38. Glamorgan RO, D/D G copy letters 1782–94, fos. 16–19, J. Guest to T. Harris, 19 August 1782.

39. Glamorgan RO, D/D G 1806 A–T, fo.32, J. Fowler to ?, 6 April 1806.

40. NLW, Maybery 2484, R. Hill to J. Powell, 30 July 1794.

41. NLW, Maybery 2490, R. Hill to W. and J. Powell, 20 January 1795. See also: other correspondence in the Maybery collection (NLW, Maybery 2482–83); the proceedings of the case in the Court of Chancery (PRO, C13/2394/Hill vs. Glamorgan Canal Navigation); and materials *re* the canal in the Bute MSS deposited at Cardiff Central Library (CCL), Bute I. Crawshay's domination of the canal was eventually to create bad feeling with all the neighbouring ironmasters: see C. Hadfield, *The Canals of South Wales and the Border* (1967), 95–7.

42. Glamorgan RO, D/D G copy letters 1782–94, fo. 209, W. Taitt to S. Homfray, 1 February 1786.

43. CCL MS 2.716(1/3), fos. 23 and 31, Diary of John Bird, 9 September 1791 and 22 August 1792.

44. Glamorgan RO, D/D G copy letters 1782–94, fo. 637, R. Thompson to W. Taitt, 12 December 1793.

45. Glamorgan RO, D/D G Section B, Box 8, memorandum dated 18 July 1794.

46. Glamorgan RO, Q/SR 1810 A, unsorted, miscellaneous depositions; Glamorgan RO, Q/SI 5/1197, indictment of J.J. Guest, Thomas John Harry and Evan Evans.

47. Glamorgan RO, D/D G Section B, Box 8, S. Homfray to Dowlais Company, 19 November 1810.

48. Merthyr Public Library (MPL), Merthyr Tydfil Vestry Minutebook, 1799–1833, fo. 118, 8 and 21 July 1808.

49. *Cambrian*, 30 September 1809.

50. *Cambrian*, 11 November 1809.

51. MPL, Merthyr Vestry Minutebook, fos.154–5, 22 June 1811, and fos.170–3, 1 May 1812. The profile of parish expenditure for the years 1813–15, given in 'Abstract of returns relative to the expense and maintenance of the poor', *BPP* 1818, Vol.XIX, 616–17, hints at the harsher regime.

52. NLW, Cyfarthfa MSS Vol. 1, William Crawshay Letterbook 1813–16, W. Crawshay to W. Crawshay jr., 21 August 1813.

53. Glamorgan RO, D/D G 1810 T–W, fo. 210, W. Taitt to A. Kirkwood, 30 April 1810.

54. NLW, Cyfarthfa MSS Vol. 1, W. Crawshay to W. Crawshay jr., 18 May 1813; Glamorgan RO, D/D G 1813 T–W, fo. 299, W. Taitt to A. Kirkwood, 6 June 1813.

55. See D. Jones and A. Bainbridge, 'The "Conquering of China": crime in an industrial community', *Llafur*, 2 (1979), 28–31 for details of the 'conservative cultural forces' operating in Merthyr by the 1850s and for comparison with developments in industrial towns in England.

9 Urbanization, social structure and population circulation in pre-industrial times: flows of people through Vadstena (Sweden) in the mid-nineteenth century

John Langton and Göran Hoppe

The tendency for urban and rural to be conceptualized separately in the study of social and economic change during early modern times has increased as work has become both more theoretically informed and more quantitatively based. Furthermore, it is now common to treat the level of 'demographic urbanization' (i.e. the proportion of the population of a territorial area that lives in places designated as towns) as a reflection of, and therefore an easily calculable surrogate for, the degree of economic advancement and social modernization that has occurred within a territory.[1]

This interpretation is supported by a wide variety of general ideas about the interaction of economic and social change incorporated into research on the pre-industrial period. These suggest that modern economies and societies came into being when rural backwardness was eroded by the penetration into rural areas, through market exchange and other forms of interaction, of quite different, more 'modern' economic imperatives, social values and cultural traits developed in towns. Markets and money are urban in provenance.[2] So are bourgeois, then industrial-capitalist modes of economic production[3] and 'large-scale, co-ordinated activities' of all kinds.[4] The social relations consequent upon this mode of production (i.e. when work is financed and organized in pursuit of maximal monetary profit by a bourgeoisie owning the means of production, and done by a proletariat in return for money wages) have enormous social and cultural significance. They produce 'societies' rather than 'communities', in which interpersonal relations between alienated individuals are mediated by the cash nexus rather than moral obligation. Towns thus encapsulate both a 'way of work' and a 'way of life'.[5] The involvement of larger and larger proportions of national populations in these modes of working and living can for brevity's sake be termed the process of 'socio-economic urbanization'. Eventually, as this proportion becomes preponderant, all areas, both urban and rural, become homogenized according to these imperatives, so that 'today one speaks of the urbanization of society'.[6]

Thus, the purely quantitative process of demographic urbanization is readily equated with the qualitative transformation brought by the development, intensification and diffusion of dynamic economic systems, social institutions and human values of a recognizably 'modern' form. Equally readily, these can be contrasted with and set against the economic backwardness and social archaism of rural peasantry. The upshot is a conceptualization which attributes enormous significance to the changing proportions of people who live in towns rather than in the countryside. Moreover, it is not simply that urban and rural are separated and opposed in this conceptualization, before the latter becomes an archaic residuum: both categories are tacitly imbued with intrinsic natures which are both coherent and autonomous, and thus capable of historical and geographical generalization.[7]

The emphasis on the fundamental and universal differences between urban and rural, and of the significance of the former as the motor of long-run historical change, have been given further support by the increased use of quantitative data (mainly derived from decennial censuses) which has accompanied the growing concern with generalization. 'For the innocent theorist, to live somewhere sometime implies a durable attachment to the place. For the actual collector of the information, however, physical presence on census day ... is commonly all that matters.'[8]

Cross-sectional data inevitably display for us, after we have solved (or fudged) the preliminary problem of classifying places consistently through time and space as either urban or rural, two mutually exclusive sets of people. No one can be in two places at once. Everyone must be *either* urban *or* rural in cross-sectional data. Because of this, it is easy to slip into the calculation of urban population growth rates, and beyond them in various directions. We can calculate the changing proportional shares of the two groups, or speculate about the economic and social implications of urban size distributions and their changes,[9] or about the extent and significance of the process of rural-urban migration which causes the proportional shares to alter.[10] Thus, the statistical categories we use to organize our data are inextricably related to the general conceptions deployed in the theoretical speculations we incorporate (even if only implicitly) into our empirical work.

Of course, a considerable body of research has now accumulated, which suggests that early development may be primarily a rural process – whether in the 'Green Revolution' of the Third World or in the development of agrarian capitalism or of rural proto-industrialization in early modern Western Europe.[11] However, these interpretations usually keep the urban/rural distinction intact, merely switching attention from one separated component to the other.

Whilst the conceptual and empirical separation between urban and rural has gained widespread currency in historical work on Europe, the opposite view that a primal distinction between urban and rural obscures much more than it reveals about the processes of economic and social change has also been expressed.[12] Although not widely accepted (or, at least, not widely reflected in the conceptualization of research and synoptic writings), this view is given considerable support by detailed research in currently developing countries. It may well be instructive for researchers into the development of early modern Europe to discover why this is so.

Statistical indices of urban population growth rates and the extent of rural-urban migration in Third World countries used to be calculated as avidly as they now are for early modern Western Europe. But they rarely seemed to correlate as well as urbanization theory predicts they should with other indicators of social and economic change. Urban populations have increased massively in numerical and proportional terms, but without the diffusion of capitalist economic structures or social transformation: demographic urbanization has occurred without socio-economic urbanization.[13] Tribalism, the extended family and other 'traditional' or 'rural' systems of social interaction based upon moral obligation rather than the cash nexus not only survive, but seem to be intensified by urban living in Africa.[14] Just as urban life is not associated, as urbanization theory predicts it should be, with personal individuation and alienation, neither are the townsfolk of the developing world proletarianized, but they are massively dependent on irregular, informal sources of income outside the wage labour market in the so-called 'bazaar economy' or 'lower circuit of capital'.[15] The cities of the developing world have a 'dual economy' in which a small Westernized enclave, which does represent urban economic and social life as represented in theory, coexists with, and does not destroy, a much larger sector. What were once thought to be 'pre-urban', 'traditional' or 'rural' values, patterns of behaviour and modes of economic organization and interaction not only survive, but flourish there and ramify as demographic urbanization proceeds.

A homogeneous urban reality does not exist. A vast numerical and proportional expansion of the urban population is not necessarily associated with fundamental economic and social changes. The statistical process of demographic urbanization cannot, in the presently developing world, be used as a surrogate for the economic, social behavioural and psychological changes usually taken to comprise the socio-economic process of urbanization.

Census-type cross-sectional data of the kind used to calculate urban and rural or economic sectoral proportions and rates of rural-urban migration give a very misleading picture of the social and economic attributes of a population. The rapid demographic urbanization which they reveal is a chimerical indicator of economic and cultural changes, because in developing countries most urban dwellers live in towns for very short periods of their lives and depend on particular sources of income for even shorter spells. Very few individuals are either 'rural' or 'urban', peasant or wage-earning, 'traditional' or 'modern', throughout their lives, or exclusively one or the other for significant lengths of time. There are not 'urban-rural migration streams' and a consequent 'urbanization' of the population, but vast and ceaseless circulations of people back and forth between town and country, traditional and modern economic sectors and cultures.[16]

It might be argued that these findings have no relevance to Europe in the past because they represent the economic and social consequences of colonialism and systems of rural land tenure that serve, particularly over much of Africa, to retain for life people's contact with the land they have a right to work, preventing them from capitalizing its value. However, it may well be the case that the difference between what is happening in Africa and what is believed to have been the case in nineteenth-century Europe results from the reliance on census data for our knowledge of the latter case, whereas in the former we can actually make observations of current reality.

Indeed, recent research has discovered that net migration figures disguise an enormous throughflow of short-stay migrants in cities on the north-eastern seaboard of the United States in the nineteenth century,[17] and there is evidence that things were not very different, either, in nineteenth-century Europe. Circulation rather than rural-urban migration was characteristic of late nineteenth-century Russia where, in consequence, an urban proletariat failed to develop, and of Rhineland-Westphalia at the same time.[18] Anderson's work demonstrates that there were symptoms of a similar state of affairs in nineteenth-century England.[19] If this pattern was widespread, we would need to think very hard about the relevance of most received theorizing about the process of urbanization in early modern and nineteenth-century Europe, and about the dichotomous rural/urban conceptualization upon which this theorizing is based.[20] Certainly, we would have to question what economic and social significance can be read into statistics which simply chart changing proportions of people living in towns rather than the countryside.

And it might well simply be that this situation has not so far been recognized as widespread because the available quantitative source materials generally provide only cross-sectional data which are by nature incapable of revealing it. As soon as people are considered longitudinally – that is, as living continuously through whole life-times rather than momentarily whilst a census count is made – some awkward questions about the urbanization process arise immediately. What does a statement such as '10 per cent of the country's population lived in towns on the day that a count was taken' actually mean? Only if 10 per cent of the people spent the whole, or most, of their lives in towns would the statistic automatically carry the interpretation that '10 per cent of the country's population was urban' in the full theoretically meaningful economic, social and cultural sense of the term 'urban' as elucidated above. But what if the statistic reflects a situation in which everyone in the population spent 10 per cent of their life-times in towns? It might then be the case that 'urban' social and economic attributes would in consequence spread more quickly through the whole population. However, it might also be that the opposite would occur. Towns might be 'ruralized', with the traditional cultural attributes, social structures and economic values of the countryside being characteristic of town life. We then have 'cities of peasants', to use the title of a recent book on Third World urban growth.[21] What the particular effect would be might be questioned, but that there would be *some* real difference in the 'degree of urbanization' of the two '10 per cent urban' populations cannot be disputed. And surely in the second case it would not only be futile, but positively misleading, to classify the population into separate and different 'urban' and 'rural' categories, implying that the distinction carried unequivocal economic and social meaning?

How can we learn the extent to which these cautions should be applied in the interpretation of the development process in Western Europe? To discover the extent of urban-rural circulation in a population requires longitudinal rather than cross-sectional data. That is, information not simply on how many people were where doing what at particular points in time, but exactly who was where doing what throughout the whole of their life-times. Perhaps it is the general absence of such data which is responsible for our not having addressed historically the kinds of questions which exercise demographers, geographers, economists and sociologists working on modern developing countries. However, it is possible in some places to assemble longitudinal data sets, and therefore to examine these kinds of questions. One country where this can be done from the eighteenth century onwards is Sweden. What follows is an examination of some aspects of the flows of people through the Swedish town of Vadstena in the early nineteenth century. Situated on the eastern shore of Lake Vättern, and complete with castle, pre-Reformation monastery, guilds and the Swedish equivalent of burghal status, Vadstena was the chief central place and mercantile centre of the fertile arable plain of western Östergötland (the plains are depicted as the unshaded area within the provincial boundary on Fig. 9.5). From the early eighteenth century, the region of the Östergötland plains around Vadstena was largely under peasant freehold tenure.[22]

A priori, Sweden might be expected to fit the model which equates development with urbanization very well. In European terms, it was a peripheral and backward country in the early nineteenth century. In 1860, Scandinavian GDP per head was only 49 per cent of that in Great Britain and 88 per cent of that in Eastern and Western Europe as a whole. According to its excellent censuses, 72 per cent of Sweden's labour force was still employed in agriculture in 1870 (comparable with Spain, Portugal and Hungary, and considerably more than in Denmark and Norway).[23] It was well on the road to becoming one of the continent's wealthiest and most socially progressive nations by the second quarter of the twentieth century.[24] The province of Östergötland followed these national trends quite closely. The transformation was associated with a massive increase in the urban proportion of the population, which had only grown from 9.8 per cent to 11.3 per cent between 1800 and 1860.[25] Stockholm, the largest city by far, grew from 75,517 in 1800 to 93,070 in 1850, when only five towns had more than 10,000 people, and Vadstena's population of 2,225 made it Sweden's 34th and Östergötland's third largest town.[26] Quantitatively negligible as it may appear to have been, this urban system was sharply distinguished constitutionally as a separate estate of the realm, and by guild and other privileges whose purpose was to limit craft, mercantile and administrative activities to within its confines, until the wholesale economic, social and constitutional reforms which destroyed the Swedish *ancien régime* in the 1840s, 1850s and 1860s.[27] Moreover, it had functioned as an *integrated* system since long before that time, and the benificence of this for the process of economic growth and social change in this indubitably pre-industrial economy has recently been stressed.[28] By 1913, when Stockholm contained 382,085 people, the proportion of the Swedish population living in towns had reached 26.4 per cent. It had passed 50 per cent by 1950.[29]

Thus, urban seems clearly to have been separated from rural in pre-industrial Sweden, and economic development and social change seem to have marched together with demographic urbanization in the transformation of what appears previously to have been an archetypally-backward peasant society and economy.[30] The conventional model of an autonomous urban reality expanding to transform the whole national economy and society seems readily applicable to macro-economic and demographic census data for Sweden. However, because of the wealth of Swedish sources of data besides the highly-aggregated cross-sectional censuses, we can also test how far this was actually so, and discover how far rural-urban population circulation acted to dissolve any simple distinction between the urban and rural categories.

That is the general question we will be trying to answer in the following analysis of the longitudinal life-paths of people who lived in Vadstena between 1855 and 1860. In particular, we are concerned with four questions. Firstly, was there an integral town population? And how far were Vadstena's economy and society produced and reproduced by native permanent residents of the town, and how far by streams of people passing through it? Secondly, if the latter predominated, did the flows of people through the town serve to integrate Vadstena into a larger urban system, or into its rural surroundings? Thirdly, if the latter, how far is it possible to adduce from the patterns of population flows between the town and the countryside whether their net effect would be to 'ruralize' the town, or to 'urbanize' the countryside? Fourthly and more generally, how far anyway is it reasonable to imply, through data classification, that people existed in either urban or rural categories which were both mutually exclusive and internally consistent through time? In considering this particular question, we will also refer to data for the neighbouring town of Motala to illustrate the deep contrasts that existed between contemporary urban experiences and, by extension, between the very different rural systems of production with which they were linked through population movement.

Our discussion will be based on two sets of data drawn from *husförhörslängder*.[31] The first set of data we have abstracted represents information on the places of birth, last residence and next residence of all the people who lived in Vadstena as non-dependents, in their own or others' households, whilst the register for 1855–60 was in use. That is, it contains all the residential information presented for everyone except dependent children. These data are not so easy to relate to our questions as might at first sight appear. The registration of changes of address within the town as changes of place of residence, with a new household entry made at the new address, means both that there is multiple counting of internal migrants and also that a large proportion of the inhabitants have Vadstena addresses recorded as their places of last and next residence. Therefore, where they lived before coming to the town, and the date of their entry into and/or exit from it, and thus the length of time they stayed in it, cannot be discovered in this way. The second set of data comprises detailed life-path reconstructions for a sample of 87 people drawn from the registers of Vadstena and some neighbouring rural parishes in 1855 and traced forward and backward through the registers of all the other parishes in which they lived between birth and death. Some individuals could not, in fact, be discovered in the registers of one of the parishes to or from which they were recorded, elsewhere, as having moved, so that they pass out of observation. Yet it was possible to reconstruct complete life-paths for almost all of the people in this sample. The tables[32] and maps in Figs. 9.4 and 9.5 are drawn from the first set of data, the diagrams in Figs. 9.1–3 from the second.

Of course, it is necessary to classify people in order to analyse this mass of information. Although we have done so quite finely for other purposes and in the diagrams, we have used a crude classification in most of the tables presented here. In order to get the main general patterns across clearly, in most of the tables we have merely distinguished between 'patricians' and 'plebeians' and adults and juveniles.[33] We will discuss each of these dimensions of classification briefly before presenting our results.

The first distinguishes between those who might be expected to be most fully urban in occupation and outlook, whom we have called patricians (the craftsmen, merchants, administrators and professionals who were trained for specifically urban functions, ran the town and belonged to its institutions), and those who might be suspected of being considerably less peculiarly urban in the kind of work they did and the associations to which they belonged, whom we have called plebeians (the workmen, labourers, hands and maids). The latter group of occupations was largely identical with the menial opportunities also available in the countryside. Hands were males who fetched, carried and did other menial duties under the supervision of the head of the household in which they lived as non-kin members. Maids performed domestic duties under the supervision of the housewife on the same basis. Both hands and maids would fall within the designation 'servant', although doubtless hands gained some conversance with the more menial aspects of a craft if they lived in a craftsman's household. A workman (*arbetare*, of which 'labourer' would be as good a translation) performed the same duties as a hand, but worked for wages and lived in a household of his own and would probably have been even more involved in the menial aspects of the productive process in craftsmen's households. The large numbers of bellringers, watchmen and nightwatchmen have been classified with the labourers as adult plebeians. Whether they occupied the lowest level of service provision for the urban community full-time, or whether these were honorary ascriptions, or whether the designations simply indicate that these people were in receipt of small sinecures for the performance of occasional or part-time duties, is not clear. Whatever the exact case, they seem to have been little different from labourers, except that they were often considerably older. It seems reasonable to surmise that if any rural-urban circulation occurred, similar to that through the 'lower circuit of capital' in the towns of today's developing world, it would be through these plebeian livelihood positions.

The distinction between adults and juveniles is also based on commonsense notions. The adults maintained, worked and lived in their own family households,

Table 9.1 Average ages of the people classified into various adult and juvenile categories from the *husförhörslängder* of Vadstena 1855–60

Occupational category	N	Average year of birth	Percentage with known date of inmigration	Average age at inmigr.	Percentage moving both in and out 1855–60
Adults					
Traders (I)	50	1818	29	31 yrs.	13
Craftsmen (I)	171	1820	25	30 yrs.	6
Workmen (II)	232	1820	28	33 yrs.	5
Juveniles					
Apprentices (V)	149	1839	52	18 yrs.	17
Shop Assts. (V)	44	1837	80	19 yrs.	30
Journeymen (V)	198	1830	64	26 yrs.	43
Hands (VI)	168	1830	62	25 yrs.	26

and juveniles – apprentices, shop assistants, most journeymen, hands and maids – both lived and worked in the households of others. The distinction is not an absolutely precise one because it represents both a life-cycle stage and status relative to the head of household for whom work was done, as recorded in the occupational ascriptions of the registers, rather than simply age. It is possible that some maids in particular (because there is no equivalent terminological distinction for females to that between male hands and workmen) were, in fact, adults living in their own separate households. However, as Table 9.1 shows, those whom we have classified as juvenile on the basis of occupational ascription were generally much younger than those classified as adults on the same basis. Consultation of the town's *mantalslängder*[34] corroborates that all but a very few of them lived in the households of others. Nonetheless, the perhaps surprisingly high average ages of some of the juvenile categories reflects the existence of a small number of people who were called maid, journeyman or hand even though they were well into (or even beyond) middle age, with families and households of their own.

Table 9.2 shows the proportions of the non-dependent townspeople in each of these groups according to the *husförhörslängder* and according to the *mantals-längder* in 1850. Figures for other groups have been included for comparative purposes. They show – not surprisingly given the turnover figures in the last column of Table 9.1 – that the householding adult groups are more heavily represented in the snapshot picture given by the *mantalslängder*, and the juvenile groups much less so. Because all who lived in Vadstena at some time between 1855 and 1860 are included in the *husförhörslängder* figures of column B, groups comprising more mobile juveniles are more heavily represented there than in the tax figures of column A. However, the whole of society was astonishingly mobile. The differences between the total numbers in each group do not reflect massive population growth between 1855 and 1860, but the very high frequency with which people in all walks of life moved into and out of the town, as demonstrated by Table 9.1, and changed their address within it.

Figure 9.1 makes this point even more emphatically. On it, each line represents the life-path of an individual, with years from birth marked on the horizontal axis, tracing each change of residence from birth to death or the time at which they fall out of observation. The lines are grouped according to the occupations of the people

Table 9.2 Population structure of Vadstena according to the *mantalslängder* of 1850 (A), and the *husförhörslängder* of 1855–60 (B)

Group		Number		Percentage	
		A	B	A	B
I	Adult Patrician	135	310	19	13
II	Adult Plebeian	127	303	18	13
III	Widows & Spinsters	153	384	21	16
V	Apprentices etc.	88	391	12	17
VI	Young Hands & Maids	207	954	29	41
	Totals	710	2342	99	100

Table 9.3 Places of previous and subsequent residence of patricians and plebeians who lived in Vadstena 1855–60

A *Percentage figures*

	Total non-dependent population	Patricians		Plebeians	
		Adult	Juvenile	Adult	Juvenile
Birthplace					
Vadstena	15	13	17	12	9
Other town	13	31	24	8	6
Rural	72	56	59	80	84
Last residence					
Vadstena	57	66	34	73	49
Other town	14	18	44	5	7
Rural	28	16	23	23	44
Next residence					
No change	46	58	37	53	38
Other Vadstena	32	30	21	37	35
Other town	9	8	23	3	8
Rural	10	4	5	8	19
Unknown	2	0	14	0	0

B *Figures in A expressed as deviations away from those for total non-dependent population*

Vadstena					
Birthplace	15	–2	+2	–3	–6
Last residence	57	+9	–23	+16	–8
Next residence	78	+10	–20	+12	–5
Other towns					
Birthplace	13	+18	+11	–5	–7
Last residence	14	+4	+30	–9	–7
Next residence	9	–1	+14	–6	–1
Rural places					
Birthplace	72	–16	–13	+8	+12
Last residence	28	–12	–5	–5	+16
Next residence	10	–6	–5	–2	+9
Unknown					
Next residence	2	–2	+12	–2	–2

C *Figures in B expressed as percentage deviations away from those for all non-dependents*

Vadstena					
Birthplace		–13	+13	–20	–40
Last residence		+13	–40	+28	–14
Next residence		+13	–26	+15	–6
Other towns					
Birthplace		+138	+85	–39	–53
Last residence		+29	+214	–64	–50
Next residence		–11	+156	–67	–11
Rural places					
Birthplace		–22	–18	+11	+17
Last residence		–43	–18	–18	+57
Next residence		–60	–50	–20	+90

concerned, designated by the letter codes at the beginning of the lines (a key to this code appears in Fig. 9.2). The sample of 47 individuals included was drawn from the *husförhörslängd* of 1855–60 to give a reasonable representation of all occupational and life-cycle categories.[35] A change of residence is marked by a vertical peck across a life-line. The way in which the line is drawn designates whether the place of residence is urban or rural (solid or dotted), local, elsewhere in the province of Östergötland, elsewhere in Sweden (fine, medium or bold thickness) or abroad (wavy line). Vadstena, Stockholm and Gothenburg are indicated by their initial letters. Thus, the information on Fig. 9.1 is very generalized and the spatial categories are highly aggregated. Nonetheless, it reveals much more fully the nature of the massive residential mobility shown in the tables. It was normal for people to change their place of residence at all stages of the life-cycle. Although there was a tendency for this mobility to be at its most frenetic when people were in their twenties, everyone had moved, some two or three times, by their early teens, and everyone continued to move about until their sixties and seventies if they lived so long.

Table 9.3A shows that only 15 per cent of the people listed in the *husförhörs-längder* were born in the town (although 15 out of the 47 in the life-path sample in Fig. 9.1 were because that sample deliberately sought to concentrate on 'urbanite' groups), and that 21 per cent of them moved out of it during the five years. Table 9.3A also shows that the pattern of these movements varied considerably between the groups we have isolated for consideration. Tables 9.3B and 9.3C are attempts to make the extent of these differences clearer. The patricians had far stronger connections with other towns than had the plebeians. Although 72 per cent of the townspeople were born in the countryside, rural origins were considerably less prevalent than average among patricians and much more so among the plebeian

Table 9.4 Birthplaces of non-native born residents of Vadstena 1855–60

Group		Born in	Per cent urban	Per cent rural	Total per cent
I	a	Adjacent Hundreds	–	17	17
	b	Rest of Östergd.	9	26	35
	c	Elsewhere	27	22	49
II	a	Adjacent Hundreds	–	33	33
	b	Rest of Östergd.	3	43	46
	c	Elsewhere	6	14	20
V	a	Adjacent Hundreds	–	27	27
	b	Rest of Östergd.	7	19	26
	c	Elsewhere	22	26	48
VI	a	Adjacent Hundreds	–	44	44
	b	Rest of Östergd.	3	35	38
	c	Elsewhere	4	14	18

population. We see the opposite when we look at the proportions born in other towns, where the adult patricians were two-and-a-half times more likely to have had their birthplace than the average citizen. The juvenile patricians were rather less markedly urban-born than their adult counterparts, and the plebeians less than half as likely as average to be urban-born.

It was not simply that these social and age groupings differed in terms of the extent to which they were urban- or rural-born. Table 9.4 shows that this difference was paralleled by differences in the distances they had travelled between birth and their stay in Vadstena. Patricians, even if rural-born, generally originated at much greater distances from the town. More than twice as many adult patricians had been born outside the county of Östergötland than adult plebeians, whilst less than half as many had been born in the 23 rural parishes of the two hundreds immediately surrounding the town. The juveniles were rather different. Young plebeians were even more likely to have been born in the rural hundreds adjacent to Vadstena than their adult counterparts, whilst a much higher proportion of young patricians had been born in all rural areas, but especially the local ones, than their adult counterparts. Moreover, as Table 9.3 shows, the patricians much more frequently moved to Vadstena directly from another town. That seems to have been especially true of the juveniles (which may be because many youngsters had moved to the town very recently and not yet changed address within it, whilst adults were highly likely to have a previous Vadstena address registered as their last place of residence). Only the juvenile patricians moved on to other towns more frequently than the average, which they exceeded by a very considerable margin.

The differences between the highly-aggregated group data presented in the tables are stark enough, but there are far wider ones between some of the smaller, and therefore more precisely defined and uniform, categories that are lumped together within those groups. The differences in out-movement patterns between 'urbanized' and 'non-urbanized' townsmen, for example, are illustrated most sharply by a comparison of the destination of people described as hands (i.e. young

Table 9.5 Destinations of hands and journeymen who left Vadstena, 1855–60

	Hands	Journeymen
Number recorded	168	198
Per cent changing place of residence	63	69
Per cent of moves within Vadstena	59	28
Per cent of moves to rural local Hundreds	26	2
Per cent of moves to all local places	84	28
Per cent of moves to other rural places	7	1
Per cent of moves to towns in Östergöt.	2	8
Per cent of moves to more distant towns	8	28
Per cent of moves to all distant places	16	37
Per cent of moves to unknown destinations	0	34

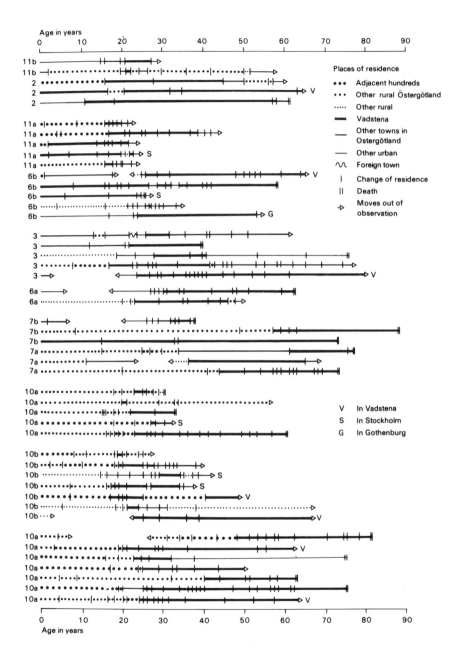

Figure 9.1. Life-time migration histories of 47 people sampled from the *husförhörslängder* of Vadstena in 1855. See legend of Fig. 9.2 for occupational categories.

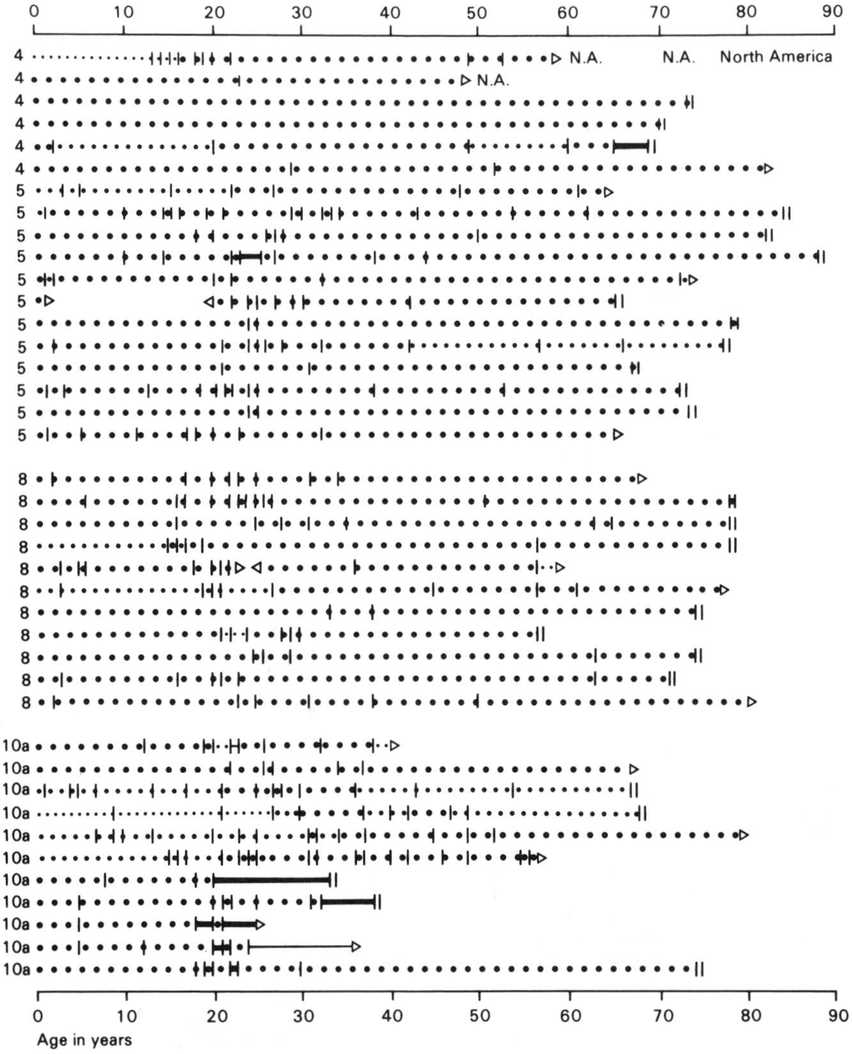

Figure 9.2. Life-time migration histories of 40 people sampled from the *husförhörslängder* of rural parishes around Vadstena in 1855. Classification of places on life-lines as on Fig. 9.1

Occupational categories

1	Official	6a	Independent craftsman	10a	Hand; labourer; workman
2	Trader	6b	Journeyman	10b	Maid
3	Master craftsman	7a	Widow	11a	Apprentice
4	Farmer > quarter mantal	7b	Spinster	11b	Shop assistant
5	Farmer ≤ quarter mantal	8	Crofter; soldier	12	Living in
		9	Cottager	13	Destitute

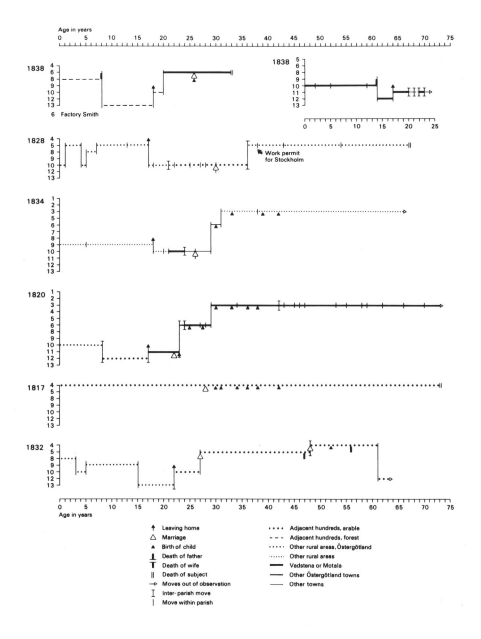

Figure 9.3. Changes in place of residence, social and family status of 7 people sampled from the *husförhörslängder* of Vadstena and neighbouring rural parishes in 1855.

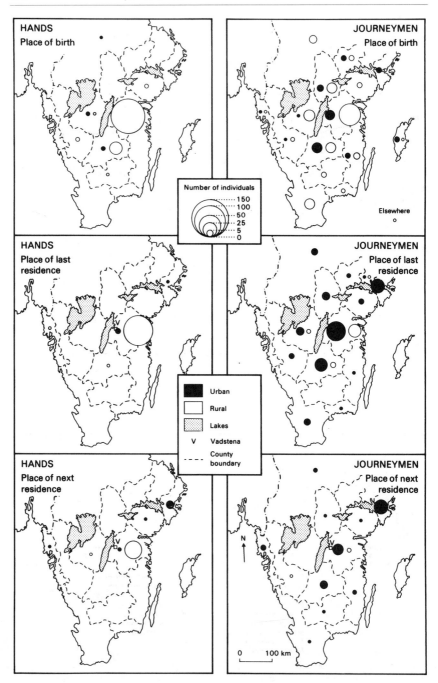

Figure 9.4. Places of birth, last residence and next residence of journeymen and hands registered in the *husförhörslängder* of Vadstena, 1855–60, by county.

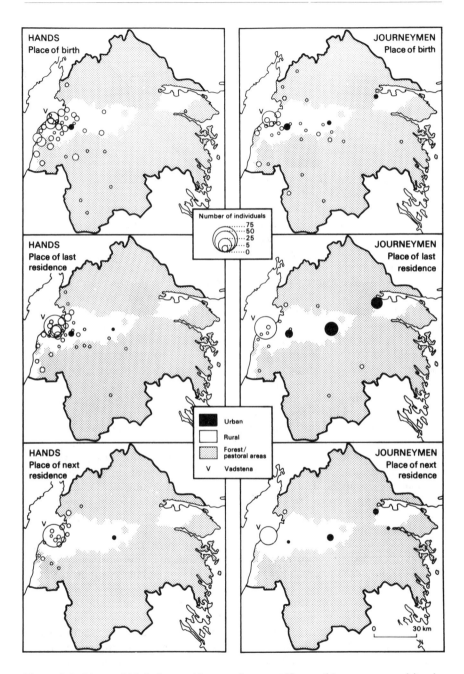

Figure 9.5. Places of birth, last residence and next residence of journeymen and hands registered in the *husförhörslängder* of Vadstena 1855–60, by parish within the county of Östergötland.

plebeians) and journeymen (i.e. young patricians whose training was complete) when they left Vadstena. Table 9.5 and Figs. 9.4 and 9.5 show this contrast. Although the hands were more likely to move out to another town (especially Stockholm) than they were to have moved into Vadstena from one, their destinations were still, like their origins, overwhelmingly narrowly local and rural. The journeymen moved even more frequently than the hands. In further and greater contrast, 8 per cent of them moved on to urban destinations in Östergötland, nearly 40 per cent to towns further afield, and it can reasonably be assumed that the additional 34 per cent who were permitted to move speculatively to an unknown destination[36] were most likely to end up in similar places.

The differences we have described in proportions born, last resident and next resident in towns and rural areas and in the geographical catchment areas of the different groups show some strong general contrasts in the characteristic life-paths of patricians and plebeians, contrasts which are displayed equally starkly and in considerably more detail by the diagrammatic representations of sample life-paths on Figs. 9.1–3. The sizes of the locational categories used in the construction of these diagrams ensures that most movements occurred within them. Even so, over 40 of the life-lines of the Vadstena residents depicted in Fig. 9.1 contain at least one transition from rural to urban (dotted to solid line) or local to or from more distant places (thicker to thinner line or vice versa). The urban birthplaces of most patricians, and their uniformly urban adult life-times, with a substream of apprentices drawn from rural homes for future urban lives, are also clearly depicted in Fig. 9.1. So are the uniformly rural origins of the urban plebeians, although the movement back and forth between urban and rural places of residence, though apparent on eleven of the life-lines, was not so prevalent amongst this sample as it was amongst the whole population, or the hands in particular, as depicted in the tables. The 40 rural life-paths depicted in Fig. 9.2 show the movements of people sampled from the 1855 *husförhörslängder* of three rural parishes near Vadstena. They offer a complete contrast. Most of these residents of the countryside in 1855 had spent the whole of their lives there, even though, except for the larger farmers, they moved about with an alacrity equal to that of the townsmen, sometimes over considerable distances. Thus, as in the modern developing world, although a majority of townsmen had rural origins, and moved back and forth between town and countryside, the proportion of the total rural population with any experience at all of urban living was very small indeed.

Fig. 9.3 provides even more detailed information on the life-paths of seven individuals, including occupational changes and vital and family events. Of course, it would be improper to generalize from this small sample, but these more complex life-lines can be used to illustrate in more detail some of the general points we have already made. The second-from-bottom example illustrates even more clearly than Fig. 9.2 the spatial immobility of the freeholding farming population, which sharply marked off those who inherited land from the rest of society. The example above it shows the career of a rural-born person who became first an apprentice, then a journeyman, then a master craftsman in town, and who continued to change places of residence through the process of family formation, which also spanned his progression from apprentice to master: life-cycle stages were not so neatly related to changes in occupation and place of domicile as we might expect them to have been. The second-from-top and bottom examples show the careers of persons who were, at their peak, small farmers.[37] Both were considerably more mobile than the large farmer discussed earlier, the second only acquiring his farm when, as a widowed crofter,[38] he married a farmer's widow. The third-from-top example shows the typically short urban sojourn of a rural cottager's son who, after shifting around between town and country as a hand, then spent two years as an urban independent craftsman before acquiring the lease of a large farm. As far as any single individual can, this man typifies the complete interpenetration between urban and rural occupations amongst the plebeian population.

Thus, the tables and figures show an identical general pattern, embellished by progressively greater amounts of detail. Urban plebeians were country born, moved to the nearest town for a short while, then usually subsided back into the local countryside. Their changes of place of residence were frequent throughout their life-cycle, but only very rarely did these moves take them to town, most usually, as in the third-from-top example in Fig. 9.3, in their early twenties. Some stayed in the local town for the rest of their lives; a few moved on to other towns, especially the capital city, or distant rural areas; but a large majority stayed only a short while and went off to shuffle around again through a variety of menial occupations in the immediately surrounding countryside. The urban plebeian population was highly transient and its members' numerous sojourns and moves in the local rural area suggest that that is where they were at home. The patricians were also highly likely to have been rural born, and to go to a nearby town for training in craft or mercantile skills. However, afterwards they moved around almost wholly within the urban system (though they might retire to rural areas), often over very great distances.

Our figures and diagrams suggest, then, that there were two quite different 'urban societies' in the pre-industrial town of Vadstena. Or, rather, that there were two societies of which only the smaller one was 'urban' in any economically or socially meaningful sense. The patrician third was 'urbanite', operating in the economic system that transformed and redistributed rural surpluses, trained in towns in the skills necessary to do so, and fully at home anywhere within a geographically widespread extent, across which it coursed with alacrity. The plebeian half was not 'urban' in anything except place of residence. Its links were with the rural population of a severely restricted geographical area and of an archetypally 'circulatory' nature. When in town, the plebeians were concerned with serving patrician society in menial occupations, comprising tasks that were little different from those performed by the hands and maids of farmers in the countryside, and there was very little mobility across the socio-economic divide which separated them from the trained craftsmen, merchants, administrators and professional people of the town. The widows and spinsters, who headed the remaining sixth or so of households, were in between the patricians and plebeians in terms of their patterns of mobility. Most townspeople were, therefore, not distinctly 'urban' in terms of the work they did or the social positions they occupied, and this was reflected in their patterns of geographical movement.

Does this simply tell us, in terms of our introductory remarks, that the 'urban system' and the degree of 'urbanization' was much smaller in pre-industrial times than population statistics would imply because most townsfolk were economically, socially and culturally 'rural', as they are in the dual economies of towns in developing countries at the present time? Probably. It is certainly true that the differences between the two social groups were so profound in Vadstena that the patricians' urbanism could not possibly have been eroded, however numerically predominant the plebeian group. There were, therefore, strong similarities between the situation in early nineteenth-century Vadstena and the dual economies of today's developing world. Although they were not, of course, reinforced by ethnic differences and the legacies of colonial status, the economic and behavioural differences between a classically urban minority population and a majority of 'urban countrymen' were clearly, nonetheless, very deep. It is also clear from the geographical patterns of patricians' movements that Vadstena, small and remote though it was, functioned as a fully integral part of an urban *system* in the pre-industrial economy of early nineteenth-century Sweden. That being so, the patrician urbanites of Vadstena must have been both alive to and affected by whatever was going on in higher tiers of the urban hierarchy.[39]

On the other hand, even though the economic links between Vadstena's plebeians and the patricians who employed them were far closer than those between people in the upper and lower circuits of capital in the cities of the now-developing world, it is difficult to see how usually brief urban residence in menial dependent positions can have affected the economic capacities, social behaviour or cultural values of Vadstena's plebeians, who comprised a majority of the townsfolk, to any significant extent. It is even more difficult to see how any such effect could have been transmitted back into rural society, despite all the shuttling back and forth that occurred. It is much more likely that the large plebeian sector of the urban population maintained rural characteristics in terms of behaviour, aspirations and attitudes, due to their circulatory patterns of movement. Thus, the sizes of urban populations and their changes do not necessarily tell us anything at all about the extent of economic and social processes of 'urbanization'. The assumption that urban and rural differences, real though they were in this pre-industrial system, can be measured in terms of the numbers and proportions of people who happened to live in town and country at a particular time is quite unwarranted.

Yet there are some signs of profound changes from this perhaps unsurprisingly pre-industrial situation in our figures and diagrams, particularly in some of the detailed life-paths illustrated in Figs. 9.1–3, which indicate strongly that there was no continuity in the economic, social and cultural contents of the categories we have distinguished above as 'urbanite townsmen' and urban and rural plebeians. The monopoly of the guilds in urban craft and mercantile work together with their power over the scope of their members' activities, were formally removed in 1846. Many other liberating economic reforms were enacted in Sweden at about the same time. Certain aspects of our data can be interpreted as a consequence of this (or perhaps more probably of the underlying changes to which the liberating legislation was a response).

The young patricians of the late 1850s were not only more rural and local in origin than their elders, but were also generally from humbler rural homes. Nearly half of the hands, labourers and workmen shown (as 10a) in Fig. 9.2 moved to town. Four of the five ended their lives there, whereas only two farmers followed a similar path, one upon retirement and the other for a short period at a stage in the life-cycle when residence away from home was common in traditional peasant society. It may be that, in earlier generations, freehold farmers' sons had entered urban craft positions in Sweden. Although we are by no means certain of this, it is what we might expect in pre-industrial society, and apprenticeship was certainly the only conduit through which rural people became urbanized according to our data: apprentices were rural-born, but after qualification as journeymen or masters they moved around solely and very widely in the urban system. However, as fewer and bigger businesses emerged, access to the position of employer was greatly restricted and the demand for employees greatly expanded. The relatively high proportion of juvenile patricians who had been born in Vadstena itself and other towns perhaps signifies the keenness of fathers to hold onto their privileges for their own or their associates' children. There were other corollaries of the growth in the size of urban workshops after the removal of guild controls, too. Whatever may have been the case earlier, it was now the homes of the rapidly increasing number of people without access to land which provided boys from the countryside for apprenticeships in town.[40] All the rural-born apprentices of 1855–60 (as exemplified by the second of the life-paths beginning in 1838 and that beginning in 1820 in Fig. 9.3) were the children of proletarians. In three of the five examples (signified by 11a) in Fig. 9.1, their parents had at times been destitute. In so far as it is possible to trace them (see the bottom row of Table. 9.2B) few seem to have become master craftsmen themselves after qualifying. Instead, they remained perpetual journeymen, frantically wandering from town to town (see Fig. 9.1, categories 11a and 6b) in search of a niche where they might become a master craftsman or, more likely, find a more congenial wage-earning position. Indeed, their wandering was sanctioned by a law which limited the period of residence of a journeyman in one place to three years (although this law had little effect on many of the journeymen in our samples).

Thus, the vast majority of the apprentices of the 1850s were not juvenile patricians at all. Few of them would become master craftsmen with their own independent workshops later in life. So the categories we have used to structure the urban population were becoming anachronistic as the rapidly growing proletarian segment of the population of the arable plain was becoming fused with, and was in fact providing, a nascent urban proletariat. Farmers' sons were staying at home on expanding arable holdings; the children of craftsmen and merchants were gaining a tighter grip on employer positions in the towns, whilst the sons and daughters of those without any command over resources – other than what could be gained in exchange for their labour power – were surging hither and thither in search of work and advancement.

They searched around urban and rural areas alike, and also in places like Motala, 15 kilometres north of Vadstena, where copious water power, engineering for the Göta Canal (opened in 1832) and the canal itself spawned a new settlement around a rapidly expanding mass of new industrial plant. By 1860, the Motala Engineering Works alone employed 659 people and there were numerous other water-powered works, ranging from cornmills through breweries and a paper mill to a gunpowder manufactory and an ironworks, as well as a market settlement (*köping*) laid out in the 1830s. They straggled along the river Motala and the adjacent Göta Canal, where there had previously been little more than rocks, forest and a number of riverine mills of medieval provenance. Although it was not classified as a town for administrative or statistical purposes until the twentieth century, Motala was already twice the size of Vadstena by 1860, when the *köping* and the clusters of houses amongst the canal-side, water-powered works contained a population of 4,480.[41]

Nearly all of the industrial wage workers of Motala Engineering Works, as exemplified by the first life-path depicted in Fig. 9.3, came from rural areas.[42] Although some of them were designated as apprentices and journeymen, the vast majority were called workmen. However, there was a vast difference between their working patterns and those of the workmen who ministered to the needs of the craftsman and merchant households of Vadstena. Their patterns of recruitment and subsequent movements also differed from those of Vadstena's workmen and resembled more closely those of its apprentices and journeymen. They were young when they came to the town, on average 25 years of age, like the hands and journeymen of Vadstena, compared with the 33 years of the workmen there (see Table 9.1). Only about half of them came from the proletariat of the large farms of the arable plains that supplied Vadstena's transient plebeian population. The rest came, often over very considerable distances, from forested pastoral areas where farm sizes were not only small, but shrinking,[43] with long traditions of domestic manufacture and, often, ironmaking and ironworking in furnaces and forges which provided employment outside the home.[44] Indeed, a sprinkling of the most skilled engineering workers came directly from England, Scotland and many widely separated places in continental Europe. None came from Vadstena and very few from other pre-existing towns, although some of the traders and craftsmen of the *köping* did. Most of the rural immigrants to Motala Engineering Works worked in corn mills for a short while beforehand, and most moved on to further destinations. However, only between 5 and 13 per cent of the 1,066 workmen registered in the *husförhörslängder* moved out from Motala Works to rural areas; 64 per cent moved within the works (which provided some housing) and 23 per cent moved out to towns, 19 per cent to towns outside Östergötland. Only 9 of the 50 employees of Motala Works in 1855 whose detailed life-paths have been traced returned to the countryside.

Perhaps we can see in the Motala data the very beginnings of what may be considered a modern industrial-urban society. Certainly, they depict a situation very different from that in Vadstena. Perhaps there is some validity in the hoary notion that the new industrial towns of modern Europe were *sui generis*, after all. In no sense was industrial urbanism in this case a lineal evolution from what had existed specifically and solely in towns before, not even in a whole national (or international) urban system. It was completely inseparable from what was happening in the countryside of Östergötland, the rest of forested Sweden and, indeed, in (usually rural) ironworking areas throughout Europe.

As large-scale capitalist methods of production penetrated rural and urban economies alike they changed: Vadstena's workshops, shops and warehouses were slowly evolving into fully capitalist enterprises with larger, wage-earning, labour-forces. The erstwhile peasant farms on the plains were moving faster and further in the same direction. Ironworking and domestic industry provided supplementary farm income in pastoral forested areas and farm sizes shrank, whilst water power and water transport together spawned what were at the time enormous manufacturing plant. As different rural and urban areas were changing in these very different ways, so were the relationships between them. (It is worth recalling here that the Swedish economy and society were almost completely quiescent and archaic at this time, according to national aggregate statistics derived from censuses).

Quite different kinds of work were associated with quite different sorts of societies and individuals in pre-industrial Vadstena; and, as the nature of work was totally different in burgeoning Motala from what it had been in Vadstena, so was the society it produced. In the first case 'urban' work was done by a minority of townsfolk. In the second, it was neither common to all towns nor confined to them. The transition from bourgeois to industrial capitalism was neither produced nor contained within the urban system. Moreover, the pattern of links between the towns and rural areas also changed fundamentally. Vadstena's plebeian population was transient and circulatory, its apprentices and journeymen equally transient but destined for much more distant urban opportunities. Both came from proletarian niches on the arable plain. Motala's industrial proletariat was only partially recruited from this source, and equally strong links were evident with forested proto-industrial and ironworking areas where small family-manned farms were multiplying. Few of these were circular migrants, and most moved off to similar urban opportunities elsewhere.[45]

Thus, although for quite different reasons, in both the pre-industrial and industrializing economies revealed in our data, it is inappropriate to separate urban and rural populations, with the automatic and unquestioned implication that they comprised coherent and unitary economic, social or cultural categories. It is even more inappropriate to look for evolutionary development or cataclysmic changes within the separated and implicitly continuous confines of one or the other of the abstracted categories. What 'urban' and 'rural' comprised differed fundamentally and changed in very different ways as the resources and societies of different kinds of physical environment provided different kinds of opportunities to and responded in different ways to the penetration of capitalist production. Moreover, the nature of urban economy and society in a particular region, and the ways in which they were changing, were inextricably linked to the particular nature of local rural economy and society and the ways in which they were changing.

This strongly human ecological dimension is obscured by, but in fact renders otiose, both a categorical distinction between and any generalization about urban and rural systems of production and social organization in the part of Sweden to which our research relates.[46] We believe that the same situation might be discovered in the rest of early modern and early industrial Europe, as it has been throughout the modern developing world, if data were available to allow us to look for it.[47]

Notes

1. The notions are now so common that a list of works containing them would run to many pages. Some general and notable recent expositions may be found in P. Abrams and E.A. Wrigley (ed.), *Towns in Societies* (1978); B.J.L. Berry, *The Human Consequences of Urbanization* (1973); D. Harvey, *Consciousness and the Urban Experience* (1985) and *The Urbanization of Capital* (1985); P.M. Hohenberg and L.H. Lees, *The Making of Urban Europe 1000-1950* (Cambridge, Mass., 1985); H. Schmal (ed.), *Patterns of European Urbanization since 1500* (1981); J. de Vries, *European Urbanization 1500-1800* (1984); and E.A. Wrigley, *People, Cities and Wealth* (1987).
2. F. Braudel, *Capitalism and Material Life 1400-1800* (1973).

3. For a neo-classical economic view, see for example: O. Handlin and J. Burchard, *The Historian and the City* (Cambridge, Mass., 1963), esp. Part II; and for a Marxist point of view, D. Harvey, *Social Justice and the City* (1973), esp. Chapter 6, and D. Harvey, *Consciousness*.

4. De Vries, op. cit., 12.

5. The phrase was coined by Louis Wirth, 'Urbanism as a way of life', *American Journal of Sociology*, 44 (1938), 1–24. For reviews of the theories linking urban living to cultural change, see Berry, op. cit., and P. Saunders, *Social Theory and the Urban Question* (1981).

6. De Vries, op. cit., 12. Full descriptions of these processes can be found in the references cited in note 1.

7. It is, of course, only on this basis that separate and systematic urban and rural branches of history, geography, anthropology and sociology can be predicated.

8. C. Tilly, 'Migration in modern European history', in *Time, Space and Man*, ed. J. Sundin and E. Söderlund (Umeå, 1979), 176–7.

9. The thesis that it is the degree to which towns cohere into holistic systems, diagnosed by their size distributions, which is significant for development, rather than simply the aggregate sizes of urban populations, has been advanced in a European context by de Vries, op. cit., and by B.T. Robson, *Urban Growth: An Approach* (1973).

10. The depiction of people who were registered at a particular time as living in towns but born in the countryside as rural-urban migrants, without questioning whether they might have moved about in the interim or subsequently, is widely current. See, for example, D. Souden, 'Migrants and the population structure of later seventeenth century provincial cities and market towns', in *The Transformation of English Provincial Towns*, ed. P. Clark (1984).

11. See for example: for today's developing world, J. Harriss (ed.), *Rural Development: Theories of Peasant Economy and Agrarian Change* (1982); for European agrarian capitalism, T.H. Aston and C.H.E. Philpin (ed.), *The Brenner Debate: Agrarian Class Structure and Economic Development in Pre-industrial Europe* (1985) and K. Tribe, *Genealogies of Capitalism* (1981); and for proto-industrialization L.A. Clarkson, *Proto-Industrialization: The First Phase of Industrialization?* (1985) and P. Kriedte, H. Medick and J. Schlumbohm, *Industrialization before Industrialization: Rural Industry in the Genesis of Capitalism* (1981). These ideas, and those which located the processes of change in towns, are reviewed in J. Langton and G. Hoppe, *Town and Country in the Development of Early Modern Western Europe* (Historical Geography Research Series 11, 1983).

12. Indeed, by both of the editors of *Towns in Societies*. See E.A. Wrigley, 'The process of modernization and the Industrial Revolution in England', repr. in *Industrialization and Urbanization*, ed. T.K. Rabb and R.I. Rotberg (Princeton 1981), 23–57, and P. Abrams, 'Towns and economic growth: some theories and problems', in *Towns in Societies*, ed. Abrams and Wrigley, 9–33, where (p. 10) it is argued that 'in an important sense the city is not a social entity; that we have been victims of the fallacy of misplaced concreteness in treating it as such; and that one object of urban history and urban sociology now might be to get rid of the concept of the town'.

13. See, for example, T.G. McGee, *The Urbanization Process in the Third World: Explorations in Search of a Theory* (1971); and A. Gilbert and J. Gugler, *Cities, Poverty and Development: Urbanization in the Third World* (1981).

14. See ibid; K. Little, *Urbanization as a Social Process: An Essay on Movement and Change in Contemporary Africa* (1974); and J.C. Mitchell, *Cities, Society and Social Perception* (1987).

15. M. Santos, *The Shared Space: The Two Circuits of the Urban Economy in Underdeveloped Countries* (1979).

16. See, for example, T.G. McGee, 'The rural-urban continuum debate, the pre-industrial

city and rural-urban migration', *Pacific Viewpoint*, 5 (1964), 159–81; B.M. du Toit and H.I. Safa (ed.), *Migration and Urbanization: Models and Adaptive Strategies* (Paris, 1975); L. Kosinski and R.M. Prothero (ed.), *People on the Move: Studies in Internal Migration* (1975) and R.M. Prothero and M. Chapman (ed.), *Circulation in Third World Countries* (1985).

17. S. Thernstrom and P. Knights, 'Men in motion: some data and speculations about urban population mobility in nineteenth-century America', in Rabb and Rotberg (ed.), op. cit., 171–99.

18. R.E. Johnson, *Peasant and Proletarian: The Working Class of Moscow in the Late Nineteenth Century* (1979); S. Hochstadt, 'Migration and industrialization in Germany', *Social Science History*, 5 (1981), 445–68.

19. M. Anderson, *Family Structure in Nineteenth-Century Lancashire* (1971) and his 'Urban migration in nineteenth-century Lancashire: some insights into two competing hypotheses', *Annales de Démographie Historique* (1972), 13–26.

20. This point is developed in detail in Thernstrom and Knights, op. cit. and in M. Anderson, 'Indicators of population stability and change in nineteenth-century cities: some sceptical comments', in *The Structure of Nineteenth-Century Cities*, ed. J.H. Johnson and C.G. Pooley (1982), 283–98.

21. B. Roberts, *Cities of Peasants: The Political Economy of Urbanization in the Third World* (1978). See also Mitchell, op. cit.

22. The work reported here is a small part of our current research, which is concerned with the role of rural-urban and inter-regional interaction in the transformation of the peasant farming system of western Östergötland in the early nineteenth century. A fuller presentation of the aggregate data given below can be found in J. Langton and G. Hoppe, 'Small towns in peasant society: migration paths of people resident in Vadstena between 1855 and 1860', in *The Strategy of Migration in Demographic and Cultural History*, ed. P. Kreager (Journal of the Anthropological Society of Oxford, forthcoming).

23. I.T. Berend and G. Rànki, *The European Periphery and Industrialization* (1982), 16–17.

24. See S. Koblik (ed.), *Sweden's Development from Poverty to Affluence 1750-1970* (Minneapolis, 1975) and C.G. Gustavson, *The Small Giant: Sweden Enters the Industrial Era* (Athens, Ohio, 1986).

25. E. Arosenius, 'Demography', in *Sweden: Historical and Statistical Handbook*, ed. J. Guinchard (Stockholm, 1914), I, 109.

26. Ibid., 120.

27. See E. Heckscher, *An Economic History of Sweden* (Cambridge, Mass., 1954) and F. Scott, *Sweden: The Nation's History* (Minneapolis, 1977).

28. K. Stadin, *Småstäder, småborgare och stora samhällsförändringar* (Uppsala, 1979).

29. M. Hellspong and O. Löfgren, *Land och stad: Svenska samhällstyper och livsformer från medeltid till nutid* (Lund, 1974), 184.

30. Ø. Østerud, *Agrarian Structure and Peasant Politics in Scandinavia: A Comparative Study of Rural Response to Economic Change* (Oslo, 1978) and G. Hoppe and J. Langton, 'Time-geography and economic development: the changing structure of livelihood positions on arable farms in nineteenth-century Sweden', *Geografiska Annaler*, 68B (1986), 115–37.

31. This source is discussed more fully in A-S. Kälvemark, 'The country that kept track of its population', in J. Sundin and E. Söderlund (ed.), op. cit. Literally translated, *husförhörslängder* means 'household examination registers'. They were compiled for every Swedish parish, in principle from the seventeenth century, although in fact they are often difficult to use or non-existent before the 1780s. Their primary purpose was to record the results of annual checks on the religious knowledge of each member of the population. *Inter alia*, they record the name and address of every household head and the

age, places of birth, last and next residence, relation to household head and occupation of each member of each household. They were up-dated continuously by church ministers.

32. Totals on tables do not always sum exactly to 100 per cent due to rounding before summation.

33. Our basic classification comprises six groups of occupational and status categories, each group designated by a Roman numeral. For consistency, we have kept our usual numbering conventions here, even though group IV, the poor, are omitted. The groups contain the following categories:- I: officials, traders and craftsmen; II: independent craftsmen (i.e. craftsmen without guild status or privileges, invariably practising less skilled crafts such as carpentry and bricklaying), workmen, ex-farmers, labourers, bell ringers, watchmen and people involved in transportation. III: widows and spinsters (the latter including seamstresses); V: apprentices, shop assistants (who were normally youngsters training in traders' businesses) and journeymen; VI: hands and maids. Our distinction between plebeian and patrician social groups is similar to that normally used for urban social classification in Sweden at that time, except that we have amalgamated the officials with craftsmen and traders, whereas they are usually defined as a separate higher social stratum. See G. Paulsson, *Svensk stad* (Stockholm, 1953); B. Hanssen, 'Samhällsklasser i de svenska småstäderna under 1850- och 1860-talen', *Historisk Tidskrift*, 3 (1978), 243–62 and K. Stadin, op. cit.

34. *Mantalslängder* are annual taxation ledgers which list all inhabitants and the taxes assessed on their land, other property, salaries, profits, wages and persons, and in which people taxed as servants in others' households are distinguished.

35. The sample was stratified so that a number of individuals from each occupational group would be included. We were not concerned to make the occupational proportions in the samples of life-paths correspond with their proportions in the total *husförhörslängder* population; indeed, we deliberately over-represented the 'urbanite' groups in the life-path sample. Within each group, individuals were selected randomly.

36. The entry *obest. ort.* ('unknown destination') was exclusive to journeymen and apprentices in the Vadstena *husförhörslängder*.

37. A *mantal* was a unit of taxation, which originally represented a homestead capable of fully supporting one family. Variations in farm size are reflected quite accurately by the proportions of a *mantal* for which they were assessed.

38. A crofter was a person who had the right to cultivate for a fixed number of years a small parcel of land belonging to a farmer in return for a contractual number of days' work each year.

39. Our findings in this respect corroborate de Vries's idea that *systems* of towns developed in pre-industrial Europe: see de Vries, op. cit.

40. The changes occurring at the time in the social structure of the arable plains around Vadstena, involving a rapid and massive expansion of farm holdings and proletarianization of labour, are discussed in Hoppe and Langton, 'Time-geography'.

41. It is possible to estimate the population of the cluster of settlements along the Motala river from the *mantalslängder*, which give very precise locations for the households it lists.

42. For a detailed analysis of the socio-economic and geographical origins of the labour force of Motala Engineering Works in the 1850s, see G. Hoppe, 'Från jordbruk till järnverk? kopplingar mellan jordbruk, förindustriell massproduktion och formel industri ur ett geografiskt perspektiv med exempel från 1850–talets Motala', *Bebyggelsehistorisk Tidskrift*, 16 (1988). It is impossible to calculate statistics for the urban settlement at Motala which are comparable with those for Vadstena because it was not distinguished in ascriptions of places of birth, last and next residence in the *husförhörslängder* from the large rural parish in which it lay. Distinctions were made between places of residence in Motala Engineering Works, the *köping* and at the Göta Canal terminus, but not

between other industrial locations along the river and those in the large rural parts of the parish. Thus, moves within the urban settlement, between these places and the numerous other works and mills along the river, cannot be distinguished from those between these locations and the large rural parts of the parish. This means that the figures of turnover and in- and out-migration calculated for the Engineering Works and the *köping* will be much higher than those for the town as a whole would have been, and that it is impossible to identify whether origins and destinations registered as 'Motala parish' were in the industrial settlement or the countryside.

43. J. Langton, 'Habitat, economy and society revisited: peasant ecotypes and economic development in Sweden', *Cambria*, 13 (1986), 5–24.

44. It has recently been strongly emphasized that the growth of manufacturing and consequent urban development in Sweden generally in the second half of the nineteenth century emerged from rural handicrafts, and that town manufactories and workshops depended heavily on hand skills brought by people from the countryside. M. Isacson and L. Magnusson, *Proto-Industrialization in Scandinavia: Craft Skills in the Industrial Revolution* (1987), 39.

45. Åkerman discovered an identical difference in his study of migration in Västmanland province, 1895–1930, distinguishing between '*circular* migration' and '*effective* migration'. The former was characteristic of agricultural and the latter of industrial parishes. Effective migration increased in proportion to the level of demographic urbanization. S. Åkerman, 'Internal migration, industrialization and urbanization (1895–1930): a summary of the Västmanland project', *Scandinavian Economic History Review* (1975), 149–58.

46. The argument is developed in terms of the whole of Western Europe in Langton and Hoppe, *Town and Country*.

47. This was also the conclusion of the anthropologist Hanssen's work on the social structure of the Österlen region, situated on the southern tip of Sweden, in the eighteenth and early nineteenth centuries. 'As the research proceeded, it proved fruitful to regard this complex object as a congeries of social fields . . . which made it easier to understand and describe a complex whole, which could not have been so easily described with the help of such concepts as urban people, rural people and other conventional terms': see B. Hanssen, 'Commonfolk and gentlefolk', *Ethnologia Scandinavica* (1973), 67.

10 The taxonomy of occupations in late eighteenth-century Westminster[1]

Edmund M. Green

'It was imprudent to propose Lord Lincoln,' declared Edward Gibbon at the start of the Westminster election in 1780, 'he is disliked by the substantial tradesmen: but they abhor Fox.'[2] Analysis of political behaviour in terms of social and economic structures is now commonplace. But this is by no means only a modern preoccupation: the eighteenth-century's greatest historian also commented on political allegiance in terms of interest groups and the social hierarchy.[3]

Occupation is an unavoidable social indicator for sociologists and historians. This essay not only explores different principles of economic and social classification of occupations, but also probes inside the occupational label itself to explore the apparent similarity within the occupational group. It questions some received wisdom about occupational classification in the light of evidence from eighteenth-century Westminster.

In practice, perceptions of social structure are intricate and fluid. They are the product of a host of different characteristics, such as skill, education, status, position in authority structures, relationship to the means of production, and income. In general, occupation stands proxy for these multiple indices; it can be applied to the majority of household heads in the population, and is regarded as the best single indicator of social class in modern Britain. There remain numerous problems in the classification of the unemployed, the retired, and those who are not household heads. In particular these problems apply to the social classification of women.

Sociologists have sought to standardize the allocation of occupations to social classes in modern Britain, and to rank them in a hierarchy;[4] and, with due caution, historians have followed suit.[5] For some eighteenth-century constituencies details of the voters' occupations are preserved in the poll books of parliamentary elections. These record the names, addresses, and self-ascribed occupations of the voters, together with their political choices.[6] But while poll books can be used to describe the occupational distribution of Westminster's male householders in the late eighteenth and early nineteenth centuries, evidence is lacking to place these into the ranked order that is a prerequisite of further social analysis. Gibbon's assertion cannot be tested unless the 'substantial' tradesmen can be distinguished from their 'insubstantial' neighbours. It is in an attempt to remedy that deficiency, at least in part, that the present essay has been written. Its focus is upon the social analysis of occupational descriptions, rather than upon work processes pure and simple.

I

This essay reports on some of the first fruits of a research project into the relationship between the social structure and the political allegiance of the voters of Westminster between 1774 and 1820. The surviving poll books of the Westminster elections[7] provide a reasonable guide to the occupational distribution of the male householders of that part of London. It was the largest constituency regularly to go to the polls in the period. Poll books survive for eleven of the twelve contested elections between 1774 and 1820. Over 12,300 voters polled in 1784, representing over four-fifths of the male householders in the constituency.[8] It was one of the large 'open' constituencies to which commentators throughout the country looked for evidence of popular political behaviour.

A database of 55,000 voting acts between 1774 and 1820 has yielded over 1,800 occupational descriptions, including all variant spellings, combined occupations and synonymous descriptions. But the distribution of these occupations is highly irregular. Taking just the 11,423 voters, for whom records survive from the 1784 election,[9] half of them are found under sixteen major occupations and status labels: these included not only gentlemen and esquires, but also cordwainers (shoemakers), victuallers, butchers, and so on. Meanwhile, there is a long tail of 5,000 voters, with hundreds of different occupational descriptions: only one voter in Westminster in 1784 described himself as a 'dog doctor', and only one was a 'bug destroyer'.

In an ambitious attempt to devise a general system of occupational classification, Treiman has constructed a ranking of occupations from societies as different as

Table 10.1 The frequency of common occupations and status labels among Westminster voters in 1784

Occupation	Observations	Percentage of all voters
Gentleman	1,120	9.8
Victualler	878	7.7
Tailor	565	4.9
Cordwainer	548	4.8
Carpenter	541	4.7
Esquire	456	4.0
Butcher	270	2.4
Hairdresser	203	1.8
Baker	175	1.5
Chandler	158	1.4
Other voters	6,509	57.0
Total	11,423	100.0

those of fourteenth-century Nepal and the present-day United States.[10] But what such a classification gains in terms of comparability of data between periods and places it loses in terms of sensitivity to the social and cultural context. The caste of *Gayane* (bard singers) in the Nepali caste ranking of 1395 is classified with 'musical entertainers' in the standard classification. The assumption of the immutability of occupational descriptions is a questionable one; and it is necessary to devise an occupational taxonomy for eighteenth-century London in the absence of survey data on income and the social perception of work, skill, and status.

Historians have devised a number of different ways of classifying occupations, falling into the two main types of economic and social classification.[11] The inference of a social classification from occupational descriptions alone is fraught with difficulty. The simple occupational descriptions found in the poll books reveal little about the precise nature of the work being undertaken: shoemakers might be classified as makers of shoes, as vendors of shoes, as workers in leather, or as all of these. And whereas the early urban directories might be presumed to contain a population essentially of business proprietors,[12] there is little evidence in the poll books to determine a voter's relationship to the means of production, to distinguish the master from his man.

In the Westminster election of 1774 the government candidates, Lord Percy and Thomas Pelham Clinton, roundly defeated their Wilkite opponents, Lords Mountmorres and Mahon.[13] The vanquished candidates responded with a petition against the election result. An analysis of this petition is preserved in the papers of Abraham Bayley, election agent to Pelham Clinton.[14] This analysis explicitly divides the petitioners against the election result into four classes: those 'trades dependent upon the consumption of provisions', the 'trades of the lower class', the 'trades of a higher class', and those petitioners 'of the addition of gentleman'.

The occupations of 255 of the signatories to the petition were classified by the unknown contemporary analyst. Of these, 93 (36 per cent) were tradesmen 'dependent upon the consumption of provisions'. A further 22 signatories (9 per cent) were acknowledged to be tradesmen 'of a higher class', and a mere 12 petitioners (5 per cent) were 'of the addition of gentleman'. By contrast, fully half of the petitioners, 128 of the 255, were aggregated as belonging to the 'trades of the lower class'. In each section of the classification there is a proportion of undifferentiated 'others' ranging from 5 per cent of the purveyors of provisions to 31 per cent of the 'trades of the lower class' and 40 per cent of the 'trades of a higher class'.

Among the 'trades of the lower class' are found most artisan and dealing occupations. Those involved in the building trades include bricklayers, carpenters, glaziers, and painters. Among the retailers were to be found brokers, chandlers, hatters, pawnbrokers, tallow chandlers, and tobacconists. The artisans who may also have sold their products form a miscellaneous group: cabinet-makers, carvers, cutlers, hatters, paper stainers, peruke-makers (makers of wigs), shoemakers, silk-dyers, stay-makers, tailors, and watchmakers. The stable-keepers are also reckoned among these 'trades of the lower class', although it is likely that they were a group requiring considerable capital to start in business. Among the purveyors of provisions are to be found: bakers, brewers, butchers, cheesemongers, cooks, fishmongers, grocers, oilmen, victuallers, and wine merchants. The 'trades of a higher class' constitute the semi-professional callings, the luxury trades of the eighteenth-century metropolis, and those perhaps requiring more capital than the run-of-the-mill artisan and trade callings. Those 'trades of a higher class' comprise the following: apothecaries, coach makers, coal merchants, jewellers, linen drapers, and upholders (furniture-makers/dealers).

Contemporary analyses of the social structure reflected perceptions of society ranked by status and income. From Gregory King's calculations of 1695 (back-dated by him to 1688), through to Joseph Massie's analysis from the mid-eighteenth century, and to Patrick Colquhoun's recalculations based on data from 1803, there ran a tradition of ranking both by status and by household income.[15] Recognizing the complexity of the social structure in their investigation of a dual approach, they all eschewed the simplicities of a single hierarchy.

Further contemporary impressions of the relative status of occupations may be obtained from publications intended to assist in the choice of a career. Campbell's *London Tradesman* (1747) gives details of the apprenticeship premiums required in a variety of trades, the capital necessary to become established as a tradesman, the hours of work, and the remuneration.[16] But a master's profits are likely to have varied with his ability and the location of his business, and Campbell's imprecision doubtless reflects such factors: for example, he gives the capital sum required to set up as an appraiser as anything between £50 and £2,000.

Indeed, while the poll books record the occupations or status descriptions of Westminster voters, they cannot by themselves reveal the process of change in the careers of individual voters. The mutability of occupations is shown by the vicissitudes of the peripatetic career of Simon Place, as recorded in the autobiography of his son Francis, 'the radical tailor of Charing Cross'.[17] Thrice ruined by 'his propensity for drinking and gaming', Simon Place's career was characterized by social, occupational and residential mobility. A journeyman baker in Clapham, Simon Place rose to become a master baker in the Borough, Southwark, before moving to a baker's shop in Windmill Street in St James's parish, Westminster. But he lost £800 of his savings by gambling, and was obliged to sell his house and business. By about 1770, Simon and his wife were living in Russell Court, near Temple Bar. He worked as a bailiff, though in the poll book of the 1774 election he was described as 'gentleman'. He seems to have prospered in his new calling, but the passage of a statute in 1779 against frivolous and vexatious arrests removed much of his business. Selling his office, he took the lease of the King's Arms in Arundel Street, just off the Strand. It was from this address that Simon Place voted in the elections of 1780 and 1784. Lest Simon Place's career seem unusual in its vicissitudes, his son adds a note that 'such men as he was, were by no means uncommon in his time'.

In aggregate, the economic contours of Westminster's male householders are revealed by the occupational descriptions of the voters recorded in the poll books. The occupations have been allocated to nine broad economic sectors, using a classification first devised by Charles Booth in 1886 for the analysis of nineteenth-century census data and subsequently amended by modern historians.[18] This is not a social classification, but an economic distribution. It therefore avoids some of the pitfalls of adapting the Registrar-General's twentieth-century classification of occupations into social classes to eighteenth-century data, but by the same token it leaves the data devoid of any hierarchical classification for social analysis.

II

Eighteenth-century Westminster was no mean suburb of metropolitan London. Financial services, commodity trading, and the wharves were concentrated in and around the City of London, eastwards and downstream of Westminster. But the constituency of Westminster contained the royal court at St James's Palace; the centre of government at Whitehall and the Palace of Westminster; the socially-select residential developments of the Grosvenor estate in Mayfair; the legislature at the Palace of Westminster; the centre of the legal profession at Lincoln's Inn; the centre of the theatre world around Covent Garden; a service sector economy for all these; and many thousands of artisans and tradesmen living cheek-by-jowl in the streets and alleyways behind and between the main thoroughfares and in close propinquity to the rich and powerful of the realm.[19] With a population of around 150,000, Westminster would have been considered as Britain's second city in the late eighteenth century had it been a discrete entity not subsumed by the metropolitan sprawl.[20] The relationship of Westminster to the burgeoning metropolis of the period is shown in Fig. 10.1.

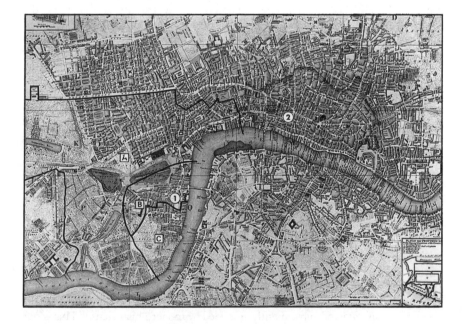

Figure 10.1. London and Westminster in the late eighteenth century. Extract from John Fairburn's plan, published in 1797. 1) denotes Westminster Abbey, and 2) St Paul's Cathedral. The boundaries of the city of Westminster and of the parishes of St Margaret (containing 1) and of St John, Westminster, are shown in heavy outline.
Copyright: Guildhall Library, London.

Although London was a great manufacturing centre at the time, such production as there was in Westminster was organized in small units and not in vast factories. It was essentially an artisan and trading economy with a large service sector of professionals. It was not the home of an archetypal dispossessed and immiserated factory proletariat; and the inherent bias of the poll books towards those with some property means that those in acute poverty are hidden from sight. But through this same medium of the poll books of an 'open' constituency with a householder franchise, the eighteenth-century petty bourgeoisie may be rescued 'from the overwhelming condescension of posterity'.[21]

Even among small industries and services, the occupational structure was characterized by a high degree of economic specialization. In the luxury trade of coachmaking, which flourished around Long Acre in the parish of St Martin-in-the-Fields, there were to be found: coach builders, coach carvers, coach draftsmen, coach founders, coach frame makers, coach harness-makers, coach harness-platers, coach joiners, coach liners, coach livery lace-makers, coach-makers, coach painters, coach-platers, coach smiths, coach spring-makers, coach trimmers and coach wheel-

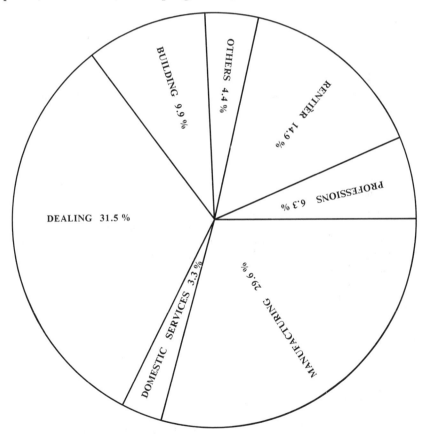

Figure. 10.2. Distribution of voters' occupations in Westminster, 1784, using Booth's occupational classification.

wrights. The processes of manufacture and dealing were broken down into their constituent elements, and voters identified themselves in terms of those specializations.[22] Whilst the creation of meaningful groups for social analysis requires that this riot of specialization be aggregated into fewer, larger groups, this must be done with great sensitivity to the nuances of eighteenth-century trade and industry.

Predominantly, the economic structure of late eighteenth-century Westminster was dominated by three main groups. There were the artisan trades and handicrafts, the large service sector, and a substantial leisure class. If the poll book for the 1784 election may be taken as a proxy for an occupational survey of male household heads, it will be found that almost a third of them worked in the retail and distributive trades, and almost a third in a broad manufacturing sector. Some voters, of course, sold the goods that they made: doubtless many shoemakers and hatters, and most of the bakers, fell into this category. Meanwhile, nearly a sixth of all voters described themselves as gentlemen, esquires, or men with some status title, who were classified in a sector of *rentiers*. A smaller but still significant tenth of the voters worked, mostly in artisan trades, in the building industry. Together these four sectors of dealers, manufacturers, *rentiers*, and builders accounted for fully 86 per cent of Westminster's voters in 1784, as shown in Fig. 10.2.

The commonest occupations have already been given in Table 10.1, but there were also some unusual ones. These included: an artificial flower maker, a bird stuffer, a comedian, a dogs' meat seller, an earl, a fiddle-case maker, a glass scalloper, a harp maker, an ivory turner, a jack maker, the keeper of a fives court, a lavender-water merchant, and a mouse-trap maker, through to a tea-tray manufacturer, an umbrella maker, a venetian-blind maker, and a water-closet maker.[23]

III

The franchise of the parliamentary constituency of Westminster lay in male householders assessed to pay rates, though arguments persisted as to precisely who was entitled to vote.[24] The survival of the parish rate books as well as the constituency poll books raises the possibility of linking the two documents to create a composite file. This would allow a numerical value of the rack-rent of the property occupied by the voter to be related to his occupation and his vote. The rate book data exist for a substantial proportion of the voters, and allow interval data to be associated with more voters than do comparable sources such as fire insurance policies and probate records.[25]

Rack-rent values of property may be used to give additional meaning to the raw occupational descriptions.[26] Occupations for which a number of the voters had rated properties may be ranked in a hierarchy by the average rack-rental values. And for those few titles of status or occupation for which there are many observations, the dispersion of values within each occupation may be examined to reveal the degree of homogeneity of the descriptive label.

Taking a detailed look at one area, a fifth of the voters in 1784 came from the parishes of St Margaret and St John. These parishes, which adjoined Westminster Abbey, polled together. They have been selected for more detailed study because of the exceptional wealth of data that have survived for them: poll books have survived for each contested election between 1774 and 1820, with the exception of that of 1807; and the parish poor rate books are complete and readily available.[27]

Although a fifth of Westminster's voters lived in the parishes of St Margaret and St John, the overall figure conceals differences between the economic sectors. Only one in seven of all of Westminster's voters in the dealing sector lived in these parishes, and almost one in five of all those in the manufacturing sector. But almost two-fifths of all those in the sector of professions and public service, and a similar proportion of those in the agricultural sector and in the transport sector, lived there.

Market gardeners and graziers were concentrated on the low-lying undeveloped marshland in the west and south of the constituency; and the westward spread of housing may account for a slightly higher proportion of those in the building trades than the average for the constituency as a whole. But the small proportion of manufacturers and dealers, and the high proportion of professionals and public servants in St Margaret and St John, is a greater problem. Many of those public servants were soldiers stationed in the parishes who were dragooned to the hustings in Covent Garden: 29 sergeants from the regiment of guards voted in 1784, of whom 27 cast straight votes for the two government candidates, Lord Hood and Sir Cecil Wray. And among the soldiery have been classified the 136 yeomen who voted in St Margaret and St John, whose presence has greatly inflated the total of public servants there.

Rate book entries have been found for just over half the voters in St Margaret and St John. Given that the assessment for rates was held to be a necessary condition of voting, this is a disappointment.[28] The proportion of voters for whom poor-rate data can be found varies from one economic sector to another. Such data can be found for less than a quarter of those in the agricultural sector, and for less than a third of those in the sector of industrial services. But rate data are available for almost two-thirds of the voters with occupations in the sector of dealers, and for nearly three-quarters of the *rentiers*.

The discrepancy between those appearing in the poll books and those for whom rate data can be found is an undeniable problem. Sometimes the rate collectors merely recorded the surname and address of the householder. In other cases, it seems likely that voters gave addresses where rates were paid by someone else: a parent, a sibling, a child, a business partner, or a landlord. And in the west of the parishes, where market gardens and pastures were as yet unsupplanted by urban development, houses were scattered rather than laid out in streets; whilst the names of areas were sometimes vague ('Tothill Fields', 'Palmer's Village', or 'Knightsbridge') and sometimes variable ('York Street', also known as 'Petty France'). In the more easterly and urbanized parish of St Anne, Soho, where the rate collectors almost always included both the Christian name and surname of the occupier of a property, rate data have been found for about three-quarters of the voters in 1784.

Nonetheless, having noted the difficulties, a file of 1,249 rate-paying voters in St Margaret and St John in 1784 was created, with information on their votes, their occupations, and their rates. That information can be tested against the record of the 2,337 who voted in those parishes in that year. Rate data are available for only a quarter of the agricultural workers there; and for less than a third of the transport workers and the industrial servants (a miscellany of clerks and labourers). The proportion of voters for whom rack rental assessments can be found is greater among the larger economic sectors. Assessments exist for about half the builders, the domestic servants, the manufacturers, and the professionals. The level of linkage between poll books and rate books is highest among the dealers and the *rentiers*. Assessments have been linked to slightly under two-thirds of the dealers and slightly over this proportion of the *rentiers*.

This raises the possibility that the records of the rich are more readily linked than those of the poor. If so, it would mean that caution must accompany any interpretation of results based on data linked in this manner. The *rentiers* were undoubtedly the most well-off economic sector: rate assessments exist for 249 of St Margaret's 353 *rentier* voters, and those 249 had a mean rack-rent of £33.95. The next best-off group were the transport workers, who turn out to have a low level of record linkage. The third sector in the ranking by mean rack-rental assessments are the dealers, almost two-thirds of whom have been linked to the rate books. Established shopkeepers would have been a permanent part of the community; and shopkeepers may have required larger premises, often in main streets, in which to live and from which to conduct their businesses.

The different profiles of the occupational and status groups can be compared by splitting the rack-vent values into £5 bands. Hence, for example, the two artisan trades of carpenters and cordwainers stand out as very homogeneous groups: over 60 per cent of the carpenters and 70 per cent of the cordwainers, for whom data survive, occupied property with a rack-rent of £10 or less. The victuallers, who may be presumed to have carried on their retailing businesses from their rated premises, were a more heterogeneous group: few of them occupied property with a rack-rent of £10 or less, though 86 per cent of them occupied property with a rack-rent of £25 or less; and a higher proportion of them occupied property in the upper teens and twenties of pounds than did the carpenters and cordwainers. No esquires occupied property in the two bands of £10 or less, in which were found 70 per cent of the cordwainers. But esquires were well represented in each band between £11 and £75, and then more sporadically over this sum. Self-styled gentlemen were even more widely dispersed, occupying properties with rack-rents from under £5 to over £100. The career of Simon Place is a reminder of the imprecision of titles of gentility in the eighteenth century.

The relationship between occupation and the rack-rent of property occupied may be examined at four levels, with varying degrees of comprehensiveness and accuracy. Analysis by economic sector has the advantage of creating larger groups for study, but it aggregates many between whom there may be little social connection, such as, for example, the clerks and the labourers, both of whom are classified among the industrial servants. Alternatively, the analysis may proceed at the level of the economic sub-sector: those dealing in coals are distinguished from those dealing in drink, and the clerks are distinguished from the labourers. That brings rather more precision to the analysis, though the numbers involved for each group are necessarily smaller. Thirdly, the relationship of occupation to rack-rent may be explored at the level of groups of closely-related occupations: within the sub-sector of the drink trade the victuallers, publicans and beer sellers may be distinguished from the wine merchants. And fourthly the groups may be analysed at the level of the actual occupational description which voters gave to the poll clerks: at this level the victuallers may be distinguished from the publicans, and the silversmiths from the goldsmiths and jewellers. But at this level the evidence is much scantier, given a population of rate-paying voters of just 1,249 in St Margaret and St John.

Returning, therefore, to the top level of analysis for St Margaret and St John, the mean rack-rent values by economic sector of occupation varied considerably between £11.00 among the industrial servants and £33.95 among the *rentiers*. The mean rack-rent for the whole population of 1,249 identified rate-paying voters in St Margaret and St John in 1784 is £18.74, with a standard deviation of £20.77. The results of the analysis by economic sector are tabulated below:

Table 10.2 Mean rack-rent values of property inhabited by all identified rate-paying voters in St Margaret and St John, Westminster, 1784 (£)

Economic Sector	Mean	Std Devn	Sd/Mean	Observations
Rentier	33.95	34.93	1.03	249
Transport	20.00	20.56	1.03	33
Dealing	18.18	11.85	0.65	324
Agriculture	16.87	15.95	0.95	15
Manufacturing	13.95	13.43	0.96	298
Professions & Public Service	13.30	12.71	0.96	126
Domestic & Personal Service	11.72	6.64	0.57	39
Building	11.30	9.75	0.88	159
Industrial Service	11.00	5.90	0.54	6
All Sectors	18.74	20.77	1.11	1,249

Mean values, however, reveal little about the dispersion of the individual rack-rent figures in each sector. That can be shown by the standard deviation figure, which has also been shown in a standardized form by being divided by the mean. Quartile and median values give a good idea of the dispersion within each economic sector, as shown in Table 10.3.

Table 10.3 Quartile dispersions of rack-rents of property occupied by all identified rate-paying voters in St Margaret and St John, Westminster, 1784 (£)

Economic Sector	Quartile 1	Median	Quartile 3	(Q3-Q1)/2
Rentier	12	23	40	14.0
Dealing	11	15	23	6.0
Transport	6	14	23	8.5
Agriculture	6	12	21	7.5
Manufacturing	8	11	15	3.5
Domestic & Personal Service	7	9	17	5.0
Industrial Service	6	9	15	4.5
Professions & Public Service	6	9	15	4.5
Building	7	9	12	2.5
All Sectors	8	12	21	6.5

Table 10.4 Mean and median rack-rents of property, inhabited by identified rate-paying *rentiers* in St Margaret and St John, Westminster, in 1784 (£)

Economic Sub-sector	Mean	Std Deviation	Observations	Median
Titled Nobility	150.00		1	
Knights & Baronets	107.17	81.45	6	85
Esquires	57.46	39.27	69	45
Gentlemen	21.36	17.62	173	15
All *Rentiers*	33.95	34.93	249	23

As the very high standard deviations and interquartile ranges show, the mean for each economic sector conceals wide variations in rack-rents. Analysis of the data in more detailed sub-groups corresponds more closely to the reality 'on the ground' of late eighteenth-century Westminster. For example, the sector of *rentiers* has been divided, in imitation of an ascending social hierarchy, into sub-sectors of gentlemen, esquires, knights and baronets, and titled nobility. These do indeed reveal progressive increases in mean rack-rent values commensurate with their rising status, though paucity of data indicates that the results for the two smallest sub-groups must be treated with caution (see Table 10.4).

Similarly, the mean rack-rent of £13.30 among the professionals and public servants conceals wide variations, particularly between members of the armed forces and the learned professions: those in the army sub-group had a mean rack-rent of £8.64 with a standard deviation of £5.82 in 84 observations, the mean being kept low by the urban yeomanry, 58 of whom had a mean rack-rent of less than £8. Meanwhile, the medical men, who included apothecaries, physicians, and surgeons, had a mean rack-rent of £28.50 with a standard deviation of £19.23 in 22 observations.

The large sector of dealers makes a particularly appropriate test case for splitting into sub-sectors: whereas the manufacturers fall into as many as thirty-one sub-groups of separate specialisms, making all but a few of them too small for serious comparative analysis, the dealers are divided into thirteen sub-groups. And dealing occupations may be allocated to their sub-goups with rather more confidence than with the manufacturers. One of the weaknesses of Booth's classification is that his categories are not necessarily exclusive: thus within the manufacturing sector the woodworkers are separated from the furniture makers. Booth's sub-groups within the manufacturing sector cut across materials and finished products: but rather than devise a wholly new classification, consistent rules have been followed in the allocation of occupations to sub-sectors, and problem areas have been noted.

It should be remembered, of course, that the occupations in Table 10.5 are grouped by the classification devised by Booth for analysing nineteenth-century census returns. His classification necessarily smooths and simplifies the rough edges of the original data, though at the more detailed level it remains good. For example, the coal trade consists of coal dealers and coal merchants, with a mean rack-rent of £15.84, and coal porters, coal heavers, and coal carters, who have a mean rack-rent of only £5.[29] In the sub-sector of the drink trade, victuallers have a mean

Table 10.5 Mean rack-rents of property occupied by identified rate-paying voters in St Margaret and St John, Westminster, in 1784 by sub-groups of the dealing sector (£)

Economic Sub-sector	Mean	Std Devn	Sd/Mean	Observations
Clothing Materials	37.40	12.50	0.33	5
Stationery	31.29	21.65	0.69	7
Raw Materials	29.00	18.99	0.65	16
Coffee Houses	27.67	4.04	0.15	3
Household Goods	26.00	11.78	0.45	4
Dress	22.36	9.24	0.41	11
Drink	19.97	10.44	0.52	102
Unspecified	18.00	14.13	0.79	20
Furniture	16.50	3.80	0.23	8
Food	15.35	9.30	0.61	84
Tobacco	14.75	6.04	0.41	4
Coal	13.96	7.15	0.51	23
General	10.48	6.06	0.58	37
All Dealers	18.18	11.85	0.65	324

rack-rent of £18.85, but vintners have a mean rack-rent of £30.13.[30] Finally, within the medical sub-sector of the professions, the humbler apothecaries have a mean rack-rent of £23.46, the surgeons have a mean rack-rent of £30.20, and the exalted physicians have a mean rack-rent of £52.33.[31] Like the detailed breakdown of the mean rack-rentals of *rentiers*, these details among the coal dealers and the drink trade, and among the medical men, look very plausible.

IV

It is clear that many of the results at this level of detail must be jeopardized by the infrequency of observations. Sociologists today seek to grade occupations by asking respondents to rank occupations in a hierarchy of status and prestige, or to attach multiple scores to occupations for various criteria such as skill and status. That is clearly impossible for a study of eighteenth-century society. But it might be possible to use rental values as a proxy for incomes, and to rank at any rate some of the larger occupations. The ability to rank all occupations on this basis is still elusive, and too much emphasis should not be placed on small differences of mean rack-rents between small groups.

Concentrating, therefore, on cases where data are plentiful, Table 10.6 shows a ranked hierarchy of those occupations in St Margaret and St John in 1784, with seven or more observations of rate-paying voters. It appears to support the idea that those who may have had business premises, such as the stable-keepers and the dealers, were in general more highly rated than the artisans in the building trades, who did not. The anomalous position of the stable-keepers stands revealed here: although the analyst of the electoral petition of 1774 reckoned them to be tradesmen 'of the lower class', they were clearly one of the better-off callings in Westminster at the time, with a mean rack-rental higher than the upper quartile of the *rentiers*. Also revealed is the striking distinction between the shoemakers and the cordwainers, whereby the cordwainers appear as the occupiers of higher-rated properties and the shoemakers as amongst the poorest artisan groups.[32] A print by Rowlandson of the Westminster election campaign of 1784 (reproduced as Fig. 10.3) shows one such shoemaker at work in Peter Street. The Duchess of Devonshire sits on Fox's knee, paying for a minor repair to her shoe by a cobbler who leers at the finely-turned aristocratic ankle.[33]

The need for caution in the interpretation of occupational titles is moreover confirmed by the case of the yeomen, of whom 136 voted in St Margaret and St John in 1784. Far from being the sturdy independent farmers of the seventeenth century, they turn out to be among the lowest rated of the major occupational groups, with a mean rack-rental of under £8.00. They have been classified among the professionals and public servants in the economic classification of occupations, on the assumption that the urban yeomen were in fact soldiers. This has undoubtedly greatly reduced the mean rack-rental figure for that sector.[34]

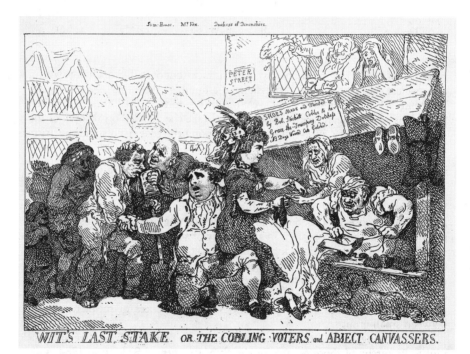

Figure 10.3. Fox and the Duchess of Devonshire at the 1784 Westminster election: print satirizing the enthusiastic canvass undertaken by Charles James Fox and his aristocratic supporter, the Duchess of Devonshire, before the 1784 Westminster election. They are shown here wooing the poorest shoemakers, although in the event the Poll Books show that, while some artisan occupations did give strong support to Fox, the shoemakers' votes were evenly divided between the rival parties.
Copyright: British Museum.

Table 10.6 Ranking of occupations with seven or more identified rate-paying voters in St Margaret and St John, Westminster, in 1784, by mean rack-rent values (£)

Occupation	Mean	Std Devn	Sd/Mean	Observations
Esquire	57.46	39.27	0.68	69
Stable-keeper	42.38	28.81	0.68	8
Vintner	30.13	23.11	0.77	8
Apothecary	23.46	12.95	0.55	13
Gentleman	21.36	17.62	0.82	173
Grocer	20.94	10.25	0.49	17
Publican	20.86	7.38	0.35	7
Cheesemonger	19.23	8.80	0.46	13
Victualler	18.85	8.07	0.43	81
Gardener	17.86	21.77	1.22	7
Wood Turner	17.71	9.23	0.52	7
Hairdresser	16.29	7.49	0.46	14
Baker	16.19	8.93	0.55	26
Coal Merchant	16.00	6.02	0.38	8
Coal Dealer	15.73	6.90	0.44	11
Butcher	14.60	9.99	0.68	20
Cordwainer	13.55	15.34	1.13	60
Painter	13.31	7.17	0.54	13
Tailor	13.13	9.40	0.72	39
Wheelwright	12.86	6.72	0.52	7
Cooper	12.82	7.82	0.61	11
Carpenter	12.49	13.25	1.06	73
Broker	11.50	3.23	0.28	14
Bricklayer	10.38	4.21	0.41	16
Peruke-maker	9.92	3.82	0.39	13
Greengrocer	9.50	3.50	0.37	12
Chandler	9.50	3.52	0.37	26
Sergeant	9.40	4.12	0.44	10
Plasterer	9.00	3.74	0.42	18
Stonemason	8.40	2.99	0.36	10
Yeoman	7.93	4.34	0.55	58
Coachman	6.93	2.28	0.33	15
Shoemaker	6.00	2.12	0.35	9
All Rate-paying Voters	18.74	20.77	1.11	1,249

V

Analysis by occupation must always remain central to much historical research since the data are available from many sources. But, while occupational groups may reveal aspects of those 'interest groups' that fascinate historians of the eighteenth century, they are imperfect guides to social differentiation. The construction of a new hierarchy based on a combination of occupational and tax data is beset with problems: partly because of the vast quantities of data required for such an exercise;

partly because definitions of class involve much more than the product of income and occupation; partly because of the problems of record linkage; and partly because tax data themselves are imprecise proxies for the wealth, status, and income of the taxpayers.

What has been shown is that occupational data themselves are imprecise and fluid. Even allowing for the assumption that Westminster's voters actually did what they said they did, the precise meaning of what they said remains unclear. The combination of both occupational and tax data in the analysis of a third variable makes a contribution greater than the sum of its parts, allowing a means of ranking and comparing items from the database.

There is no easy basis for the inference of a social classification from eighteenth-century occupational data. The poll books allow the identification of the tradesmen to whom Gibbon referred, and the rate books facilitate the distinction of at least some of the 'substantial' ones among them. Gibbon rightly drew attention to the social context of political behaviour. Eighteenth-century Westminster was not a simple two-class society, and political behaviour was conditioned by the interaction of more complex social forces than trade and 'substance' alone. But only if an adequate social classification is devised can Gibbon's *obiter dictum* be tested. The supplementing of information about the work done by the inhabitants of what was probably the world's largest city with information about their relative prosperity may go some way towards achieving that.

Notes

1. This essay is based on research-in-progress for a London University PhD thesis entitled 'Social Structure and Political Allegiance in Westminster, 1774–1820'. I am grateful to my supervisors, Dr P.J. Corfield and Dr Charles Harvey, and to the Computer Centre at Royal Holloway and Bedford New College, for advice, assistance, and encouragement. The research was supported by the Economic and Social Research Council, the Central Research Fund of the University of London, and Royal Holloway and Bedford New College.

2. J.E. Norton (ed.), *The Letters of Edward Gibbon* (3 vols, 1956), II, 251.

3. The right to vote in parliamentary elections was not uniform. In county constituencies the franchise was vested in forty-shilling freeholders. In the boroughs there were wide variations in the franchise, which could lie with burgages, with the corporation, among the freemen, or among the male inhabitants at large. Westminster had a 'Scot and Lot' franchise of rate-payers. In general elections, such as those of 1774 and 1784, both of Westminster's parliamentary seats were contested; voters had two votes at their disposal, though they were not obliged to use both.

4. See R.H. Hall, *Occupations and the Social Structure* (Englewood Cliffs, N.J., 1975); K. Hope (ed.), *The Analysis of Social Mobility: Methods and Approaches* (1972); and J. Goldthorpe and K. Hope, *The Social Grading of Occupations: A New Approach and Scale* (1974). Meanwhile, A. Stewart, K. Prandy, and R.M. Blackburn, in their *Social Stratification and Occupations* (1980), challenge the assumption that occupations can be used to indicate status or social class. A.P.M. Coxon and C.L. Jones in *The Images of Occupational Prestige* (1978) also challenge conventional use of occupational information.

5. M.B. Katz, 'Occupational classification in history', *Journal of Interdisciplinary History*, 3 (1972), 63–88.

6. Poll books are the records of voting in parliamentary elections prior to the introduction of the ballot. See J. Sims, *A Handlist of British Parliamentary Poll Books* (1984); and J.A. Phillips, *Electoral Behavior in Unreformed England: Plumpers, Splitters and Straights* (Princeton, N.J., 1982).

7. Printed poll books survive for the Westminster elections of 1774, 1780 and 1818: *A Correct Copy of the Poll for electing Two Representatives for the City and Liberty of Westminster* (1774); *Copy of the Poll for the Election of Two Citizens to serve in the Present Parliament for the City and Liberty of Westminster* (1780); *The Poll Book, for electing Two Representatives in Parliament for the City and Liberty of Westminster* (1818). The printed poll book for the election of 1780 lacks occupational data. These have been supplemented by manuscript poll books in the Greater London RO: WR/PP/1784, /1788, /1790, /1796, /1802, /1806, /1819, and /1820.

8. An investigation (recorded in the Chatham Papers) after the election of 1788, in which 11,961 voted, found that there were 17,291 households, of which 897 were unoccupied and 1,845 were headed by women, leaving 14,549 which may be presumed to have had a male householder: PRO, PRO30/8/237, f. 784.

9. Greater London RO, WR/PP/1784.

10. See D.J. Treiman, *Occupational Prestige in Comparative Perspective* (New York, N.Y., 1977), 120; and D.J. Treiman, 'A standard occupational prestige scale for use with historical data', *Journal of Interdisciplinary History*, 7 (1976), 283–304. Some evidence of the comparability of twentieth-century classifications to nineteenth-century data is presented in R.M. Hauser, 'Occupational status in the nineteenth and twentieth centuries', *Historical Methods*, 14 (1982), 111–26.

11. Among others, occupational classifications are discussed in M.B. Katz, 'Occupational classification in history', *Journal of Interdisciplinary History*, 3 (1972), 63–88; in J. Patten, 'Urban occupations in pre-industrial England', *Transactions of the Institute of British Geographers*, n.s. 2 (1977), 296–313; in F. Bédarida, 'Londres au milieu du XIXe siècle: une analyse de structure sociale', *Annales E.S.C.*, 23 (1968), 268–95; in P.H. Lindert, 'English occupations, 1670–1811', *Journal of Economic History*, 40 (1980), 685–712; in J. Ellis, 'A dynamic society: social relatons in Newcastle upon Tyne, 1660–1760', in *The Transformation of English Provincial Towns 1600–1800*, ed. P. Clark (1984), 217–20; and in Phillips, op. cit.

12. P.J. Corfield with S. Kelly, '"Giving Directions to the Town": the early town Directories', *Urban History Yearbook 1984* (1984), 22–35.

13. L.B. Namier and J. Brooke (ed.), *The House of Commons 1754–90* (1964), I, 335–7.

14. BL, Add. MS 33,123, f. 101.

15. For Gregory King, see G. Holmes, 'Gregory King and the social structure of pre-industrial England' in his *Politics, Religion and Society in England 1679–1742* (1986). Massie's analysis is described and reproduced in P. Mathias, 'The social structure in the eighteenth century: a calculation by Joseph Massie', *Economic History Review*, 2nd ser. *10* (1957), 30–45. Colquhoun's tables, published in his *Treatise on Indigence* (1806), are reproduced in M.D. George, *England in Transition* (1953), 152–3. See also below, 229 n. 81.

16. R. Campbell, *The London Tradesman* (1747, reprinted 1969).

17. M. Thale (ed.), *The Autobiography of Francis Place 1771–1854* (1972), 22–34.

18. C. Booth, 'Occupations of the people of the United Kingdom, 1801–81', *Journal of the Statistical Society*, 49 (1886), 314–444. W.A. Armstrong, 'The use of information about occupation', in *Nineteenth-Century Society: Essays in the Use of Quantitative Methods for the Study of Social Data*, ed. E.A. Wrigley (1972), 191–310. It is assumed that the voters did what they said they did: but the census authorities in 1891 drew attention to 'the foolish but very common desire of persons to magnify the importance of their occupational condition' (Census, 1891, IV, General Report, 36: cited in Armstrong, op. cit.). Occupations have been classified into nine economic sectors of

Agriculture, Building, Dealing, Domestic Service, Industrial Service, Manufacturing, Professions and Public Service, *Rentiers* and Transport. The Mining sector in the Booth-Armstrong classification is redundant in Westminster; it has been replaced by a sector of *Rentiers* to accommodate those many voters described as 'gentleman', 'esquire', and so on.

19. Useful accounts are contained in: M.D. George, *London Life in the Eighteenth Century* (second edn., 1966); G. Rudé, *Hanoverian London 1714-1808* (1971); N. Rogers, 'Aristocratic clientage, trade and independency: popular politics in pre-radical Westminster', *Past and Present*, 61 (1973), 70-106; and J. Stevenson (ed.), *London in the Age of Reform* (1977).

20. The Census Return of 1801 recorded a population of 153,272 in Westminster, of whom 33,934 were engaged in 'trade, manufacture, or handicraft': *British Parliamentary Papers, Abstract of the Answers and Returns made pursuant to an act . . . intituled, 'an Act for taking an Account of the Population of Great Britain'* (1801), 215.

21. This phrase is taken from E.P. Thompson, *The Making of the English Working Class* (1968), 13. The nineteenth-century artisan has received the attention of G. Crossick, *An Artisan Élite in Victorian Society: Kentish London 1840-80* (1978). But little work has been done on the eighteenth-century petty bourgeoisie, though much can be gleaned from E.P. Thompson, op. cit., *passim*.

22. For a contemporary view of the division of labour, its causes and consequences, see A. Smith, *An Enquiry into the Nature and Causes of the Wealth of Nations*, ed. R.H. Campbell and A.J. Skinner (2 vols, 1976), I, 13-24.

23. This miscellany of occupational specializations are taken from all the poll books between 1774 and 1820, as were those specialists in the coach-making trades.

24. There has been some confusion over the right to vote in Westminster, reflecting uncertainties and variations in eighteenth-century practice. After the election of 1749 the High Bailiff gave his opinion that 'The right of election for the City and Liberty of Westminster is in the Inhabitant Householders within the said City and Liberty paying or being liable to pay scot and lot' (PRO, PRO30/8/237, f. 795r). Under cross-examination before the Parliamentary Committee in 1789 Thomas Corbett, the High Bailiff of Westminster, followed the precedent and repeated the confusion that the franchise lay 'in the Inhabitant householders paying or being liable to pay scot and lot' (ibid., f. 791v). Thereafter would-be voters who had not paid their rates were liable to be successfully challenged on these grounds at the hustings and to be denied the vote.

25. See discussions on these sources in: L.D. Schwarz and L.J. Jones, 'Wealth, occupations and insurance in the late eighteenth century: the policy registers of the Sun Fire Office', *Economic History Review*, 2nd ser. 36 (1983), 365-73; and W.R. Ward, *The English Land Tax in the Eighteenth Century* (1953). Probate inventories become scarce for the period after the early eighteenth century, and other probate data are unavailable until the nineteenth century.

26. Rack-rents are valuations of property based upon the imputed annual rental value of the property. They may bear little similarity to the actual rents paid. The parish rate income in Westminster depended on three variables: the rack-rent, the rate levied upon this, and the frequency of collection. These could be different between parishes, or in the same parish over time. But within one parish in any year the rack-rent valuations should be comparable. The problems involved in using parish rates as a source are discussed by E. Baigent in her thesis, 'Bristol Society in the later Eighteenth Century, with special reference to the handling by computer of fragmentary historical sources' (D Phil thesis, University of Oxford, 1985) and in her article 'Assessed taxes as sources for the study of urban wealth: Bristol in the late eighteenth century', *Urban History Yearbook 1988* (1988), 31-48. On parish rates more generally considered, see E. Cannan, *The History*

of *Local Rates in England* (1896), and J.V. Beckett, *Local Taxation: National Legislation and the Problems of Enforcement* (1980).

27. I am grateful to Miss M. Swarbrick, Archivist at Westminster City Libraries Archives and Local History Department, for the loan of a microfilm of the poor rate books for St Margaret and St John in 1784: E/504–6.

28. Poll books have been linked to rate books of the same year on the basis of matching strings of characters for surnames and Christian names, and either matching or compatible addresses. Vowels and repeated consonants were stripped out of the personal name field in an attempt to apply a consistent correction to the uncertain and inconsistent orthography of the poll clerks and rate collectors. Matching at the level of compatible addresses was necessary because voters frequently were recorded as living in a main thoroughfare whilst paying rates on a property in a contiguous side-street. If more than one property was rated under the name of a voter, then the single highest-valued property was linked, on the assumption that this corresponded most closely with the income of the voter. See also E.A. Wrigley (ed.), *Identifying People in the Past* (1973), for discussion of problems in record linkage.

29. Information is available in: M.W. Flinn, *The History of the British Coal Industry, Vol II 1700–1830: The Industrial Revolution* (1984); T.S. Ashton and J. Sykes, *The Coal Industry of the Eighteenth Century* (1964); H.S. Jevons, *The British Coal Trade* (1915); and R. Smith, *Sea Coal for London* (1961).

30. On drink, see variously: P. Mathias, *The Brewing Industry in England 1700–1830* (1959); S. and B. Webb, *The History of Liquor Licensing in England* (1903); and P. Clark, *The English Alehouse: A Social History 1200–1800* (1983).

31. Detailed information on these occupations can be found in the following studies: B. Hamilton, 'The medical profession in the eighteenth century', *Economic History Review*, 2nd ser. 4 (1951–2); I. Waddington, *The Medical Profession in the Industrial Revolution* (Dublin, 1984); and I. Loudon, *Medical Care and the General Practitioner* (1986).

32. In this connection, it is interesting to note a usage of the words from Hawick in 1722 in which the cordwainers petitioned to be incorporated and separated from the shoemakers 'or those who make single-soled shoes': *O.E.D.*, 'Cordwainer'. For earlier variations in terminology in shoemaking trades, see above: 44, 65.

33. A wealth of material documents the significance of the political print in this period. See M.D. George, *Catalogue of Political and Personal Satires*, vols. V–X (1938–52), esp. vol VI, *1784–92* (1938); M.D. George, *English Political Caricature* (2 vols., 1959); J. Brewer, *The Common People and Politics 1750–90s* (1986); and H.M. Atherton, *Political Prints in the Age of Hogarth: A Study in the Ideographic Representation of Politics* (1974).

34. The imprecision of the eighteenth-century term 'yeoman' is discussed by G.E. Mingay, *English Landed Society in the Eighteenth Century* (1963), 88. Among the definitions of 'yeoman' recorded in *O.E.D.* are: a servant in a royal or noble household; a member of the bodyguard of the sovereign of England; and a man serving as a (foot) soldier. These last two senses are the reason for classifying them among the soldiery, although the sense of the royal servant might be more appropriate. These definitional problems will be discussed further in my thesis.

11 Working and moving in early-nineteenth-century provincial towns[1]

John A. Phillips

Shrewsbury began the nineteenth century as a small provincial town and continued in that capacity over the first decades of the century. Its population of only 15,000 at the turn of the century grew sluggishly to a peak of 21,000 in 1831 before declining slightly. By 1841, Shrewsbury contained only 18,000 residents. Life in nineteenth-century Shrewsbury appears to have been most remarkable for its calm in the face of England's vibrant population and economy. Shrewsbury seems not to have even been aware of many of the events that transformed England's urban face, and some of its inhabitants shared the town's general torpor. James Evan Adams, cabinet-maker, lived in Castle Gates in St Mary's parish, Shrewsbury in 1826. Four years later, he continued to follow the same occupation, and since he occupied the same house it is no surprise to find that he also paid rates on an assessed rental of four pounds in both years.

Other inhabitants of this ancient town on the Severn, first chartered by King John in AD 1200, were less fixed in their jobs and homes. While J.E. Adams remained absolutely static residentially and occupationally, his fellow parishioner Thomas Cheshire, a writing clerk, moved from Chester Street to Castle Foregates and in the process increased his poor rate assessment, as his new premises were valued two pounds higher than his previous rental of four pounds. Over the same years James France, another parishioner of St Mary's, also moved house, but unlike Cheshire's, his move resulted in no change in his tax assessment; the assessed rental of his new dwelling in Chester Street matched that of his old place in Back Street. France worked at the same job over these years, plying his trade as a whitesmith in 1826 and in 1830. Another Shrewsbury freeman, William Pryce, paid the same poor rate over these years for the same residence in Hill's Lane, but Pryce's life must have changed significantly when he changed jobs from maltster to victualler. Yet another freeman, with the unlikely name Richards Richards, changed abode, occupation, and tax status over these years. He called himself a tailor in 1826 and paid poor rates on a Castle Gates house assessed at £2 10s. 0d.; 1830 found him claiming to be a tinplate worker and living in Castle Street in a house rated at exactly three pounds. So much about his life changed that only his unusual name permits reasonable certainty that the two sets of records pertained to the same individual.[2]

Changes like these in the occupational, residential, and relative socio-economic positions of individuals living in early-nineteenth-century English towns were far from rare, even in Shrewsbury. Nearly a quarter of all of the residents of Shrewsbury's St Mary's parish moved house in 1830 alone. By 1834 the residential mobility rate in St Mary's had increased to almost 30 per cent.[3] Many of these moves resulted in a higher or lower poor rate for the household, but many of them yielded no net change. At the same time men in Shrewsbury – and elsewhere – were changing jobs with considerable frequency. Their movements up, down, or laterally in the economy seem to have been as complicated and as common as their changes of residence.

This essay examines as closely and as frequently as the available data permit the relationship between working and moving in Shrewsbury and two other towns, Bristol and Northampton, during the second, third and fourth decades of the nineteenth century. Many important questions about working and moving cannot be answered satisfactorily, but the questions are so central to an adequate understanding of the lives of those working and living in towns that they demand consideration regardless of their susceptibility to answers. Before examining the complex relationship between working and moving in these three towns, however, the problems inherent in occupational analyses require careful consideration. It is difficult enough to measure residential mobility among historical populations, but from virtually every perspective working is a much trickier concept than moving.

I Occupations and Social Stratification

When Messrs. Gore and Son, printers, of Castle Street, published the Liverpool poll book of 1818, they included an occupational analysis of the voters, but the rationale behind it is far from obvious.[4] After beginning rather conventionally with 'Gentlemen, Merchants, and Brokers' taken together, the listing moved on to 36 other occupational categories containing sometimes a single occupation, sometimes several. Coopers appeared alone, as did masons, hatters, and jewellers, while painters were clumped with plumbers and glaziers. Bricklayers were forced into the company of slaters and plasterers. The Gores may have conceived of the list as a hierarchical structuring of occupations since it began with 'gentlemen' and almost ended with 'labourers', but if so the hierarchy is not always apparent. What exactly they intended to demonstrate or thought they *had* demonstrated with their list also remains obscure. Their presentation of the voting patterns of the 37 groupings is as complex as the groupings of occupations, and it would tax anyone's imagination to conclude anything about the relative support among any particular group for any of the three candidates standing for Liverpool. The publishers of the pollbook chose to present the table without comment, just as they chose not to discuss the accompanying geographical analysis of the non-resident voters at the election. They must have believed the information to be of some value, because it cannot have been particularly easy to categorize nearly 3,000 voters in such detail, but the value escapes a modern reader. Information about the behaviour of individual occupations of groups or related occupations is potentially interesting, but for any *systematic* analysis of urban occupational structure, then or now, the Liverpool list is virtually useless. Knowing the political preferences of tobacconists or enamellers or musicians (all categories in the Liverpool list) advances our knowledge of political behaviour very little; finding enamellers listed nine categories after tobacconists and the solitary musician ranked last without explanation reveals even less.

That same year, the editors of the *Sussex Advertiser* introduced their own, far simpler, occupational scheme for an analysis of the hotly contested parliamentary election in Lewes.[5] Attached to the published list of votes was a breakdown of the voters into two groups: 'clergy, gentry, yeomen, and tradesmen' on the one hand, and 'clerks, journeymen, handicraftsmen, and labourers' on the other. In such fashion, the *Advertiser* believed it had demonstrated conclusively that the incumbent Tory candidates had attracted greater support from Lewes's 'respectable' voters. In one respect, the *Advertiser*'s list is preferable to the one the Gores devised because the rationale underlying its categorization is much clearer. The Liverpool occupational categories may have meant many things, but the editors of the *Advertiser* imposed a distinct, albeit rather simple, hierarchical structuring upon the residents of Lewes who had participated in the election. Even so, the *Advertiser* list is almost as useless analytically. Without knowing the specific occupations that made up the broad categories devised by the Lewes editors, much less their reasons for counting particular occupations in particular groups, the Lewes listing cannot be compared to any other contemporary listing such as the one for Liverpool. It also cannot provide the basis for the construction of a comparable listing. Neither list vouchsafes much insight into contemporary perceptions of social structure, nor does either facilitate analysis of urban social structure. The apparent perception of respectable and less respectable voters in Lewes is barely noteworthy and too general to be of much value.

Unfortunately, there are no generally acceptable alternative listings or rankings of occupations that could be used to facilitate an interpretation of the Liverpool and Lewes lists. And just as certainly as historians would refuse to use these published divisions of occupations in Lewes and Liverpool, even if the two sets of publishers had explained their schemes far more adequately, historians are virtually certain to disagree over any alternative division of specific occupations into larger occupational categories.

Virtually every attempt to construct meaningful occupational categories for eighteenth- and nineteenth-century populations has failed as badly to meet with general acceptance as the efforts of these Sussex and Lancashire publishers. The reason, of course, is what appears to be a universal inability to grapple effectively with the infinitely complicated questions raised in discussing social relationships. Ultimately, the problem becomes one of defining 'class', a task that seems to have baffled Marx himself.[6] Penelope Corfield recently described some of the 'highly eclectic' eighteenth-century usages of 'class', from James Nelson's five classes of 1753 to Adam Smith's 'three great, original, and constituent orders of every civilized society' of 1776.[7] Daniel Defoe in 1705, Joseph Massie in 1756, and Patrick Colquhoun in 1814 all used seven occupational categories to describe English society, but their groupings share little besides numerical equality.[8] The conflation of 'class' and older concepts of 'rank and degree' tended to confuse the issue for observers in the eighteenth century; not that it has become any clearer subsequently.

The fluidity of eighteenth and nineteenth-century society compounded the problems encountered by those wishing to describe it. Census takers themselves have constantly wrestled with occupational categories, but they have failed to achieve either consistency or precision.[9] W.A. Armstrong tried to turn necessity into a virtue by suggesting that historians simply define class as occupational status. As R.J. Morris has observed, this solution is unsatisfactory. According to Morris, occupational title cannot define class, but might permit historians to make intelligent estimates of an individual's social class.[10] Others have suggested that class cannot be defined by economic or material criteria, or indeed by any criteria at all since class is, and was, a relationship and thus inaccessible to historians even if they try to take this relationship into account.[11] Moreover, R.S. Neale has argued persuasively that virtually all of those involved in the long debate over the existence of an English working class have fallen notably short of demonstrating the presence of 'classes' in England that evinced the sort of class-consciousness Marx had in mind most of the time when he discussed the concept.[12] Thus idiosyncracy has been the principal attribute of occupational descriptions of English society; it is hardly surprising that historians have been unable to achieve consensus.

Some have attempted to avoid the problems inherent in occupational groupings by examining occupations individually. This approach has facilitated neither systematic nor comparative analysis, but has provided better information than reports of various, unexplained, and therefore useless 'clusters' of occupations such as Vincent reported in his pioneering look at Victorian pollbooks.[13] Examining individual occupations, though, cannot provide a reasonable solution to the problem facing most historians because of the sheer number of occupations encountered in an examination of most historical communities. Urban history is particularly ill-served by the individual-occupation approach, and the problem increases as one moves across time. Examining solitary occupations in fifteenth-century Northampton might be possible, but nineteenth-century Northampton defies any such attempt. By 1841, even a small, shoemaking town like Northampton contained men who claimed hundreds of different occupational titles.

On the other hand, those who have suggested occupational classification schemes for general use usually have seen them disappear without measurable impact. Even a major collaborative effort like the American 'Five Cities Project' failed to create consensus. Historians have not responded positively to suggestions that 'any scholar can link his own data by using *our* rules and can achieve results which, at the least, may be compared to ours with some confidence'.[14] As a result, the published research of historians, demographers, and the like, usually has not been comparable. Also as a result, the following examination of the relationship between occupational and residential mobility in three nineteenth-century towns must be prefaced by the suggestion of an occupational scheme appropriate for the task.

Although useful, existing occupational categorizations for nineteenth-century urban populations do not fully capture social realities in the three towns selected for this essay on the basis of both randomness and the iron law of available data. Given the striking differences between Bristol, Shrewsbury, and Northampton, it would be an extraordinarily effective categorization that could be employed for all three without alteration or emendation. Bristol dwarfed both Shrewsbury and Northampton at the accession of George IV. With a population of about 60,000, Bristol still ranked as England's seventh largest town at the beginning of the nineteenth century. It fell to eighth place by 1831, but managed to grow at a pace closely approximating that of the whole country. Originally contained in twenty-two parishes covering a restricted area surrounded by or adjacent to the River Avon, the early nineteenth-century city expanded into its large out-parishes, St Paul, Saints

Philip and Jacob, Bedminster, and Clifton, all of which ultimately were incorporated into the city in the political reforms of 1832 and 1835, resulting in a roughly circular city within a diameter of eight to ten kilometres.

Bristol's population growth occurred in the face of a long economic decline that plagued the city even before the end of the eighteenth century. Bristol had never fully recovered from the trade disruption occasioned by the war with the American colonies, and the problems associated with transatlantic trade generally were exacerbated by Liverpool's emergence late in the eighteenth century as England's slaving capital. Many efforts to shore up the local economy, some of them desperate, failed. The massive construction project that revamped Bristol's harbour between 1804 and 1809 proved to be so expensive that shipping costs to and from Bristol reached prohibitive levels. The sad result was a further decline in trade rather than the prosperity promised by the Bristol Dock Company. In the decade following 1822, the value of exports from Bristol dropped by a third, and imports suffered similarly. The end of the slave trade meant that after 1807 it was no longer possible for a man like John Cam Hobhouse's father to turn a gross profit of more than £6,000 from a single and relatively small cargo shipped to the West Indies.[15] With the sharp decline in the triangular trade even before the actual abolition of the slave trade, the sea dominated Bristol's trades to a lesser extent than earlier. Improvements in other areas such as the various metals industries helped to remedy some of the deficit, but the overall picture was far from positive.

Although much smaller than Bristol or Shrewsbury in 1800, Northampton benefited both from a growing specialization in the manufacture of shoes and from the opening in 1815 of a branch canal connected to the Grand Union Canal. With such stimuli, Northampton doubled its initial nineteenth-century population by 1831 and tripled it by 1841, surpassing Shrewsbury in the process. But growth does not always mean prosperity, and in Northampton development did not mean improvement. Between a quarter and a third of the electorate, and probably nearly the same proportion of the entire adult male population, occupied their days with some usually poorly-paid aspect of shoemaking. Spread over four parishes of increasingly impoverished aspect moving from east to west, Northampton's early nineteenth-century workers lived in a particularly desolate, albeit expanding, environment.[16]

Three such diverse towns posed serious challenges to a systematic comparison of occupations. Bristol's inhabitants claimed hundreds of different occupational titles, as did Shrewsbury's and Northampton's despite their relatively small size. Other studies of nineteenth-century urban occupations assisted materially in accomplishing the task. The 'Five Cities' scheme, for example, considered many similar occupational titles and dealt with many comparable problems. This collaborative effort attempted to achieve consensus among scholars examining five nineteenth-century North American cities: Philadelphia; Hamilton, Ontario; and the New York State trio of Kingston, Buffalo, and Poughkeepsie. The original goal was to eliminate disagreement over occupations containing very few people and to devise groupings only for those occupations that accounted for 75 per cent of the workforce. Only 30 occupations accounted for three-quarters of workers in Buffalo, New York, in 1860 while 80 were required for Philadelphia. The combined list of 113 occupations for each city were then grouped vertically and horizontally. Subsequently, occupations with smaller numbers were added.[17] Just as most of the occupations in nineteenth-century Bristol, Shrewsbury and Northampton were best described as 'skilled' labour, most of the jobs encountered by the 'Five Cities' project were best described as 'craftsman'. Nevertheless, too many differences, specific and general, existed to permit its wholesale adoption. The Five-Cities distinction of manufacturers (Vertical Category 2) and makers (Vertical Category 3) is inappropriate since the terms maker and manufacturer were often interchangeable in early-nineteenth-century English towns. William Peach of Bridgwater called himself a rope-maker *or* rope manufacturer. James Ager of Northampton used the titles shoemaker and shoe manufacturer indiscriminately, just as Stephen Ald, Henry Auld, and John Faulkner also of Northampton, called themselves at different times shoemakers, boot manufacturers, or shoe manufacturers. Bedstead makers did not distinguish themselves from bed manufacturers, nor chocolate makers from chocolate manufacturers. Nor could all 'merchants' be clustered with all 'gentlemen' without sacrificing too much potential information about social status.[18]

One of the few efforts to examine English towns from comparable sources and for a comparable period demands special consideration. In an effort to understand the intricacies of the early nineteenth-century middle classes, R.J. Morris examined England's frenetic woollen metropolis, Leeds. Rather than examining the jobs followed by all of the city's inhabitants, though, Morris focused on those occupations listed in the pollbooks of 1832 and 1834 as well as those in the city directory of 1834.[19] He found 636 specific occupational titles and considered them from virtually every conceivable perspective except the one of greatest concern in this analysis – relative socio-economic status. By considering a new (post-Reform) borough whose voters were all qualified through their occupation of premises valued at £10 per annum or more, Morris dealt with a definitionally 'middle-class' population and so the question of relative socio-economic status never arose. The three towns examined here, on the other hand, were constituencies long before 1832. Their franchise varied enormously, but *each* of them contained considerable numbers of men who fell below the ten-pound qualification and who cannot be counted among Morris's 'middle-class'. Additionally, caught squarely in the midst of the industrial revolution, Leeds contained a very different population than less economically-advanced towns like Shrewsbury.

The potentially insurmountable difficulties associated with measuring local stratification even in the best of circumstances are compounded enormously by deficiencies in the data available for early nineteenth-century towns. By any normal historical standard, the data are extraordinarily rich, but they are nevertheless inadequate to meet the extraordinarily rigorous demands made upon them by attempts to analyse social stratification. Occupational title is often the sum total of the socio-economic data for any individual. Occasionally, journeymen are distinguished from masters, which allows some additional economic discrimination, but the surviving data usually reveal only the grossest distinctions. The mere existence of the journeyman/master distinction in the Lewes pollbook of 1818 and in other towns on occasion does not necessarily indicate a desire to distinguish voters economically, but if the information had been gathered more frequently it could now be put to that use, whatever the intentions of the original gatherers.[20]

Assessing the social status of some occupations poses few difficulties, although even a title as unambiguous as 'clergyman' can require difficult decisions about the relative status of Nonconformist ministers and Anglican clergymen. Other categories, such as handicraftsmen, pose far greater obstacles. Should 'tailors' be counted as 'handicraftsmen' or as 'tradesmen'? Were tailors as a group distinguishable from grocers as a group? Neale has demonstrated the economic heterogeneity of shoemakers and others in Bath during the early years of the century, yet surely shoemakers *as a group* can be distinguished economically and socially from bankers *as a group*. Nor were worsted weavers likely to rate at all well in comparison to large merchants or woolstaplers.[21] Even more serious problems arise in trying to make finer distinctions, and most of these questions have only the most general and unsatisfactory answers.

The occupational data presented here are derived from urban pollbooks and their consequent electoral bias raises a number of other problems that cannot be overcome.[22] Certainly these voters cannot be expected to represent any complete urban population. In addition to the obvious gender bias, the voters in Bristol and Shrewsbury were less likely to have come from the lower end of the socio-economic spectrum than in Northampton, where a 'potwalloper' franchise requirement resulted in virtual universal manhood suffrage. Only the very poor, those without a 'pot to boil', were systematically excluded from voting in Northampton's parliamentary elections. The 'freeman/freeholder' franchises in Bristol and Shrewsbury resulted in far fewer voters at the lower end of the social spectrum, but in each of these towns as well, men pursued a wide variety of occupations.

The men examined in this analysis used more than 900 specific titles to describe themselves when the polling clerk asked them their occupations immediately prior to the poll, but substantial numbers of voters in each town could claim no better occupation than 'labourer'. Many others clearly spent their days in jobs requiring few if any skills.[23] Between half and two-thirds of the Northamptoners in this study claimed skilled occupations while between six and twelve per cent were unskilled. But even with its more restrictive franchise, a similarly broad range of occupations marked Bristol's electorate, even in the skilled and unskilled sectors. In the 1830s, the proportion of skilled workers in the Bristol electorate dropped to about 40 per cent, but before 1832 they accounted for as much as 62 per cent of the electorate. Unskilled workers actually improved their share of the electorate after the Reform Act, making up fully ten per cent of the voting population by 1841. Shrewsbury's occupational make-up resembled Bristol's prior to 1832 and followed the same post-Reform trends.

The electoral bias of these data is partially offset by a number of distinctive strengths. The research strategy employed combined all the information related to individuals into single, inclusive records spanning the three decades of the extant pollbooks for these three towns. Thus John Acourt's occupation and address in Northampton in 1818 were linked to similar information about him in 1820. In like fashion, the information recorded at each appearance of James Evan Adams in Shrewsbury's elections was combined into a single history of his occupation and residence each year. Comprehensive, individual-level panel data of this sort permit a longitudinal examination of the lives of thousands of men. Both the self-ascription involved in occupational titles and the relatively short intervals between the occasions on which individuals described their occupations greatly increase the confidence with which they can be approached. Many other studies of occupational structure have relied on decennial census data, but only a few months or at most a few years separated these occupational self-ascriptions.[24] The sheer number of episodes improves the perspective on these individuals considerably by permitting occupational and residential attributes of individuals to be examined in considerable detail over quite a long period. Occupations and addresses for the same individuals were recorded as many as nine times over the two or three decades involved.

Socio-economic Strata: Another Attempt

Finding no generally acceptable solution to the problem, not wishing to break with tradition, and being compelled to create clusters of occupations to deal with 929 distinct occupational titles, this research employed yet another idiosyncratic set of occupational categories.[25] But rather than a proposal for general adoption which would undoubtedly meet the ignominious fate of previous efforts at categorization, the occupational strata devised for and employed in this research are intended only as indices of socio-economic status that are sufficient to permit an analysis of occupational and residential mobility. The appendix to this essay lists the eleven strata used in this analysis, but the overwhelming majority (over 90 per cent) of the occupations being examined were contained in only five categories: professional/ gentle, merchant élite, retail, skilled, and unskilled.[26]

The general utility of these admittedly crude occupational strata are demonstrated in two tables, the first of which merely presents suggestive corroborative, longitudinal, relational evidence of the consistency of the occupational claims of the residents of these towns. Much of the longitudinal consistency apparent in Table 11.1 results from the tendency of the bulk of these men to claim identical occupational titles year-in and year-out. George Aman of Northampton called himself a shoemaker in each of the nine years in which he was asked his occupation in the process of polling. Richard Morris of Shrewsbury was a hairdresser in 1819 and continued to follow that trade each year until he disappeared from view after 1841. Neither of these men changed strata because their occupations remained absolutely stable. Most of their fellows in all three towns proved to be as settled in their jobs.

There were substantial numbers of men who described themselves differently from year to year, as is revealed in Table 11.4, yet the occupational strata in Table 11.1 proved very stable nonetheless. This stability suggests that specific occupational titles are positioned relatively well among the several occupational strata, because many misplaced occupations would have created inconsistency across strata over time. If, to use a common example, 'clickers' (shoe-leather cutters) had been grouped with retailers, an individual who called himself a 'clicker' in one year and 'shoemaker' in another would have been placed in two different occupational strata at the two points in question. Changes of exactly this kind resulted in the relatively poor consistency of those classified as 'merchant élite'. Many of these men called themselves 'bankers' for a number of years, but either ended their careers by calling themselves 'gentleman', or chose to use another descriptor like 'esquire' at some point, thus pushing them into the highest stratum. In addition to subtle occupational moves that may or may not indicate socio-economic change, some individuals *did* effectively change their occupational stratum over time through genuine success or failure. Including both subtle shifts like banker to gentleman and more dramatic shifts such as William Gibson of Northampton's move from servant to shoemaker to beerseller over time, Table 11.1 reveals that remarkable consistency marks the occupational strata used in this analysis.

Perfect consistency (100 per cent) from year to year is not uncommon, as Table 11.1 shows, and consistency levels generally remained well above 90 per cent for most strata for each pair of years considered despite changes in specific occupational titles. For example, Table 11.4 reveals that 16 per cent of the men in Shrewsbury claimed different job titles in 1841 than the ones they had used in 1837. In Bristol, more than 30 per cent of the men described their jobs in 1841 differently from 1837, and in Northampton the figure topped 36 per cent. In light of that level of change in specific occupational titles, the consistency of strata in Table 11.1 is reassuring. Eight of the 15 categories in the 1837–41 comparison in Table 11.1 measured above 90 per cent, and the remainder with one exception measured above 80 per cent. Between 60 and 69 per cent of those men in Bristol, Northampton and Shrewsbury who changed their specific job description remained in the same occupational strata. And most of the movement into and out of strata occurred between adjacent

Table 11.1 Consistency of occupational descriptions among groups of voters (percentages)

	1819–26	1826–30	1830–31	1831–32	1832–35	1835–37	1837–41
Shrewsbury							
Professional	85.0	84.2	89.9	85.7	93.5	95.9	97.3
Merchant Elite	61.9	81.0	92.3	100.0	95.8	83.8	79.0
Retail	93.9	86.9	91.4	96.0	96.2	90.4	89.1
Skilled	97.7	96.3	98.2	100.0	98.0	96.6	97.4
Unskilled	95.8	96.4	97.3	88.9	100.0	87.2	87.2
Northampton							
Professional	87.5[1]	100.0	95.0	89.1	94.4	88.2	96.7
Merchant Elite	100.0	92.5	95.8	93.2	93.3	90.0	95.1
Retail	91.7	87.1	97.1	89.8	90.5	90.7	91.8
Skilled	94.6	97.0	93.4	91.4	92.1	89.5	96.6
Unskilled	97.4	90.8	97.6	96.7	98.6	89.6	91.4
Bristol							
Professional	87.5[2]	100.0[3]		92.3[4]	NA	80.3	84.0
Merchant Elite	90.9	75.0		93.3		89.3	80.0
Retail	93.2	91.9		94.7		87.3	82.4
Skilled	98.1	98.1		98.6		94.2	92.4
Unskilled	100.0	91.7		100.0		87.8	81.8

NA Data not available
[1] Elections 1818–20
[2] Elections 1812–20
[3] Elections 1820–30
[4] Elections 1830–32

Sources: Database created from occupational titles contained in printed or manuscript poll books. See John Sims (ed.), *A Handlist of British Parliamentary Poll Books* (1984).

strata in this hierarchical scheme. Thus men in the 'merchant élite' grouping either remained there or moved slightly upward into the 'professional' category or slightly downward into the ranks of the 'retailers'.

Table 11.2 reveals the degree to which these strata are also related to economic variations in the populations in question. Evidence of the economic status of these individuals is both extremely rare and terribly flawed, but it tends to underscore the utility and reliability of the occupational groups. Neither wealth nor income data exist for any group. In fact, the only economic evidence available for reasonable numbers of Englishmen are land-tax assessments and poor-rate levies. Donald Ginter has shown that by the second decade of the nineteenth century, the redemption option available to land-tax payers rendered it useless as a guide to economic status, but the poor rates were not affected by this change in the land-tax. Elizabeth Baigent's close study of eighteenth-century Bristol has identified serious problems with the poor rate as well.[27] Poor-rate data can appear to be orderly and reliable when in fact their apparent accuracy is spurious. At best, the poor rates indicate only estimated rental values of property, and as such pose an extremely nebulous and inflexible guide to the economic status of an individual. Moreover, regardless of the relative accuracy and appropriateness of an individual's assessment in one ratebook for a specific property, the individual's overall relative economic status can be measured only if *all* of his assessments are recovered. Despite these problems, poor-rate assessments can be used to make extremely broad distinctions between rich and poor, and it is this very limited task to which they are turned in Table 11.2.[28]

Two mid-nineteenth-century publishers used poor rates unapologetically as a guide to individual economic status. Printed pollbooks for Banbury (1859) and Bath (1855) included rate assessments for each voter and used them to analyse the relative 'respectability' of the support for the candidates involved. By simply totalling the rateable values of the voters for each candidate, the Banbury publishers demonstrated what they believed to be the inequity involved in the one-vote victory of Bernhard Samuelson over John Hardy in the face of an 'excess of assessment of Mr. Hardy's voters over Mr. Samuelson's' of nearly £5,000, and an 'excess of assessment of Mr. Hardy's voters over *all* the other electors', of almost £68.[29] Similarly, Harvard and Payne, printers of the Bath pollbook of 1855, pointed to the disparity in the election of William Tite instead of William Whateley even though the assessments of Whateley's supporters provided an 'excess' of more than £22,000 over those who voted for Tite.[30]

Poor-rate assessments are not put to such an unusual and unconvincing task here. Instead, Table 11.2 presents the results of comparison of the assessed rental values contained in all extant Shrewsbury poor-rate lists (divided into quartiles) and the occupational group of each individual for whom economic data could be found.[31] The results broadly support the suggested occupational stratification. Considerable economic variation existed in the 'retail' and 'skilled' categories used, as might be expected, but the relationship between occupational strata and economic position is strongly positive. A broad positive correlation between occupational stratum and relative economic status is apparent in each of the years examined, and these strata would appear, therefore, to serve their function as crude socio-economic indicators.

Such rough socio-economic strata do not entirely sidestep the question of 'class', but resolve some of the problems involved with class terminology. These 'strata' are

Table 11.2 Shrewsbury – assessed property values of occupational groups of voters (percentages)

		Assessed Property Value (Quartiles)				
		I	II	III	IV	N
Year	Occupation Group					
1826	Professional	100	–	–	–	
	Merchant Elite	100	–	–	–	
	Retail	51	20	21	8	
	Skilled	11	27	30	32	
	Unskilled	–	28	29	43	
						173
1830	Professional	80	20	–	–	
	Merchant Elite	63	25	12	–	
	Retail	31	38	16	15	
	Skilled	13	20	31	36	
	Unskilled	6	18	35	41	
						198
1835	Professional	85	15	–	–	
	Merchant Elite	66	23	8	3	
	Retail	24	36	31	9	
	Skilled	9	16	30	45	
	Unskilled	–	10	35	55	
						251
1841	Professional	83	17	–	–	
	Merchant Elite	68	32	–	–	
	Retail	39	28	26	7	
	Skilled	19	31	32	19	
	Unskilled	–	25	37	38	
						122

Sources: Shrewsbury Parliamentary Pollbooks, 1825, 1830, 1835, 1841. Parish Poor Rate Assessments for St Mary's, St Julian's, and St Alkmund's. Shropshire Record Office, Shrewsbury.

not asked to carry such an impossibly heavy burden. Far from accepting, or even testing, Thompson's argument that 'the working class presence was, in 1832, the most significant factor in British political life',[32] the figures in Table 11.2 only suggest that roughly identifiable socio-economic lines of demarcation can be drawn around the various occupations in which nineteenth-century townsmen engaged, and that these lines can convey simultaneously, albeit crudely, economic and social differences. At any rate, neither Bristol nor Shrewsbury would be the place to look for class warfare, and Foster has shown how poorly Northampton would serve as a testing ground for class struggle. Northampton workers proved incapable of organization and exhibited no signs of class consciousness.[33]

II Residential and Occupational Mobility

The real concern of this essay is the relationship between occupational and residential mobility. Richard Dennis observed that 'residential mobility is frequently associated with social mobility', but his own study of later nineteenth-century Huddersfield proved inconclusive on that point.[34] He found a greater tendency among renters to move residence than among owner-occupiers, which certainly would have been expected, but the relationship between social status and residential mobility in Huddersfield was unclear. No clear relationship between working and moving presents itself in the available data from these three towns either, but an examination of residential mobility and changes in specific occupational titles among these urban workers is suggestive.

After the difficulties involved in describing and measuring occupations and socio-economic stratification, measurements of the residential mobility patterns of these urban workers, while also fraught with problems of their own, seem both easily accomplished and interpreted. The peripatetic tendencies of past populations are now well known. Nineteenth-century urban populations were constantly on the move, though physical mobility often spanned very short distances. Those near the bottom of the social scale moved frequently but 'rarely beyond the range of local shops, pubs, and churches.'[35] Pollbook data, flawed in so many other ways, also fail to provide residential information beyond street and parish. Thus some residential mobility in these towns escapes observation, since all moves within the same street as well as very rapid moves away from a street and back again are undetectable.[36] Nor can out-migration and in-migration be examined; the former cannot be distinguished from death on the one hand and the latter is indistinguishable from household formation. The restricted nature of the populations being examined also is likely to understate overall residential mobility.[37]

Nevertheless, the populations of these towns were strikingly mobile. And, as with occupational mobility, more variation occurs within single towns than across the three towns. Men like Benjamin Fox, chairmaker, of Northampton who listed his address as Fetter Lane eight times between 1818 and 1841, and George Aman, cabinet maker, who also appears to have lived in the same place in Northampton throughout all of those years, were the exception to the rule. More typical was Northampton's other Benjamin Fox, sometime butcher, shoemaker, cowkeeper, and farmer who lived on occasion in Gold Street, Silver Street, Scarlett Well Lane, and Bath Street. Another 'mover' was Northampton shoemaker John Auburn. He lived on Bridge Street in 1818 and 1820, had moved to Mill Lane by 1826, then to Green Street until 1832, to Mayorhold by 1835, St Andrew's Street in 1837, and ended up in St Andrew's Square in 1841. Northampton occupied a rather small space that could easily be encompassed by a circle with a radius of only 2,000 feet in 1810, and even with the rapid growth of the town's population between 1810 and 1840, its physical dimensions could never be described as imposing. Yet even within the narrow limits of Northampton's four small parishes, the household moves of both Fox and Auburn covered short distances.

Nor did Shrewsbury's relatively small size prevent many household moves by those permanently resident in the town. William Hulme, a Shrewsbury hairdresser, moved from Ox Lane to the Castle Gates to Fish Street to St Mary's Place, before moving finally to Castle Street in 1841. William Schofield claimed to be a bellman

Table 11.3 Residential mobility – voters moving within town (percentages)

	1819–26	1826–30	1830–31	1831–32	1832–35	1835–37	1837–41
Shrewsbury	27.7	30.9	14.5	17.1	10.8	21.9	24.9
N	343	476	276	193	714	776	818
Northampton	38.4[1]	45.0	18.8	20.5	24.8	21.0	31.1
N	234	280	382	424	404	352	294
Bristol	61.9[2]	69.8[3]	20.4[4]		18.0	33.6	37.8
N	302	255	647		748	634	688
Bristol Movers Between Parishes	47.3	50.0	10.9		8.4	17.1	20.0
N	296	252	652		749	633	659

[1] Elections 1818–26
[2] Elections 1812–20
[3] Elections 1820–30
[4] Elections 1830–32

Sources: See Table 11.4.

while living in Kiln Lane in 1819 but called himself a butcher, before he moved to Claremont Street at some point before 1830. He moved, appropriately enough, to Gullet Passage while still a butcher, and then moved to Pride Hill in 1837 where he remained while changing his job description from butcher to carpenter in 1841. John Nicholls, a Bristol butcher, moved even more often. First occupying dwellings in Lime Kiln Lane, he reported a different address in each of the six other years when asked. He moved first a very short distance to Lime Kiln Dock, then to Pinnell Street, Kingsdown Parade, Alfred Hill, and West Street before moving to Redcliffe Place in 1841. These moves occurred between Bristol's new gaol and Temple Meads in the delta formed by Bristol's floating harbour and the new course of the River Avon, in the parish of St Mary Redcliffe.[38] A Bristol minister, Richard G. Bedford occupied five different residences between 1812 and 1837, none of which involved a move further than a contiguous parish.

In Bristol between 1820 and 1830, roughly 10 per cent of the locally-persistent population moved house each year, resulting in an overall change of almost 70 per cent over the decade.[39] These moves often involved very small distances. As the second set of figures for Bristol in Table 11.3 reveals, typically only about half of these changes of residence entailed even a shift beyond the boundary of the parish. Approximately 15 per cent or more of the 'persisters' in Shrewsbury moved house in the single years of 1830 and 1831, while almost 20 per cent of Northampton's residents moved house in those particular years. Thus the voters in these towns conformed to the expected standard; a great deal of physical mobility was normal even for those who remained within their respective towns. Indeed, moving house was the norm in these towns.

As far as occupational mobility is concerned, changes in specific occupational titles are also easily measured, though the meaning of the changes is often less easily determined. Despite the stability within occupational *groups* demonstrated in Table 11.1, the men in these three towns frequently changed their specific occupational titles from one time to the next. As Table 11.4 indicates, the very few men (less than five per cent) in Shrewsbury who described themselves differently in 1835 from 1832, were the exception, both in Shrewsbury and in the other towns. More typically, 12 per cent of the men who voted in the Shrewsbury election of 1831 used a different occupational title from the one they had given the polling clerk in 1830. Generally, these men shared a relatively high level of specific occupational mobility, and except for Shrewsbury, the proportion of men changing their occupational titles showed a decided upward trend over the period.[40] By 1841, between a fifth and a third of the 'persisters' in Bristol and Northampton described themselves differently at two elections separated by only a few years.

Some of these changes were purely nominal; the use of synonymous titles resulted in spurious occupational shifts. William Ward's claim in Bristol to the title stonemason in one year and stone cutter in another year probably meant no change in his actual occupation, just as plumber and glazier could be used on different occasions without indicating an alteration in an individual's job. George Abby, William Gates, and William Flesher of Northampton exhibited an unusual nominal shift since all of them used the titles 'solicitor' and 'barrister' interchangeably and indiscriminately, thus creating the illusion of mobility. The ambivalent attitude of the practitioners of the law in Northampton towards their titles suggests that the significant distinction between these titles in London hardly seemed relevant in the context of early nineteenth-century Northampton, where 30 per cent of the population lived beneath the poverty line.[41] Whether they claimed to be a solicitor or a barrister from one year to the next had nothing to do with their relative status;

Table 11.4 Changes in specific occupational titles (percentages)

	1819–26	1826–30	1830–31	1831–32	1832–35	1835–37	1837–41
Shrewsbury	16.1	15.0	12.0	9.3	4.9	17.0	15.6
N	341	474	276	193	713	787	826
Northampton	20.6[1]	21.4	19.9	21.3	24.3	22.0	36.4
N	233	280	381	423	404	352	294
Bristol	11.2[2]	15.7[3]	5.8[4]		11.6	20.7	30.4
N	331	297	708		768	638	687

[1] Elections 1818–20
[2] Elections 1812–20
[3] Elections 1820–30
[4] Elections 1830–32

Sources: Printed parliamentary poll books; see John Sims (ed.), *A Handlist of British Parliamentary Poll Books* (1984) and manuscript pollbook for Bristol, 1820, B4419, County of Avon Reference Library, Bristol.

they simply rested comfortably at the top. Similarly, Thomas Baker of Shrewsbury referred to himself as a draper or as a linen merchant as the mood struck him; there is no pattern to his choice of title, nor is it likely that his occupation changed perceptibly over these years.

Shifts by many other men within the same stratum reflected what appear to have been genuine occupational changes, but usually of a rather small order. Moving over one's years of employment from journeyman shoemaker, to shoemaker, to closer, to cordwainer, to clicker were real enough moves related primarily to life-cycle, but all fell into the same general category.[42] The 'skilled' stratum in Table 11.1 accounted for more than half of *all* specific occupational titles in these towns, and it is not surprising therefore that these 'skilled' workers accounted for the bulk of the changes in specific occupational titles indicated in Table 11.4. In other words, most of the occupational title shifts were claimed by men who persisted in the 'skilled' stratum, year in and year out. In Northampton, for instance, an average of nearly 94 per cent of the 'skilled' individuals in one year continued to claim a 'skilled', but possibly a different 'skilled' occupation the second time they were asked. Some shifts that were probably related to life-cycle could not be contained within a single stratum. Thomas Mills, who appeared first in the Northampton pollbook of 1818 as a labourer, called himself mason by 1830, but had fallen back to mere labourer by 1841. After twenty years of calling himself a gardener, Thomas Reeves of Northampton also fell to labourer status by 1841. Evan Griffith of Shrewsbury moved steadily downward from shopkeeper to overlooker to labourer over these years.

Other shifts in occupational titles appear to have been more directly related to success or failure, and these frequently broached the limits of a single occupational stratum. William Gibson of Northampton could only claim to be a servant in 1818, but he had become a shoemaker by 1826, a job he claimed until he listed himself as a clicker in 1835. This move from servant to skilled shoemaker was impressive enough, but he followed it with a move to beer selling in 1837 and could style himself a liquor merchant in 1841. Philip Allan Ward, a Bristol glasscutter originally became a glassmaker before moving on first to pawnbroking and then to accounting. Samuel Watton of Bristol followed the opposite track. He aspired to Esquire in 1830 yet fell to mere miller and then to porter over the succeeding years.

III Moving and Working

Table 11.4 conveys a powerful impression of substantial occupational mobility in these towns, just as Table 11.3 indicated massive residential mobility, but neither answers the basic question about the relationship between working and moving. In fact, the very high level of residential mobility in Shrewsbury, Northampton, and Bristol actually obscures the answer. So many people moved house that it is impossible to distinguish precisely their reasons for doing so, and the relationship between the very high level of residential mobility in these towns and the relatively high level of occupational mobility can only be guessed at from hints in the data rather than measured quantitatively.

The first and perhaps most revealing of these hints stems from the apparent discrepancy between the occupational *instability* revealed in Table 11.4 and the notable *stability* of the occupational strata indicated in Table 11.1. The stability revealed in Table 11.1 resulted from the fact that the majority of the specific job changes recorded by these men occurred *within* a single stratum. The 'skilled' stratum encompassed most of the household movers in each town whether or not they actually changed their occupational title at all. Moreover, nearly two-thirds of those who moved house maintained their specific occupational title across the years of their household move. Those who were residentially mobile were not also occupationally mobile; many were, but many more were not. This percentage varied very little from town to town or from year to year. Thus, since most of the residentially mobile either kept their original job description or made a job change that did not involve a significant change in socio-economic status, most of those people who were moving house must have done so in response to relatively small economic changes in their lives.

Moreover, most of those who moved occupied the lower rungs on the economic scale; the two lowest quartiles consistently contributed more than 60 per cent of those who were residentially mobile. Therefore, small economic shifts, either connected to an actual occupational title change or within the same specific job description, appear to have driven this peripatetic populace. The residentially mobile seem to have been responding to small income increments or decrements whether connected with relative success or failure within the same job, life-cycle changes, or actual changes in jobs related to either relative success or age. As they moved up the earnings ladder in a craft, they quickly adjusted their abode to match their income. They also responded to the other end of the cycle. Advancing years were often accompanied by movement down the occupational scale, and the resulting economic adjustments were also often quickly translated into residential adjustments.[43] The result was the kind of town revealed in Tables 11.3 and 11.4. Within very limited economic and geographic boundaries, these provincial urban dwellers led lives of perpetual, but often barely perceptible, motion.

IV Measuring Movement

These data provide tantalizing glimpses of the relationship between residential and occupational mobility in several provincial towns during what has often been called the age of reform. They point to the concentration of residential mobility among the lesser orders in these towns, and hint at the connection between this mobility and relatively minor changes in occupational or economic status, also particularly among the lesser sort. Ultimately, however, just as Richard Dennis's data failed to reveal more than the 'association' of social and residential mobility, these data also do not permit the impact of occupational and economic change on residential mobility, if any, to be measured with sufficient specificity. Their failure to clarify the relationship stems in part from the remarkable degree of residential mobility found in *every* occupational stratum – and indeed within virtually every specific occupational category – in these towns. With so much movement, isolating the impact of occupational change proves to be an exceedingly ticklish task, one requiring an extraordinary level of detailed knowledge of the population in question. While far more detailed and more chronologically complete than many other databases used to investigate either occupational or residential mobility, these data are nevertheless insufficiently detailed to permit the more intricate testing necessitated by the sheer volume of residential mobility encountered in these towns.

It is possible, however, that the lives of these nineteenth-century townsfolk can be captured with the degree of intimacy that would permit a more effective test of the relationship. This examination illustrates the deficiencies of pollbooks; they clearly do not provide an adequate foundation for such a test, despite the wealth of information they contain. The relative infrequency of elections and the relative occupational exclusivity of pollbooks (or electoral registers) greatly reduce their general utility, and these deficiencies are compounded by the less serious but troublesome gender bias that hampers any data set created from records pertaining to an entirely male electorate. The exclusion of women who were both employed and household heads may not be a fatal flaw for an examination of a male-dominated society, but it raises additional problems of interpretation. Nor can the surviving city directories be used as a substitute. Their gender bias is less severe, but their occupational biases are certainly as severe. Nor can the census serve as the framework upon which to build, for a variety of reasons, the most serious of which is the chronological imperative operating upon such a study. Residential mobility must be examined through frequent looks at the relevant population, and a decennial census fails abysmally to meet that requirement. Instead, what might be required is a database incorporating a wide range of sources, including pollbooks, directories, census returns, and the as yet relatively-underused rate books.[44]

Only at that point will it be possible to move beyond Dennis's no doubt accurate, but nonetheless unsatisfying, contention that residential mobility was 'associated with' occupational mobility, or the equally unsatisfactory links between residential mobility and minor occupational and economic change suggested by the movements of electors in Shrewsbury, Northampton, and Bristol. Only then will it be possible to know with a reasonable degree of certainty whether Richards Richards's move from a house in Castle Gates, Shrewsbury, to a more expensive house in Castle Street at some point between 1826 and 1830 was indeed an example of mobility prompted by a job change, or whether residential movement was so ubiquitous within these populations, that occupational mobility simply occurred in the presence of residential changes dictated by a wide variety of factors, economic and otherwise.[45]

Notes

1. This research has been supported by the Research Committee of the Academic Senate of the University of California, Riverside. I am particularly indebted to my colleague, Charles Wetherell, of the Laboratory for Historical Research, UC Riverside for his assistance with this project.
2. Shropshire Record Office, (hereinafter SRO) St Julian's, 2711/p.4; 2711/p.5b; St Chad's, 1048–84; St Alkmund's, 1049/A; 1049B; 1049/9; St Mary's, 1041/1n/11; 1041/ch. 31–49.
3. SRO, St Mary's, 1041/ch. 43; 1041/ch. 47.
4. *The Poll for the Election . . .* (Liverpool, 1818), 62.
5. *The Sussex Advertiser*, 18 June 1818. Such a concern was of long standing in Lewes, but fortunately for the Tories, the concern had shifted somewhat over two centuries. At the Lewes election of 1628, 'the gentry . . . refused to have themselves numbered with the meaner sort at the poll, presumably considering their names should not be rated on

paper on an equal basis with those of the commons, and in consequence saw the candidate they supported suffer'. Derek Hirst, *The Representative of the People? Voters and Voting in England under the Early Stuarts* (1975), 14.

6. P.N. Furbank, *Unholy Pleasure: The Idea of Social Class* (1985), 40–50.

7. Penelope J. Corfield, 'Class by name and number in eighteenth-century Britain', *History*, 72 (February, 1987).

8. Daniel Defoe, *A Review of Affairs in France* (1705); Joseph Massie, *Calculations of the Present Taxes Yearly Paid by a Family of Each Rank, Degree, or Class* (1761); Patrick Colquhoun, *A Treatise on Wealth, Power, and Resources of the British Empire* (1814).

9. W.A. Armstrong has suggested the use of other kinds of information, such as the employment of servants, as a means of discriminating within specific occupations, but the relevant information was not available for these populations. See W.A. Armstrong, 'The use of information about occupations', in *Nineteenth-Century Society: Essays in the Use of Quantitative Methods for the Study of Social Data*, ed. E.A. Wrigley (1972), 191–310.

10. R.J. Morris (ed.), *Class, Power, and Social Structure in British Nineteenth-Century Towns* (1986), 3. See also Richard J. Dennis, *English Industrial Cities of the Nineteenth Century* (1984), 186–99; and Richard J. Dennis, 'Intercensal mobility in a Victorian city', *Trans. Inst. of British Geographers*, 2. 3 (1977), 349–63.

11. Furbank, *Unholy Pleasure*, 21.

12. R.S. Neale, *Class in English History 1680–1850* (1981).

13. John Vincent, *Pollbooks: How Victorians Voted* (1967).

14. Michael B. Katz, *The People of Hamilton, Canada West* (Harvard, 1975), 121; Theodore Hershberg and Robert Dockhorn, 'Occupational Classification', *Historical Methods Newsletter*, 9. 2–3 (1976), 59–98; and Theodore Hershberg (ed.), *Philadelphia: Work, Space, Family, and Group Experience in the Nineteenth Century* (1981).

15. John Corry, *The History of Bristol* (2 vols, 1816), II, 297–313; John Latimer, *Annals of Bristol in the Nineteenth Century* (1887), 50–257; R.E. Zegger, *John Cam Hobhouse* (1973), 34.

16. V.A. Hatley, 'Some aspects of Northampton history, 1815–51', *Northamptonshire Past and Present*, 3.6 (1966).

17. Theodore Hershberg *et al.*, 'Occupation and ethnicity in five nineteenth-century cities: a collaborative inquiry', *Historical Methods Newsletter*, 7.3 (1974), 174–216.

18. Few claimed to be 'manufacturers' of anything in Bristol and Shrewsbury; virtually everyone claimed to be a 'maker'. The Five Cities project employed ten 'vertical' categories in distinguishing the residents of these towns including (1) high white-collar, (2) low white-collar, (3) craftsmen, (4) unskilled specific, (5) unskilled unspecific, (6) residual unskilled, (7) ambiguous, (8) not employed, (9) unclassifiable, and (0) blank. Of these, category 2 and 3 contained more than 60 per cent of the individuals examined in 1870: Hershberg and Dockhorn, 'Occupational classification', 71.

19. R.J. Morris, 'The Leeds middle class, 1820 to 1850', Report to SSRC, June 1983; and R.J. Morris, 'Property titles and the use of British urban poll books for social analysis'. *Urban History Yearbook 1983* (1983). Morris's 636 specific occupational titles considerably overstate the number of actual occupations followed in Leeds because Morris counted separately *every* variation in recorded job title. Thus 'Stuff manu' and 'Stuff manufact' constituted two occupations, as did 'Woolen manufr' and 'woolen manf'. 'Solicitor and notary', 'solicitor', 'solr', and 'solic' were all counted separately. Morris is convinced that merchants were inherently superior to dealers, but the pollbooks in these three towns did not make that distinction apparent. One exception in the rule against longitudinal analysis is Katz's comparison of 3 census and tax assessments separated by an interval of three months. His remarkably low level (61 per cent) of identical occupations may well be attributable to other causes: Michael Katz, 'Occupational classification in history', *Journal of Interdisciplinary History*, 1.1 (1972), 63–88.

20. Roger Penn, *Skilled Workers in the Class Structure* (1986) used occupational data and marital endogamy to test for social structure. Armstrong, of course, suggested using the employment of servants to distinguish between individuals claiming the same occupation: Armstrong, 'The use of information about occupations', in *Nineteenth-Century Society*, ed. Wrigley, 191–310. Distinctions between journeymen and masters were made, inexplicably, in the Lewes pollbooks of 1818, 1830, and 1841. See *A Poll taken by Mr. Wm. Smart and Mr. Thos. Whiteman* (Lewes, 1818); and *Borough of Lewes: A Poll taken by Messrs. Benjamin Ridge and George Bailey* (Lewes, 1830).

21. R.S. Neale, *Class and Ideology in the Nineteenth Century* (1972). Inter-urban variations also play havoc with stratification. Cowleeches existed in quantity in Bristol, but not at all in Shrewsbury, where cowkeepers abounded despite their complete absence in Bristol. Shrewsbury leather workers were also much less likely to adopt the description 'cordwainer' than their Bristol counterparts. Pilots in Yarmouth were the social equivalent of labourers, yet those who called themselves pilots in Bristol often also described themselves as 'gentlemen'. No barrier separated solicitors from barristers in Northampton, yet one surely existed elsewhere.

22. Other studies have used election data to examine mobility despite their deficiencies. Pritchard used electoral rolls to compare 1871 and 1872 knowing that approximately 30 per cent of all householders were excluded from that list: R.M. Pritchard, *Housing and the Spatial Structure of the City* (1976), 57–67.

23. There was one exception to the self-ascription of the occupations of these voters. A polling clerk with a strange sense of humour systematically recorded a number of very lowly voters as 'gentlemen' at the Northampton election of 1831. His joke was revealed only in the process of linking the records of these men over time.

24. As few as 10 (1830–31) and as many as 75 months (1820–26) separated these general elections, with an average for the period of just less than 3 years.

25. An examination of electorates in four eighteenth-century towns required only 140 occupations to cover the range of possibilities. For a discussion of the linkage techniques used in this research, see J.A. Phillips, *Electoral Behaviour in Unreformed England: Plumpers, Splitters and Straights* (Princeton, 1982), Appendix 1. This research considered the entire electorates of Lewes and Shrewsbury, but only used letter-cluster samples of the other electorates. See J.A. Phillips, 'Achieving a critical mass while avoiding an explosion', *Jnl. Interdisciplinary History*, 19.2 (1979).

26. A complete listing of the nearly 1,000 occupations considered in this analysis is available upon request from the Laboratory for Historical Research, University of California, Riverside, CA 92521, USA.

27. Donald Ginter, 'The incidence of revaluation'; and Margaret Noble, 'The land tax assessment in the study of the physical development of country towns', in *Land and Property: The English Land Tax 1692–1832*, ed. M. Turner and D. Mills (1986). See also Elizabeth Baigent, 'Bristol Society in the later Eighteenth Century' (D. Phil. thesis, University of Oxford, 1985).

28. Comparisons based upon tax assessments are complicated by possibly incomplete tax assessment for individual rate-payers. To avoid the problems raised by comparisons of apples and oranges, rental values were included for consideration *only* if a figure for a house could be found. This does not eliminate possible under-assessment from incomplete data, but provides a minimal comparability for each rated person. The economic analysis of Lewes and Shrewsbury employs all surviving poor-rate data. Other disciplines appear to have fewer qualms about using data like these. J.T. Jackson, 'Housing areas in mid-Victorian Wigan and St. Helens', *Trans. Inst. of British Geographers*, 6 (1981), 413–32.

29. *The Banbury Poll Book 1859* (Banbury: Rusher, 1859).

30. *The Bath Poll-Book* (Bath: Peach, 1855). The facsimile of the Bath pollbook published by the Open University refers to its assessment as 'somewhat unusual'; in fact, the only other pollbook to report each voter's rateable value was Banbury, 1859.

31. The economic data available for Shrewsbury posed problems, the greatest of which involved the steadily rising median rentals in Lewes and Shrewsbury coupled, usually, with stable rate assessments. Thus estimated rental values in these two towns had little to do with real worth and can only be used for *relative* comparisons. By comparing only quartiles for each year, the effect of the upward movement in recorded rental values is eliminated. The upper ranges of the bottom three quartiles in Shrewsbury for each year considered were (in decimalized pounds sterling): 1826 = 2, 3.5, 7; 1830 = 2.5, 4.5, 11; 1835 = 3.5, 7.5, 14; 1841 = 5, 12, 23.75.

32. E.P. Thompson, *The Making of the English Working Class* (1963), 14. For a bibliography pointing to the voluminous and occasionally acrimonious debate over class, see Craig Calhoun, *The Question of Class Struggle: Social Foundations of Popular Radicalism during the Industrial Revolution* (Chicago, 1982). Also see R.J. Morris's extraordinarily insightful introduction to *Class, Power and Social Structure in British Nineteenth-Century Towns* (1986). For a discussion of class in a slightly later context, see Penn, *Skilled Workers*.

33. John Foster, *Class Struggle and the Industrial Revolution: Early Industrial Capitalism in Three English Towns* (1974), 84–127.

34. Dennis, 'Intercensal mobility', 358.

35. Dennis, *English Industrial Cities*, 150–69 summarizes the discussion.

36. Residential mobility is measured from pollbook records which are at best street specific. The high levels of very short-distance residential mobility indicated in studies of both seventeenth- and nineteenth-century towns suggest that such street-level comparisons underestimate actual mobility. C. Pooley, 'Residential mobility in the Victorian city', *Trans. Inst. British Geographers*, n.s. 4.2 (1979), 259–61; Jeremy Boulton, 'Residential mobility in seventeenth-century Southwark', *Urban History Yearbook 1986* (1986), 1–14.

37. A brief look at the entire population of St Mary's parish, Shrewsbury, suggests that a quarter of the residents moved house annually: Shropshire Record Office, 1041/43; 1041/47. Between 1830 and 1831, 23 per cent of the inhabitants of St Mary's parish moved from their abode; by 1834–5 the percentage had risen to 29. This level of movement pales, of course, in comparison to the Swedish populations that J. Langton has compared to sodium on water: for a case-study, see above, Ch. 9.

38. See the excellent map of Bristol *c.* 1820 in M.D. Lobel (ed.), *Historic Towns*, II (1975).

39. By taking into account the 'population at risk', it is possible to estimate a 10 per cent change per annum among the Bristolians from the 70 per cent who had changed their residence over the decade. The following table illustrates the reduction in the overall change that results from the reduction of the original population each year. Each time the original population is diminished by one tenth, the residual change is definitionally smaller since there are fewer of the original population remaining. The annual movement of 10 per cent of the original group results in a 60 per cent change in the original population over a decade.

Year	Proportion of Original Population Remaining	Residual Percentage Change
1	100	10
2	90	9
3	81	8
4	73	7
5	66	6
6	60	6
7	54	5
8	49	5
9	44	4
10	40	4
		60

40. The reality of these apparent occupational shifts is elusive. The title cordwainer, for example, often seems to have been used as a synonym for shoemaker, but Edmund Green has found a substantial difference in the mean rack-rents of Westminster cordwainers (£13.55) and shoemakers (£6.0): above, 176–7.
41. Gareth Stedman Jones, *Languages of Class: Studies in English Working-Class History* (1983), 34 (summarizing John Foster's study of Northampton).
42. A move from 'shoemaker' to 'closer' probably indicated an improvement in a worker's status in Northampton's heavily specialized shoe trade. Also, in Northampton and occasionally in other towns, 'cordwainer' may have indicated a higher status since use of the term may have indicated a higher quality product. A 'clicker' in Northampton acted as an overseer and should have earned proportionately more than a mere shoemaker.
43. Much of the debate over Victorian towns focuses on the spatial differentiation based upon socio-economic differences. See David Cannadine, 'Victorian cities: how different?', *Social History*, 2 (1977) 457–82; and David Ward, 'Environs and neighbours in the "Two Nations": residential differentiation in mid-nineteenth-century Leeds', *Journal of Historical Geography*, 6.2 (1980), 133–62. The debate over the individual or generic quality of nineteenth-century urban development has not been addressed in this essay. Certainly, these three towns cannot be assumed to represent all English urban working and moving patterns, but the conclusions of the essay are not unlike those of Dennis, Pritchard, and others. For a related discussion of the effects of ageing on occupational structure in the United States, see Roger Ransom and Richard Sutch, 'The labour of older Americans', *Journal of Economic History*, 46.1 (1986).
44. For a discussion of the problems with ratebooks and land-tax records, see Baigent, 'thesis', op. cit., and Turner and Mills, *Land and Property*. Nineteenth-century rate books appear to be more detailed and less idiosyncratic than their eighteenth-century counterparts.
45. For a further discussion of problems, possible remedies, and attempted remedies in both American and English contexts for the succeeding decades, see Eric Monkkonen, 'Residential mobility in England and the United States, 1850–1900' in the Open University's *Themes in British and American History* (1985) 77–83. Also see Eric Monkkonen, *America Becomes Urban: The Development of U.S. Cities and Towns 1780–1980* (Berkeley, California, 1988).

Appendix

The following provides a sample of the categories assigned for the purposes of the analysis above.

A Sample occupations and assigned occupational strata

Occupation	Occupational Strata	
accomptant/accounter/bookkeeper	5	clerical
agent/collector	2	merchant élite
alderman	2	merchant élite
almsman	11	unclassifiable
anchorsmith	9	skilled
apothecary	2	merchant élite
appraiser (land)	2	merchant élite
archdeacon	1	professional/gentle
artist	3	lesser professions

attorney	1 professional/gentle
auctioneer	2 merchant élite
bacon merchant	2 merchant élite
bailiff	7 government employees
baker	4 retail
ballast burner	10 unskilled
banker	2 merchant élite
banker's clerk	5 clerical
barber	4 retail
barge owner	8 skilled service sector
baronet	1 professional/gentle
barrister	1 professional/gentle
beachman	10 unskilled
beadle	7 government employees
bed joiner	9 skilled
beer agent	2 merchant élite
beer seller	4 retail
bell founder	9 skilled
bellman	11 unclassifiable
bill poster	10 unskilled
billbroker	2 merchant élite
bird + dog fancier	4 retail
blacksmith	9 skilled
bleacher	9 skilled
boat builder	9 skilled
boatman	8 skilled service sector
bone burner	10 unskilled
bookbinder	9 skilled
bookseller	4 retail
bootcloser	9 skilled
brandy merchant	2 merchant élite
brass finisher	9 skilled
brazier	9 skilled
brewer	2 merchant élite
brick merchant	2 merchant élite
bricklayer	9 skilled
bridle cutter	9 skilled
brightsmith	9 skilled
broker	2 merchant élite
brushturner	9 skilled
builder	2 merchant élite
burner	10 unskilled
butcher	4 retail
butter dealer	2 merchant élite
cabinet carver	9 skilled
cablesmith	9 skilled
calenderer	9 skilled
canal carrier	8 skilled service sector

caneworker	9	skilled
carman, carter, driver	10	unskilled
carpenter	9	skilled
carrier	10	unskilled
carver	9	skilled
cattle dealer	2	merchant'elite
caulker	9	skilled
cellarman	11	unclassifiable
chaff cutter	9	skilled
chair turner	9	skilled
chamberlain	1	professional/gentle
chandler	4	retail
cheese factor	2	merchant élite
cheesemonger	4	retail
chemist	2	merchant élite
chimneysweeper	10	unskilled
china dealer	2	merchant élite
china painter	9	skilled
chinaman	4	retail
cider dealer	2	merchant élite
city employee	7	government employees
civil engineer	2	merchant élite
clerk	5	clerical
clerk (clergy)	1	professional/gentle
clerk (dissenting)	3	lesser professions
clicker	9	skilled
closer	9	skilled
cloth worker	9	skilled
clothes dealer	2	merchant élite
clothesman	4	retail
clothier	4	retail
coach builder	9	skilled
coach carver	9	skilled
coach driver/chaise driver	10	unskilled
coach liner	9	skilled
coach painter	9	skilled
coach proprietor	8	skilled service sector
coach trimmer + harness maker	9	skilled
coachman	10	unskilled
coachmaster	8	skilled service sector
coachsmith	9	skilled
coal + iron merchant	2	merchant élite
coal breaker	10	unskilled
coal dealer	2	merchant élite
coal merchant	2	merchant élite
coal miner	10	unskilled
coal porter	10	unskilled
coalheaver	10	unskilled

coalmeter	11	unclassifiable
collecting clerk	5	clerical
collector of town dues	7	government employees
collector/agent	2	merchant élite
collier	10	unskilled
colour seller	4	retail
colourman	4	retail
comedian/musician	3	lesser professions
commerical traveller	4	retail
commissary	4	retail
commission agent	2	merchant élite
confectioner	4	retail
conveyancer	5	clerical
cook	9	skilled
cooper	9	skilled
coppersmith	9	skilled
cordwainer	9	skilled
cork cutter	9	skilled
cork cutter + glass dealer	4	retail
corn dealer	2	merchant élite
corn factor	2	merchant élite
corn measurer	5	clerical
corn merchant	2	merchant élite
corn porter	10	unskilled
cornchandler	4	retail

B *Occupational strata and sample occupations*

Occupational strata

I *Professional/gentle:*
Archdeacon; attorney; baronet; barrister; chamberlain; clerk (clergy)

II *Merchant elite:*
Agent/collector; alderman; apothecary; appraiser (land); auctioneer; bacon merchant; banker; beer agent; billbroker; brandy merchant; brewer; brick merchant; broker; builder; butter dealer; cattle dealer; cheese factor; chemist; china dealer; cider dealer; civil engineer; clothes dealer; coal and iron merchant; coal dealer; coal merchant; collector/agent; commission agent; corn dealer; corn factor; corn merchant

III *Lesser professions:*
Artist; clerk (dissenting); comedian/musician

IV *Retail:*
Baker; barber; beer seller, bird and dog fancier; bookseller; butcher; chandler; cheesemonger; chinaman; clothesman; clothier; colour seller; colourman; commercial traveller; commissary; confectioner; cork cutter and glass dealer; corn chandler

V *Clerical:*
Accomptant/accounter/book-keeper; banker's clerk; clerk; collecting clerk; conveyancer; corn measurer

VII *Government employees:*
Bailiff; beadle; city employee; collector of town dues

VIII *Skilled service sector:*
Barge owner; boatman; canal carrier; coach proprietor; coachmaster

IX *Skilled:*
Anchorsmith; bed joiner; bell founder; blacksmith; bleacher; boat builder; bookbinder; boot closer; brass finisher; brazier; bricklayer; bridle cutter; brightsmith; brush turner; cabinet carver; cablesmith; calenderer; cane worker; carpenter; carver; caulker; chaff cutter; chair turner; china painter; clicker; closer; cloth worker; coach builder; coach carver; coach liner; coach painter; coach trimmer and harness maker; coachsmith; cook; cooper; coppersmith; cordwainer; cork cutter

X *Unskilled:*
Ballast burner; beachman; bill poster; bone burner; burner; carman/carter/driver; carrier; chimney sweeper; coach/chaise driver; coachman; coal breaker, coal miner; coal porter; coal heaver; collier; corn porter

XI *Unclassifiable:*
Almsman; bellman; cellarman; coalmeter

12 Defining urban work

Penelope J. Corfield

'Specialization' is the way to fame, sang Monroe, herself specializing with doomed brilliance as modern Hollywood megastar. Her lighthearted hymn to the impact of the division of labour celebrated a key element in the social organization of work, that underpinned all economic systems.[1] Even in the simplest communities – and few societies, on close inspection, qualify for such an appellation – the daily tasks deemed necessary for survival are apportioned unequally between different individuals, depending upon a great variety of factors that include age, sex, aptitude, economic necessity, personal status, and social custom.[2] Because human time is finite, no one, however busy, can do everything. There is an opportunity cost to action as well as to inaction: that is, for every activity undertaken, another is postponed or not done at all. Even Robinson Crusoe, fictive epitome of individual resourcefulness and hard work, had to ration his time between different chores; and when, after years in isolation, he saved a fellow castaway, he promptly demarcated their roles by training the 'useful, handy and helpful' Man Friday as his servant.[3]

Fully functioning communities, meanwhile, are organized on a considerably larger scale to sustain thousands or indeed millions of people. They depend for their survival upon an interlinking and usually unequal division of labour – an inequality that has had important influence upon inequalities in social status and wealth. That does not imply, of course, that all economies are similarly sub-divided into minute specialisms, nor all tasks similarly specialized.[4] On the contrary: while work itself is a historic constant, in that no society has yet survived without at least the basic chore of food-gathering, the nature, organization, intensity, status, and remuneration of work have all varied greatly between different communities, and certainly over time. In practice, the division of labour has proved historically very adaptable in response to a multitude of imperatives. The demands of the economy, the state of technology, and the nature of population resources between them play a highly significant role. Yet, equally importantly, cultural and social expectations strongly influence the availability of labour and the organization of work;[5] and, in addition, past and present societies have known a variety of political, legal, religious, or other institutional controls upon the supply and regulation of labour.

Even in definition, the concept of 'work' is not a simple one. Through long usage, it has acquired many shades of meaning. In English, it has up to 34 nuanced implications,[6] and complex associated vocabularies; and there are many cultural variations. Past societies have defined it very diversely. At its most generalized, it is invoked to refer to any kind of intensive effort, application, or sustained endeavour. With synonyms of labour, toil, travail, chores, and drudgery, its connotations are active, energetic, earnest, onerous, and time-consuming. In this widest sense, 'work' is whatever people consider as work. It is not applied exclusively to unpleasant or back-breaking tasks, nor solely to those prescribed by others. It is possible to labour energetically at private pastimes, just as it is possible to dawdle at official duties. Human effort breaks through formal structures and roles, so that the boundaries between 'work' and 'non-work' are in practice very often obscure.

Yet there has long been a more specific economic application to the term. 'Work' refers collectively to all the daily labours, routine and otherwise, involved in the production, management, and dissemination of resources and skills for sustaining a living. It entails the application of human energy to generate social as well as economic value, widely construed.[7] Those daily tasks include both the efforts of men and women working for themselves and their families, and the huge range of tasks carried out in the pay or service of others. Successfully coordinated, such activities constitute the bedrock of the survival, economic production, social reproduction, social adaptation, and further growth of whole communities.[8] The centrality of work (broadly defined) meant that it has generally been common for a sizeable majority of adults to work – whether that was within or outside the home – and not unusual for older children to do likewise.[9] In particular, poor societies with labour-abundant agrarian economies and limited poor-relief schemes often saw very high proportions of the population engaged in economic activity, even if many were underemployed in terms of strict efficiency and were liable to be accused of 'laziness' by uncomprehending visitors.[10] By contrast, wealthy modern societies with market economies and with some welfare provision have been able to contain without crisis a certain proportion of the population who are categorized as economically inactive, although even then neither the 'idle rich' nor especially the 'idle poor' have been immune from social criticism.

'Work', in other words, is the generic term for the toil and sweat by which post-lapsarian humanity labours to get its daily bread; for, as an unsmiling Samuel Smiles asserted in 1887, 'The life of man in this world is, for the most part, a life of work'.[11] He did not refer specifically to 'woman', and he wrote at a time when female labour was given only grudging social recognition; but there is no shortage of evidence to show that women have also been familiar with toil, not only as plentiful workers in fields, markets, shops, workshops, and factories, but, in addition, very often as the chief suppliers of the routine support services within the household.[12] The relentlessness of these domestic chores was proverbial. In 1570, for example, Thomas Tusser quoted the familiar observation that 'Huswives affaires have never none ende'; and he added an uncompromising motto for the hard-pressed housewife: 'I serve for a day, for a week, for a year/For a lifetime, for ever, while man dwelleth here.'[13]

Its frequency and ubiquity made work an earnest matter rather than a topic for casual frivolity or ready jest. It helped to give social definition to individuals as well as to whole communities. Whether lamented as Jehovah's curse upon Adam[14] or praised by Voltaire as the favoured antidote to boredom, vice and poverty,[15] work had a cultural as well as an economic impact. It was usually inculcated as a social necessity, but some waxed more rhapsodic. 'All work, even cotton-spinning, is noble', urged Thomas Carlyle in 1843, scourging England's 'do-nothing' nobility with the assertion that 'work is alone noble'.[16] No doubt, past workforces had their own views on its benefits and disbenefits. Certainly, work has been saluted with a very diverse array of reactions, ranging from celebration through boredom to outright aversion.[17] But, while it was a matter for much chronic grumbling and complaint, it was also the subject of communal traditions that affirmed positive elements of work experience, such as the distillation of work-place lore into maxims, sayings, and proverbs,[18] the commemoration of rhythms of work in ballad and song,[19] and the consolidation of working practices in customs and rituals.[20]

At the same time, the economic and social importance of these activities made them a central arena for disputes and conflict of interests, especially since the raw materials and resources for human livelihood have not been evenly distributed either geographically or socially. There was therefore a dynamic tension to work, which demanded complementarity of effort on the one hand but which readily engendered competition or friction over resources, remuneration, and control on the other. Unequal status in work was registered in systematic inequalities in the public prestige of different livelihoods. While social systems were generally complex in detail, simplified dichotomous contrasts were invoked in the conventional allocation of praise or disdain. Hence, 'men's work' was in many societies rated more highly than 'women's work', although the precise sexual division of labour was not immutable over time. Similarly, mental labour was often accorded loftier prestige than manual tasks, or, in modern sartorial terminology, white collars rated above blue collars. But a modern rival variant has countered that, at least to some extent, by applauding 'productive' labour (the generation of tangible goods) over 'unproductive' services.[21] Classic targets for disapproval in the latter category were all allegedly wealth-draining 'parasites', such as uniformed flunkies, whose inactivities were derided, and tax officials, whose activities were heartily deplored.

I: Work in Towns

Historians are interested in the past both of work and of its changing social definition. Indeed, the two are related, although not identical. The history of work in towns can be viewed through both perspectives. Thus there was a long tradition of perceived tension between urban and rural labour. On the one hand, the sturdy countryman characteristically expressed resentment at the gilded urbanite, who consumed the fruits of agrarian diligence but seemed to confer little or nothing in return. Rural life was seen as primordial, essential, divinely-sanctioned, while city life was unnatural, parasitic, artificial. 'God made the country, and man made the town', wrote William Cowper in 1785, denying that divine omnipotence had extended to intervention in urban affairs.[22] Conversely, there was an emphatic pro-town tradition, which took a rather different stand. It did not deny the reality of rural labour but pointed instead to its prosaic, repetitive, and numbing nature, and to the consequent barbarism and uncouthness of country life, in comparison with urban skills, culture, and creativity.[23] If townees were prepared on occasion to eulogize the physical countryside, the grinding toil of rustic 'yokels' and 'bumpkins' was not the customary stuff of city dreams.

Stereotypes such as these employed more than a little artistic exaggeration, although few were as sweeping as the Victorian sage who denounced the nineteenth-century division of labour as leading to an unpalatable choice between 'clownish boors' on the land and 'emasculated dwarfs' in the towns.[24] In practice, work was not divided neatly into a binary categorization of rural or urban. Instead, the perennial migration of people into and out of towns was eased by an overlapping of tasks and skills. Some jobs were more locationally exclusive than others. For example, it was rare to find town shepherds tending urban flocks, other than metaphorically, while town criers have by definition given voice within an urban environment. On the other hand, shoemakers have been found as stalwarts of either village or city society; and there is a wide spectrum of industries, trades, and professions that have not been confined to one type of settlement.

Urban work was not therefore defined by its uniqueness in terms of the labour process. It was rather the characteristic concentration of certain sorts of economic activity into one relatively densely-settled location that helped to define an urban community. Towns have been – and are still – very varied in their size, role, and history. They were not established to a precise formula, and their development did not automatically follow a linear progression towards growth and greatness. There is often scope for argument about the status of particular places and hence for disagreement about the proportionate number of urban residents within any given state or society. As in the case of 'work', definitions of 'towns' are neither timeless nor culture-free. No language-based terminology can be sundered from its temporal or social context. Yet the concept of a town has attained a longevity and cross-cultural recognition that gives it a generic, if not absolute, application. Definitions are best tested against multiple criteria,[25] although the historical evidence is not always easily assembled. Factors commonly adduced include: a certain population size and locational density; an element of institutional organization; some social heterogeneity; a cultural identity; and acceptance as a 'town'. In addition, work also plays an integral part in characterizing a settlement as urban.

Towns were and are concentrated locations for a variety of non-agrarian activities, drawn from the so-called secondary (manufacturing) and tertiary (service) sectors of an economy.[26] In other words, while work in industry, trade, and services was not by any means monopolized by urban residents, they were predominantly engaged in those occupations rather than in primary (agricultural) production. Equally, while food production was sometimes carried out by townspeople working on their own plots or on nearby estates, that was not usually the staple business of an urban economy, which tended instead to play a role in food processing and distribution. The division between a substantial village and a small town was certainly not a neat and simple one. Settlement patterns have proved both flexible and diverse. There have been small but non-agrarian mining villages that evade easy categorization; while there have been large 'agro-cities' on great landed estates, housing a landless and proletarianized agrarian workforce that travelled daily to labour in the fields.[27] Work is therefore not the sole indicator; but economic activity nonetheless remains one important criterion of urbanism. The larger and more distinctively pluralist a settlement, the less likely it was to have a major role in primary production, other than some specialist suburban businesses such as market-gardening and dairying to provide fresh supplies in urban markets.

The existence of a town therefore itself implied an element of agricultural specialization within its own economic hinterland, whether that was close at hand, or, as in the case of some colonial settlements, in a distant 'parent' economy linked by long-distance trade. Urban populations inescapably required food and raw materials on a scale that greatly outdid their own capacity to supply. In emergencies, town tables were sometimes replenished by direct plunder from the countryside, but that predictably discouraged local agriculture and afforded neither security nor regularity of provision. Hence in anything but the very short term, urban settlements needed a basic functional viability for their own survival, requiring not only a supply of staple resources from the countryside but also a sufficient demand for their own goods and services (of all sorts) in return. But the economic linkages ran both ways. While towns depended upon the countryside, virtually all rural dwellers also depended upon at least a minimal urban network, to provide a trading forum; in addition, they habitually went to town for consumer goods and a wide array of services, as well as for the town's resources of skilled populations, administrative mechanisms, financial capital, and informational know-how. It was a process of bilateral exchange, although rarely an equal one, binding both together, if often with mutual jealousies at the fluctuating terms of power and trade.

Hence the history of towns is as old as that of settled agriculture, both stretching back through thousands of years of human history.[28] Trade and traffic between urban and rural economies constituted an essential nexus. It was to the undoubted antiquity of such transactions that Friedrich Engels referred, when he wrote that 'The first great division of labour in society is the separation of town and country'.[29] In practice, there were yet older elements of economic differentiation by age, capacity, and to an extent by sex, in pre-urban hunting and foraging societies, even if social and economic roles seem to have been relatively flexible.[30] Nonetheless, the emergence of permanent towns, regular trade, and settled agriculture marked a significant consolidation of occupational and locational specialization. From ancient Babylon to modern megalopolis, the state of urban development, with its industries and services, has constituted a dynamic indicator of the concomitant development of agricultural productivity and trading networks. There was, too, an integral demographic component to the nexus, as town populations, themselves highly mobile, have repeatedly recruited to their numbers by a net in-migration, especially of young adults from the countryside.[31]

Exchange – the circulation both of rural produce and of urban goods and services – was thus a staple source of urban work. Regular trading depended upon known places of concourse. There urban and rural vendors and consumers were able to meet safely, gather information, and transact business in reasonable security. As a result, towns were integrally connected with markets,[32] even if some modern ideologues of 'the market' appear less than enthusiastic about its customary habitat. Of course, not all exchange was confined to urban venues. Nor did all market foundations automatically develop into fully urban settlements.[33] Yet all towns inescapably depended upon known venues for exchange, just as new towns rapidly systematized them. Because crowds multiplied the scale of business, so the largest cities had the greatest range of traders and dealers, from great merchants to petty hucksters; but all urban centres had some traders within their ranks.[34] Business contacts operated between towns as well as between town and country, as, for example, the sixteenth-century Shrewsbury drapers who acted as middlemen between the weavers of North Wales and the great overseas dealers in London.[35] The success of urban trading networks was consequently closely linked with the development of safe transport and communications, as towns depended upon and further generated traffic in goods, people and information.[36] The ancient Egyptian ideogram for the city, which depicted a cross in a circle to symbolize the junction of roads within walls, was not a complete representation of urban economic life, but it identified well the salience both of communications and security.[37]

As trade crucially required a modicum of social, legal and fiscal order, towns have habitually emerged and flourished within successfully functioning polities. Indeed, government bureaucracies once above a certain size have generally been agglomerated into urban centres, though the interests of rulers – not necessarily themselves urban residents – and citizens were far from always identical. Town authorities displayed constant concern to nurture the frameworks of custom and regulation that underpinned urban production and distribution. Specialization entailed not only economic exchange but also an element of social confidence, or, in Durkheimian terms, of 'moral density'. That meant that, while town societies have often appeared amorphous to onlookers and have often been unruly in practice, they were far from totally inchoate. Their successful continuance indicated a basic economic and social organization, which indeed served to sustain the notable urban resilience over the long term, in the face of challenges from both man-made and natural disasters.

Far from operating within closed systems, therefore, the work carried out in towns integrally implied their situation within wider economic networks. The urban capacity to regenerate and expand its role was one of its important features. But it was not the case that towns always grew, or were invariably altered fundamentally in growing. There are long continuities in the basic range of goods and services required to sustain an urban population, even while the technology and scale of work organization has been liable to change substantially. Many staple activities,[38] producing goods and services for both urban and rural consumers, were routinely carried out in towns, whether growing or not. This variegated urban supply not only proffered a return trade with the countryside in exchange for incoming agricultural produce, but it also catered for urban requirements, since a concentrated urban population created its own market. Those staples commonly included the processing and sale of food and drink, the supply and care of clothing and furnishings, the building and repair of housing, the provision of services and entertainment, the distribution of goods and information, the organization and servicing of transport and communications, plus some cleansing and management of the urban fabric. The variety of these staple activities gave ballast and flexibility to the urban economy, as did their great capacity to absorb labour.[39]

In addition, a number of towns had a further specialist role, catering for a wider than local demand. Here the flexibility of urban networks and their capacity to encompass change, including the growth of new towns, has also been notable. Places that outgrew the size and status of the smallest market centres did so by virtue of one or more special roles, each with its own pattern of labour recruitment, which attracted and sustained population at above-average rates. In predominantly agrarian economies, the number of such specialist towns was usually relatively small, perhaps confined to the national and provincial capitals, plus some leading ports and manufacturing centres. But in more commercialized and particularly in industrialized economies, situated within extensive international markets, the number of towns and the range and number of highly specialized towns have alike risen dramatically.[40]

These roles have included: the capital city and centre of government; the garrison town; the finance capital; the manufacturing centre; the transport staging post; the railway town; the dockyard town; the port for coastal and/or for long-distance trade; the university town; the ecclesiastical or cathedral city; the health or holiday resort; and the regional commercial centre. Nor were all those roles mutually exclusive. Some cities have grown great by a plurality of special functions. For example, in 1700 the large and protean London conurbation was the capital of a nation that was not then very populous nor yet very powerful, but it successfully combined a role as the focus for court, government, and administration, as hub of banking and financial services, as social capital, as industrial centre, as great coastal and international port, and as the headquarters for legal, medical and professional services.[41] A century later, with a population of 950,000, it had developed into an imperial metropolis with a global trading network, unsurpassed in size anywhere in the world other than by the two great eastern capitals of Edo (Tokyo) and Peking.

Much urban history has stemmed from the waxing and waning of these urban specialisms. With their quintessential concentrations of human resources, towns relied upon the production and consumption of non-agricultural goods and services as their basic stock-in-trade. That work has served many markets, and prompted an immense range of skills and organization, depending upon the size and context of each urban economy. It encompassed both general labourers and the most recondite of specialists, such as Georg Simmel's metropolitan exotics of later nineteenth-century Paris; the *quatorzièmes* or professional guests 'who hold themselves ready at the dinner hour . . . so they can be called upon on short notice in case thirteen persons find themselves at the table'.[42]

II Occupation and employment

Circulating information was vital in towns for the successful exchange of information about work. The aggregative urban economy was thereby disaggregated into the frictional interplay between supply and demand for labour. Much recruitment was informal, regulated not only by the long-term macro-economic context but also by the short-term seasonalities of each local economy. The whole urban *ambiance* in a sense constituted a general labour mart, as news about work was circulated between social, familial, and business contacts in both town and country, long before the process was formalized with the advent of newspaper advertisements and job registries. Many engagements were made privately, regulated by law or custom. In cities where sections of the urban workforce were unfree, slave markets provided a forum for the public sale and hire of labour;[43] otherwise there were informal places of *rendez-vous* – often near the central markets or wharfs – which acted as hiring marts, where labour was recruited for a specific task or term, whether daily or annually.[44]

Unofficial and casual labour therefore flourished alongside formal commitments, especially in the larger cities with their multiplicity of people and job opportunities.[45] Indeed, in urban economies where work was very closely regulated or its earnings highly taxed, it was not unusual for a considerable amount of informal business to be deliberately concealed from the record, creating an unquantified 'black economy' semi-hidden in the shadow of an 'official' economy – both concepts, however, postdating the advent of formal economic accounting.[46] Municipal authorities therefore did not generally know, or indeed need to know, the full extent of all the work that was carried out within their jurisdictions. The range of daily tasks was so extensive, their requirements often so immediate, that they eluded full public accounting.

Nonetheless, considerable information about work in towns can be derived from a great variety of sources. These do not depend exclusively upon written records, but can also be based upon inference from archaeological and material evidence, as well as from economic analysis, or indeed both. Given that full information never survives, much depends upon a careful scrutiny of incomplete data. That applies as essentially to the many written sources, both public and personal, that provide historians with direct and circumstantial evidence about work. Towns had existed for many centuries before there were attempts at gathering systematic evidence or modern censuses for the whole gamut of urban occupations. But there were, by contrast, various specific tallies and listings, of diverse origin, which were compiled with reference to specific groups for specific purposes, whether those purposes were political, administrative, fiscal, commercial, or simply the interest of private individuals. All information, however selective, is helpful, provided that its genesis

16   A DIRECTORY   OF SHEFFIELD.   17

Wild William, Trinity-ftreet -	GLOBE	Dungworth Jonathan, Meadow-ftreet -	1772
Wilkinfon John, Lambert Croft -	AN & C	Drabble Enoch, Green-lane -	USE
Withers Benjamin, and Co. Far-gate -	ESPANGE	Fox John, Park - -	+ FOX
Wright William, John, and Robert, Smithfield -	♦♡ ✚ ♡ ⚓ 8 cv ⅄	Hancock Charles, Scotland-ftreet -	QUEBEC
		Hibbert Samuel, Bailey Field -	SOL
Manufacturers in the NEIGHBOURHOOD.		Hutton Henry, Coalpit-lane -	HUTTON
		Lindley William and Son, Ponds -	SAILOR BOLD
BARLOW Samuel, Neepfend -	N ♦↩	Littlewood and Hatfield, Park -	Ⓞ I L
Baxter John, Bridgehoufes; *Hunters only*	24 N	Marfh Hannah, Park -	UPHONY
Carr John, Neepfend - -	CARR	Oates John, Little Sheffield -	⬇️ Y ●
Hawkfworth Thomas and Jonathan, At-tercliff - -	+ + SX CASAN +	Ofborne George, Porto Bello -	OATES
Warburton Samuel, Bridgehoufes -	LIFE	Parkin Thomas, Scotland-ftreet -	DRAFT
Yates George, Bridgehoufes - -	⬧ R 3	Prieft Jofeph, Young-ftreet -	LOUIS
		Revel Joseph, do. - -	DUNBAR
			+ PINK
Common POCKET and PEN KNIVES.		Revel Benjamin, Pea Croft -	JOLLY SAILOR
		Spencer Widow, Weftbar-green -	∽ ↩◁
Manufacturers in SHEFFIELD.		Smith Widow, Broad-lane End -	+ ∽ + ●
A LSOP Luke, Coalpit-lane -	HA	Swinden Matthew, Holles Croft -	⬇️ M S
Bifhop Thomas, China Square -	+ STATE	Taylor Paul, Pond-lane -	⬇️ P T
Butler Stephen, Townhead Well -	BAKU	Turner Samuel, China-fquare -	Ⓞ IVORY
Crookes Jonathan, Scotland-ftreet -	↩ ◁	Twigg Jonathan, Broadlane End -	⚓ TWIGG
Dixon James, Campo-lane -	+ DIXON	Ward James, Spring-ftreet -	W DS
Duke Henry, Trinity-ftreet -	READ	Waterhoufe Jeremiah, Scotland-ftreet -	> O +
Dungworth		Wild John, Holles Croft -	✚ WILD
		C *Manufacturers*	

Figure 12.1. Extract from *A Directory of Sheffield* (1787), published by Joseph Gales, printer and bookseller, and David Martin, engraver, as an introduction to 1,103 leading cutlers and metal-manufacturers in the Sheffield area, numbering among them 72 women: the makers of pocket- and pen-knives, including here Hannah Marsh, Widow Smith and Widow Spencer, could then be traced via their street address and their distinctive trade-mark, as shown in the right-hand column.

Figure 12.2. 'The Sheffield Cutler', from George Walker, *The Costume of Yorkshire* (1814): the small urban workshop was characteristic of businesses that needed special working conditions, outside the home but without a large-scale factory organization. The room was well-lit, with tables braced to facilitate precision work with hand-powered tools. Cutlery was predominantly a male occupation, but a number of these Sheffield businesses were owned and possibly run by women.

and implications are understood.[47] For example, a commercial directory of 1,103 cutlers, metal-manufacturers, and leading citizens in Sheffield in 1787 (see extract in Fig. 12.1) did not offer a full census of economic activity in a town of some 18,000 adult inhabitants, but instead provided a guide to the men and women who were considered to be the local leadership of the staple industry. It thereby confirmed the plurality of many small and medium-sized workshops (see Fig. 12.2), rather than dominance by only a few very large businesses.

Indeed, not only the nature of the record but also the forms in which work was socially defined and identified constitute an important part of the evidence. Both concepts and languages have their own complex histories, whether in general application or in the special idioms of particular avocations.[48] It is generally the case that the terminology of work has tended to become much more specialized as work itself has become more specialized, but the chronologies of language change are often complex. Again, it is not argued here that urban modes of nomenclature were systemically different from those in the countryside. Neither work nor vocabularies were halted at city boundaries. But it is important to note that literate town societies have often been creative language leaders and language consolidators, so that changes in broad concepts and specific terminologies of urban work also need full examination.

One long-standing definitional criterion was that of an individual's primary 'occupation', with its huge and open-ended associate vocabulary of occupational titles. In English, there were a number of synonyms for this central idea. Thus, the more colloquial 'job' referred to a specific or finite task but was also applied to long-term work. Meanwhile, an 'occupation' denoted any continuous business that engaged time and attention for more than a passing moment; and was thence extended to refer to an individual's habitual means of getting a living.[49] Initially, it may also have had some connotations of possession, in reference to gaining mastery of specific trade skills; but, as usage developed, it was found in application to unskilled as well as to skilled tasks. Certainly, it implied a degree of continuous work differentiation, whereby one occupation was distinguishable from others. But the use of these descriptive terms was also governed by convention. Thus membership of a craft guild entitled an individual to be known by that trade, whatever his or her actual livelihood. Furthermore, the use of singular designations did not preclude people from having by-employments or multiple occupations, particularly in the case of closely-associated jobs such as 'painter and glazier'.[50] However, as work and its terminology became more precise, it tended to discourage claims to working pluralism.

Occupational labels therefore offered a convenient, if sometimes simplified, means of social as well as economic recognition. Work was at once familiar but individually distinct. 'Occupation' could become close to personal identity. Indeed, that was the sense in which Shakespeare used it. When Othello lamented that 'Othello's occupation's gone!', he mourned not the literal loss of a job but the deeper collapse of his once-assured military persona.[51] At lesser levels of intensity, work was a relatively flexible form of individual identification, responsive to changing experiences during a working lifetime, in contrast to the rigidity of inherited rank or lineage. But 'occupation' was not always a simple alternative to hierarchy as defined by birth and family status. In traditional caste societies, for example, access to work was closely related to inherited social position, so that information about one also conferred information about the other, although there were also subtle gradations within castes.[52]

Another variant, found in a number of other cultures, was to derive family names directly from occupational titles, closely associating work with personal identification. That included not only urban Butchers and Bakers but also rural Farmers and Shepherds.[53] But conventions in personal nomenclature were also subject to change. As surnames themselves became standardized and heritable, the stock of names was gradually formalized, and eventually new occupations ceased to be translated into family surnames. In medieval England, people used a great variety of informal social identifiers. In addition to personal names, references were made to parentage, to free or nonfree status, to appearance, or to place of origin.[54] But at least by the twelfth century, when written records multiply – and probably before that in practice – it was not uncommon to find people described in relation to their 'occupation' or 'calling' or, later, their craft 'mystery' or (in one of its meanings) their 'profession'.

The late-medieval standardization of English, consolidated and influenced as that was by the centripetal pull of the large capital city, encouraged the growth of a standard vernacular terminology; and in sixteenth-century towns, it was relatively routine as an informal means of identification, at least for men. Meanwhile, women were habitually known by their marital or familial status, as wife, widow, or daughter. Yet some also recorded a narrower but visible range of publicly-defined occupations, in addition to their standard domestic chores. Indeed, the work of the 'spinster' in the preparatory stages of textile production was so ubiquitous that the term had acquired by the seventeenth century a dual currency as the standard sobriquet for unmarried womanhood.[55]

Undoubtedly, past town societies have displayed many cultural variants in both conventional and informal styles of identification. But the greater the degree of economic specialization and of occupational diversification – historically associated with the growth of towns and trade – the greater the social specificity of 'occupation' and the greater the tendency of individuals to be so identified. It did not conceal or obviate inequalities, but it gave scope for flexibility in response to life-cycle occupational changes. Furthermore it put people into a common framework of effort and economic contribution. Indeed, in modern democracies, 'gentlemen' and rulers have notably ceased to be defined by a leisured existence but instead prefer to stress Carlylean imperatives of work and duty. Reference to 'occupation' was a secular as well as utilitarian usage, but it was not without theological sanction. In the Christian tradition, St Paul had urged mankind to 'Walk worthy of the vocation wherewith ye are called',[56] initially interpreted with reference to priesthood. But, in sixteenth- and seventeenth-century Europe, the text was given a much more universalist emphasis, with Protestant preachers being particularly credited with inculcating an individual ethic of hard work at God's 'calling'.[57]

An occupation was a badge of social acknowledgement as well as economic role. It had connotations of respectability, albeit not necessarily of high status. Consequently, there were often unwritten cultural and legal constraints upon the sorts of livelihoods that were publicly admitted. Unlawful and semi-licit work was only rarely confessed, and not only because much criminal activity was part-time and adventitious. Thus, although professional criminals had their own language of 'jobs' and were known in their own circles and sometimes to the police, official censuses habitually excluded all illicit occupations, such as burglars, smugglers, or pickpockets, and generally excluded others of dubious legality, such as prostitutes, pimps, and bawds. Indeed, the amorphous 'immoral economy',[58] that flourished particularly in capital cities, ports, and some resorts, did its best to shun clarification at all times. However, a greater range of occupations was frequently to be found in casual sources, especially when the law did not command full social sympathy. In the later eighteenth century, for example, Parson Woodforde frequently noted in his diary purchases of luxury goods from one Richard Andrewe, identified variously as 'the smuggler' or 'my smuggler'.[59] Meanwhile, to take another equivocal occupation, begging, whether deemed holy or raffish, was not tallied officially as work, unless some tender of service was made; but for full-time beggars it frequently constituted a distinctive way of life and essential livelihood.[60]

Claims to occupational title were either allocated by others or made by self-ascription, both affording some leeway for evasion and exaggeration. Statements that were made publicly and especially on oath, as in legal proceedings, may have been more reliable – depending upon the circumstances in which declarations were made – than those made casually. But official proceedings sometimes used rather formalized designations (such as a guild affiliation), while other records can provide much fuller detail of actual work experiences. It is particularly notable that many occupational titles confined themselves to the generic business and did not specify status at work. A 'weaver' could therefore be either a master of substance or a modest journeyman, leaving to historians the manifold problems of classification.[61] By contrast, some terminology was constructed around explicit hierarchy, as in the case of service occupations: the colonel outgunned the private, the 'gentleman's gentleman' outranked the 'boots', the cook outclassed the maid-of-all-work. But, in a wide array of jobs, and especially those of craftsmen and manufacturers, it was unusual for people to describe themselves via functional status at work: hence the rarity of a self-ascribed 'journeyman' in England in the eighteenth century, or a self-named 'capitalist' in the nineteenth.

Questions of social prestige were involved, as occupations were often loosely grouped into unofficial hierarchies of esteem.[62] Again, it is probable that attitudes in practice were very variegated – and specialist groups, such as skilled craftsmen, were sustained by their own craft pride.[63] But in competitive societies, social snobberies had an impact, encouraging a tendency for unpopular roles to be regilded with smarter names. Maria Edgeworth in 1807 was sarcastic: 'There are no such things as *attorneys* now in England, they are all turned into solicitors and agents, just as every *shop* is become a *warehouse*, and every *service* a *situation*'.[64] Here she accurately prefigured change among the legal fraternity, for in 1873 the Judicature Act finally confirmed that England's attorneys were to be renamed as solicitors, linguistically at least shedding their age-old association with 'pettifogging'.

Meanwhile, the concept of 'occupation' itself had begn to be tugged into the orbit of a later and increasingly powerful definition of work. That was 'employment' and its obverse. In periods of sluggish economic activity, people who had occupations might not have work. The abstract term for 'unemployment' was not coined until the 1880s, but it developed from an earlier seventeenth- and eighteenth-century vocabulary that defined inactive labour as 'unemployed', 'idle', or 'at play'.[65] As work became more highly disciplined and more strictly differentiated from leisure, whether voluntary or involuntary,[66] 'employment' became the new term for active and contractual labour. It overlapped with the meaning of 'occupation', but it generally had a sharper focus, with connotations of purposive use. Hence 'employment' indicated an engagement that was actively in progress to carry out a specific task or to work for a specified span of time, in exchange for financial or other remuneration.[67] With it, there followed gradually a new vocabulary of status at work, especially in manufacturing and retailing. Instead of 'masters', 'apprentices' and 'journeymen', there were new 'employers' and, eventually, 'employees'. It invoked a world of formalized labour relations, but it did not refer exclusively to alienable labour, for the concept was broadened to include the 'self-employed', provided that they were actively in business.

This new definition began to gain currency in England's increasingly commercialized and contractualized labour markets from the later seventeenth century onwards, and, with the acceleration of commercial, urban, and then industrial expansion, the predominant concept of 'work' has become that of paid or gainful employment. Its usage was not simply a response to the advent of money wages – for monetary payments can be traced back well into medieval times, and conversely, some wages have continued to be given in a mix of goods and perquisites as well as in cash, into the twentieth century.[68] Nor did it demarcate a simple declension from independent into dependent labour, since many 'occupations' had been carried out in the pay or service of others. But it certainly highlighted a market-oriented and contractual approach to work, and indeed to a much stricter economic accounting, in terms of people who were in or out of work. It marked a significant streamlining of definition. It also meant, importantly, that pre-modern listings of occupations cannot automatically be read as straightforward censuses of employment.[69]

Women's work was particularly overshadowed by these definitional changes. The daily business of getting a living – in or out of town – required a great array of time-consuming support services, including childcare. Those tasks were routinely undertaken, usually by the female 'housewife' and/or her servants, within the household and family unit.[70] For many centuries, those domestic chores were carried out in close conjunction with other economic activities, in which women and older children participated as a matter of course. But the prestige of 'housework', never high, went deeper into social limbo, as work became increasingly defined as paid employment. Indeed, the centrality of the home as workplace – which had anyway varied considerably according to gender and also according to the nature of the urban economy – was increasingly eroded, once the predominant location of much non-familial economic activity moved outside the home.[71] And that development accelerated in eighteenth- and nineteenth-century England with the growth of shops, offices, factories, and other specialist workplaces.

'Housewife' meanwhile remained in use as an occupational designation, but its public acceptance as 'real' work was rendered highly uncertain. The Victorian censuses, for example, accepted as 'occupied' those wives who worked with their husbands, but classified all remaining wives and unmarried daughters without stated occupations into the non-working 'residue' of the population, a miscellaneous category which also included the dependent young, people with independent means, and all paupers and vagrants.[72] Because women's efforts as mothers and housekeepers were taken for granted, these aspects of their lives are poorly recorded and difficult to assess. Furthermore, cross-temporal analysis is rendered yet more complex by the fact that the context of childcare and housework has not remained static over time. Not only have technologies changed but over the long term a substantial number of once-domestic chores (such as, for example, teaching, healing, baking, brewing, and clothes-making) have gradually been taken over by extra-domestic specialist providers.

Similar problems beset the recording and measurement of women's non-familial economic activity, whether located inside or outside the home. There is growing evidence, however, of their participation in a range of occupations, varying with the nature of each urban economy. Some women worked in tandem with their spouses (especially in craft production and shopkeeping). But such working partnerships seem to have been much less ubiquitous than old mythologies implied.[73] Instead, many women had full- or part-time jobs in marketing, retailing, the processing and distribution of food and drink, craft production, and miscellaneous services – and notably in domestic service, which continued, up until the mid-twentieth century, to be a major source of urban employment for young women before they set up a household of their own.[74]

How far the range and remuneration of female occupations has or has not changed substantially over time is the subject of continuing research. But it seems clear that town economies were able to draw women into a range of work, in addition to traditional domestic chores. Hence it was from them, even more than from the ranks of the unemplöyed, that a real 'reserve army of labour' was potentially available to the urban economy. That was especially the case because many large towns have historically housed a majority of women among their residents, and because large towns could moreover provide women with a wider range of opportunities in the labour market.[75] Cultural expectations meanwhile also remained important, so that the nature as much as the extent of women's economic participation was influenced by social definitions of women's roles. But those too could change, particularly when skilled economies needed to draw upon the full range of human resourcefulness. Neither the theory nor the practice of the sexual division of labour was immutable. Access to important work outside the household was not an invariant male prerogative. 'Our right is the same with theirs to all public employments', asserted the pioneering 'Sophia' in 1739, contemplating – with an equanimity not universally shared by her readers – a future prospect of women doctors, women professors, women politicians, and even women generals.[76]

III Specialization

Definitions of urban work, whether in terms of aggregative economic role or in terms of disaggregative occupations, invariably point to their external economic and cultural ramifications as well as to intra-urban significance. Towns were not closed communities, sealed off from the surrounding world. On the contrary, external contacts were their life-blood. The importance of urban work does not, therefore, depend upon demonstrating its severance from a wider economy and culture. Towns were undeniably in and of their encompassing societies.[77] But that did not preclude them from having a specialist role of significance within that wider context. Indeed, the larger and more numerous the towns and cities, the greater was the concentration of human resources and the concentration of social and economic value generated by their work, and, consequently, the greater their general cultural impact.

How work has been allocated and socially defined within towns has been a matter of great diversity. Much remains to be learnt, about chronologies, about economic organization, about working experiences and perceptions, and about the languages in which these were described. As well as formal structures of work, it is important not to forget, in addition, the extent of casual and unofficial labour, which often gave town economies their *ad hoc* flexibility. Understanding urban work thence helps to illuminate the basic role of any given urban economy, as well as the extent and nature of its specialization on the urban spectrum. With the many provisos noted above, data on 'occupations' give some important clues. They are least problematic for synchronic analysis, providing comparative information about how many and what occupations are recorded at any given time, and how they are distributed among urban populations and between towns. That offers some guide both to urban function and scale. In fifteenth-century England, for example, a small market centre, such as Thornbury in Gloucestershire, had 20 to 30 separately-specified occupations. Similarly, it is suggested that in Suffolk in 1522 the small towns recorded at least 18–23 separate occupations, while rural villages had fewer than 18.[78] No doubt, these tallies were incomplete, but they were still indicative. By contrast, a medium-sized but economically-struggling county town like Winchester in 1500 recorded 52 separate occupations, while the thriving capital city had earlier in 1300 housed a population of some 80,000 people, mustering between them at least 175 separate occupational·titles.[79]

Diachronic comparisons are more difficult, because over the long term it is necessary to make allowance not only for changes in the terminologies of work but also for changing work processes described by continuing terminology. Again, precise totals are less important than general scale, because addition is further complicated by better record-keeping and by the impact of regional vocabularies, particularly in Scotland, but also including such relative rarities as the West Country 'grutt-makers', who processed oatmeal, the provincial 'helliers', who were slaters or tilers, and the Tyneside 'raffmen', who worked in Newcastle timber yards.[80] Even allowing for these changes in context, however, it seems clear that England's resumed urban growth from the later seventeenth century onwards was accompanied by a marked expansion in the recorded number of specialist urban occupations. For example, in the 1690s, tax listings in the City of London alone, excluding Westminster and the huge circumjacent urban parishes, listed at least 720 occupations, which was incidentally almost twice the number profiled in a standard handbook to London trades in 1747.[81] Even a very small place like Wetherby in Yorkshire, whose role as market town and staging-post on the Great North Road had hardly changed over many centuries, saw from the eighteenth century onwards a broadening and refining of its range of trades, crafts, and professional services.[82]

By the nineteenth century, the number of known urban occupations ran into hundreds in the middle-ranking provincial towns, and into thousands in the metropolis. The multiplication in types of jobs occurred partly as a result of the sub-division of labour, breaking down production processes into more and more specialist stages – a process that had begun long before mechanization, as Adam Smith had recognized, and which accelerated thereafter. At the same time, the multiplication of jobs was also promoted by the creation of new trades, industries, and services, in response to the growing extent and affluence of urban consumer markets. With that, the number of places with marked sectoral concentrations of labour also increased. More than 30 per cent of the adult workforce in one trade or industry was already a sign of specialization within the urban spectrum. But some places, especially single-industry manufacturing towns, showed yet higher figures: for example, the 1861 census listed 50.34 per cent of the occupied male population in the borough of Sheffield as engaged in metal-manufacturing (32.45 per cent of all Sheffield men). By contrast, the resort city of Bath at the same time kept its male workforce busy in a range of manufacturing and retailing jobs, while a high 62.06 per cent of its occupied female population named their occupation as domestic service (26.13 per cent of all Bath women) and another 22.11 per cent were engaged in dressmaking.[83]

Overall, the joint processes of individual and locational specialization marked a differentiation of economic specialisms that also entailed an economic complementarity – albeit not one that was always friction-free – between town and town, and between town and countryside. But divisions of labour were complex in all societies; and there was no universal pattern of evolution from one discrete stage or pattern of economic development to another.[84] Towns, whether experiencing growth, steady state, or decline,[85] constituted significant pointers to the complexities of wider continuities and change. Moreover, they themselves were part cause as well as part consequence of those processes.[86] If not all specialization led inexorably to fame, then it did at least underpin sustainable urban work, and thence much history.

Notes

1. Special thanks for helpful discussions of early versions of these ideas go to colleagues at the Queen's University Belfast economic history seminar and the 1986 Urban History Conference; as well as to Tony Belton, Peter Clark, Peter D'Sena, Chris Evans, Edmund Green, Vanessa Harding, Serena Kelly, Paul Laxton, Gervase Rosser; and particularly to Derek Keene for his amicable cooperation, including advice on clarifying text and curbing footnotes.

2. For the classic economic analysis, see Adam Smith, *An Inquiry into the Nature and Causes of the Wealth of Nations* (1776), ed. R.H. Campbell and A.S. Skinner (2 vols, 1976), I, 13–36, positing the increasing division of labour as an indicator of economic progress. And for the classic sociology of work, see Emile Durkheim, *De la division du travail social* (Paris, 1893) and *idem, Selected Writings*, ed. A. Giddens (1972), 146–7, 150–4, endorsing Tönnies's dichotomous model of social evolution from traditional *Gemeinschaft* (community) to modern *Gesellschaft* (contractual society) but rejecting an atomistic view of modern work. Meanwhile, Marilyn Monroe sang in a duet to 'Specialization' in G. Cukor's film, *Let's Make Love* (1960).

3. D. Defoe, *The Life and Strange Surprising Aventures of Robinson Crusoe of York, Mariner* (1719; 1926), 51–2, 150.

4. 'Specialization' in an economic application was used in 1865 by John Stuart Mill, referring to the impact of the process earlier analysed by Adam Smith as the subdivision of labour in production: see *O.E.D.* The term is sometimes reserved for 'advanced' economies with highly-skilled workforces, but it can be applied with reference to any continuous process whereby different tasks and skills are systematically divided between different groups within a workforce – so that the extent and nature of job specialization may be examined as an index of economic activity.

5. Work has been much studied, often by implication, in economic history, and recent research is also alert to its social and cultural dimensions, thereby rejecting the view that the economy can be analysed simply as an autonomous 'infrastructure'. See S.L. Kaplan and C.J. Koepp (ed.), *Work in France: Representations, Meaning, Organization and Practice* (Ithaca, N.Y., 1986), and P. Joyce (ed.) *The Historical Meanings of Work* (1987). For a select Bibliography of the history of work in towns, see below, 231–41.

6. *O.E.D* defines 'work' (Old English: *weorc*) under fully 34 sub-headings. See also R. Williams, *Keywords: A Vocabulary of Culture and Society* (1976), 281–4; S. Wallman, 'Introduction', in *idem* (ed.), *Social Anthropology of Work* (A.S.A. Monograph 19, 1979), 1–3, 20; R.H. Hall, *Dimensions of Work* (Beverly Hills, Calif., 1986), 9–38; Joyce, 'Introduction', in *Historical Meanings*, 2–14; and R.E. Pahl (ed.), *On Work: Historical, Comparative and Theoretical Approaches* (1988), 7–20.

7. That is, the impact of work is implausibly confined to economics. Its social value is defined as the production of benefits (whether social, cultural, spiritual, ideological or any other) as perceived by individuals and communities; economic value as the production of goods and services for the use or exchange. This holistic definition does not assert, however, that there is universal agreement about what constitutes social value. Nor does it deny that other factors, such as scarcity, affect economic value. It therefore accepts a greater complexity than did the classic labour-based theories that were so influential in eighteenth- and nineteenth-century economic and political

thought. For labour as the origin of value and of private property, see John Locke, *Two Treatises of Government* (1690), Bk. ii, c. 40: 'For it is labour indeed that puts the difference of value on everything'. That assumption was not only retained in classical economics but also incorporated into Karl Marx's radical assertion of labour as the source of 'surplus value' (profits) appropriated from the workforce by capitalists: see K. Marx, 'Wages, price and profit', in K. Marx and F. Engels, *Selected Works* (2 vols, Moscow, 1962), I, 431: 'Rent, Interest, and Industrial Profit are only different names for different parts of the surplus value of the commodity, or the unpaid labour enclosed in it, and they are equally derived from this source, and from this source alone'.

8. Social reproduction refers to the capacity of societies to reproduce not only their numbers but also their social and cultural patterning. It includes biological reproduction (which has its own intrinsic division of labour), since that may be experienced as economic task or even chore. But it is important to note that definitional boundaries are permeable and overlapping, as many aspects of social reproduction – let alone of human sexuality – are not convincingly confined within the concept of 'work'.

9. Definitions of childhood are therefore influenced by the socio-economic roles allotted to children. See P. Ariès, *L'enfant et la via familiale sous l'ancien régime* (Paris, 1960), transl. by R. Baldick as *Centuries of Childhood: A Social History of Family Life* (1962), 25–9, 125–30; J.R. Gillis, *Youth and History: Tradition and Change in European Age Relations 1700 - Present* (New York, 1974), 1–18; and V.A. Zeliger, *Pricing the Priceless Child: The Changing Social Value of Children* (New York, 1985).

10. Although the term dates only from 1909 (see *O.E.D. Supplement*), the phenomenon of 'underemployment' has a long history. See D.C. Coleman, 'Labour in the English economy of the seventeenth century', *Economic History Review*, 2nd ser. 8 (1955/6), esp. 288–92. And on the cultural relativity of 'laziness', see L.P. Mair, *Studies in Applied Anthropology* (1957), 75.

11. S. Smiles, *Life and Labour: Or, Characteristics of Men of Industry, Culture and Genius* (1887), 1.

12. For a pioneering study, see C.P. Gilman, *Women and Economics: A Study of the Economic Relation between Men and Women as a Factor in Social Evolution* (1899), esp. 1–22. Although women's work has long been analytically under-estimated by many anthropologists, sociologists, economists, and historians, the subject has recently begun to attract proper research attention, following surveys such as E. Boserup, *Woman's Role in Economic Development* (1970). See comments in Pahl (ed.), *On Work*, 349–54; and Bibliography, below, 238–40.

13. T. Tusser, *A Hundred Good Points of Husbandry, lately Married to a Hundred Good Points of Huswifery* (1571), 26.

14. The traditional Judaeo-Christian view of work was based upon God's curse on Adam after the Fall: 'In the sweat of thy face shalt thou eat bread', *Old Testament*, Genesis, iii, 19; later emphasized in Pauline Christianity: 'If any would not work, neither should he eat', *New Testament*, 2nd Epistle of St Paul to the Thessalonians, iii, 10. However, Christ's injunction to 'Consider the lilies of the field', in ibid., St Matthew, vi, 25–34, and St Luke, xii, 24–9, allowed scope for alternative attitudes to work.

15. F.M. Arouet de Voltaire, *Candide, ou l'optimisme* (Paris, 1759), 162: 'Le travail éloigne de nous trois grand maux, l'ennui, le vice et le besoin.'

16. T. Carlyle, *Past and Present* (1843), 207.

17. For cultural theorizations, see: A. Tilgher, *Work: What it has Meant to Men throughout the Ages*, transl. by D.C. Fisher (New York, 1930); C. Mossé, *Le travail en Grèce et à Rome* (Paris, 1966), transl. by J. Lloyd as *The Ancient World at Work* (1969); P.D. Anthony, *The Ideology of Work* (1977); and J. Le Goff, *Time, Work and Culture in the Middle Ages* (Chicago, 1978). Meanwhile, how far past workforces have shared or ignored the changing cultural canons is as yet unknown.

18. But A. Taylor, *The Proverb* (Cambridge, Mass., 1931), 12–15, points out that some sorts of work have proved more proverb-prone than others.

19. For examples and discussion, see R. Palmer, *The Sound of History: Songs and Social Comment* (1988), esp. 61–120.

20. An exemplary study of the power of workplace custom is provided in M. Sonenscher, *The Hatters of Eighteenth-Century France* (Berkeley, Calif, 1987).

21. For this influential if controversial distinction, see Smith, *Wealth of Nations*, I, 330–5, esp. 330: 'A man grows rich by employing a multitude of manufacturers: He grows poor, by maintaining a multitude of menial servants'. But, while the social value of services may be debatable and their economic productivity highly variable, there is no reason to deny value to 'intangible' services – any more than there is to discount 'invisible' earnings in the balance of overseas trade. For the history of the distinction, see S.H. Coontz, *Productive Labour and Effective Demand: Including a Critique of Keynesian Economics* (1965), esp. 28–40; and for its radical application, see ibid., 53–75; and I. Gough, 'Marx's theory of productive and unproductive labour', *New Left Review*, 76 (1972), 47–72.

22. W. Cowper, *The Task: A Poem* (1785), in *The Complete Poetical Works of William Cowper*, ed. H.S. Milford (1905), 145.

23. See R. Williams, *The Country and the City* (1973) for a survey of English literary expressions of these attitudinal polarities over many centuries.

24. D. Urquhart, *Familiar Words: As Affecting the Character of Englishmen and the Fate of England* (1855), 119, urging that 'the sub-division of labour is the assassination of a people'.

25. E. Jones, *Towns and Cities* (1966), 1–12. Influential in inculcating multivariate approaches have been M. Weber, *The City*, ed. D. Martindale and G. Neuwirth (Glencoe, Ill., 1958), esp. 65–89; and L.B. Wirth, 'Urbanism as a way of life', *American Journal of Sociology*, 44 (1938), reprinted in *Cities and Society: The Revised Reader in Urban Sociology*, ed. P.K. Hatt and A.J. Reiss (New York, 1957), 46–63.

26. The service (tertiary) sector is sometimes further sub-divided to indicate the extent of research, government, and information (quaternary) services, but those also remain characteristically, if not exclusively, urban in location.

27. For the 'agro-cities' of early twentieth century Italy, see F.M. Snowden, *Violence and Great Estates in the South of Italy: Apulia 1900–22* (1986), 21–6, 41–61. These places housed sizeable populations of unskilled day labourers, employed in manual labour as *zappatori* (hoers and diggers). These labourers did not cultivate their own plots for food but worked on the surrounding great estates, producing foodstuffs for distant markets.

28. The earliest urban civilizations were found in fertile river valleys and had extensive trading contacts, as shown by archaeological recovery of stones, metals, and woods from distant places. See L. Mumford, *The City in History: Its Origins, its Transformations, and its Prospects* (1961, 1966), 40–7, 70–6; V.G. Childe, *What Happened in History* (1942), Ch. 5; and R.M. Adams, *Heartland of Cities: Surveys of Ancient Settlement and Land Use on the Central Floodplain of the Euphrates* (Chicago, 1981), 52–81, 248–52.

29. F. Engels, *Herr Eugen Dühring's Revolution in Science (Anti-Dühring)* (1878), ed. C.P. Dutt (1934), 318; and also K. Marx, *Capital: A Critical Analysis of Capitalist Production* (1887), ed. D. Torr (1946), 345: 'The foundation of every division of labour that is well developed, and brought about by the exchange of commodities, is the separation between town and country. It may be said, that the whole economical history of society is summed up in the movement of this antithesis'. Only a post-revolutionary society could therefore expect a 'gradual abolition of the distinction between town and country': K. Marx and F. Engels, *The Communist Manifesto* (1848) in *Karl Marx: Selected Writings*, ed. D. McLellan (1977), 237.

30. See M. Sahlins, *Stone Age Economics* (Chicago and New York, 1972), 10, 14–32; and

thought-provoking analysis and conjectures in M. Ehrenberg, *Women in Prehistory* (1989), 41–52, 80–90, 99–107.

31. Over many centuries, towns with high mortality rates have relied upon net immigration from the countryside to replenish numbers and to grow; and, even after the secular reduction in urban mortality rates, many modern towns remain attractive to rural recruits. For twentieth-century patterns, see B.M. Du Toit and H.I. Safa (ed.), *Migration and Urbanization: Models and Adaptive Strategies* (The Hague, 1975); and B. Roberts, *Cities of Peasants: The Political Economy of Urbanization in the Third World* (1978), 98–107.

32. For references and introduction to debates, see B.L. Anderson and A.J.H. Latham (ed.), *The Market in History* (1986); and R. Hodges, *Primitive and Peasant Markets* (1988). In addition, there is much information in detailed studies of the marketing of industrial and agricultural products.

33. Thus the history of markets is not simply coterminous with that of towns: see, for example, the instructive case-histories in R.H. Britnell, 'The proliferation of markets in England, 1200–1349', *Economic History Review*, 2nd ser. *34* (1981). In eighteenth-century England, many ancient markets had decayed into small villages but were still known as 'market towns': see P.J. Corfield, *The Impact of English Towns 1700–1800* (1982), 20–1.

34. For an exposition of the cultural diversity of trading and marketing practices, see C. Geertz, *Peddlers and Princes: Social Change and Economic Modernization in Two Indonesian Towns* (Chicago, 1963), 32–47.

35. T.C. Mendenhall, *The Shrewsbury Drapers and the Welsh Wool Trade in the Sixteenth and Seventeenth Centuries* (1953), 36–47.

36. For a case-study of those linkages, see A.R. Pred, *Urban Growth and the Circulation of Information: The United States System of Cities 1790–1840* (Cambridge, Mass., 1973).

37. R.S. Lopez, 'The crossroads within the wall', in *The Historian and the City*, ed. O. Handlin and J. Burchard (Cambridge, Mass., 1963), 27–43, and brief critique by A. Gershenkron, 'City economies – then and now', in ibid., 56–62, also republished in his *Continuity in History and Other Essays* (Cambridge, Mass., 1968), 249–54.

38. Production and services are categorized as 'maintenance' (serving local markets) as opposed to 'export' (extra-local) activities in A.J. Reiss, 'Functional specialization of cities', in *Cities and Society*, ed. Hatt and Reiss, 555–7; but it should be noted that the local basis of urban 'maintenance' activities included local exports into the rural hinterland.

39. Thus Roberts, *Cities of Peasants*, 175, notes the modern Third World town's intensive use of cheap labour in craft production and in repair, personal, and commercial services. In a case-study, R.V. Kemper, *Migration and Adaptation: Tzintzuntzan Peasants in Mexico City* (Beverly Hills, 1977), 135–48, found a high participation rate in the urban economy among a group of rural migrants to the huge Mexican capital, with few household heads unemployed and many households containing more than one earner.

40. For the extensive history of towns, see Bibliography, below, 232–3. A new overview of European data is presented in P. Bairoch, J. Batou and P. Chèvre, *La population des villes européennes: banque de données et analyse sommaire des résultats 800-1850/ The Population of European Cities: Databank and Short Summary of Results* (Geneva, 1988); with a general analysis in P. Bairoch, *De Jéricho à Mexico: villes et économies dans l'histoire* (Paris, 1985); transl. by C. Braider as *Cities and Economic Development: From the Dawn of History to the Present Day* (1989).

41. London's protean economy is analysed and debated in E.A. Wrigley, 'A simple model of London's importance in changing England's economy and society, 1650–1750', *Past and Present*, 37 (1967), 44–70; A.L. Beier and R. Finlay (ed.), *London 1500-1700: The Making of the Metropolis* (1986); and J. Alexander, 'The economic structure of the City

of London at the end of the seventeenth century', *Urban History Yearbook 1989* (1989), 47–62.

42. G. Simmel, 'The metropolis and mental life' (1903), in *idem, On Individuality and Social Forms*, ed. D.N. Levine (Chicago, 1971), 335.

43. For regulation of slave markets in classical antiquity, see documents cited in T. Wiedemann, *Greek and Roman Slavery* (1981), 108–14; and note in M. Massey and P. Moreland, *Slavery in Ancient Rome* (1978), 18–22. In the pre-Emancipation American South, large slave markets, where slaves were both sold and hired to town and country masters, were located at the great trading depots, such as New Orleans, Richmond, and Charleston, with smaller subsidiaries elsewhere: see R.C. Wade, *Slavery in the Cities: The South 1820-60* (New York, 1964), 197–208; C.D. Goldin, *Urban Slavery in the American South 1820-60: A Quantitative History* (Chicago, 1976), 27, 35–40; and R.N. Rosen, *A Short History of Charleston* (San Francisco, 1982), 63–5.

44. An example is cited by Keene, 'Continuity and development', above, 8.

45. A sympathetic study of tramping labourers in nineteenth-century England, as they seasonally crossed and recrossed town/country boundaries, is given in R. Samuel, 'Comers and goers', in *The Victorian City: Images and Reality*, ed. H.J. Dyos and M. Woolf (2 vols, 1973), I, 123–60.

46. For 'formal' and 'informal' work in modern Sheppey, Kent, see R.E. Pahl, *Divisions of Labour* (1984), esp. 17–20, 46–54, 89–113. Appropriately enough, the history of the 'black economy' is very difficult to recover, although its extent can sometimes be estimated by economic calculus.

47. There are a number of parallel debates about the use of selective records relating to English urban occupations. For references and contributions to these debates, see variously: Keene, 'Continuity and development', above, 9–11; H. Swanson on medieval guild affiliations in 'Artisans', above, 42–53; as well as J.F. Pound, 'The validity of the freeman's lists: some Norwich evidence', *Economic History Review*, 2nd ser. *34* (1981), 48–59; and G. Shaw, 'The content and reliability of nineteenth-century trade directories', *Local Historian, 13* (1978), 205–9.

48. The languages of work in definition and in social use await further analysis, but for a lively account of one loquacious occupational group, see R. Porter, 'The language of quackery in England, 1660-1800', in *The Social History of Language*, ed. P. Burke and R. Porter (1987), 73–103.

49. *O.E.D.* dates these English usages of 'occupation' from the fourteenth century, and 'job' from the seventeenth, although it may have had an earlier colloquial use. See also Williams, *Keywords*, 183–4. Occupational designations were, however, much older than both these generic terms.

50. Local sources often reveal occupational pluralism, such as a weaver who also kept an alehouse or a washerwoman who also took lodgers, although it is possible that those were family rather than one-person businesses. By contrast, formal listings tended to record large majorities with single jobs. A study of 16 urban directories in Britain in the 1770s and 1780s found that, of the 29,733 individuals and firms with occupations, 88.0 per cent had single occupations, another 11.4 per cent had two (often closely linked), and only 0.6 per cent had three or more – the exception to prove all the rules being the Bristolian (1775) who was simultaneously glover, hosier, parchment-maker, orange-man, and undertaker (entrepreneur): see P.J. Corfield, 'Urban occupations in Britain in the early Industrial Revolution', unpublished report on research-in-progress, for which the support of the Economic and Social Research Council (Ref: BOO/23/0031; 1983–85) is gratefully acknowledged. For further comment on the problems posed by multiple occupations for calculations of social and occupational structure, see also P.H. Lindert, 'English occupations, 1670-1820', *Journal of Economic History, 40* (1980), 691–2, 706.

51. W. Shakespeare, *Othello*, Act III, scene iii.

52. E. Blunt, *The Caste System of Northern India: With Special Reference to the United Provinces of Agra and Oudh* (1931), esp. 229–52. See also L. Dumont, *Homo Hierarchicus: le système des castes et ses implications* (Paris, 1966), 123–42; and M. Moffatt, *An Untouchable Community in South India: Structure and Consensus* (Princeton, N.J., 1979), 89–98, 212–18.

53. In the English-speaking world, occupational/status labels constituted one of four main sources of surnames, the others being personal/family names; place/location names; and nicknames/descriptive terms. See P.H. Reaney, *A Dictionary of British Surnames* (1958), ix–xxxviii. For the geography of surnames as indicator of long-term male migrational patterns, see F. Leeson, 'The history and technique of surname distribution studies', *Family History*, 3 (1965), 35–7, 45; and M. Ecclestone, 'The diffusion of English surnames', *Local Historian*, 19 (1989), 63–70.

54. G. Bourcier, *An Introduction to the History of the English Language*, in Engl. adaptation by C. Clark (1981), 177–83, points to the standardization of spelling, grammar and vocabulary in the later Middle Ages, and the pull of London and the Home Counties in that process.

55. *O.E.D.* cites 'spinster' as occupation from the fourteenth century onwards; and as standard term for an unmarried women from the seventeenth.

56. *New Testament*, St Paul's Epistle to the Ephesians, iv, 1.

57. Luther preached that to work was to serve God: see M. Luther, 'The sum of a Christian life', in *Thirty-Four Sermons . . .* (1816), 139. And for an English Presbyterian examplar, see J. Collinges, *The Weavers Pocket-Book: Or, Weaving Spiritualized, in a Discourse, wherein Men Employed in that Occupation are Instructed how to Raise Heavenly Meditations* (1675). But both the uniqueness and the social impact of Protestant economic teaching have been disputed. See debates in: M. Weber, *The Protestant Ethic and the Spirit of Capitalism* (1905; 1971); R.H. Tawney, *Religion and the Rise of Capitalism* (1926); C. Hill, 'Protestantism and the rise of capitalism', in *Essays in the Economic and Social History of Tudor and Stuart England*, ed. F.J. Fisher (1961), 15–39; and G. Marshall, *In Search of the Spirit of Capitalism: An Essay on Max Weber's Protestant Ethic Thesis* (1982).

58. The 'immoral economy' comprised work that was illegal or immoral or both; it was not identical to the 'black economy', which included work that was not illegal in itself, even if illegally concealed from authority.

59. Examples are recorded in J. Beresford (ed.), *The Diary of a Country Parson: The Reverend James Woodforde* (5 vols, 1924–31), I, 197, 201, 221.

60. For repeated attempts to distinguish between holy poverty, involuntary want, and conscious roguery, see references in B. Tierney, *Medieval Poor Law: A Sketch of Canonical Theory and its Application in England* (Berkeley, Calif., 1959), 11–12, 130–1; P. Slack, *Poverty and Policy in Tudor and Stuart England* (1988), 104–6, 115–16, 123–8; A.L. Beier, *Masterless Men: The Vagrancy Problem in England 1560-1640* (1985), 3–13; and literary descriptions in C.J. Ribton-Turner, *A History of Vagrants and Vagrancy, and Beggars and Begging* (1887), 576–665.

61. Occupations may be classified into significant economic groupings, but even that poses many problems, because single occupations often straddle sectoral boundaries. It is still more problematic to classify occupations into social status groups or classes, because similar occupational titles may include individuals of divergent wealth, power and working status. See discussions in: J. Patten, 'Urban occupations in pre-industrial England', *Transactions of the Institute of British Geographers*, n.s. 2 (1977), 296–313; M. Katz, 'Occupational classification in history', *Journal of Interdisciplinary History*, 3 (1972), 63–88; W.A. Armstrong, 'The use of information about occupation', in *Nineteenth-Century Society: Essays in the Use of Quantitative Methods for the Study*

of Social Data, ed. E.A. Wrigley (1972), 191–310; D. and J. Mills, 'Occupation and social stratification revisited: the census enumerators' books of Victorian Britain', *Urban History Yearbook 1989* (1989), 63–77; J.H. Goldthorpe and K. Hope, *The Social Grading of Occupations: A New Approach and Scale* (1974); and works cited in Bibliography, below, 240–1. These classification problems also crucially affect analyses of wealth distribution by social class, when class is defined solely by occupation. For pertinent comments on the large extent of wealth dispersion within occupational groups, see J.A. James, 'Personal wealth distribution in late eighteenth-century Britain', *Economic History Review*, 2nd ser. *41* (1988), 554; and Green, 'Taxonomy', above, 174–7.

62. Very little work has been done on historic hierarchies of esteem, but, for modern data, see the emphasis upon pluralism and subjectivity in A.P.M. Coxon and P.M. Davies with C.L. Jones, *Images of Social Stratification: Occupational Structures and Class* (1986), 1–3, 202–13. That differs from D.J. Treiman, *Occupational Prestige in Comparative Perspective* (New York, 1977), esp. 2, 22–3, arguing for an invariant hierarchy of occupational esteem, applicable 'in all complex societies, past and present'.

63. It is possible that many occupations, even the 'lowliest', were able to generate some occupational solidarity, although it tended to be most marked among those with restricted entry or hard-won skills. 'Books of Trades', celebrating the diversity of occupational skills rather than their hierarchy, were a popular genre of publication in Enlightenment Europe: see for examples J. and K. Luiken, *Het Menselyk Bedryf, vertoond in 100 Verbeeldingen* (Amsterdam, 1694; and many later edns.); and Anon., *The Book of Trades: Or, Library of the Useful Arts* (2 vols, 1804).

64. Compare M. Edgeworth, *Patronage* (3 vols, 1814), II, 269; and Statute 36 & 37 Victoria (1873), cap. 66, sect. 87. But 'attorney' survived elsewhere in the English-speaking world, notably in the United States of America.

65. 'Unemployment' as an abstract noun dates from the late 1880s, although the adjective 'unemployed' was used for individuals at least since the 1660s: see *O.E.D*; Williams, *Keywords*, 173–5; and J.A. Garraty, *Unemployment in History: Economic Thought and Public Policy* (1978), esp. 4–5.

66. For the evolution of the work/leisure dichotomy, see K. Thomas, 'Work and leisure in pre-industrial society', *Past and Present*, 29 (1964), 50–62; E.P. Thompson, 'Time, work discipline and industrial capitalism', *Past and Present*, 38 (1967), 70–97; and H. Cunningham, *Leisure in the Industrial Revolution c.1780–c.1880* (1980), esp. 15–56, 192–212.

67. *O.E.D.* notes 'employment' in reference to specific tasks from the ·1590s, and to occupation or business from the mid-seventeenth century. 'Employer' shared a similar chronology, but 'employee' was a nineteenth-century American innovation, that was slow to gain currency in England. See also Williams, *Keywords*, 282–3.

68. For a sceptical overview of monetization, see M.M. Postan, 'The rise of a money economy', *Economic History Review*, 14 (1944), 123–34; reprinted in *Essays in Economic History*, ed. E.M. Carus-Wilson (1954), 1–12. Changing forms of pay, their typicality, and their impact upon attitudes to work, all merit further research. See for discussion: C. Hill, 'Pottage for freeborn Englishmen: attitudes to wage-labour', in *idem*, *Change and Continuity in Seventeenth-Century England* (1974), 219–38; and, for a case study: P. D'Sena, 'Perquisites and casual labour on the London wharfside in the eighteenth century', *London Journal*, 14 (1989), 130–47.

69. See, for example, the debate about the special Venetian guild censuses (undertaken for fiscal purposes) as indicators of employment: R.T. Rapp, *Industry and Economic Decline in Seventeenth-Century Venice* (Cambridge, Mass., 1976), 14–15, 22–32, 54–7, 82–106; and a review by B. Pullan, *Economic History Review*, 2nd ser. *30* (1977), 207–8.

70. This complex subject is introduced in C. Hall, 'The history of the housewife', *The Politics of Housework*, ed. E. Malos (1980), 44–71.

71. Some towns (e.g. with household-based staple industries) had traditionally seen a much higher proportion of work in the home than had others (e.g. ports and dockyard towns) but all had a considerable number working outside the home (e.g. in building, marketing, transport, entertainments). When most shopkeeping and manufacturing had shifted to specialist venues, and home was left to specialize as residential accommodation, tended by 'housewives' and (up until the mid-twentieth century) by domestic servants.

72. E. Higgs, *Making Sense of the Census: The Manuscript Returns for England and Wales 1801–1901* (1989), 78–96; and census tabulations, such as those for 1841 in *British Parliamentary Papers*, 27 (1844) and 'Preface', in ibid., 9. The manifold problems in identifying working women and in classifying their work are explicated in E. Higgs, 'Women, occupations, and work in the nineteenth-century censuses', *History Workshop Journal*, 23 (1987), 59–80. Subsequently, a new category of 'homeworker' was introduced in 1901, in reference to people (mainly women) who were engaged in paid employment in the home but for an external employer.

73. See Roberts, 'Women and work', above, Ch. 6; P. Earle, 'The female labour market in London in the late seventeenth and early eighteenth centuries', *Economic History Review*, 2nd ser. 42 (1989), 328–52; and the growing corpus of new research as cited in Bibliography, below, 238–40.

74. For informative evidence (not confined to towns), see: J.J. Hecht, *The Domestic Servant Class in Eighteenth-Century England* (1956); S.C. Maza, *Servants and Masters in Eighteenth-Century France: The Uses of Loyalty* (Princeton, N.J., 1983); and T.M. McBride, *The Domestic Revolution: The Modernization of Household Service in England and France 1820–1920* (1976).

75. A combination of female longevity and high levels of female migration to town gave all large towns in eighteenth- and nineteenth-century Britain a preponderance of women among their residents, and particularly in resorts such as the city of Bath. But for contrasting examples of some modern Third World towns, which are male-dominated either through government restrictions upon female migration or through cultural constraints upon the public appearance of women, see Boserup, *Women's Role*, 85–7. Much current research is examining the range of working opportunities available to women in towns. See for example: P.J.P. Goldberg, 'Women in fifteenth-century town life', in *Towns and Townspeople in the Fifteenth Century*, ed. J.A.F. Thomson (1988), 107–28; and works cited in Bibliography, below, 238–40.

76. 'Sophia', *Woman not Inferior to Man: Or, a Short and Modest Vindication of the Natural Right of the Fair-Sex to a Perfect Equality of Power, Dignity, and Esteem with the Men* (1739), 60: 'public employments' in this context meant public office rather than waged employment. A rebuttal followed from 'A Gentleman', *Man Superior to Woman . . .* (1739); and a yet stronger surrebuttal from *'Sophia', Woman's Superior Excellence over Man* (1740).

77. A somewhat similar point is made, but with a different emphasis and conclusion, in P. Abrams, 'Towns and Economic Growth: Some Theories and Problems', in *Towns in Societies: Essays in Economic History and Historical Sociology*, ed. P. Abrams and E.A. Wrigley (1978), esp. 9–10; and Langton and Hoppe, 'Urbanization', above, Ch. 9.

78. Compare information on Thornbury in R.H. Hilton, 'Towns in English feudal society', in *idem, Class Conflict and the Crisis of Feudalism: Essays in Medieval Social History* (1985), 177–8; with scalogram analysis of Suffolk towns and villages in J. Patten, 'Village and town: an occupational study', *Agricultural History Review*, 20 (1972), 1–16, esp. Figs. 3 and 4.

79. Keene, 'Continuity and Development', above, 7. For leading occupations in three Midland provincial towns in the 1510s and 1520s, see also W.G. Hoskins, 'English provincial towns in the sixteenth century', *Transactions of the Royal Historical Society*, 5th ser. 6 (1956), 12–17; but contrast with discussion in N. Goose, 'English pre-industrial urban economies', *Urban History Yearbook 1982* (1982), 24–30.

80. Data from Corfield, 'Urban occupations', as cited above, note 50.

81. Compare figures cited by Keene, 'Continuity and development', above, 7; and information in R. Campbell, *The London Tradesman: Being a Compendious View of All the Trades, Professions, Arts, Both Liberal and Mechanic, Now Practised in the Cities of London and Westminster* (1747), 331–40. Fresh research and analysis of eighteenth-century occupations is much needed, especially as the extent of economic change then is strongly contested. For pioneering, if speculative, exercises in reconstructing England's socio-economic profile from occupational listings and probate inventory data, see: Lindert, 'English occupations', 685–712; and P.H. Lindert and J.G. Williamson, 'Revising England's social tables, 1688–1812', *Explorations in Economic History, 19* (1982), 385–408.

82. R. Unwin, *Wetherby: The History of a Yorkshire Market Town* (1986), 29–33, 66–71, analysing occupations in medieval and eighteenth-century Wetherby.

83. Data from the 1861 census for Bath and Sheffield are tabulated in Armstrong, 'Use of occupations' in *Nineteenth-Century Society*, 250.

84. Since the intellectual weakening of the great Victorian organizing concepts of Whiggish 'progress' or a Marxist sequence of revolutions in the mode of production, there has been considerable uncertainty and eclecticism among historians about the organizing concepts and the significant chronologies of long-term historical development, with some preferring instead to stress deep continuities and the rarity of fundamental change. It may be hoped that out of these debates will come successful resynthesis; and it is already clear that simple binary contrasts, such as premodern/modern, pre-industrial/industrial, underdeveloped/developed, *Gemeinschaft/Gesellschaft*, fail to encompass the full diversity and complexity of long-term development.

85. Specialization was not invariably a cause of growth; it could lead to economic problems, if economic conditions changed. Recently, research attention has been fruitfully devoted to questions of urban decline. For overviews of two regional urban systems that experienced relative eclipse, see essays in H. Van der Wee (ed.) *The Rise and Decline of Urban Industries in Italy and the Low Countries (Late Middle Ages – Early Modern Times)* (Leuven, 1988), esp. summary chaps. 7 and 15.

86. For urban growth as a component of wider equations of economic and social change in eighteenth-century England, see Corfield, *Impact*, 95–8.

Select bibliography:
work in towns 850–1850

Note by the editors

A full list of the many studies that refer, directly or indirectly, to work and town life would cover much of the output of urban and economic history and fill many volumes. This bibliography is therefore designed as a selective introduction. It focuses chiefly upon the history of Britain, plus other historical, sociological and anthropological studies that have provided a number of conceptual reference points for research and discussion. Some exemplary case-histories of specific employments and specific towns have been included, although it is impossible to list them all. Additional references are also listed in the footnotes to the essays in this volume. For further information, the standard social and economic history bibliographies should be consulted, including not only references to 'work' and 'towns' but also to many contiguous subjects such as: population growth; migration; gender; children; apprenticeship; the family; servants; the professions; services; markets; consumerism; trade; transport; industry; technology; management; labour; workplace culture; occupational clothing; occupational illness; factory reform; guilds; trade unions; wages/earnings; poverty and poor relief; unemployment; socialist and other political ideas; economic thought. Overall, despite a recent surge of interest, it is notable how much yet remains unknown about the historic experience of actual work processes in towns and its cultural and social evaluation, both within and outside the household.

Contents of Bibliography

1 Work
2 Urbanization/general
3 Work and towns
   3.1 Medieval
   3.2 Early modern
   3.3 Eighteenth century
   3.4 Post-1801
4 Gender and work
   4.1 Medieval
   4.2 Early modern/eighteenth century
   4.3 Post-1801
5 Occupations and their classification

1 - Work

P.D. Anthony, *The Ideology of Work* (1977)

T. Caplow, *The Sociology of Work* (Minneapolis, 1954)

T. Carlyle, *Past and Present* (1843)

E. Durkheim, *De la division du travail social: études sur l'organisation des societés supérieures* (Paris, 1893); transl. by W.D. Halls as *The Division of Labour in Society* (1984).

A. Fox, 'The meaning of work', in *The Politics of Work and Occupations*, ed. G. Esland and G. Salaman (1980)

J.A. Garraty, *Unemployment in History: Economic Thought and Public Policy* (New York, 1978)

A. Giddens and G. MacKenzie (ed.), *Social Class and the Division of Labour: Essays in Honour of Ilya Neustadt* (1982)

C.P. Gilman, *Women and Economics: A Study of the Economic Relation between Men and Women as a Factor in Social Evolution* (1899)

M. Godelier, 'Work and its representations: a research proposal', *History Workshop Journal, 10* (1980)

R.H. Hall, *Dimensions of Work* (Beverly Hills, Calif., 1986)

P. Joyce (ed.), *The Historical Meanings of Work* (1987)

C. Littler (ed.), *The Experience of Work* (1985)

K. Marx, *Das Kapital: Kritik der Politischen Ökonomie* (1867), transl. by S. Moore and E. Aveling as *Capital: A Critical Analysis of Capitalist Production*, ed. F. Engels (1887)

K. Marx, *Grundrisse der Kritik der Politischen Ökonomie*, transl. as *Pre-Capitalist Economic Formations*, ed. E.J. Hobsbawm (1964)

K. Marx and F. Engels, *Die Deutsche Ideologie*, transl. as *The German Ideology*, ed. C. Arthur (1970).

R.E. Pahl, *Divisions of Labour* (1984)

R.E. Pahl (ed.), *On Work: Historical, Comparative and Theoretical Approaches* (1988)

A. Smith, *An Inquiry into the Nature and Causes of the Wealth of Nations*, ed. R.H. Campbell and A.S. Skinner (2 vols, 1976)

P. Thompson, *The Nature of Work: An Introduction to Debates on the Labour Process* (1983)

S.H. Udy, *Work in a Traditional and Modern Society* (Englewood Cliffs, N.J., 1970)

S. Wallman (ed.), *Social Anthropology of Work* (ASA Monograph 19, 1979)

M. Weber, *The Theory of Social and Economic Organisation: Being Part I of Wirtschaft und Gesellschaft*, ed. T. Parsons (1947)

2 - Urbanization/general

P. Abrams and E.A. Wrigley (ed.), *Towns in Societies: Essays in Economic History and Historical Sociology* (1978)

P. Bairoch, *De Jéricho à Mexico: villes et économies dans l'histoire* (Paris, 1985), transl. by C. Braider as *Cities and Economic Development: From the Dawn of History to the Present* (1989)

P. Bairoch, J. Batou and P. Chèvre, *La population des villes européennes: banque de données et analyse sommaire des résultats 800-1850/The Population of European Cities: Data Bank and Short Summary of Results* (Geneva, 1988)

B.J.L. Berry, *The Human Consequences of Urbanization: Divergent Paths in the Urban Experience of the Twentieth Century* (1973)

D. Denecke and G. Shaw (ed.), *Urban Historical Geography: Recent Progress in Britain and Germany* (1988)

P. Hauser and L. Schnore (ed.), *The Study of Urbanization* (New York, 1965)

P.M. Hohenberg and L.H. Lees, *The Making of Urban Europe 1000–1950* (Cambridge, Mass., 1985)

B.F. Hoselitz, 'Generative and parasitic cities', *Economic History and Cultural Change*, 3 (1954/5)

J. Jacobs, *The Economy of Cities* (1969)

E.E. Lampard, 'The history of cities in the economically-advanced areas', *Economic Development and Cultural Change*, 3 (1954/5)

E.E. Lampard, 'The urbanizing world', in *The Victorian City: Images and Realities*, Vol. I, ed. H.J. Dyos and M. Wolff (2 vols, 1973)

R.S. Lopez, 'The crossroads within the wall', in *The Historian and the City*, ed. O. Handlin and J. Burchard (Cambridge, Mass., 1963)

T.G. McGee, 'The rural-urban continuum debate, the pre-industrial city and rural-urban migration', *Pacific Viewpoint*, 5 (1964)

L. Mumford, *The City in History: Its Origins, its Transformations and its Prospects* (New York, 1961)

T.K. Rabb and R.I. Rotberg (ed.), *Industrialization and Urbanization* (Princeton, N.J., 1981)

G. Sjoberg, *The Preindustrial City: Past and Present* (New York, 1960)

M. Weber, *The City*, ed. D. Martindale and G. Neuwirth (Glencoe, Ill., 1958)

L. Wirth, 'Urbanism as a way of life', *American Journal of Sociology*, 44 (1938); reprinted in *Cities and Society: The Revised Reader in Urban Sociology*, ed. P.K. Hatt and A.J. Reiss (New York, 1951, 1957)

3 – Work and towns 3.1 – Medieval

P.V. Addyman (ed.), The Archaeology of York series published 1976 onwards

J. Allan, *Medieval and Post-Medieval Finds from Exeter 1971–80* (Exeter Archaeological Reports 3, 1984)

B.L. Anderson and A.J.H. Latham (ed.), *The Market in History* (1986)

F. Barlow, M. Biddle, O. von Feilitzen and D.J. Keene, *Winchester in the Early Middle Ages: An Edition and Discussion of the Winton Domesday*, ed. M. Biddle (1976)

W.J. Blair and N. Ramsay (ed.), *Medieval English Industry: The Craftsmen and their Products* (1990)

A.R. Bridbury, *Economic Growth: England in the Later Middle Ages* (1962)

R.H. Britnell, *Growth and Decline in Colchester 1300–1525* (1986)

R.H. Britnell, 'The proliferation of markets in England, 1200–1399', *Economic History Review*, 2nd ser. 34 (1981)

A. Chédeville, J. Le Goff and J. Rossiaud, *La ville médiévale* (Paris, 1980), Vol. II in G. Duby (ed.), *Histoire de la France urbaine*

H.B. Clarke and A. Simms (ed.), *The Comparative History of Urban Origins in Non-Roman Europe: Ireland, Wales, Denmark, Germany, Poland and Russia from the Ninth to the Thirteenth Century* (British Arch. Reports, internat. ser. 255, 2 vols, 1985)

J. Cooper and A. Crossley, 'Medieval Oxford', in *V.C.H. Oxfordshire*, Vol. IV: *The City of Oxford* (1979)

E. Coornaert, 'Les ghildes médiévales (Ve-XIVe siècles): définition – évolution', *Revue Historique*, 199 (1948)

P. Davey and R. Hodges (ed.), *Ceramics and Trade: The Production and Distribution of Later Medieval Pottery in North-West Europe* (1983)

B. Dobson, 'Admissions to the freedom of the City of York in the later Middle Ages', *Economic History Review*, 2nd ser. 26 (1973)

C. Dyer, *Standards of Living in the Later Middle Ages: Social Change in England c. 1200–1520* (1989)

C. Dyer, 'The consumer and the market in the later Middle Ages', *Economic History Review*, 2nd ser. 42 (1989)

E. Ennen, *Die Europäische Stadt des Mittelalters* (Göttingen, 1975), transl. by N. Fryde as *The Medieval Town* (Amsterdam, 1979)

B. Geremek, *Le salariat dans l'artisanat parisien aux XIIIe-XVe siècles* (Paris, 1968)

B. Geremek, *Les marginaux parisiens aux XIVe et XVe siècles* (Paris, 1976), trans. by J. Birrell as *The Margins of Society in Late Medieval Paris* (1987)

R.H. Hilton, *Class Conflict and the Crisis of Feudalism: Essays in Medieval Social History* (1985)

R.H. Hilton, 'Small town society in England before the Black Death', *Past and Present, 105* (1984)

R. Hodges, *Dark Age Economics: The Origins of Towns and Trade AD 600-1000* (1982)

R. Hodges and B. Hobley (ed.), *The Rebirth of Towns in the West AD 700-1050* (Council for British Archaeology Research Report 68, 1988)

D. Keene, *Survey of Medieval Winchester* (1985)

D.J. Keene, 'Shops and shopping in medieval London', in *Medieval Art and Architecture in London*, ed. L.M. Grant (British Arch. Assocn. Conference Transactions 10, 1990)

J.I. Kermode, 'Merchants, overseas trade and urban decline: York, Beverley and Hull, *c.* 1380-1500', *Northern History, 23* (1987)

J. Le Goff, *Time, Work and Culture in the Middle Ages*, transl. by A. Goldhammer (Chicago, 1980)

M. Lynch, M. Spearman and G. Stell, *The Scottish Medieval Town* (1988)

E. Miller, 'Medieval York', in *V.C.H. Yorkshire*, Vol. I: *The City of York* (1961)

H. Pirenne, *Medieval Cities: Their Origins and the Revival of Trade*, transl. by F.D. Halsey (Princeton, N.J., 1925)

C. Platt, *Medieval Southampton: The Port and Trading Community AD 1000-1600* (1973)

C. Platt, *The English Medieval Town* (1976)

S. Reynolds, *An Introduction to the History of English Medieval Towns* (1977)

S.H. Rigby, 'Urban decline in the later Middle Ages: the reliability of the non-statistical evidence', *Urban History Yearbook 1984* (1984)

F. Rörig, *Die Europäische Stadt* (1932), transl. by D. Bryant as *The Medieval Town* (1967)

G. Rosser, *Medieval Westminster 1200-1540* (1989)

P.H. Sawyer, 'Fairs and markets in early medieval England', in *Danish Medieval History: New Currents*, ed. N. Skyum-Nielsen and N. Lund (Copenhagen, 1981)

A.D.F Streeten, 'Craft and industry: medieval and later potters in south-east England', in *Production and Distribution: A Ceramic Viewpoint*, ed. H. Howard and E.L. Morris (1981)

H. Swanson, *Medieval Artisans: An Urban Class in Late Medieval England* (1989)

H. Swanson, 'The illusion of economic structure: craft guilds in late medieval English towns', *Past and Present, 121* (1988)

S.L. Thrupp, *The Merchant Class of Medieval London 1300-1500* (Chicago, 1948)

E.M. Veale, 'Craftsmen and the economy of London in the fourteenth century', in *Studies in London History presented to P.E. Jones*, ed. A.E.J. Hollaender and W. Kellaway (ed.) (1969)

3.2 - Early modern

J. Alexander, 'The economic structure of the City of London at the end of the seventeenth century', *Urban History Yearbook 1989* (1989)

I. Archer, C.M. Barron and V. Harding (ed.), *Hugh Alley's Caveat: The Markets of London in 1598* (London Topographical Society 137, 1988)

J.M. Baart, 'Dutch material civilization – daily life between 1650-1776: evidence from archaeology', in *New World Dutch Studies*, ed. R.R. Blackburn and N.A. Kelley (Albany, N.Y., 1987)

A.L. Beier and R. Finlay (ed.), *London 1500-1700: The Making of the Metropolis* (1986)

J. Boulton, *Neighbourhood and Society: A London Suburb in the Seventeenth Century* (1987)

P. and J. Clark, 'The social economy of the Canterbury suburbs: the evidence of the census of 1563', in *Studies in Modern Kentish History*, ed. A. Detsicas and N. Yates (1983)

P. Clark and P. Slack (ed.), *Crisis and Order in English Towns 1500-1700: Essays in Urban History* (1972)

P. Clark and P. Slack, *English Towns in Transition 1500-1700* (1976)

P. Clark and D. Souden (ed.), *Migration and Society in Early Modern England* (1987)

D.C. Coleman, 'Labour in the English economy in the seventeenth century' *Economic History Review*, 2nd ser. 8 (1955/6)

P.J. Corfield, 'Urban development in England and Wales in the sixteenth and seventeenth centuries', in *Trade, Government and Economy in Pre-Industrial England: Essays Presented to F.J. Fisher*, ed. D.C. Coleman and A.H. John (1976)

J. de Vries, *European Urbanization 1500-1800* (1984)

O.J. Dunlop and R.D. Denman, *English Apprenticeship and Child Labour: A History* (1912)

R. Duplessis and M.C. Howell, 'Reconsidering the early modern urban economy: the cases of Leiden and Lille', *Past and Present*, 94 (1982)

A.D. Dyer, *The City of Worcester in the Sixteenth Century* (1973)

P. Earle, *The Making of the English Middle Class: Business, Society and Family Life in London 1660-1730 (1989)*

A. Everitt, 'The English urban inn, 1560-1760', in *idem* (ed.), *Perspectives in English Urban History* (1973)

F.J. Fisher, 'London as an "engine of economic growth"', in *Britain and the Netherlands, IV: Metropolis, Dominion and Province*, ed. J.S. Bromley and E.H. Kossman (The Hague, 1971); reprinted in F.J. Fisher, *London and the English Economy 1500-1700: Collected Essays*, ed. P.J. Corfield and N.B. Harte (1990)

N. Goose, 'English pre-industrial urban economies', *Urban History Yearbook 1982* (1982)

C. Hill, 'Pottage for freeborn Englishmen: attitudes to wage labour', in *idem, Change and Continuity in Seventeenth-Century England* (1974)

J.R. Kellett, 'The breakdown of gild and corporation control over the handicraft and retail trade in London', *Economic History Review*, 2nd ser. 10 (1957/8)

J. Langton and G. Hoppe, *Town and Country in the Development of Early Modern Western Europe* (Historical Geog. Research Series 11, 1983)

W.T. MacCaffrey, *Exeter 1540-1640: The Growth of an English County Town* (Cambridge, Mass., 1958)

T.C. Mendenhall, *The Shrewsbury Drapers and the Welsh Wool Trade in the Sixteenth and Seventeenth Centuries* (1953)

J. Merrington, 'Town and country in the transition to capitalism', *New Left Review*, 93 (1975)

D.M. Palliser, *Tudor York* (1979)

J. Patten, *English Towns 1500-1700* (1978)

C. Phythian-Adams, *Desolation of a City: Coventry and the Urban Crisis of the Late Middle Ages* (1979)

J.F. Pound, 'The social and trade structure of Norwich, 1525-75', *Past and Present*, 34 (1966)

J.F. Pound, 'The validity of the freeman's lists: some Norwich evidence', *Economic History Review*, 2nd ser. 34 (1981)

M. Power, 'Shadwell: the development of a London suburban community in the seventeenth century', *London Journal*, 4 (1978)

R.T. Rapp, *Industry and Economic Decline in Seventeenth-Century Venice* (Cambridge, Mass., 1976)

M. Reed, 'Economic structure and change in seventeenth-century Ipswich', in *Country Towns in Pre-Industrial England*, ed. P. Clark (1981)

D.R. Ringrose, *Madrid and the Spanish Economy 1650-1850* (1983)

D. Souden, 'Migrants and the population structure of later seventeenth-century provincial cities and market towns', in *The Transformation of English Provincial Towns 1600-1800*, ed. P. Clark (1984)

W.B. Stephens, *Seventeenth-Century Exeter: A Study of Industrial and Commercial Development 1625-88* (1958)

K. Thomas, 'Work and leisure in pre-industrial society', *Past and Present, 29* (1964)

G. Unwin, *Industrial Organisation in the Sixteenth and Seventeenth Centuries* (1904)

G. Unwin, *The Gilds and Companies of London* (1908)

H. Van der Wee (ed.), *The Rise and Decline of Urban Industries in Italy and the Low Countries (Late Middle Ages - Early Modern Times)* (Leuven, 1988)

R.B. Westerfield, *Middlemen in English Business, particularly between 1660 and 1760* (New Haven, Conn., 1915)

E.A. Wrigley, 'A simple model of London's importance in changing England's economy and society, 1650-1750', *Past and Present, 37* (1967); reprinted in *idem, People, Cities and Wealth: The Transformation of Traditional Society* (1987)

3.3 - Eighteenth century

M. Berg, *The Age of Manufactures: Industry, Innovation and Work in Britain 1700-1820* (1985)

M. Berg, P. Hudson and M. Sonenscher (ed.), *Manufacture in Town and Country before the Factory* (1983)

P. Butel and L.M. Cullen (ed.), *Négoce et industrie en France et en Irelande aux XVIIIe et XIX siècles* (Paris, 1980)

P. Clark (ed.), *The Transformation of English Provincial Towns 1600-1800* (1984)

L.A. Clarkson, *Proto-Industrialization: The First Phase of Industrialization?* (1985)

L.A. Clarkson and B. Collins, 'Proto-industrialization in an Irish town: Lisburn 1821', in *La Protoindustrialisation: théorie et realité*, ed. P. Deyon and F.F. Mendels (2 vols, 1982)

A.W. Coats, 'Changing attitudes to labour in the mid-eighteenth century', *Economic History Review*, 2nd ser. *11* (1958/9)

D.C. Coleman, 'Proto-industrialization: a concept too many', *Economic History Review*, 2nd ser. *36* (1983)

P.J. Corfield, *The Impact of English Towns 1700-1800* (1982)

M.R. Dobson, *Masters and Journeymen: Prehistory of Industrial Relations 1717-1800* (1980)

M.D. George, *London Life in the Eighteenth Century* (1925; revised 1965)

R. Glen, *Urban Workers in the Early Industrial Revoluation* (1984)

J.L. and B. Hammond, *The Town Labourer 1760-1832: The New Civilization* (1917)

J.J. Hecht, *The Domestic Servant Class in Eighteenth-Century England* (1956)

W.G. Hoskins, *Industry, Trade and People in Exeter 1688-1800* (1935)

S.L. Kaplan and C.J. Koepp (ed.), *Work in France: Representations, Meaning, Organization and Practice* (Ithaca, N.Y., 1986)

M. Kriedte, H. Medick and J. Schlumbohm (ed.), *Industrialization before Industrialization: Rural Industry in the Genesis of Capitalism* (1981)

J. Langton and P. Laxton, 'Parish registers and urban structure: the example of late eighteenth-century Liverpool', *Urban History Yearbook 1978* (1978)

C. Lis, *Social Change and the Labouring Poor: Antwerp 1770-1860* (New Haven, Conn., 1986)

R.W. Malcolmson, *Life and Labour in England 1700-80* (1981)

P. Mantoux, *The Industrial Revolution in the Eighteenth Century: An Outline of the Beginnings of the Modern Factory System in England* (Paris, 1906; London, 1928)

S.C. Maza, *Servants and Masters in Eighteenth-Century France: The Uses of Loyalty* (Princeton, N.J., 1983)

F.F. Mendels, 'Proto-industrialization: the first phase of the process of industrialization', *Journal of Economic History*, 23 (1972)

J. Meyer *et al.*, *Études sur les villes en Europe occidentale: milieu du XVIIe siècle à la veille de la Révolution Française* (2 vols, Paris, 1983)

H-C. and L.H. Mui, *Shops and Shopkeeping in Eighteenth-Century England* (1989)

M. Noble, 'Growth and development in a regional urban system: the country towns of eastern Yorkshire, 1700–1850' *Urban History Yearbook 1987* (1987)

M.B. Rowlands, *Masters and Men in the West Midland Metalware Trades before the Industrial Revolution* (1975)

J. Rule, *The Experience of Labour in Eighteenth-Century Industry* (1981)

W.H. Sewell, *Work and Revolution in France: The Language of Labour in France from the Old Regime to 1848* (1980)

M. Sonenscher, *The Hatters of Eighteenth-Century France* (Berkeley, Calif, 1987)

M. Sonenscher, *Work and Wages: Natural Law, Politics and the Eighteenth-Century French Trades* (1989)

E.P. Thompson, *The Making of the English Working Class* (1963; 1968)

E.P. Thompson, 'Time, work discipline and industrial capitalism', *Past and Present*, 38 (1967); reprinted in *Essays in Social History*, ed. M.W. Flinn and T.C. Smout (1974)

L. Weatherill, *The Pottery Trade and North Staffordshire 1660–1760* (1971)

R.G. Wilson, *Gentlemen Merchants: The Merchant Community in Leeds 1700–1830* (1971)

E.A. Wrigley, 'Urban growth and agricultural change: England and the continent in the early modern period', in *idem, People, Cities and Wealth: The Transformation of Traditional Society* (1987)

3.4 – Post-1801

D. Alexander, *Retailing in England during the Industrial Revolution* (1970)

A. Armstrong, *Stability and Change in an English County Town: A Social Study of York 1801–51* (1974)

C. Behagg, 'Secrecy, ritual and folk violence: the opacity of the workplace in the first half of the nineteenth century', in *Popular Culture and Custom in Nineteenth-Century England*, ed. R. Storch (1982)

J. Bienefeld, *Working Hours in British Indusry: An Economic History* (1972)

H. Braverman, *Labour and Monopoly Capitalism: The Degradation of Work in the Twentieth Century* (New York, 1974)

J. Brown, *The English Market Town: A Social and Economic History 1750–1914* (1986)

D. Bythell, *The Sweated Trades: Outwork in Nineteenth-Century Britain* (1978)

L. Chevalier, *Classes laborieuses et classes dangereuses à Paris pendant la première moitié du XIXe siècle* (Paris, 1958); transl. by F. Jellinek as *Labouring Classes and Dangerous Classes in Paris during the First Half of the Nineteenth Century* (New York, 1973)

G. Crossick, *An Artisan Elite in Victorian Society: Kentish London 1840–80* (1978)

G. Crossick and H-G. Haupt (ed.), *Shopkeepers and Master Artisans in Nineteenth-Century Europe* (1984)

R.J. Dennis, *English Industrial Cities of the Nineteenth Century: A Social Geography* (1984)

A. Everitt, 'Country, county and town: patterns of regional evolution in England', *Transactions of the Royal Historical Society*, 5th ser. 29 (1979)

R.Q. Gray, *The Labour Aristocracy in Victorian Edinburgh* (1976)

E.J. Hobsbawm, *Labouring Men: Studies in the History of Labour* (1964)

E.J. Hobsbawm, *Worlds of Labour: Further Studies in the History of Labour* (1984)

M. Holbrook-Jones, *Supremacy and the Subordination of Labour: The Hierarchy of Work in the Early Labour Movement* (1982)

E. Hopkins, *Birmingham: The First Manufacturing City in the World 1760-1840* (1989)

P. Horn, *The Rise and Fall of the Victorian Servant* (New York, 1975)

E.H. Hunt, *British Labour History 1815-1914* (1981)

M. Isacson and L. Magnusson, *Proto-industrialization in Scandinavia: Craft Skills in the Industrial Revolution* (1987)

P. Joyce, *Work, Society and Politics: The Culture of the Factory in Later Victorian England* (1980)

S.A. Marglin, 'What do bosses do? The origins and function of hierarchy in capitalist production', in *The Division of Labour: The Labour Process and Class-Struggle in Modern Capitalism*, ed. A. Gorz (1976)

C. More, *Skill and the English Working Class 1870-1914* (1980)

R. Penn, *Skilled Workers in the Class Structure* (1984)

S. Pollard, *A History of Labour in Sheffield* (1959)

S. Pollard, *The Genesis of Modern Management: A Study of the Industrial Revolution in Great Britain* (1965)

R. Price, *Labour in British Society: An Interpretative History* (1986)

I.J. Prothero, *Artisans and Politics in Early Nineteenth-Century London: John Gast and his Times* (1979)

W.M. Reddy, *The Rise of Market Culture: The Textile Trade and French Society 1750-1900* (1984)

D.A. Reid, 'The decline of Saint Monday, 1776-1876', *Past and Present*, 71 (1976)

B.T. Robson, *Urban Growth: An Approach* (1973)

C. Sabel and J. Zeitlin, 'Historical alternatives to mass production: politics, markets and technology in nineteenth-century industrialization', *Past and Present*, 108 (1985)

R. Samuel, 'The workshop of the world: steam power and hand technology in mid-Victorian Britain', *History Workshop Journal*, 3 (1977)

R. Scola, 'Food markets and shops in Manchester, 1770-1870', *Journal of Historical Geography*, 1 (1975)

P.N. Stearns, *Paths to Authority: The Middle Class and the Industrial Labour Force in France 1820-48* (Urbana, Ill., 1978)

P.J. Waller, *Town, City and Nation: England 1850-1914* (1983)

A.F. Weber, *The Growth of Cities in the Nineteenth Century: A Study in Statistics* (New York, 1899; reprinted Ithaca, N.Y., 1963)

J. Zeitlin and R. Harrison (ed.), *Divisions of Labour: Skilled Workers and Technological Change in Nineteenth-Century England* (1985)

V.A. Zeliger, *Pricing the Priceless Child: The Changing Social Value of Children* (New York, 1985)

4 - Gender and work 4.1 - Medieval

J.M. Bennett, Review – '"History that stands still": women's work in the European past', *Feminist Studies*, 14 (1988)

M.K. Dale, 'The London silkwomen of the fifteenth century', *Economic History Review*, 4 (1933)

H. Dillard, *Daughters of the Reconquest: Women in Castilian Town Society 1100-1300* (1984)

P.J.P. Goldberg, 'Female labour, service and marriage in the late-medieval urban north', *Northern History*, 22 (1986)

P.J.P. Goldberg, 'Women in fifteenth-century town life', in *Towns and Townspeople in the Fifteenth Century*, ed. J.A.F. Thompson (1988)

B. Hanawalt (ed.), *Women and Work in Pre-Industrial Europe* (Bloomington, Indiana, 1986)

R. Hilton, 'Women traders in medieval England', in *idem, Class Conflict and the Crisis of Feudalism: Essays in Medieval Social History* (1985)

M.C. Howell, *Women, Production and Patriarchy in Late Medieval Cities* (Chicago, 1986)

M. Kowaleski and J.M. Bennett, 'Crafts, gilds and women in the Middle Ages: fifty years after Marian K. Dale', *Signs: Journal of Women in Culture and Society 14* (1989)

K.E. Lacey, 'Women and work in fourteenth- and fifteenth-century London', in *Women and Work in Pre-Industrial England*, ed. L. Charles and L. Duffin (1985)

S. Lewenhak, *Women and Work* (1980)

C. Middleton, 'The sexual division of labour in feudal England', *New Left Review, 113-14* (1979)

J. Rossiaud, *Medieval Prostitution*, transl. by L.C. Cochrane (1988)

M. Wensky, 'Women's guilds in Cologne in the later Middle Ages', *Journal of European Economic History, 11* (1982)

4.2 - Early modern/eighteenth century

V. Brodsky, 'Widows in late Elizabethan London: remarriage, economic opportunity and family orientations', in *The World We Have Gained: Histories of Population and Social Structure*, ed. L. Bonfield, R.M. Smith, and K. Wrightson (1986)

L. Charles and L. Duffin (ed.), *Women and Work in Pre-Industrial England* (1985)

A. Clark, *The Working Life of Women in the Seventeenth Century* (1919), ed. M. Chaytor and J. Lewis (1982)

P. Earle, 'The female labour market in London in the late seventeenth and early eighteenth centuries', *Economic History Review*, 2nd ser. *42* (1989)

M.W. Ferguson, M. Quilligan and N.J. Vickers (ed.), *Rewriting the Renaissance: The Discourses of Sexual Difference in Early Modern Europe* (Chicago, 1986)

B. Hill, *Women, Work and Sexual Politics in Eighteenth-Century England* (1989)

R.A. Houston, 'Women in the economy and society of Scotland, 1500–1800', in *Scottish Society 1500-1800*, ed. R.A. Houston and I.D. Whyte (1989)

O. Hufton, 'Women and the family economy in eighteenth-century France', *French Historical Studies, 9* (1975)

O. Hufton, 'Women in history: early modern Europe', *Past and Present, 101* (1983)

J.H. Quataert, 'The shaping of women's work in manufacturing: guilds, households and the state in Central Europe, 1648–1870', *American Historical Review, 90* (1985)

E. Richards, 'Women in the British economy since about 1700: an interpretation', *History, 59* (1974); reprinted in *The Woman Question: Readings on the Subordination of Women*, ed. M. Evans (1982)

L. Roper, *The Holy Household: Women and Morals in Reformation Augsburg* (1989)

E. Shorter, 'Women's work: what difference did capitalism make?', *Theory and Society, 3* (1976)

W. Thwaites, 'Women in the market place: Oxfordshire, *c.* 1690–1800', *Midland History, 9* (1984)

M.E. Wiesner, 'Women's work in the changing city economy', in *Connecting Spheres*, ed. M.J. Boxer and J.H. Quataert (New York, 1987)

M.E. Wiesner, *Working Women in Renaissance Germany* (New Brunswick, N.J., 1986)

D. Willen, 'Guildswomen in the City of York, 1560–1700', *The Historian, 46* (1984)

M.W. Wood, 'Paltry peddlers or essential merchants? Women in the distributive trades in early modern Nuremberg', *Sixteenth-Century Journal, 12* (1981)

4.3 - Post-1800

S. Alexander, *Women's Work in Nineteenth-Century London: A Study of the Years 1830-50* (1983)

R.D. Barron and G.M. Norris, 'Sexual divisions and the dual labour market', in *Dependence and Exploitation in Work and Marriage*, ed. D.L. Barker and S. Allen (1976)

V. Beechey, 'Women and production: a critical analysis of some sociological theories of women's work', in *Feminism and Materialism: Women and Modes of Production*, ed. A. Kuhn and A.M. Wolpe (1978)

E. Boserup, *Woman's Role in Economic Development* (1970)

P. Branca, 'Image and reality: the myth of the idle Victorian woman', in *Clio's Consciousness Raised: New Perspectives on the History of Women*, ed. M.S. Hartman and L.W. Banner (New York, 1974)

S. Burman (ed.), *Fit Work for Women* (1979)

L. Davidoff and C. Hall, *Family Fortunes: Men and Women of the English Middle Class 1780-1850* (1987)

C. Hall, 'The history of the housewife', in *The Politics of Housework*, ed. E. Malos (1980)

M. Hewitt, *Wives and Mothers in Victorian Industry* (1958)

A. John (ed.), *Unequal Opportunities: Women's Employment in England 1800-1918* (1986)

J. Lown, 'Not so much a factory, more a form of patriarchy: gender and class during industrialization', in *Gender, Class and Work*, ed. E. Garmarnikow *et al.* (1983)

T.M. McBride, *The Domestic Revolution: The Modernization of Household Service in England and France 1820-1920* (1976)

W.F. Neff, *Victorian Working Women: An Historical and Literary Study of Women in British Industries and Professions 1832-50* (New York, 1929)

S. Pennington and B. Westover, *A Hidden Workforce: Homeworkers in England 1850-1985* (1989)

I. Pinchbeck, *Women Workers and the Industrial Revolution 1750-1850* (1930; 1969)

E. Roberts, *Women's Work 1840-1940* (1988)

S.O. Rose, '"Gender and work": sex, class and industrial capitalism', *History Workshop Journal*, 21 (1986)

J.W. Scott, 'Men and women in the Parisian garment trades: discussions of family and work in the 1830s and 1840s industry', in *The Power of the Past: Essays for Eric Hobsbawm*, ed. P. Thane, G. Crossick and R. Floud (1984)

J.W. Scott and L.A. Tilly, *Women, Work, and Family* (New York, 1978)

E. Sullerot, *Histoire et sociologie du travail féminin: essai* (Paris, 1968)

S. Walby, *Patriarchy at Work: Patriarchal and Capitalist Relations in Employment* (1986)

5 - Occupations and their classification

W.A. Armstrong, 'The use of information about occupation', in *Nineteenth-Century Society: Essays in the Use of Quantitative Methods for the Study of Social Data*, ed. E.A. Wrigley (1972)

C. Booth, 'Occupations of the people of the United Kingdom, 1801-81', *Journal of the Royal Statistical Society*, 49 (1886)

A.P.M. Coxon and P.M. Davies, with C.L. Jones, *Images of Social Stratification: Occupational Structures and Class* (1986)

A.P.M. Coxon and C.L. Jones, *Class and Hierarchy: The Social Meaning of Occupations* (1979)

J.H. Goldthorpe and K. Hope, *The Social Grading of Occupations: A New Approach and Scale* (1974)

E. Gross, 'Plus ça change...? The sexual structure of occupations over time', *Social Problems*, 16 (1968)

R.M. Hauser, 'Occupational status in the nineteenth and twentieth centuries', *Historical Methods*, 14 (1982)

E. Higgs, 'The tabulations of occupations in the nineteenth-century census, with special reference to domestic servants', *Local Population Studies*, 28 (1982)

E. Higgs, 'Women, occupations and work in the nineteenth-century censuses', *History Workshop Journal*, 23 (1987)

M.B. Katz, 'Occupational classification in history', *Journal of Interdisciplinary History*, 3 (1972)

P. Lindert, 'English occupations, 1670–1811', *Journal of Economic History*, 40 (1980)

D. and J. Mills, 'Occupation and social stratification revisited: the census enumerators' books of Victorian Britain', *Urban History Yearbook 1989* (1989)

L. Murgatroyd, 'Women, men and the social grading of occupations', *British Journal of Sociology*, 35 (1984)

T.L. Parcel and C.W. Mueller, 'Occupational differentiation, prestige and socio-economic status', *Work and Occupations*, 10 (1983)

J. Patten, 'Urban occupations in pre-industrial England', *Transactions of the Institute of British Geographers*, n.s. 2 (1977)

J. Patten, 'Village and town: an occupational study', *Agricultural History Review*, 20 (1972)

A.J. Reiss *et al.* (ed.), *Occupations and Social Status* (New York, 1961)

G. Routh, *Occupations of the People of Great Britain 1801–1981: With a Compendium of a Paper 'Occupations of the People of the United Kingom, 1801–81' by Charles Booth* (1987)

A. Stewart, K. Prandy, and R.M. Blackburn (ed.), *Social Stratification and Occupations* (1980)

S.R.S. Szreter, 'The genesis of the Registrar-General's social classification of occupations', *British Journal of Sociology*, 35 (1984)

D.J. Treiman, 'A standard occupational prestige scale for use with historical data', *Journal of Interdisciplinary History*, 7 (1976)

D.J. Treiman, *Occupational Prestige in Comparative Perspective* (New York, 1977)

Index

Page references in italics indicate tables, maps and figures.

Index compiled by Meg Davies (Society of Indexers)